Networking Personal Computers with TCP/IP

Networking Personal Computers with TCP/IP

Craig Hunt

O'REILLY®

Beijing · Cambridge · Köln · Paris · Sebastopol · Taipei · Tokyo

Networking Personal Computers with TCP/IP
by Craig Hunt

Copyright © 1995 O'Reilly & Associates, Inc. All rights reserved.
Printed in the United States of America.

Editor: Mike Loukides

Production Editor: Stephen Spainhour

Printing History:

> July 1995:   First Edition.

This book is printed on acid-free paper with 85% recycled content, 15% post-consumer waste. O'Reilly & Associates is committed to using paper with the highest recycled content available consistent with high quality.

ISBN: 1-56592-123-2

[4/99]

Table of Contents

List of Figures

List of Tables

Preface

NetWare, LAN Manager, NETBIOS, DOS, Windows, Windows for Workgroups, Windows NT, Windows 95 . . . confused? Many of us are. *Us* being the administrators of TCP/IP-based networks. In a world dominated by IBM-compatible Personal Computers (PCs) it is inevitable that you will be asked to add some PCs to your TCP/IP network. A bewildering variety of operating systems and networks are offered for PCs. Finding your way through this maze of options can be a daunting task.

This book will help you understand these options and tame these Pesky Critters (PCs) by giving you the practical information you need to internetwork PCs. *Networking Personal Computers with TCP/IP* will help you anticipate the problems that arise when connecting PCs to an internet, and it will help you find solutions to those problems. It contains detailed configuration examples for popular TCP/IP software packages for DOS, Windows, Windows 95, and Windows NT—operating systems that are commonly used on PCs. Additionally, you'll learn techniques for incorporating NetWare and NETBIOS networks into your TCP/IP internet.

Networking Personal Computers with TCP/IP is a book about TCP/IP networking for IBM-compatible personal computers and is a companion to *TCP/IP Network Administration*, which is also published by O'Reilly & Associates. This book stands on its own. *TCP/IP Network Administration* provides details of the TCP/IP protocol suite as well as detailed instructions for setting up UNIX workstations and servers on a TCP/IP network. *Networking Personal Computers with TCP/IP* provides the detailed instructions for attaching PCs to a TCP/IP network and its UNIX servers.

Audience

This book is intended for anyone who wants to attach a PC to a TCP/IP network. This obviously includes the network manager and the PC support personnel who are responsible for setting up and running systems and networks. Administrators of PC LANs that are attached to TCP/IP backbones will also find this book useful. The audience also includes any user who is interested in knowing how his or her computer is configured to communicate with other computers. A key group of users who would benefit from this book are the PC "power users." These users are interested in knowing how their computers function, and they have the skills necessary to use this knowledge to their advantage.

We assume that you have a good understanding of computers and their operation, and that you are familiar with TCP/IP network administration. If you're not, the Nutshell Handbook *TCP/IP Network Administration* will fill you in on the basics.

Organization

This text begins with a description of the challenges you'll face when adding PCs to a TCP/IP internet, and with general advice on how to deal with these challenges. Everyone can benefit by reading these chapters. Even if you're a PC expert, you can gain a fresh perspective on these systems as seen through the eyes of a network administrator.

The initial section is followed by a series of chapters that provide basic TCP/IP configuration information for some of the popular PC operating systems. Each of these chapters is complete and stands on its own. If you're only interested in DOS, you can, if you wish, read only the DOS chapter and skip the others. However, if you're like most of us, sometime in the future you will probably have to deal with all of the operating systems covered here.

Next is a series of chapters that cover advanced configuration topics and the configuration of specific applications such as email. Each of these chapters stands on its own, and again you only need to read the sections that deal with your own requirements. However, if you have the time (please control your laughter), reading these chapters may give you insight into additional services that you could be providing on your network.

The book concludes with a chapter on NetWare, the most popular PC LAN system software. This package is not based on TCP/IP, but you may need to integrate it into your internet. The chapter provides the information necessary to interconnect NetWare LANs over a TCP/IP backbone.

The book contains the following chapters:

Chapter 1, *The PC Dilemma*, discusses the nature of PC hardware and software, pointing out why these powerful, versatile computers are a real challenge for the network administrator.

Chapter 2, *Dealing with the Dilemma*, provides advice on ways to reduce the problems that PCs can cause for network administration.

Chapter 3, *Network Tools*, covers several hardware and software tools that help a network administrator support PCs attached to a TCP/IP network.

Chapter 4, *DOS TCP/IP*, provides detailed examples of TCP/IP configuration under the PC Disk Operating System (DOS).

Chapter 5, *Windows on the Network*, covers the configuration of TCP/IP in a Windows environment. It covers Windows 3.1 and Windows for Workgroups.

Chapter 6, *Windows 95 TCP/IP*, covers TCP/IP configuration for Microsoft's new desktop operating system Windows 95.

Chapter 7, *Windows NT Networking*, provides detailed information on TCP/IP for the Windows NT operating system. The chapter also provides information on integrating NETBIOS networks into a TCP/IP internet. NETBIOS is the native network protocol for Windows for Workgroups, Windows 95, and Windows NT.

Chapter 8, *Configuration Control*, discusses alternatives to custom, system-by-system configuration. It covers techniques for centrally controlling the configuration of a large number of systems using RARP, BOOTP, DHCP, and **rdist**.

Chapter 9, *Personal Email*, covers the configuration of the Post Office Protocol (POP) servers and clients that allow PC users to receive email directly at their desktops. Gateways to LAN-based email systems are also discussed.

Chapter 10, *File and Print Servers*, covers the configuration of the two classic PC LAN services: file sharing and printer sharing.

Chapter 11, *NetWare and TCP/IP*, discusses ways in which Novell's NetWare Network Operating System (NOS) can be integrated into a TCP/IP network. The problems and possibilities of getting these two distinctly different networking systems to cooperate are discussed.

Appendix A, *Installation Planning Form*, is a helpful planning guide that covers the configuration information necessary to plan a successful TCP/IP installation on a PC.

Appendix B, *Contacts and References*, lists vendor contacts for the various commercial software packages mentioned in this text. It also lists the books and RFCs referenced in the text.

Appendix C, *Sendmail Configuration*, provides a complete *sendmail.cf* file that contains all of the modifications mentioned in Chapter 9.

Appendix D, *Changes to System Files*, highlights the modifications that are made to the DOS boot files and the Windows initialization files by a sample TCP/IP installation.

Appendix E, *Public Domain Software*, builds a Windows TCP/IP system using Crynwr packet drivers, Trumpet Winsock software, and the Eudora 1.4 mailer.

Software Versions

The examples in this book come from a variety of different operating systems. The UNIX server examples are based on SunOS 4.1.3. The PC examples are based on the following operating systems:

- DOS 6.0

- Windows 3.1

- Windows 95 (March 95 Beta)

- Windows for Workgroups 3.11

- Windows NT 3.5

- NetWare 3.11

These are the current major releases as of this writing.[*] However, PC software changes at a rapid rate. New versions of these operating system may soon be released. Remember to check the documentation that comes with your operating system for the exact details.

Several versions of TCP/IP are referenced in this book. See Appendix B for contact information. The bulk of the TCP/IP examples are drawn from these packages:

- FTP Software's PC/TCP 2.2

- Novell's LAN Workplace 4.2

- SuperTCP 3.00 and 4.00

- Chameleon NFS 4.0

- Microsoft's TCP/IP for Windows for Workgroups

Conventions

This book uses the following typographical conventions:

Italic	is used for the names of hostnames, domain names, UNIX files, UNIX directories, and to emphasize new terms when they are first introduced.
UPPERCASE	is used for PC filenames and commands.
Bold	is used for command names and selectable window items such as menu items, buttons, and checkboxes.

---

[*] NetWare 4.0 has been released but it is not as prevalent as version 3.11.

`Constant-width`	is used to show the contents of files or the output from commands.
Constant-bold	is used in examples to show commands or text that would be typed literally by you.
constant-italic	is used in examples to show variables for which a context-specific substitution should be made. (The variable *filename*, for example, would be replaced by some actual filename.)
`C:>`, `%`, `#`	are used to indicate commands that you give interactively. The `C:>` prompt indicates a command that is entered at the DOS command line. For UNIX commands we normally use the default C shell prompt (`%`). If the UNIX command must be executed as root, we use the default superuser prompt (`#`).
[*option*]	When showing command syntax, we place optional parts of the command within brackets. For example, **ls** [-l] means that the -l option is not required.

Acknowledgements

I want to thank my wife Kathy for her patience. As you'll be able to tell from the first paragraph of the first chapter, I began this book on Halloween. That Halloween was more than a year ago. Many months of work followed. During that time I wasn't much help around the house, and Kathy has been a real trooper. I also want to thank my kids, Sara, David and Rebecca, for understanding why I've been so distracted. I couldn't have done this without the support of all of my family. They're the greatest!

I'd like to thank my editor, Mike Loukides. Mike keeps me on track and helps keep me sane. His suggestions have been invaluable.

I also received many excellent suggestions and corrections from the reviewers. Ron Petrusha and Clement T. Cole both suggested major changes that improved the book. Jim Bound and Paul Ebersman provided very useful comments. My thanks to all of the reviewers.

The people at O'Reilly are the best in the business. Stephen Spainhour pushed the book through production on an accelerated schedule. Chris Reilley produced the figures. Edie Freedman designed the cover. Nancy Priest provided the book design. Seth Maislin produced the index. Clairemarie Fisher-O'Leary wrote the colophon. Invaluable help came from John Files, Kismet McDonough, Nicole Gipson, Kiersten Nauman, Len Muellner, and Sheryl Avruch. My thanks to everyone. I couldn't have done it without you.

We'd Like to Hear From You

We have tested and verified all of the information in this book to the best of our ability, but you may find that features have changed (or even that we have made mistakes!). Please let us know about any errors you find, as well as your suggestions for future editions, by writing:

```
O'Reilly & Associates, Inc.
101 Morris Street
Sebastopol, CA 95472
1-800-998-9938 (in the US or Canada)
1-707-829-0515 (international/local)
1-707-829-0104 (FAX)
```

You can also send us messages electronically. To be put on the mailing list or request a catalog, send email to:

info@oreilly.com

To ask technical questions or comment on the book, send email to:

bookquestions@oreilly.com

1

The PC Dilemma

They're everywhere! They're everywhere! Personal Computers (PCs) are everywhere. They're in every office and on every network. Like the birds in Alfred Hitchcock's film, PCs are easily dealt with in small numbers. But when they flock together in large mobs and roost on your internet, a network administrator can quickly be overwhelmed and picked to pieces by the demands of these small systems.

Don't get me wrong. I love my PC. It is a powerful, useful and usable system; I used it to write this book. But a legend exists, particularly among the managers who fund technical support, that PCs are less complicated and less challenging than other systems, and therefore less in need of professional technical support. That's just not true. Network administrators need to understand PCs and need to be ready to support them.

Why PCs are the biggest support challenge faced by most network administrators is the question answered in this chapter. Perhaps if the people who manage your organization understand the scale of this support problem they will provide sufficient resources to deal with it. (Oh well, we can always dream!)

Popular Computers

Supporting PCs is the largest task of most network administrators. This is not because these systems are exceptionally troublesome, it is simply because they are exceptionally numerous. PCs dominate the world of computing for some very good reasons. Some of the reasons are obvious and some are more subtle.

The most obvious reason for PC popularity is their low cost. PC hardware is an incredible bargain. But selecting a PC simply on the basis of initial cost is one reason why PCs are a major support burden. The cost difference between a "commodity" PC and a "network-ready" workstation is, in part, an illusion.[*] While the initial outlay for a low-end system is less, the system engineering and installation effort is greater. Part of what you pay for in a workstation is *system integration*. With a commodity system, you are your own integrator, and system integration is a major task when the PC is networked.

The decision of which system is most cost effective in your environment is similar to the make/buy decision that managers are always puzzling over. "Should we buy a system with integrated network hardware and software, or should we build a system from third-party hardware and software?" In the past, managers usually favored building a system because relatively few computers were networked. Most organizations had large numbers of stand-alone PCs and much smaller numbers of networked systems. As networks continue to grow and the long-term savings of having integrated network hardware and operating systems becomes more apparent, we'll see a growth in the number of vendors offering higher cost PCs that have networking hardware and operating systems pre-installed and fully integrated. Meanwhile, a huge market has sprung up for add-on hardware and software to network existing PCs. It is into this sometimes confusing world of "add-ons" that network administrators are drawn.

The great abundance of low-cost, high-quality software available for PCs is another reason for their tremendous popularity.[†] New hardware technologies often suffer from a lack of available software, but PCs have been around a long time in computer technology terms—over a decade. In that time the amount of high quality PC software has reached a "critical mass" that attracts customers. At the same time, the large numbers of PCs make the market for that software big enough to keep prices down. This is a situation that the manufacturers of other types of systems only dream of.

There is no free lunch, and like everything else this low-cost software does have its hidden cost. The great success of the PC is closely tied to the treasure trove of great PC software, but this software is largely dependent on DOS, the original PC operating system. Efforts to modernize DOS or to replace it with a modern operating system like Windows NT are slowed by the absolute requirement to support existing applications software. The limitations of DOS, and the reasons that Microsoft and others are working to update or replace it, are particularly apparent when you network PCs.

A less commonly recognized reason why PCs are so popular is the open architecture of the PC bus. Many people will dispute anything that appears to apply an

---

[*] For this discussion, a "commodity" PC is any PC selected solely on the basis of low initial cost, and a workstation is a well-equipped system. See the glossary.
[†] PC software is so popular that even UNIX workstations frequently have emulators or interpreters to allow their users to run it.

open system label to a PC. They point out that the DOS operating system is proprietary software from Microsoft and that all PC hardware is based on Intel CPUs. How can a system based on proprietary software that runs on only one type of processor be called "open"?

To understand this point don't think about how open systems are currently defined. Think instead about the market in which the original PC competed. The microcomputer market leader was the Apple II system: a computer that had an open bus architecture with an abundance of unique third-party attachments, ranging from music synthesizers to optical disk readers. In that context "open" meant that third-party vendors were allowed to develop products for the bus without restrictive licenses or fees. IBM, with its name recognition and powerful sales organization, was introducing an open bus architecture system at the same time Apple was beginning its move to a closed bus architecture for the new Macintosh system. IBM encouraged third-party hardware development by not charging a license fee for use of the PC bus design. Many third-party hardware developers took this opportunity to move to the new IBM system, and the new system quickly acquired the unique attachments that make small systems useful to so many people. Additionally, the large market and tremendous competition among third-party hardware vendors kept the cost low.

Unfortunately this abundant, low-cost hardware also carries a hidden cost for the network administrator. Just as the huge pool of software has prevented users from moving rapidly to new operating systems, the desire for backward compatibility in hardware has slowed the development of improved PC bus architectures. Later in this chapter we'll discuss PC bus architectures and see why adding new hardware to a PC can be one of the network administrators biggest headaches.

The final point we'll raise about why PC popularity is often overlooked. PCs are popular in the office because they are also affordable enough to be installed in the home. There are, of course, many more PCs and PC users in the office than there are in the home. However, technical managers, technical support personnel, software developers, and key users are all likely to have PCs in their homes. These people make or influence computer purchasing decisions for their offices, and while they may be liberal with office funds, they are probably very conscious of the money they spend at home. They select PCs for home use because of the low initial cost. They naturally favor office equipment that is compatible with their home equipment. For the network administrator, this means that not only will PCs continue to be popular in the office, it also means that there will be pressure to extend TCP/IP access to the users' homes soon after the users network their office computers.

Oddly enough, many of the things that contribute to the PCs popularity may also contribute to making your support task more difficult. "Low-cost" can mean increased system integration duties. "Abundant software" can mean more operating systems and networking packages to learn about. "Third-party hardware" can mean supporting several different network adapters. The following sections examine the architecture of PCs and look at the unique challenges these systems bring to network administration.

PC Hardware

In the computer center, you'll find minicomputers operated by a full-time technical staff and covered by full software and hardware support contracts. In the engineering department, you'll find fully integrated workstations, which may also be covered by vendor support contracts. But in the front office, you're likely to find no-name PCs purchased via mail-order without any support at all. It is a paradox of the computer world that the people who most need support are the ones that are least likely to buy it. And it is a paradox of the Personal Computer that these systems so well known for their user-friendly software have some of the most difficult hardware that a network administrator has to deal with.

The CPU of the PC is a powerful state-of-the-art CISC processor. The Intel CPU has evolved rapidly over the years: 8088, 8086, 80186, 80286, 80386, 80486, Pentium.[*] This is a litany of modern processors that have kept pace with technological change. However, the CPU is not the only part of the hardware that the network administrator deals with. Networks are really I/O devices. Therefore the I/O bus architecture is a part of the system that the network administrator must also work with, and it is here that the PC becomes really troublesome.

The Bus

There are at least five different bus architectures now used in PCs: two local bus architectures and three peripheral bus standards. The local bus standards are discussed in the next section. The three commonly used peripheral bus architectures are: Industry Standard Architecture (ISA), Extended Industry Standard Architecture (EISA), and Micro Channel Adapter (MCA).

The original PC bus was a low-speed, 8-bit bus. It was outmoded by the introduction of the 80286. The ISA bus is also called the AT bus because it was introduced with the PC AT. The ISA bus expanded the original PC bus from 8 to 16 data lines but retained full physical and electrical compatibility with the existing 8-bit cards of the original bus.

Backward compatibility was also a design principle for the EISA bus. The EISA bus expanded the ISA bus to a full 32-bit data path while retaining full support for the old 16-bit and 8-bit adapter cards. Unlike the older MCA bus, a 32-bit bus that IBM introduced with the PS/2, the EISA bus was compatible with the ISA and PC buses.

---

* The 8086 and 80186 did not see widespread use in PC systems.

IBM's strategy with the MCA bus was to hope that users and hardware developers would adopt it and abandon their old adapter cards. Many of the people in the PC industry rejected this approach, and the EISA bus was the result.*

The EISA bus and the MCA bus are both *intelligent buses*. These intelligent designs provide hardware in the bus and in the adapter cards that allow the systems to identify new hardware adapters when they are plugged into the bus. The hardware of EISA and MCA systems is largely self-configuring. If you have experience with workstations, this is just what you expect. You expect Ethernet interfaces to come pre-installed and to require no hardware configuration, and when you install other network hardware, you expect the system to take care of some of the work. Right now you are probably smiling to yourself to hear that the EISA and MCA buses provide similar levels of service. Well, don't smile yet!

The ISA bus is the dominant PC bus. The EISA bus is much less common and the MCA bus is generally confined to the IBM PS/2. Even when you find a system that has an EISA bus, many of the adapter cards in that system may be old ISA cards. These old 8 and 16-bit cards are often used because they are cheaper. But they lack the EISA hardware and cannot be automatically configured. They can even interfere with the EISA cards that are installed in the system, preventing them from using some of their advanced features. (See the discussion of IRQs later in this section.) Using the old cards defeats some of the best features of the EISA bus. But they are cheaper, and low initial cost is very important in the PC market.

What's so bad about old ISA adapter cards? Nothing really. Just have your screwdriver and needle-nosed pliers handy when you're installing one. ISA cards often require the hardware configuration to be set directly on the board via DIP switches and jumpers.

Figure 1-1 is a diagram of an imaginary multi-I/O card. This card shows examples of the three ways that configuration values are commonly set in PC hardware: DIP switches, single position jumpers, and two position jumpers. DIP switches are simply small switches that are set or cleared by being switched on or off. Single position jumpers are set by placing a shorting jumper on the prongs and are cleared when the jumper is removed. Two position jumpers use the shorting jumper to connect either the left or the right prong to the central prong.

Some new ISA cards can be configured through software. This is helpful, but the real difficulty is not in setting configuration values, it is in learning the correct values to set. The best new ISA cards have intelligent software configuration programs that help you avoid setting the wrong configuration value. These improved cards are well worth the price.

PC adapter cards require up to four distinct hardware configuration parameters. The parameters are the Interrupt Request number (IRQ), Direct Memory Access (DMA) Request number (DRQ), I/O Port Address, and Adapter Memory Address.

---

* Backward compatibility was not the only motivation for the EISA bus. IBM charged manufacturers a license fee for the MCA bus.

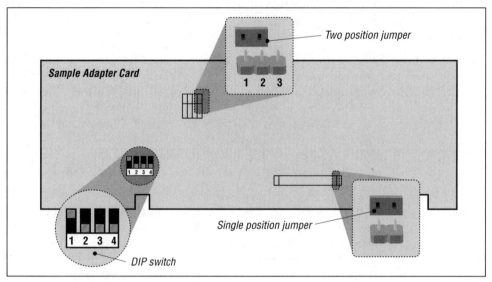

Figure 1-1: Sample Adapter Card

Each parameter has a range of possible values:

• The IRQ values available for adapter cards are 2-7, 9-12 and 14-15. IRQs 0, 1, 8, and 13 are used by functions on the system board.[*]

• The available DRQ values are 0-3 and 5-7. DRQ 4 is used by the system board.

• The I/O Port Addresses available for peripheral bus I/O are hex values in the range from 100 to 3FF. The I/O addresses from 000 to 0FF are reserved for the system board. Table 1-1 lists some of the common I/O address assignments.

• The Adapter Memory Address is the address in *system memory* where the ROM on the adapter card is mapped. System memory is explained later in this chapter. The addresses available for adapter memory are from C0000 to DFFFF. See the memory map in Figure 1-4.

Take care to ensure that each card has unique configuration values. Cards cannot share configuration values or I/O conflicts can occur.

---

* See Table 1-2 for common IRQ assignments.

Table 1-1: Common I/O Port Address Assignments

I/O Port	Assignment
1F0-1F8	Hard disk controller
200-207	Game port I/O
278-27F	Parallel printer port 2 (LPT2)
2F8-2FF	Serial port 2 (COM2)
378-37F	Parallel printer port 1 (LPT1)
3B0-3BF	Monochrome display adapter
3D0-3DF	Color graphic adapter
3F0-3F7	Floppy disk controller
3F8-3FF	Serial port 1 (COM1)

Of the four configuration values, IRQ assignment causes the most trouble. A quick look at the information in the previous paragraphs might make you think that the configuration resource in shortest supply is the DRQ. That's not the case. Seven DRQ numbers are usually enough because few cards use Direct Memory Access to perform I/O. However, almost all ISA cards use interrupts and require an IRQ number. Some cards use more than one. Figure 1-1 is based on a multi-I/O card that uses four IRQ numbers! Additionally, several of the IRQ values are "pre-assigned" to commonly used I/O devices, which further limits your choices. Table 1-2 shows the traditional assignments of IRQs.

Table 1-2: Traditional IRQ Assignments

IRQ Number	Assignment on ISA Systems
0	System timer
1	Keyboard
2	Cascade to second interrupt controller
3	Second serial port (COM2)
4	First serial port (COM1)
5	Second parallel printer port (LPT2)
6	Floppy disk controller
7	First parallel printer port (LPT1)
8	Real-time clock
9	Available for general use
10	Available for general use
11	Available for general use
12	Available for general use
13	Coprocessor
14	Hard disk controller
15	Available for general use

Cascade Interrupt

The IBM AT design uses two 8259 programmable interrupt controllers. The first controller handles IRQ lines 0 to 7, just as it did on the original PC. The second controller handles lines 8 to 15. The second controller is linked to the system through IRQ line 2 on the first controller. IRQs 8-15 are *cascaded* through IRQ 2, thus the name *cascade interrupt* for IRQ 2. So what happened to the real interrupt number 2? It is activated by IRQ 9! IRQ 9 is linked via software to the interrupt routine for interrupt 2.

IRQs not only signal an interrupt, they indicate its priority. In the original PC, IRQs are given priority in ascending order. IRQ 0 is the highest priority and IRQ 7 is the lowest. Because IRQs 8-15 are linked through IRQ 2 in the AT design, IRQ 7 is still the lowest priority! The IRQ priorities on an ISA system are: 0-1, 8-15, 3-7. The priority of IRQs that you can actually assign are 9-15 and then 3-7.

The IBM AT design described above and the IRQ assignments shown in Table 1-2 are used by most ISA systems. There are, of course, variations for non-ISA systems, and there are exceptions even among ISA systems. For example: the PC XT, which uses the PC bus, assigns IRQ 5 to the hard disk controller and makes IRQ 2 available for general use. The PS/2 makes IRQ 5 available for general use and assigns IRQ 12 to mouse I/O. But none of this is cast in stone. Users can assign IRQs to other uses. The network administrator needs to realize this and be ready to deal with the problems.

Avoid using an IRQ that is traditionally assigned to another I/O device when installing network hardware.[*] It's not always possible, but it's a good idea even if the device that uses the interrupt is not currently installed in the system. In the future someone may install an I/O card that contains the device, and it will probably default to its traditional IRQ assignment. If you've already installed a network card using that IRQ, expect a call saying that the "network is broken," because IRQs cannot be shared reliably.[†] The reason they can't goes back to the design of the original PC bus. Interrupts on the PC bus are *edge-triggered*, which means that the transition of the signal on the IRQ line causes the system to detect an interrupt. Specifically, IBM defined this interrupt as a transition from low to high. If more than one card attempts to use a single IRQ line the interrupts can be lost.

This limitation of the PC bus caused IBM to increase the number of interrupt request lines when they designed the ISA bus. Figure 1-2 shows the changes in the peripheral I/O bus starting with the PC bus, moving to the ISA bus, and ending

---

[*] Chapter 3, *Network Tools*, covers software tools that can help you avoid configuration conflicts.
[†] Some devices can share an IRQ because of how they are used. A network adapter is not one of those devices.

PC BUS

GND	IO CH CHK-
RESET DRV	D7
+5V	D6
IRQ 2	D5
-5V	D4
DRQ 2	D3
-12V	D2
N/C	D1
-12V	D0
GND	IO CH RDY
SMEMW-	AEN
SMEMR-	A19
IOW-	A18
IOR-	A17
DACK3-	A16
DRQ3	A15
DACK1-	A14
DRQ1	A13
REFRESH-	A12
CLK	A11
IRQ7	A10
IRQ6	A9
IRQ5	A8
IRQ4	A7
IRQ3	A6
DACK2-	A5
TC	A4
BALE	A3
+5V	A2
OSC	A1
GND	A0

ISA BUS

GND	IO CH CHK-
RESET DRV	D7
+5V	D6
IRQ 2	D5
-5V	D4
DRQ 2	D3
-12V	D2
N/C	D1
-12V	D0
GND	IO CH RDY
SMEMW-	AEN
SMEMR-	A19
IOW-	A18
IOR-	A17
DACK3-	A16
DRQ3	A15
DACK1-	A14
DRQ1	A13
REFRESH-	A12
CLK	A11
IRQ7	A10
IRQ6	A9
IRQ5	A8
IRQ4	A7
IRQ3	A6
DACK2-	A5
TC	A4
BALE	A3
+5V	A2
OSC	A1
GND	A0
MEM CS16-	SBHE-
I/O CS16-	LA23
IRQ10	LA22
IRQ11	LA21
IRQ12	LA20
IRQ15	LA19
IRQ14	LA18
DACK0-	LA17
DRQ0	MEMR-
DACK5-	MEMW-
DRQ5	D8
DACK6-	D9
DRQ6	D10
DACK7-	D11
DRQ7	D12
+5V	D13
MASTER-	D14
GND	D15

EISA BUS

GND	GND	IO CH CHK-	
+5V	RESET DRV	D7	
+5V	+5V	D6	CMD
MFG SPEC	IRQ 2	D5	START-
MFG SPEC	-5V	D4	EXRDY
(KEY)	DRQ 2	D3	EX32-
MFG SPEC	-12V	D2	GND
MFG SPEC	N/C	D1	(KEY)
+12V	-12V	D0	EX16-
M-IO	GND	IO CH RDY	SLBURST-
LOCK-	SMEMW-	AEN	MSBURST-
RESERVED	SMEMR-	A19	W-R
GND	IOW-	A18	GND
RESERVED	IOR-	A17	RESERVED
BE3	DACK3-	A16	RESERVED
(KEY)	DRQ3	A15	RESERVED
BE2-	DACK1-	A14	(KEY)
BE0-	DRQ1	A13	BE1-
BND	REFRESH-	A12	LA31
+5V	CLK	A11	GND
LA29	IRQ7	A10	LA30
GND	IRQ6	A9	LA28
LA26	IRQ5	A8	LA27
LA24	IRQ4	A7	LA25
(KEY)	IRQ3	A6	GND
LA16	DACK2-	A5	(KEY)
LA14	TC	A4	LA15
+5V	BALE	A3	LA13
+5V	+5V	A2	LA12
GND	OSC	A1	LA11
LA10	GND	A0	GND
			LA9
LA8			
LA6	MEM CS16-	SBHE-	LA7
LA5	I/O CS16-	LA23	GND
+5V	IRQ10	LA22	LA4
LA2	IRQ11	LA21	LA3
(KEY)	IRQ12	LA20	GND
D16	IRQ15	LA19	(KEY)
D18	IRQ14	LA18	D17
GND	DACK0-	LA17	D19
D21	DRQ0	MEMR-	D20
D23	DACK5-	MEMW-	D22
D24	DRQ5	D8	GND
GND	DACK6-	D9	D25
D27	DRQ6	D10	D26
(KEY)	DACK7-	D11	D28
D29	DRQ7	D12	(KEY)
+5V	+5V	D13	GND
+5V	MASTER-	D14	D30
MACKn-	GND	D15	D31
			MREQn-

Figure 1−2: I/O Bus Evolution

with the EISA bus. Notice that the PC bus had only six IRQ lines. The PC bus had only five bus slots. Since there were no multi-I/O cards when the bus was designed, six interrupts seemed sufficient. However, once multi-I/O cards came into existence, the number of interrupt request lines was clearly inadequate. The designers of the AT bus added another five lines, making a total of eleven lines. But even eleven IRQs can prove inadequate when a system is stuffed full of I/O cards.

The designers of the EISA bus avoided this line inadequacy completely. The EISA bus does not increase the number of IRQ lines because no increase is necessary. Interrupts on the EISA bus are *level-sensitive*. EISA interrupts are triggered by the level of the signal on an interrupt line. Therefore it is electrically possible to have multiple adapters share a single interrupt. The problem with sharing is, of course, that most EISA systems still have lots of ISA adapter cards. ISA cards are ISA cards. They do not use level-sensitive interrupts and cannot share an interrupt line even when used in an EISA system. In all likelihood you will have to pick an unused IRQ whenever you install a network card in a PC, even in an EISA bus PC.

Local Bus

The latest improvement of PC bus technology involves the use of the local bus for peripheral I/O. The *local bus* is the pathway that connects the CPU to the memory. It is a "fast and wide" bus that is at least 32 bits wide and clocked at the CPU's external clock rate.[*] This means that the local bus can move at least 32 bits of data, a full four bytes, every clock cycle. That's fast!

The bus is fast because it needs to be. The performance of a CPU is very tightly linked to the speed with which it can move data and instructions into and out of its memory. The path between the CPU and its memory is so important that traditionally, nothing else is connected to this path. The manufacturers of PC video controllers ignored this tradition and started something that has lead to a major change in PC bus technology.

The change came because the ISA bus is simply not fast enough to provide adequate support for a Super VGA (SVGA) controller and a high performance PC. A single SVGA screen image requires the bus to move hundreds of thousands of bytes of data. Moving these data over a slow bus that is shared with all of the other system peripherals undermines the effectiveness of a high-performance video board. To solve this problem, a standard was developed that allows a video controller to connect directly to the PC's local bus. This standard is called the VESA local bus.

The VESA bus has some major limitations, but it does what it was designed to do, which is move data to a video controller at extremely high speed. The original VESA bus was not intended to be a general purpose I/O bus. Most systems equipped with it have only one VESA card connector that is used solely for the video controller board. A newer version of the standard, called VESA II, is more robust and versatile, but it is not the most widely used local bus. The leader in the local bus market is the PCI bus.

The *Peripheral Component Interconnect* (PCI) bus overcomes the limitations of earlier local bus implementations. It has these advantages:

---

[*] We say "at least 32 bits" because the local bus increases to 64 bits when a 64-bit CPU is used.

- Broad industry acceptance. The PCI Special Interest Group (SIG) was formed by Intel and many of the major PC hardware manufacturers to develop and promote the PCI standard. Hundreds of companies that make PCs and PC adapter boards have adopted the standard. Its use is not limited to video controllers. There are several different types of network adapters available for the PCI bus.

- Standard clock speed. The local bus runs at the external clock rate of the CPU. This might be 33 MHz on one system and some other speed on another. The adapter manufacturer is forced to work with several different possible clock speeds when connecting directly to the local bus. The PCI bus solves this problem. The PCI interface always provides a fixed 33 MHz clock rate, thus simplifying the manufacture of the adapter boards.

- Standard connector. The PCI bus connector is the same on all systems.

- Intelligent bus. The PCI bus protects the vital communications between the CPU and memory, and at the same time allows multiple devices, some of which may be bus masters, to use the local bus. Intel calls this feature *concurrency*. The bus also supports automatic adapter board configuration through a feature called *Plug-and-Play*. Plug-and-Play peripherals require no configuration. The board, the bus, and the system cooperate to find and assign unused hardware configuration values.

- Low cost. Compared to adapters for the EISA and the MCA peripheral buses, PCI boards are very inexpensive.

The PCI bus is good news for a PC system administrator. It is extremely high performance, with a maximum speed of 132M bytes per second. Now PCs can really take advantage of new high-speed networking technologies like FDDI and ATM, and they can do it at a lower cost.

Systems based on the new bus maintain compatibility with the older adapter cards by including a second bus. The second bus is one of the standard peripheral buses: EISA or ISA. The most common configuration is to have a PCI bus for high speed I/O and an ISA bus for compatibility with older cards and for lower speed I/O. Figure 1-3 illustrates this common board structure. Some I/O devices connect to the system through a peripheral controller built into the PCI bus. Other devices use the three PCI bus slots and still others use the five ISA bus slots.

The future looks bright. New technologies like PCI and Plug-and-Play are good reasons to upgrade to modern PCs. These features should be considered any time an upgrade is planned. However, older equipment will continue to exist on your network for some time. Things are improving but we must be aware of, and deal with, the problems that exist today.

In the next chapter we look at ways to ease the problems caused by older PC hardware. There is no way to eliminate these problems completely, however, as some of these limitations are designed into the systems.

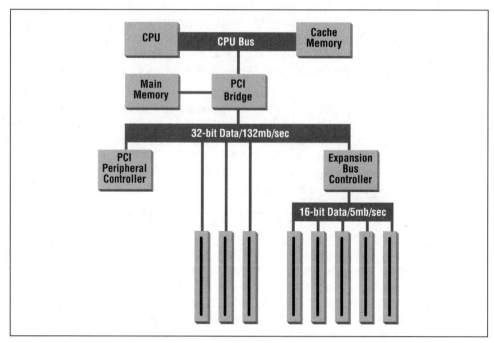

Figure 1–3: A PCI Bus System

Memory Limitation

One of the most famous limitations designed into the PC is the limit of 640K bytes of user memory. This is not strictly a hardware limitation. It is as much a part of PC software as hardware, but the roots of this problem go back to the original PC hardware design.

Back in the remote past, all the way back in 1980, a very substantial desktop computer had 64K bytes of RAM. It was common for systems to have only 16K and some sold with only 4K. It is hard to imagine now, but that was the situation, and that was the environment the PC design team was working in.

The PC designers created a system that uses all of the memory the 8088 processor can address. The processor has a 20-bit address that allows it to address 1M bytes of memory. The address is often represented as 20 contiguous bits that are written as 5 hexadecimal digits, 00000-FFFFF. In this representation, the high-order digit is said to indicate the *memory page,* and the remaining four digits indicate the address within that page. The pages are referred to as *page 0* to *page F.* This allows us to visualize the system as having 16 memory pages of 64K bytes each for a total of 1M bytes. Naturally, the way address registers are really used in the 8088 is more complex. The shorthand of using a 5-digit hex address is just a common way of describing 8088 memory and is the technique we'll use. See *8088 Addressing* if you want more details about how the address registers really work.

8088 Addressing

The 8086/8088 uses two 16-bit registers to define the 20-bit memory address that provides the 1M byte address space. They are the *segment register* and the *offset register*. To obtain the actual memory location the the registers are interpreted in this way:

1. The segment register is left-shifted 4 bits creating a 20-bit address where the low-order 4 bits are always 0.

2. The offset register is added to the 20-bit value from the first step yielding a full 20-bit address that points to a specific memory location.

This address structure creates *segment boundaries* every 16 bytes throughout memory, and each segment is 64K bytes long. Therefore there are many *segment:offset* combinations for every memory address. For example, B100:01F3 and B200:00F3 both point to the same memory location.

Segment:offset addressing is available on every processor in the 8086 family. It is called *real mode* addressing, and it is the only form of addressing used in DOS. But DOS extenders, multitasking shells, and other PC operating systems can make use of *protected mode* addressing, which is offered on newer processors in the 8086 family.

Protected mode addressing provides 80286 and later processors with access to their entire address space. It is called protected mode because it uses a *global descriptor table* that includes memory access information. This allows the memory dedicated to one process to be protected from accidental access by another process. Operating systems that use protected mode addressing do not suffer from the 1M byte memory limitation.

The designers set aside 10 pages of memory (00000-90000) for user memory and reserved 6 pages (A0000-F0000) for system use.[*] This set the limit of user addressable space to ten pages of 64K bytes each for the total of 640K, which was a full order of magnitude greater than the amount of memory commonly available on systems of that day. It appeared to everyone to be a very generous allocation of memory.

Everyone also thought that when new CPUs were developed that could address more memory, a new PC design would emerge. No one thought the original PC would be so popular it would not allow people to change the design. However, Intel felt it had to make its new processors backward compatible to the 8088 to keep its position in the PC market. Backward compatibility allowed DOS to run unchanged on succeeding generations of the 8086 family. In effect, each new

---

[*] This is an arbitrary division that appeared in DOS 2.0. DOS 1.0 had divided the memory in half with 512K for users and 512K for the system.

generation has been used merely as a faster 8088 and not to its full potential. The 8088's 1M byte memory limit has continued to this day, even on systems with the newest processors that can address 4G bytes of memory.

An additional problem with the design of PC memory is the placement of *system memory* above *user memory*. Simply stated, user memory is the memory available to application programs, and system memory is the memory reserved for use by the system. Look at the map shown in Figure 1-4.

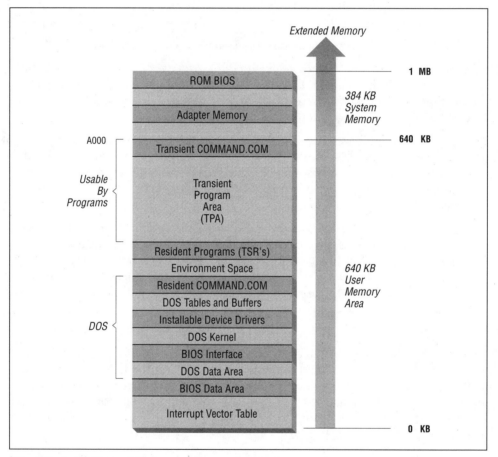

Figure 1-4: PC Memory Map

If a user program were allowed to grow beyond 640K, it would conflict with the memory reserved for the system. If additional memory is installed above the 1M byte barrier, it is called *extended memory*. Special hardware or software is necessary to link this memory smoothly into a user program running under DOS. If the system memory had been mapped into memory below the user memory, it might have been simpler for programs to grow into extended memory. It certainly would have been easier to manage contiguous blocks of memory.

Again, the reason that system memory is mapped above user memory is historical. When an 8088 starts up, it executes its first instruction from memory location FFFF0; it expects to find its startup ROM at the top of memory. Placing startup routines at the top of memory allows the operating system to load from the bottom up without interfering with the startup routine until the OS is ready to take over. It is possible for an operating system to overlay the startup area after the CPU performs initial startup.[*] However, in the early 1980's many small systems used ROM-based control programs instead of real operating systems. At that time, BASIC was frequently used in lieu of an operating system on home computers. The initial design of the PC provided this capability. If a PC powered up without a boot disk, the system would startup running BASIC. With limited expensive RAM and the BASIC program already in ROM, it made sense to place other parts of the software needed by the system in ROM also. The designers of DOS could have changed this but they didn't, so the legacy of the 8088 and ROM BASIC live to this day.

Operating Systems

IBM designed the PC from commercially available hardware components and purchased an existing operating system from a microcomputer software house so that the PC could be brought to the market as quickly as possible. This was a dramatic departure from the traditions of Big Blue. IBM, like all mainframe manufacturers, creates OS software that is designed for a specific hardware platform. The hardware and software are so tightly coupled that they create a single integrated system. The PC changed all that. PC hardware is separable from its operating system. The hardware is sold as a commodity and so is the operating system. From the very first, the PC offered a choice of operating systems. IBM introduced the original PC with DOS, CP/M-86, and P-system as possible operating system choices.[†] In succeeding years even more choices have been added.

The variety of operating systems adds to the difficulty of mastering PCs. DOS, Windows 3.1, UNIX, NetWare, and Windows NT are all in widespread use. You can't expect to become an expert in all of these. Luckily a network administrator only needs to concentrate on particular aspects of the operating system and only on those systems actually used at his site.

Disk Operating System

Almost every PC has DOS on it. Even PCs with other operating systems usually have boot loaders that allow DOS to be booted. The ubiquitous nature of DOS would be good news for the network administrator if mastering it allowed you to

---

[*] It is possible for RAM and ROM to share the same memory address. The ROM can be electrically disabled when it is no longer needed allowing the RAM to take over. This is how an operating system overlays ROM-based initialization routines, and it is how *ROM shadowing* is done.

[†] CP/M-86 and P-system never played a significant role in the PC market because IBM released all IBM brand software for DOS.

handle most of the PCs on your network. Unfortunately, of all the current PC operating systems, DOS provides the least support for network services.

Networks place special demands on the operating system. Because DOS was not designed with networks in mind, it has a few major weaknesses:

Lack of multitasking

DOS is designed to run only one task at a time. This allows the application program to have all of the resources of the system at its disposal, which is an efficient design for a small, single-user system. Networks, however, benefit from having constantly running background processes that listen for network connections and process data as it arrives. For example, most people want to be notified as soon as their email arrives, but because there is no background mail process listening to the SMTP port, DOS-based TCP/IP systems usually require the user to check a server to see if mail has arrived.

Limited memory

We've discussed the memory limits of the original PC hardware. The limit of 1M byte of memory, 640K of which is allowed for applications programs, lives on in DOS. Network software naturally requires some of this memory and the more functions the software provides, the more memory it requires. This can cause an "out of memory" error when the user attempts to load an application that ran before the network was installed. Memory management software that helps you overcome this problem is covered in Chapter 3.

Lack of standards

This item could also be titled *too many standards*, because many different approaches have been developed to get around the two DOS limitations mentioned above. Terminate and Stay Resident (TSR) programs and multitasking GUI shells like DESQview and Windows have been developed to sidestep the lack of multitasking. Extended memory standards, like EMS and XMS, third-party memory managers, and DOS extenders have been developed to get around the memory limitation. The variety of modifications creates different "flavors" of DOS that the network administrator must deal with.

Some of the memory and multitasking work-arounds are used by network software, but these are not sufficient to meet the need for truly robust networking. Entire operating systems, in particular the network operating systems such as NetWare, have been created to fill this need. All of the new PC operating systems have features specifically designed to support networking.

Heterogeneous networks, such as TCP/IP internets, bring together a diverse array of systems. The network provides users with direct access to all of the connected systems, which makes skills that are transferable from system to system very desirable. Users are happiest when a command learned on the desktop system can also be used on the mainframe. DOS runs only on Intel processors, while some other operating systems run on a wide range of processors. On a network, an operating system that runs across a range of hardware platforms is clearly desirable, so new PC operating systems like Windows NT are designed to run on a variety of computers.

For many reasons there is widespread interest in alternatives to DOS, and the growing importance of networking provides additional pressure pushing users toward other operating systems. The need for reliable, easily configured network software and the exposure that the network brings to the variety of available operating systems both contribute to the pressure. People who in the past saw DOS as a de facto standard unifying their PCs, now see it as just another operating system. Increasingly they choose PC operating systems other than DOS, and your network will have to be ready to deal with them. Mastering DOS is no longer enough.

Other Operating Systems

DOS is an important part of the PC market. Every network administrator must learn something about DOS in order to deal with the PCs on his network. However, other PC operating systems are growing in importance. Even Microsoft, the developer of DOS, offers alternatives for PCs.

Windows 3.1, another product from Microsoft, is the most popular DOS alternative. Windows 3.1 is not really a separate operating system. It is a multitasking shell that runs on top of DOS and provides a graphical user interface (GUI) very similar to the Macintosh's. The GUI is nice, but multitasking and Windows' ability to use extended memory are the important features for networking.

Windows 3.1 runs most DOS applications, but users running DOS programs under Windows are not taking full advantage of the power of Windows. For this reason, and because Windows has its own unique configuration requirements, we treat Windows as a separate operating system.

Windows for Workgroups (WfW) is a variant of Windows that we will also look at. WfW adds NetBIOS networking to the basic Windows environment. Details of NetBIOS are covered later in this text. For now it is enough to realize that there are PC networking packages in widespread use that are not based on TCP/IP that you will nonetheless be called upon to integrate into your TCP/IP network.

Another PC networking package is NetWare. NetWare is client/server networking software based on the proprietary *NetWare Core Protocol* (NCP). The client software is a small, efficient package that runs directly on PCs running DOS or Windows. The server software, however, is a complete operating system. The server provides print and file service functions similar to those provided by NFS and **lpr** on UNIX systems. We'll look at how to incorporate NetWare servers into your TCP/IP network.

Windows 3.1 and Windows for Workgroups 3.11 are built on top of DOS. Some other PC operating system choices have no direct ties to DOS. Three of these are Windows NT, Windows 95, and UNIX. UNIX, of course, turns a PC into a multitasking, multi-user system with full support for TCP/IP. UNIX is covered extensively in the full line of Nutshell Handbooks from O'Reilly & Associates, so it will not be covered here.

Windows NT, on the other hand, is covered here. Windows NT is not Windows 3.1. It is a full operating system with *preemptive multitasking* and built-in support for TCP/IP (among other networking systems). The only link between Windows NT 3.5 and Windows 3.1 is that they share a common GUI.

Windows 95 is a new operating system designed to replace DOS and Windows 3.1. Like Windows NT, it includes built-in support for TCP/IP. Operating systems like Windows NT and Windows 95 that support a full range of services are actually easier for the network administrator to configure than DOS is.

Despite their advantages, the alternatives to DOS have their own problems. The most obvious is that a greater variety of operating systems means a greater variety of network configuration commands for you to master. Another problem is the difficulties that can occur during the initial installation of a new PC operating system. The difficulties are usually that:

- The operating system cannot determine the hardware configuration because the bus or adapter cards lack the necessary intelligence.

- The operating system cannot support all of the hardware because it lacks the necessary drivers.

No operating system choice is perfect. Every choice has its own unique advantages and disadvantages. In the next chapter we'll look at ways to minimize the disadvantages and exploit the advantages for your network.

Summary

PCs are powerful, popular and easy to use. The popularity of PCs means that they will probably be the most numerous systems on your network. The "ease-of-use" of PCs is often mistaken to mean that they are easy to support. In fact, they need as much or more technical support as large systems do. The wide variety of operating system, networking, and hardware choices available for PCs add to the technical complexity of supporting them.

In the next two chapters we look at ways to deal with this technical challenge. Chapter 2 covers techniques for reducing the support burden and for widening the group of people involved in PC support.

2

Dealing with the Dilemma

As technical people, we understand that PCs have the same hardware and operating systems support requirements as any other computer, and that the sheer number of PCs makes them a network's single biggest support requirement. Unfortunately, PCs do not get the respect they deserve. Too often management views them as "office equipment." This misperception leads to PCs getting little or no technical support. However, you can bet that you'll be expected to support the PCs connected to your network whether or not this support is formally recognized by management. You may find yourself climbing into the guts of a PC to straighten out its configuration because the PC's problem is reported simply as "the network is broken." Too many such reports, even though untrue, undermine confidence in your network. You have to respond to them no matter who is officially assigned PC support.

With limited resources you need creative ways to reduce the network support workload and to extend the circle of people who can help. In this chapter we look at ways to do both of these things by:

- Planning your network and each individual system installation

- Training users and developing grassroots support personnel

- Standardizing the hardware and software components that receive full support

Attitude Adjustment

Before we get into the meat of this chapter, I want to discuss something that can get in the way of effective network support. It is your attitude toward your customers. Network users are our customers. Sometimes when we view the people on the network as "users" and ourselves as service providers, we feel we're doing them a favor. That's not the case. We're not doing anyone a favor; we're doing our jobs. We're employed to support a network, and the people on the network are the customers of our services. If we didn't have any customers, we wouldn't have any job. Of course there are going to be some idiots who try to push you around and monopolize your time. Don't let them sour you to the point that you start treating everyone like an idiot. If you do, your customers will turn to others for support, and you may lose control of your own network.

This attitude of respect even extends to the customer's computer. I know it sounds silly, but many people take criticism of their computer as a personal insult. Just look at the religious debates between Windows NT and UNIX, or PCs and work-stations that take place on various newsgroups. To the outsider these debates are ridiculous. But perfectly sane, intelligent people get drawn into these meaningless arguments because they see an attack on the computer they use as a personal attack.

Many TCP/IP network administrators have a UNIX background. If you're in this category, be careful about a bias against PC systems. In particular, don't tell your PC customers that they wouldn't have problems if they'd only switch to UNIX. As we've noted, some people take this as personal criticism. Others may think that it indicates that TCP/IP only supports UNIX systems effectively. They may turn to other networks that are marketed as PC networks. Instead of supporting one more PC, you may find yourself supporting an entire non-TCP/IP network!

Finally, don't fall into the same trap as your customers. Don't take criticism of your network personally. If you provide high quality services and ensure that your management and customers know it, occasional criticism from irate customers will not undermine the confidence people have in your network. If you react defensively to the criticism of frustrated users, you waste time and focus more importance on the criticism than it deserves. The best way to handle a user's problem is to fix it.

To sum up this digression: don't be your own worst enemy. Cultivate an attitude of professional technical support that builds confidence in your abilities, your services, and your network.

Avoiding Problems

You can't avoid all PC problems, but you can minimize the number you encounter by proper preparation. To properly prepare your network:

- Design the network to support PC users.

- Learn about the computers using your network.

- Teach users to understand their systems and the network.

- Select systems that can be easily supported and are acceptable to the users.

This is a lot to do, and you probably already have more work than you can do every day without adding any new tasks. Nevertheless, completing them can make your network easier to maintain. In the long run, developing a robust network with well-documented systems and knowledgeable users is worth the effort. In the following sections we discuss specific techniques for accomplishing these tasks.

Planning

A good network begins with good planning. We divide network planning into two categories. The first is planning the physical network architecture to minimize the problems caused by users. The second is the detailed planning of each system installation.

If you're building a new network from scratch, you're in luck. You have a chance to do it right from the start. Plan a network that can be supported with a limited staff. People are much more expensive than computers or software. If you're able to convince your management that designing the right kind of network reduces the need for increased staff, you may be able to get the materials you need to build a quality network. Those of us with old networks envy you!

If your network already exists, there are probably some things about it that can't be changed. These things are called *legacy systems*: systems that exist, must be supported, and cannot be easily replaced. You obviously can't scrap your entire network just to build one that is easier to maintain, but don't despair. Incremental improvements happen even on existing networks. As your network expands, you can design each new piece to be more easily supported. The detailed installation planning we discuss later is applied as each new system is installed. Eventually the number of documented systems will increase to the point where the old legacy systems are a small enough part of the whole to be replaced. The key is to start improving your network as soon as possible without letting the size of the task discourage you.

An Accident-proof Network

An "accident-proof" network is designed so that the actions of one user do not affect the network access of another user. We're not talking about the malicious actions that network security protects against.[*] We're talking about mistakes. Even given this limited definition, no network is really accident-proof. Our aim is to reduce the impact of a user's mistake on the other users, while knowing full well that some accidents cannot be planned for.

One key to an accident-proof PC network is physical security. Design a network that a user cannot bring down by merely disconnecting his PC, or even by accidentally cutting a wire in his office. Ideally, the network components in the user's office should be sufficiently isolated from the network so that damage to those components does not damage the entire network. Only trained support personnel

---

[*] Chapter 12, *Network Security*, in *TCP/IP Network Administration* covers this. Computer security is also covered in great detail in *Practical UNIX Security*, by Garfinkel and Spafford, O'Reilly & Assocates, 1991.

should have physical access to shared network components, and only trained support personnel should attempt to fix the hardware. Physical security is accomplished by placing critical components inside walls and behind locked doors that only the support staff can open. This type of security is essential for a reliable network, but it places certain constraints on the type of wiring used and adds to the cost of a network. To see why this is true let's look at the different types of wiring.

Ethernet wiring comes in three forms:

- *Thicknet*, a thick yellow coaxial cable that is about .5" in diameter. This cable is specified in the IEEE 10Base5 standard.

- *Thinnet*, a thin black coaxial cable that is about .2" in diameter. It is specified in the IEEE 10Base2 standard.

- *Unshielded twisted pair (UTP)*, a standard telephone cable made up of pairs of wire twisted together. Telephone people refer to this as a "Category 3" cable.[*] Its use for Ethernet is defined in the IEEE 10BaseT specification.

Our discussion of wiring does not include Token Ring, but the basic concept of physical security is the same for Token Ring and Ethernet. We concentrate on Ethernet because it holds the lion's share of the TCP/IP LAN market, and it is lower cost. Table 2-1 compares the characteristics of the three Ethernet wiring schemes.

Table 2–1: Ethernet Wiring Limits

Maximum	10Base5	10Base2	10BaseT
Segment Length	500 m	185 m	500 m[a]
Repeaters or Concentrators	4	4	4
Total Length	2500 m	925 m	2500 m[a]
Nodes per Segment	100	30	512
Workstation Cable	N/A	N/A	100 m

[a] 10BaseT concentrators can be connected to 10Base5 wiring.

Thicknet is rarely used to directly connect PCs. Thicknet is generally used for *backbone* Ethernets. A backbone network is used to interconnect other networks, as in Figure 2-1. Thicknet is used for backbones because it allows longer cable runs than thinnet. About the only time thicknet is used to connect PCs is when the thicknet cable already exists because of an old Ethernet installation. For new PC installations, 10BaseT is rapidly becoming the most popular wiring scheme.

A 10BaseT system requires a concentrator or hub to operate. In fact it is really a technique for wiring computers to concentrators. The concentrators themselves can be interconnected using any Ethernet wiring scheme. Purchasing a

---

* There is also a "Category 5" cable, which can be used for newer networking standards (like 100BaseT, or fast Ethernet) that operate at much higher data rates. Category 5 cable is harder to install correctly, but is probably a worthwhile investment.

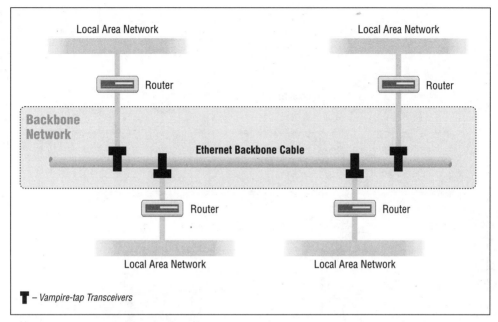

Local Area Network   Local Area Network

Router   Router

Backbone
Network   **Ethernet Backbone Cable**

▉ – *Vampire-tap Transceivers*

Router   Router

Local Area Network   Local Area Network

Figure 2–1: A Backbone Network

concentrator adds cost to the basic cost of the wiring. At first this looks like a distinct cost disadvantage for 10BaseT systems, but the cost difference is less than it first appears. Thicknet (10Base5) always requires an external transceiver that adds a cost to each system, and except for very small installations, thinnet (10Base2) also requires an external transceiver for an accident-proof network. Figure 2-2 shows why.

Notice how thinnet wiring runs from system to system. When internal transceivers are used, the shared Ethernet wire runs directly into the office, into the user's PC, and back out again. If the user opens the cable when moving his PC, the network goes down. If the user crushes the cable when moving furniture in his office, the network goes down, and the entire segment of cable may need to be replaced. Clearly this is not an accident-proof installation. In fact it is an accident waiting to happen. The installation using external transceivers is more secure because the shared cable is mostly behind the wall. But even here the shared cable may be slightly exposed if the transceiver is installed in the office to allow the status lights to be viewed.

There are some modular wiring systems that allow the thinnet cable to be kept completely behind the wall. The one I am familiar with is called *FastTap for Thin-Net*, and it is available from Black Box Corporation. The system requires a special *FastTap* barrel assembly that is attached directly to the thinnet cable, a special wall plate, and a special drop cable. The components are designed so that inserting and removing the drop cable does not interrupt service on the thinnet cable. A

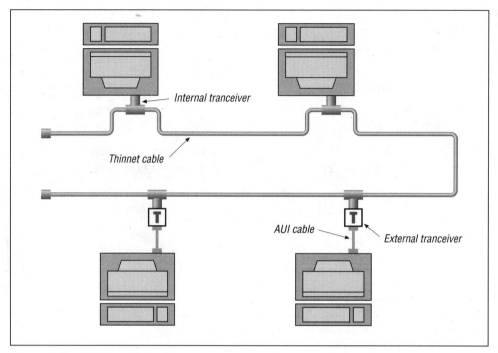

Internal tranceiver

Thinnet cable

AUI cable

External tranceiver

Figure 2–2: A Thinnet Network

modular system like *FastTap* can be used to make an existing thinnet installation more secure at a lower cost than adding external transceivers.

A 10BaseT installation does not need additional equipment to be made physically secure. Figure 2-3 shows a 10BaseT installation. An external transceiver is not required for physical security because the wire that runs to the PC is not a shared cable. If the user disconnects the computer or crushes the cable, only his computer is affected. The network continues to run and service everyone else. The hub, located in a locked closet, provides a secure, centralized service point. The only special limitation of a 10BaseT installation is that no single workstation cable run can be longer than 100 meters.

Each Ethernet specification, 10Base2, 10Base5 and 10BaseT, has limitations on the length of cable segments, total cable length, number of repeaters, etc. You may be tempted to exceed them, particularly in the case of the 100 meter limit for 10BaseT. Don't give into temptation; you'll only regret it later.

Late collisions are one example of why you'll regret violating the Ethernet specifications. Late collisions are undetected collisions caused by a cable segment that is too long. Collisions are a normal part of Ethernet operation. They occur when two or more systems transmit at the same time contending for the right to control the network. If a system transmits 64 bytes, it is considered to be in control, and the other systems are supposed to be quiet until the controlling system has finished. It

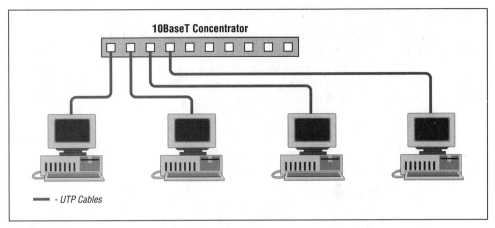

Figure 2–3: A 10BaseT Network

is possible, if the total length of an Ethernet exceeds the specifications, for a system not to know that another system has control of the network and to transmit right over the controlling system's packet. This creates a packet greater than 64 bytes long with a CRC error. The busier the network, the worse this problem becomes.

Sometimes when an installation doesn't work because the cable is too long or otherwise out of spec, people use a transceiver or network card that functions even over an out-of-spec link to "solve" the problem. Don't do it. You're not solving anything. You're just hiding a problem that may come back to haunt you in the future. There are enough problems without making your own.

Detecting problems, spotting trends, and managing devices is an important part of running a reliable network. In Chapter 3 we'll look at software and hardware tools that help with this task. You should plan for network management when you design your network. Hardware and software that collect and report information and that can be remotely managed are very desirable. In a large 10BaseT installation, hubs that can be remotely managed are almost indispensable.

Simple Network Management Protocol (SNMP) is the standard management software for TCP/IP networks.[*] The management station software normally runs on a UNIX workstation and is usually selected to be compatible with the specific routers or hubs used in the network. In this sense it is not really a PC issue, but increasingly the TCP/IP packages for PCs include an *SNMP agent*. The agent is the software that reports information about a device back to the management station. SNMP may help you manage the PCs on your network, so we'll look at configuring a PC SNMP agent in Chapter 3.

---

[*] The new version of SNMP, which includes enhanced security, is called SNMP2 or SNMPv2.

PC Installation Planning

A PC network installation requires more configuration information than the network connection for a UNIX system. Certain configuration values are required by TCP/IP for all systems that connect to the network, but a PC also has configuration parameters specific to its hardware and operating systems. Let's look first at the TCP/IP parameters required of every system:

- A unique IP address

- The correct subnet mask

- A unique hostname and a domain name

- The address of a name server

- The correct routing information, either a default gateway address or the appropriate dynamic routing protocol configuration

- The correct broadcast address

Details about why these configuration values are required by TCP/IP and what they are used for are covered in *TCP/IP Network Administration*, so the full details won't be covered here. If you're familiar with these things, skip to the section *PC-specific Requirements*. Otherwise, read on for a synopsis of the TCP/IP configuration parameters.

IP address

Every computer on a TCP/IP network is identified by a unique *IP address*. The address must be *globally unique*, which means that a computer cannot have the same IP address as any other computer with which it can communicate. Keeping addresses globally unique in a worldwide network like the Internet is a big job, which is assigned to Registration Services at the InterNIC *(rs.internic.net)*. On your network, the network administrator is responsible for keeping addresses unique.

IP addresses are generally written as four decimal numbers separated by dots, e.g., 128.66.12.1. This address format is called *dotted decimal notation*. Each decimal number represents one byte of the address, so the dot-separated decimal values can range from 0 to 255.

An IP address identifies a network and a computer on that network. The number of bytes that identify the network and the number that identify the computer vary according to the *address class*. To determine the class of an address, look at the value of the first byte:

- A first byte value less than 128 indicates a *class A* address. In a class A address, the first byte is the network number, and the last three bytes are the host number.* There are very few class A network addresses, but each one can address millions of hosts.

- A first byte value from 128 to 191 means the address is a *class B* network address. The first two bytes of a class B address are the network number, and the last two bytes are the host number. There are thousands of class B network addresses, and each class B network can address thousands of hosts.

- A first byte from 192 to 223 means the address is a *class C* address. Class C addresses use the first three bytes to identify the network and the last byte to identify the host. Therefore there are millions of class C networks, but each network has only about 250 host addresses.

- Addresses with a first byte value greater than 223 are reserved for special use. An example of a special use address is a *multicast address*. Multicast addresses are used to address groups of computers simultaneously.

If you already have a TCP/IP network, you already have a TCP/IP network address. If you are installing your organization's first TCP/IP network and you don't have an official IP address, obtain one from the InterNIC now. Remember, IP addresses must be globally unique. If there is any chance at all that your network will connect to the Internet, get an official IP network number that the InterNIC ensures is unique. Contact the InterNIC at 1-800-444-4345 for information.†

Subnets

Host addresses within a network must also be unique. Two techniques are commonly used to accomplish this. One technique is to maintain a central registry for the entire network out of which addresses are assigned one at a time. This technique works best on small networks where a single administrator can handle all of the assignments without being overwhelmed. On larger networks, blocks of addresses are delegated to local network administrators who then assign individual host addresses from the blocks. The blocks of addresses can simply be paperwork assignments, or they can be formal *subnets*.

Subnets are used for administrative reasons, as noted above, but that is not the only reason to subnet. Subnets are "real" IP networks that are identified in the routing table just like any other real network. This means that subnets can be used with routers to physically subdivide a network to deal with technical problems,

---

* In TCP/IP, a computer is called a *host*, and the network address is called the *network number*.

† There are several excellent references on connecting to the Internet. Details of the procedures and applications needed to obtain an official IP address and domain name are found in *TCP/IP Network Administration*. Descriptions of the benefits and services of the Internet are found in the *Whole Internet User's Guide and Catalog*, and a comparison of various Internet connection services is found in *Connecting to the Internet*. These three books are all from O'Reilly & Associates.

such as overcoming cable length limitations or isolating unwanted traffic onto a single segment. So subnets are used for a variety of reason.

Subnets are created by taking bits from the host portion of an address and using them to define smaller networks within the larger network. How the address is divided into the network portion and the host portion is defined by the *subnet mask*. The subnet mask is a bit mask in which the bits used for the network portion are all set to ones, and the bits used for the host portion are all set to zeros. An example should make this clear.

Address 128.66.12.1 is a class B address, which means that the network number in this address is 128.66. You might say that this address identifies host 12.1 on network 128.66. The interpretation of the address can be changed by applying a subnet mask. Assume the mask is 255.255.255.0. In this mask, all bits are one in the first three bytes and zero in the last byte. Interpreting the address with this mask gives a network number of 128.66.12 and a host number of 1. You might say that this address identifies host 1 on subnet 12 of network 128.66. As you can see, this mask effectively divides the large class B address space into approximately 250 smaller subnets.

Subnet masks are only known locally. They are specifically defined in each host configuration and are not transmitted to remote hosts. Therefore subnet masks are only applied to local network addresses and only work properly if every system on the local network uses the same subnet mask. Because remote systems do not know your subnet mask, they can only apply the address class rules, which every system knows, to interpret your IP address. In the example above, remote systems still see 128.66 as one large class B network. Only systems within 128.66 apply the subnet mask to see how the address should be interpreted. Clearly this only works correctly if every host in 128.66 has the same subnet mask.

Hostnames

When a host is assigned a unique IP address it should also be assigned a unique hostname. The name is not absolutely required by TCP/IP, but most users prefer to use names instead of numbers when dealing with networked computers. Choosing a hostname is a surprisingly emotional issue. As we pointed out earlier, many people identify with their computers and take these things personally. I'd suggest that you read RFC 1178, *Choosing a name for your computer*, and follow the guidelines set down there.

Techniques similar to those used to maintain globally unique IP addresses are used to keep hostnames unique. If a host can only communicate with the hosts on its local network, its name only needs to be unique within that local network. But if a host can communicate with systems worldwide, its name must be unique throughout the world. Again it is the role of Registration Services at the InterNIC to ensure this uniqueness. They do this by assigning globally unique *domain names* to anyone who properly requests one. This process is very similar to the assignment of a network number. The InterNIC ensures that domains are unique and delegates to the domain administrators the responsibility to ensure that the host-names within the domains are unique.

Like IP addresses, hostnames have component parts. The parts of a hostname identify a name domain and a specific host within that domain. Hostnames are written from the most specific to the most general as a series of dot separated labels. Hostnames start with a computer's name, move through locally created domains to the NIC delegated domain, and finally to the top-level domain. To make the structure clear, let's look at a sample hostname.

Assume that you have a host named *peanut* in the domain *nuts.com.** The fully qualified domain name (FQDN) for this host is *peanut.nuts.com*. Locally you may refer to the computer as *peanut*, but a user on the other side of the world refers to it as *peanut.nuts.com*. The InterNIC ensures that *nuts.com* is unique, and the local domain administrator ensures that *peanut* is unique within the *nuts.com* domain.

Again, the local organization will probably take one of two approaches to maintain unique names within the domain. Small networks usually maintain a single database of names controlled by a central administrator. Large networks usually create *subdomains* within the domain and delegate authority to assign names within the subdomains to local subdomain administrators. Once the NIC has assigned an organization a domain, that organization has the right to create subdomains within that domain without consulting the NIC.

We might create a subdomain, *sales.nuts.com*, within the *nuts.com* domain and delegate authority over that domain to Tyler McCafferty in the sales department. Tyler then creates hostnames within that subdomain, one of which might even be *peanut*. This *peanut* would not conflict with the other one because its real name (its FQDN) is *peanut.sales.nuts.com*, which is not the same as *peanut.nuts.com*. Note that it is NOT a good idea to have similar hostnames in two local subdomains. This example illustrates only that there isn't a name conflict as far as the software is concerned. The confusion this would cause for network users is another matter!

Name service

Every domain and subdomain is served by a *name server*.† The name server takes the hostnames and turns them into IP addresses for use by the TCP/IP software. If you use Domain Name Service, each PC configuration needs to identify a valid name server for its software to use for name-to-address translation.

It is not necessary to use DNS unless your network connects to the Internet. If it does, you must use DNS, and all of the information in the previous section applies

---

* The *com* domain is a top-level domain used for commercial organizations. *nuts* is the domain within *com* that the InterNIC delegated to our imaginary company.
† Domain name service is covered in Chapters 3 and 8, and Appendix D, of *TCP/IP Network Administration*, but the most complete reference is *DNS and BIND* from O'Reilly & Associates.

to you. If your system is on a small, isolated network, it's possible to map host-names to IP addresses using the *host table*. The host table is a file of hostnames and addresses that is read directly on the PC. The system administrator is responsible for keeping the table up to date. The following chapters have examples of configuring both DNS and the host table.

Routing

Routing is absolutely required for TCP/IP to function. To reach a remote destination, your computer has to know the correct path to follow. Routes identify these paths. Routes are usually defined in a simple table of destinations and the *gateways* used to reach those destinations.[*] There are two methods commonly used to enter routes into this table: *static routing* and *dynamic routing*. Static routes are configured manually by the system administrator, and dynamic routes are learned by the system via routing protocols. PCs most often use static routing, usually a single static *default route* that points to a router that forwards all data for the PC.

Configuring routing for DOS is different from configuring routing under UNIX because DOS is not multitasking. Without multitasking, a routing protocol cannot run as a background process. This is one reason that most PCs use static routes. Additionally, many PC TCP/IP implementations only permit one static route to be entered. This doesn't give you much choice, but at least you won't spend much time thinking about the routing configuration!

Figure 2-4 shows a small network with two routers and two computers. One router connects the network to other local networks, and the other connects the network to the Internet. One of the computers is a UNIX system, and the other is a PC running DOS.

The UNIX system administrator can run a routing protocol and let the routers create the routing table for his system. Alternatively, he might create a static routing table with the default route pointing to the Internet gateway *almond.nuts.com*, and individual routes for the local subnets pointing to the internal gateway *pecan.nuts.com*. On the UNIX system, *almond* is chosen as the default gateway because the greatest number of static routes are eliminated by using it as the default. You choose *almond* even if the bulk of the traffic from *hazel* is sent to the local subnets through *pecan*. In this case it is the number of routes, not how often they are used, that determines which gateway is the default.

The PC configuration is different. The PC only allows one route to be entered, even though there are two routers. It relies on ICMP Redirects for corrections when it sends data to the wrong router.[†] In this case, select the gateway that is used most often as the default gateway and allow it to correct you on the

---

[*] TCP/IP terminology defines a gateway, also called an *IP router*, as a system that forwards data between networks.

[†] *Internet Control Message Protocol* (ICMP) is part of TCP/IP. One thing it can do is direct a host to use another router when the other router provides a better path to a remote destination. The message it uses to correct the route is called an *ICMP Redirect*.

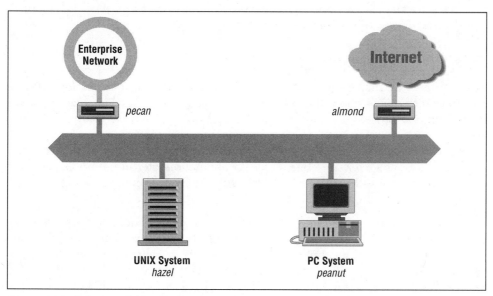

Figure 2–4: Subnet with Two Routers

occasions that your data should really be sent to the other router. In this case it is how often the routes are used, not the number of routes, that determines which gateway should be the default. Therefore the PC in our example uses *pecan* as its default gateway.

Broadcast address

The last commonly used TCP/IP configuration parameter that we discuss is the *broadcast address.* The broadcast address is a special address the system uses to speak to every computer on the local network simultaneously, something that is more common than you might imagine. This is a standardized value that really should not need to be defined in the configuration. Unfortunately it does.

The standard broadcast address is an IP address with all bits in the host portion set to ones. For example, the broadcast address for network 128.66.0.0 is 128.66.255.255; on network 201.36.12.0, the broadcast address is 201.36.12.255. Notice that an IP address with the host bits set to zeros refers to a network. 128.66.0.0 means network number 128.66, while 128.66.255.255 is the broadcast address for all hosts on network number 128.66. A network address and a broadcast address are two different things. However, due to a historical mix-up these two numbers have become confused. Some systems mistakenly get configured with the network address, 128.66.0.0 in our example, as the broadcast address, and oddly enough it works just fine. Although the standard broadcast address is preferred, either the standard broadcast address or the network address can be used as a broadcast address. The key requirement is that every system on the local network must use the same value. For this reason it is best to define the standard broadcast address explicitly for every system.

PC-specific Requirements

In the same way that the lack of multitasking limits routing choices for a PC, it changes other things about the configuration. Many of the services that are done by background processes on a UNIX system are done by remote servers for a PC. To configure a PC, you need to know what systems provide services for the network. Your PC will certainly have a mail server and will probably also have a file server and a print server. We cover server configuration later in the book. For now it is only important to know that each PC needs to know the addresses of the various servers it relies on.

A PC configuration also requires hardware specific information. In particular you need to know and record the information required to configure the network adapter card. The possible configuration items used for each adapter are: the Interrupt Request Number (IRQ), the DMA Request Number (DRQ), the I/O Port Address, and the Adapter Memory Address. These configuration items are discussed in Chapter 1, *The PC Dilemma*. Ensure that these values do not conflict with the values assigned to other adapters installed in the PC.

There are other items that should also be recorded for each PC. These aren't things that you configure; they're values that you may find useful in the future for debugging purposes. Chapter 3, *Network Tools*, covers the PC software tools that are used to obtain the values. The items that should be recorded are:

The Media Access Control (MAC) layer address
> In a TCP/IP environment this is usually an Ethernet address. Having the MAC layer address is helpful for tracking down physical layer problems, or Address Resolution Protocol (ARP) problems. Because the Ethernet cards for PCs come from many different manufacturers, attempting to identify the source of a problem by looking at the vendor identification in the Ethernet address is futile.[*] It's best to record the Ethernet address of each PC as it's installed.

A general description of the system
> PCs are built from hardware and software from many different sources. Record the name and release number of the operating system as well as the brand name and release number of the TCP/IP software. Record the hardware configuration, including the manufacturer, the processor type, the clock speed, the ROM BIOS brand name and version, the amount of RAM, the monitor type and resolution, the available peripherals, and the various adapter cards. This seems like a lot to do but it's worthwhile. Recording the initial configuration provides a baseline against which to check user modifications. It is also easiest

---

* Chapter 11, *Troubleshooting TCP/IP*, of *TCP/IP Network Administration*, lists some of the vendor Ethernet prefixes and shows how they are used to troubleshoot ARP problems. The *Assigned Numbers* RFC contains a more complete list of the prefixes.

to check the configuration before the system starts to malfunction. In the next chapter we look at tools that can help with this inventory.

A list of Terminate and Stay Resident (TSR) programs
Systems running DOS use TSRs to emulate multitasking services. TSR programs are a great source of problems. It's best to know exactly what TSRs are in use and how to boot the system without them.

The memory manager being used
If the system has a memory manager configured, you need to know what it is and how to configure the TCP/IP software to run with it. Memory managers extend DOS allowing it to use memory beyond the 1M byte limit. However, they can change the essential characteristics of DOS and can be incompatible with some applications. You need to know that your TCP/IP software runs with the specific memory managers being used.

Recording all of this information is easier if you develop a standard form and use it for every new installation. Appendix A, *Installation Planning Form*, contains a sample form that covers all of the topics we have mentioned here. Existing systems should also be documented, and the same form can be used. Finding time to document existing systems is the difficult part, but you may be able to get the users to help. If your users are knowledgeable enough, they may be able to fill in the forms themselves. In the next section we look at ways to train and develop knowledgeable users. Planning is only the first step in building a reliable network.

User Development

A little knowledge is a dangerous thing. We've all heard that old saw. Don't believe it! Knowledge, even a little, makes better users. Give your users all the information they will accept. I know that most of us can think of a know-it-all who is a danger to the network because of the knowledge he *thinks* he possesses. However, the problem is not the knowledge he really possesses, it is his mistaken view of his own abilities. Accurate information may even make the know-it-all less of a problem.

The only dangerous information is misinformation. If you don't give your users the correct information, others are perfectly willing to fill them full of rumors, speculation, and misinformation. These people are not motivated to do wrong. They genuinely think they know what they are talking about, but you're the person who has to straighten out the mess they make. You yourself can be a source of misinformation if you speculate with users about the cause of a network problem. Remember they are not your engineering colleagues; they look to you for answers, not wild guesses. When you have a clear, accurate answer to a problem, give it. Otherwise, don't be afraid to say you don't know the answer but you'll find out. Do yourself a favor. Give your users accurate, quality information before the confusion starts.

How is information disseminated to the users? We discuss three ways: training, documentation, and person-to-person communication. We begin with a section entitled *Training*. We use that word in the broadest sense of the term. In this text, training means several things, only one of which is formal training.

Training

A wide variety of formal training classes can benefit network users. The most beneficial classes are designed specifically for your network and the services it offers. Unfortunately, you're usually the person whose task it is to teach such classes. Don't fight it. The benefits gained by more knowledgeable users far outweigh the effort of creating and teaching the class. Of course if you can get someone else to teach the class, even better. Just make sure you work with them to create accurate class materials that reflect the state of your network. Tune the class to the people who will be attending. Don't overwhelm users with details that are meaningless to them, but don't forget to provide them with the details they need. Detailed information should be provided in the written classroom materials. The lecture and hands-on exercises should stick to the basics. Make sure they grasp the basic concepts of how things work and how they can use the services.

Professionally taught training classes, even when not tailored to your site, are also useful. Be careful, however, not to send people to training classes that increase their confusion. A classic example from the UNIX world is training in BSD system administration for a System V computer. To reduce this type of mistake, only circulate announcements for classes that relate to your site's configuration and encourage users to seek advice from more knowledgeable people before signing up. If your organization has a training department, enlist its help in screening training opportunities.

Training occurs in many forums. Technical conferences and user groups are the most common, but even some free product seminars are useful. However, knowing which conferences, user groups, or seminars are worthwhile is a problem, so let the attendees tell you. Create a newsgroup or mailing list that provides an electronic platform for attendees to sound off about the training they've taken. The network is a powerful tool for creating *communities of interest*, groups of people brought together because of a shared interest. Try to create an electronic community of users who stimulate interest in training and take the initiative in screening training opportunities.

Documentation

Documentation is another important method for disseminating information to your users. It's a requirement for almost every project. While it is obviously needed, it is often ignored. One reason is that writing documentation is no fun. The fun is in designing and developing new systems and services, not in writing about them once the development is done. And once a project is up and running, support often takes so much time that documentation is delayed and eventually forgotten. Even management contributes to the problem. Managers tend to reward the developers, not the writers. For these reasons and more, documentation often gets ignored.

Don't ignore yours. Good documentation is an investment of time and effort that pays for itself by answering users' questions before you have to. Of course there are some who never read the documentation no matter how good it is, but most people do read it. If it answers most of their questions, it saves you time.

The type of documentation we most often think of is traditional printed documentation. It is still the most common and plays a very important role. Printed documentation is essential for the initial system startup and for system recovery. Hardcopy documentation is also an important talisman for users to ward off evil spirits. Even if it is only crumpled up and hurled at the computer when things go wrong, printed documentation provides an important comfort factor. However, printed documentation is difficult to update and keep current. That is one of the reasons that online documentation is growing in popularity.

Traditional documentation can be stored in computer files on anonymous FTP servers and on gopher servers. This allows the documents to be updated more easily than printed documentation, and it allows the users to retrieve updated documents when needed. Anonymous FTP is limited to document retrieval, but gopher allows the user to either retrieve a document or read it online. Make all of your documentation available through the network using one or both of these techniques.

Documentation can also be stored on World Wide Web (WWW) network information servers. WWW servers provide capabilities that go beyond anything provided by either printed documentation or traditional documents stored on a network. Similar to gopher, WWW servers allow documents to be read and searched online or retrieved across the network, but because WWW is a hypertext system, it takes things a step farther. Hypertext documents can include audio and video clips, which are impressive, but the real power of hypertext is the fact that related documents are linked together. Readers can easily follow the links between documents to learn more about a particular subject. Clicking on a highlighted keyword in the current document accesses a related document that is then retrieved from anywhere in the World Wide Web network of servers and opened on your desktop.[*] The convenience and power of WWW is very impressive.

Storing plain text documents does not use WWW to its maximum advantage. Some effort must be made to properly link related documents together. Text files are first converted to Hypertext Markup Language (HTML) and then hand-edited to get the exact linkages desired. The WWW documents that have maximum impact include audio and video information. All of this makes WWW-based documentation

---

[*] See *The Whole Internet User's Guide and Catalog* for a full description of the World Wide Web.

difficult to create. Oddly enough, the technical difficulty seems to motivate some people. You may find that the technical staff prefers creating documentation for a WWW server simply because it is more technically challenging. Use this interest as a way to motivate people to write documentation. Remember all documentation, even documents destined for the WWW, start as text that can be printed as hard-copy or stored in a gopher server.

Online help systems and UNIX **man** pages are some of the oldest electronic infor-mation systems. Unlike the document retrieval systems described above, help sys-tems provide information about specific command syntax. Help systems provide online "how to" instructions for the computer user, and they can be useful for doc-umenting network services. However, they are primarily used on multi-user sys-tems and are only useful to PC users when they are logged into one of those systems. This is changing. New PC operating systems, like Windows NT and Win-dows 95, include extensive help facilities. These new help systems offer hypertext-style links to bring together related topics. They provide information about specific command syntax and online "how to" instructions for the computer user. Help sys-tems are very useful for documenting network services. Learn how to use them and pass that knowledge to your users.

No matter what medium is used to distribute documentation, developing it is simi-lar to developing good training. Make sure the documentation clearly describes the basics and gives the user enough "how to" information to get started. Include details, but don't let them interfere with the basic "how to" message of the docu-ment. Include details in an appendix or in a box so that they are not in the way of those who don't need them, but are available to those who do.

Like training, documentation that is specifically written for your network and ser-vices is the best. However, don't overlook vendor documentation and technical books. These provide the extensive details that many users crave. If documenta-tion comes with the network software, distribute it to the users. If you have only limited copies of the documentation, make at least one copy available for inter-ested users to borrow. Finally, use your internal mailing lists to announce new and updated documentation, to develop interest in appropriate publications, and to allow users to recommend books to each other.

Users can help with much more than evaluating training opportunities and docu-mentation. Many of them are motivated, talented people who want to help. Undi-rected, their help amounts to little more than interference. Properly developed grassroots support groups are a powerful aid in reducing the workload of an over-worked network support staff.

Grassroots support

Grassroots support is the help users give to each other. Creating communities of interest through the services that the network provides is one tool for developing grass roots support. It is a powerful tool not only because it provides a forum for exchanging questions and answers but because it uses the network to do it.

Network involvement as a problem-solving tool helps new users feel comfortable. But even this seemingly free support requires an investment of time from the network support staff. Monitor these electronic groups so that rumors and misinformation are quickly cut off. Keep the groups focused on answering specific questions and away from issues of network engineering and corporate policy. When a group degenerates into a debating society, its usefulness is lost.

Some electronic communities evolve into traditional user groups with regular face-to-face meetings. Traditional user groups are more difficult to start than electronic groups and are usually motivated by one or two particularly active users. The groups are helpful to network administrators because they provide a single point of contact to a group of motivated users. Work with the groups that exist in your organization. You want them on your side!

Ad hoc organizations like users groups, newsgroups, and mailing lists help identify the most knowledgeable users on the network. In PC parlance, these users are called *power users*. Frequently they are more than willing to help others. This is particularly true of the power users who take the time to respond to questions on newsgroups and mailing lists. Provide them with a clear and accurate understanding of how things really work so that when they answer user questions, which they will do anyway, they answer them correctly. Change them from mere power users into *mentors* who educate and support other users. Let them know that you appreciate the help they give others and that you want to work with them. People want to help, and they want to be appreciated.

Some organizations take the mentor concept one step farther and create *user advocates*. A user advocate is a technical stand-in for a new user. When a new employee is hired, the employee is given a user advocate who personally handles getting the computer equipment, central computer account, network connection, and training that the new employee requires. In many companies, advocates are generally computer aides recruited from the secretarial staff, trained, and assigned to the computer support staff or the personnel office. They have good knowledge of how PCs are used in the organization and detailed knowledge of the "who, what, and where" of the organization's computing and networking environment. They help new hires cut through red tape and help them get comfortable with using the computer and network services.

Others who are formally delegated a role in network support are the subnet administrators, subdomain administrators, and system administrators. We discussed the role that the subnet administrators and subdomain administrators play in assigning IP addresses and hostnames, but that is only one part of their duties. They also provide support to the users within their domains and on their subnets.

The subdomain administrator's support is limited to DNS. He answers questions about domain name service and helps users and systems administrators configure DNS for their systems. Keep the subdomain administrator abreast of all DNS information and see that he is adequately trained to do his job.

The subnet administrator has a wider role. Because the subnet administrator assigns addresses on the network, she knows exactly what equipment is connected to the network and who is responsible for that equipment. She is the most important liaison to the local system administrators. The subnet administrator uses her knowledge of the people and systems on her network to filter the large volume of network information and to forward the appropriate information to the correct system administrators. She makes sure that the system administrators on her net are not overwhelmed by meaningless information, but that they receive the information that they need.

Subnet administrators are a key to network support in a large organization. They allow the network administrator to divide a large network into manageable pieces and they give system administrators the personal support that they only get on a smaller network. Subnet administrators should be well trained to understand the details of your network.

System administrators are the last piece in the network support puzzle. They provide direct support for the multi-user systems on the network. PC users log into these systems and use them as servers. They naturally look to the system administrator for technical support. If the system administrator is trained to understand the network, he can answer many of the user's network questions without passing them on to the network administrator.

Subnet, subdomain, and system administrators need to understand their obligations relating to user support, security, and enforcement of network policies. These duties should be made clear at the time they are delegated a subdomain, subnet, or IP address. A letter that makes these duties clear should be sent before the delegation is formalized. The actual delegation is only made after the letter is agreed to by the new administrator. This entire operation must be blessed by management because these administrator roles are formal delegations of power and responsibility.

To keep them informed, create a mailing list for the subnet and subdomain administrators. Allow anyone to join the list so that the power users can also keep informed. This mailing list is the top of the network information tree. The network administrator posts information about the network and the network services to this list. The subnet administrators take the relevant information and post it to the lists of system administrators that they maintain. The system administrators take the information they receive and forward on the relevant parts to the users of their systems.[*] Each person in the information chain contributes to keeping the users properly informed.

---

[*] Every subnet should have a newsgroup or mailing list that addresses every system administrator on the subnet, and every multi-user system should have one that addresses every user of that system.

Standardization

Every network benefits from adequate planning, user training, and good documentation, but standardizing hardware and software components is a technique that is particularly applicable to PC networks. PCs are built from a wide variety of hardware and software. No network support organization can expect to master all of them. For that reason, pick a specific set of components to receive full support and let the users know what they are. All organizations make these selections, either consciously or unconsciously. No organization supports all types of computers equally, and it is best to let your users know the truth before they buy the wrong things.

For PC networking the most important hardware and software items are the network interface card[*] and the TCP/IP software package. The selection of these items is usually determined by a price/performance analysis. Price is always important to PC buyers, but true cost is more than just the initial price. A few hours of labor from a network engineer cost more than an Ethernet card, so pick a card that is easy to configure, reconfigure, and maintain. Likewise, performance is more than how fast a card can send packets. The card needs to have drivers for the software and operating systems you use. Think of all the things you require from a network card before you make a selection.

A few things worth thinking about when selecting a network card are:

Vendor support

It is difficult to determine the quality of vendor support until something goes wrong, and of course you hope it never does. In lieu of actual experience with the vendor's support organization, you can ask yourself a few questions: Does the product come from a well-known vendor? Does your organization have any experience with this manufacturer? Does the local supplier seem competent? Does the vendor have a support hotline? Answers to these questions might help in your analysis. Also look at the documentation that comes with the card. Is it a five-page pamphlet or a fifty-page book? Does the documentation answer your questions or just give vague directions? Well-thought-out documentation shows a commitment to customer support.

Ease of Configuration

A card that must be removed from the system every time it is reconfigured is not "user-friendly." Look for a card that can be configured via software. Also look for a card that supports a wide range of possible configuration values. An IRQ conflict can render a card inoperable. Don't select a card that only allows you to choose a few possible IRQ values.

---

[*] The network interface card in a PC often is called a NIC, not to be confused with the traditional TCP/IP acronym for a network information center (NIC).

Driver support

Select a card that has a wide variety of drivers for different operating systems and network software packages. If available, use the hardware compatibility lists that come with the operating system and the network software to help determine possible choices. Look for a vendor that makes new drivers and software fixes available online so you can download new software when you need it.

Selecting TCP/IP networking software is similar to selecting a network card. It is still a price/performance decision, and vendor support and ease of configuration are still important, but selecting software has some additional factors. First, there is price. No one gives new hardware away, but there are free software packages. As a UNIX user I'm naturally a big fan of free software. I used it extensively in the *TCP/IP Network Administration* book. However, the PC culture is different. Most of the people who use PCs at work do not look at a glitch as an opportunity to track down a bug and send in a fix. They expect the system to run, and they expect you to keep it running. In that environment, it's nice to have a vendor to blame. The biggest danger with free software is that support may not be there when you need it. The graduate student who wrote the package may be assigned another project, or the university may drop the project all together. Additionally, PC software is less expensive than UNIX software and often is steeply discounted when purchased via a *site license* agreement. These two reasons, lack of vendor support and lack of a clear cost benefit, make free software less attractive to the PC market than it is to the UNIX market. Examples of public domain PC software are covered in Appendix E.

Select networking software that meets your needs. The software should have the specific features required for your network services and the correct "look and feel" for your users. Windows users want a network interface that uses the Windows GUI. A TCP/IP package that requires them to use an unfamiliar interface would not be acceptable.

The DOS user interface is a simple command-line interface, remarkably like the UNIX command line. TCP/IP software for DOS should provide network commands that are similar to those provided by UNIX so that the extensive TCP/IP documentation written for UNIX is of some use to PC users. Simply put, **ping** should be **ping**. If a package consistently uses other names for the well-known TCP/IP applications, such as **ftp** and **telnet**, it may cause more confusion than it is worth. If there are just a few variations, they can be fixed with a few batch files.

For example, assume that you select a package that uses **tn** to invoke Telnet instead of the more common **telnet** command. A user following the examples in the *Simple Telnet* section of *The Whole Internet User's Guide and Catalog* could become frustrated and report a network problem because the **telnet** command is not working. You can tell him to look it up in his TCP/IP documentation, but what about the guy who calls five minutes later, and the guy after him. It is best to fix this before the user ever encounters the problem. Create a **telnet** alias for the **tn** command at the time you install the network software by creating a *telnet.bat* file in the execution path. The file might contain the following line:[*]

```
tn %1 %2
```

One or two such fixes are acceptable. Several such variations from the norm would not be.

Investigate before you buy. Don't make a big decision based on advertising. Get a copy of the software you're interested in. Evaluate its documentation and features. Test it in your environment and make sure it provides the quality of service your users will demand.

In this book we use different TCP/IP packages for DOS and Windows. This is done to provide examples from a wide variety of software vendors. You may decide to use a single package for both user interfaces so that you have only one package to master and one vendor to deal with. If you do, make sure the package effectively supports both user interfaces. If it doesn't, you're better off with two packages, each of which is optimized for a specific user interface. User confusion and complaints are harder to deal with than a second vendor!

Regardless of the hardware and software selected, limit the number of suppliers that you deal with. Try to develop a long-term relationship with your supplier. Don't jump from one source to another every time someone offers a discount. A supplier who knows he has a long term customer will give you the support you need when you need it.

Once you have decided on a standard set of hardware and software, how do you enforce these standards? First, clearly state what systems, adapters, and software are fully supported so that people who want to comply with the standards can. But what about the people who don't want to comply? Given the organizational clout most network administrators have, the stick probably won't work. You need a carrot. The best carrot you can offer is convenience. If you have a site license that offers a better price for software than people can get elsewhere, most people will order software through your site license. Stock network interface cards and make them available to the users at cost. Users will get them from you because it is quick and easy. You should do what you can to make your standards easy to implement. Most users won't care that they are buying standard hardware and software. They'll do it because it's convenient.

User advocates, like the ones described in the last section, or a central purchasing department can also help promote standards. User advocates obtain computer systems for new hires. They can easily obtain systems that meet your network standards. Advocates and other grass roots support personnel are motivated to comply with standards because they also support end users. The same things that simplify your support tasks simplify theirs. The purchasing department can enforce

---

[*] This example is specific to FTP Software's product *PC/TCP*. Another software package might require a different and more complex batch file to alias the command.

standards when computers are procured, although getting their cooperation proba-bly requires help from management.

Our discussion has been limited to network hardware and software. Organizations make other support decisions that go beyond the network to such things as oper-ating systems and hardware platforms. Some organizations don't support Mac's, or PC UNIX, or Windows NT, or any number of things. This book has made similar decisions. We cover IBM-compatible PCs running DOS, Windows, and Windows NT, but not dozens of other systems that exist. These decisions are made because no support organization (and no book) can cover everything effectively. Make it clear to your users what you can and cannot do, but don't leave your "unsup-ported" users out in the cold. Help them create their own grass roots support orga-nization through mailing lists, newgroups, and users groups.

Make your standards palatable to users by explaining why they are needed and by making them simple to implement. Most users are glad to comply. Those who don't follow the standard path knowingly choose a lower level of support.

Summary

This chapter suggests three techniques to help you effectively support the PC users on your network. These are:

- *Planning*—to anticipate where problems may occur and design a system that reduces their probability.

- *User Development*—to create a user community that can overcome problems on its own.

- *Standardization*—to concentrate support on specific hardware and software that can truly be mastered.

Throughout this chapter I have addressed you as the network administrator. In reality, that may not be your function. You may be a system administrator, a sub-net administrator, a super user, or just an average network user. You may feel powerless to implement the various suggestions from this chapter. Rubbish! You're in charge of yourself! You're in charge of your PC! (That's one of the great things about PCs.) Use the planning form in Appendix A to document your system. Prac-tice user development, even if it's confined to self development. If any exist, adhere to your organization's network standards. If they don't exist, use the guide-lines for developing those standards to select your own hardware and software. The fact that you're reading this book shows you to be a motivated, knowledge-able "networker." Use your knowledge and skill to improve the network.

The first two chapters have been general in nature, defining the challenge pre-sented by networking PCs and the approaches used to deal with the challenge. Chapter 3, which covers specific PC support tools, continues the discussion of how to deal with the challenge of networking PCs but in a more specific, detailed manner.

3

Network Tools

The first two chapters point out that there are many challenging tasks involved in keeping a network of PCs running. Luckily, you do not have to face these challenges alone. Your PC can help. It is a powerful tool that is as easily applied to network management tasks as it is to other work. No computer has a richer software library than a PC, and many of the programs in this library help manage a network.

In this chapter, we look at software that eases the installation and maintenance of networked PCs. We also look at hardware tools, some of which are based on Personal Computers, that help troubleshoot network problems.

Installation Tools

Most problems occur during a system's initial installation because most problems are caused by configuration errors. During the initial configuration, new hardware (the network adapter) and new software (the TCP/IP software) are installed at the same time. Configuration problems in one can hide problems that are lurking in the other.

It is easier to add a new network interface without causing a conflict if you understand the current configuration of the system and the network. Documenting each system's configuration is part of keeping your understanding current. It is possible to document a system with pencil and paper, but frankly it isn't much fun. If you're like me, you prefer to let the computer do the work. Happily there are several tools available that automatically document a PC's hardware configuration for you.

EISA Configuration Programs

Every EISA system comes with an EISA Configuration Utility (ECU) to configure the system and its adapter cards. Unlike many ISA cards, all EISA adapters are configured via software. EISA cards are usually delivered with a diskette that contains an adapter configuration file designed to be read by the ECU. The diskette frequently includes an *overlay* file that provides the ECU with a user interface customized for installing the specific adapter. An ECU directory that contains both adapter configuration files and overlay files is listed below. Adapter configuration files always have names that begin with an exclamation and end with a .CFG extension. The overlay files are usually identified by either a .OVR or a .OVL file extension.

```
Volume in drive C is MS-DOS_6
Volume Serial Number is 1AD2-82A2

Directory of C:\cfg

.CFG        EXE        308397 07-14-92   01:40AM
EISACFG     HLP         40196 07-14-92   01:40AM
ADP0000     OVR         24724 06-04-92   09:43AM
SMC3200     OVR         11620 01-16-92   01:41PM
!ECS1100    CFG          3097 06-02-92   04:48AM
!ECS1110    CFG          3097 06-02-92   04:48AM
ECS1110     CMS           423 01-07-94   04:02PM
ECS1110     INF          2488 01-07-94   04:02PM
!TCM5094    CFG          3555 07-08-93   02:29PM
CFG         ISA          1792 09-29-93   04:54PM
            12 File(s)      399389 bytes
                         99397632 bytes free
```

Each vendor has its own version of the ECU. Those that I am familiar with, MCS (**CF**), Phoenix (**PTLECU**) and AMI (**CFG**), are all very similar. I use the CFG program from AMI in my examples because I know it best, but all of the utilities have very similar user interfaces. Figure 3-1 shows an example of this full-screen interface.

Figure 3-1 shows the AMI ECU display after **Configure** was selected from the **Configure** pulldown menu. Selecting any adapter shown in the Manual Configuration box brings up another display showing the specific configuration values set for that adapter and allowing the values to be changed. All very slick and easy.

A major benefit of the ECU program is that it automatically detects potential configuration conflicts and allows you to fix them before you install the network software. This is not limited to EISA adapter cards. Many EISA bus PCs have some ISA cards installed. The ECU allows the settings from ISA cards to be stored in the configuration file so that they can also be checked for conflicts. Obviously the

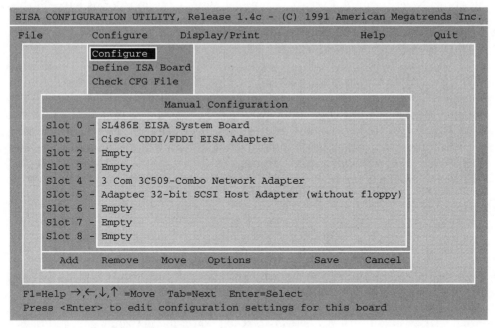

Figure 3-1: EISA Configuration Utility

ECU does not actually configure the ISA cards, which is still done by DIP switches and jumpers.* But it does provide a tool for documenting the ISA configuration settings as part of the overall system configuration.

Refer to Figure 3-1 and to the directory listing shown above. In Figure 3-1, the second entry in the **Configure** pulldown menu is **Define ISA Board**. Selecting that menu item brings up a window that allows you to identify the various ISA boards installed in the system and to define the configuration parameters used by the adapters. The information about the ISA cards is stored in the CFG.ISA file.

Selecting **Display/Print** from the menu bar brings up another menu from which you choose the information you want to print. Choices include **DMA Resources**, **IRQ Resources**, **Port Resources**, and **Memory Resources**—the four adapter configuration values discussed in Chapter 1, *The PC Dilemma*. A report of the current assignment of these values can be printed or directed to a file. The network manager keeps this listing, along with listings of the system and network configuration files, as a historical record of the state of the system's configuration at the time the network was installed. When she's called back to work on the system at some future date, she can quickly tell if the configuration has been modified. The user's mantra is "I didn't change anything. It just stopped working." This historical record provides a reality check for the user's memory.

---

* Some software-configurable ISA cards can be configured via the system's ECU. The 3COM 3C509 Ethernet card is an example.

All of this is very helpful if you have an EISA system, but most of us have ISA bus computers. Nothing similar to the ECU comes with an ISA system, but there are many add-on programs available that document the configuration of ISA systems.

Configuration Documenters

Several programs for documenting PC configurations exist. Some system documentation utilities are part of large utility packages such as the *Norton Utilities*. Others, such as *CheckIt Pro*, are standalone packages specifically designed for documenting systems. Our examples use the documentation utility that is bundled into DOS 6.22, which is the MSD command. We use MSD because it is widely available, but all of these programs provide essentially the same information.

To start the Microsoft Diagnostics utility, enter MSD at the DOS prompt. You see a full-screen display that has various boxes reporting the status of the system. Each box has a label on it, and one letter in the label is highlighted. To select a specific box, type the highlighted letter.

Many of the boxes provide a summary of the hardware installed in the system, such as the CPU type and the type of video card installed. A few of the boxes provide details that are important to a network administrator. For example, the TSR Programs box and the Device Drivers box tell you if the network TSRs and device drivers are loaded. The IRQ Status box helps you avoid an IRQ conflict. Figure 3-2 shows the IRQ Status display.

Figure 3-2 lists the IRQs, the vector address installed for each interrupt, the description of the device assigned to the interrupt, whether or not the device was detected, and the software that is handling the interrupt. MSD will not always detect the network adapter or describe it properly.[*] Look at the whole entry to determine if an interrupt is used.

In our example, the system has a 3COM card installed on interrupt 10. MSD gives it a description of (`Reserved`), which means "this interrupt is available." Additionally, MSD does not show any value for this interrupt in the `Detected` field. We know, however, that the interrupt is in use because it is assigned to ELNK3$, which is the driver for this network adapter.

The **Files** menu (see the upper left corner of Figure 3-2) provides additional useful information. This menu contains entries for all of the boot files and system initialization files. A file can be displayed on the screen or printed to the printer. The reports this generates provide much of the information a network manager needs about the current hardware configuration.

System documentation utilities provide a wider array of information than an ECU does. But the key items of information for a network manager are the adapter configuration and the contents of the system and network configuration files. All

---

[*] This problem is not particular to MSD. Other documentation utilities have the same difficulty.

```
┌─────────────────────────────────────────────────────────────────────┐
│  File      Utilities       Help                                       │
├─────────────────────────────────────────────────────────────────────┤
│                             IRQ Usage                                 │
│   IRQ  Address      Description        Detected       Handled By      │
│     0  0D0A:1875    Timer Click        Yes            Block Device     │
│     1  0D0A:1923    Keyboard           Yes            Block Device     │
│     2  06E6:0057    Second 8259A       Yes            Default Handlers │
│     3  06E6:006F    COM2:  COM4:       COM2:          Default Handlers │
│     4  06E6:0087    COM1:  COM3:       COM1:          Default Handlers │
│     5  06E6:009F    LPT2:              No             Default Handlers │
│     6  06E6:00B7    Floppy Disk        Yes            Default Handlers │
│     7  0070:06F4    LPT1:              Yes            System Area      │
│     8  06E6:0052    Real-Time Clock    Yes            Default Handlers │
│     9  F000:EED2    Redirected IRQ2    Yes            BIOS             │
│    10  0893:0530    (Reserved)                        ELNK3$           │
│    11  06E6:00E7    (Reserved)                        Default Handlers │
│    12  06E6:00FF    (Reserved)                        Default Handlers │
│    13  F000:EEDB    Math Coprocessor   Yes            BIOS             │
│    14  06E6:0117    Fixed Disk         Yes            Default Handlers │
│    15  F000:8EB7    (Reserved)                        BIOS             │
│                       ┌──────────┐                                    │
│                       │    OK     │                                   │
│                       └──────────┘                                    │
│  IRQ Status: Displays current usage of hardware interrupts.           │
└─────────────────────────────────────────────────────────────────────┘
```

Figure 3-2: Microsoft Diagnostics Utility

system documentation programs provide this information, and all use a graphic user interface similar to the one shown in Figure 3-2. These programs are easy to use and really require little explanation. The important thing is not how to operate the program but how to use the information it provides.

The adapter configuration information tells you if there are any hardware conflicts. Eliminate conflicts by carefully reconfiguring the individual adapter cards. The startup files help if there are any software conflicts. By starting with a basic network configuration and adding the other drivers and programs from the user's CONFIG.SYS and AUTOEXEC.BAT files one at a time, you can find out what software conflicts with the network. This "brute-force" approach may seem inefficient but it works well. Since it is only used during the initial installation, and then only if a software problem occurs, it is more efficient then developing a special debugging scheme for these isolated incidents.

It is not necessary to edit both startup files to control which drivers and programs are started at boot time. The DOS 6.x boot program provides an escape mechanism that lets you select the drivers started from the CONFIG.SYS file. It's easy to do:

1. Reboot the PC. As soon as "Starting MS-DOS..." is displayed, press the **F8** function key. The system then displays the message "MS-DOS will prompt you to confirm each CONFIG.SYS command."

2. Each command is displayed in this form: "DEVICE=C:\DOS\SETVER.EXE [Y/N]?" Press **Y** for each device driver you want to start and **N** for each device driver that you want to skip. Using this technique, it is easy to add drivers one at a time to the network configuration until you find the one that is causing problems.

3. After processing CONFIG.SYS the system prompts "Process AUTOEXEC.BAT [Y/N]?" Press **Y**.

4. Repeat steps 1 through 3, adding a device driver with each iteration. If the software conflict occurs, you'll know which driver is the culprit.

5. If the problem is not caused by a driver from the CONFIG.SYS file, it might be caused by a program loaded by AUTOEXEC.BAT. You must use an editor to modify the configuration of that file. Insert the the remark (REM) command at the beginning of each line you wish to comment out. Start by commenting out every resident program except the network. Uncomment one additional program with each iteration until you find the one causing the problem.

Once you find the software that is interfering with the network, what do you do about it? Sometimes there is nothing that can be done. Some TSRs operate in such a non-standard way that they don't get along with anything else and must be removed from the system. However, some software conflicts are avoided through proper memory management. Memory managers are covered in the next section.

Both of the documentation tools we mentioned, *Norton Utilities* and *CheckIt Pro*, run on a single system. There are other system documentation tools that run over a network. The advantage of the network-based tools is that they constantly update the network manager about the configuration status of the systems on her network. When a user modifies a configuration, the manager is alerted. If trouble follows, she has a good indication of the cause. The problem with most of the current network-based tools for PCs is that they are based on Novell network protocols. That's not really a technical problem, but Novell tools won't help us build a TCP/IP network. Never fear. SNMP, which is a standard protocol in the TCP/IP protocol suite, is a better network management system than any network based configuration documenter. We'll cover SNMP very soon, but first let's take a quick look at memory managers.

Memory Managers

Memory managers help install the network by avoiding memory conflicts between the network software and the other software that the user wants to run. Chapter 1 explained why DOS applications are limited to the first 640K of memory (*user memory*). Without a memory manager, the network software shares user memory with other resident programs, DOS, and DOS applications. It gets pretty crowded!

Memory managers make better use of the memory that is actually installed in a DOS system. Today minimal systems are sold with 2M bytes of RAM, while most systems have 4M of RAM and some systems have 16M or more. When you buy a system with that much memory, you want to make use of it. Memory managers permit DOS programs to use the memory beyond the 1M boundary as *extended memory*. They also make better use of the memory below the 1M boundary.

Figure 1-3 in Chapter 1 shows how the 1M bytes of memory in the original PC design is divided between *user memory* and *system memory*. User memory is the first 640K, and system memory is the remaining 384K. The allocation for system memory has proved to be overly generous. On most PCs, large portions of system memory are unused. Memory managers make use of this memory by moving software and data that normally inhabit user memory into unused areas of system memory. The relocated software and data remain completely addressable from DOS. This memory management feature is often the most useful for installing TCP/IP on a DOS system.

The confusing terminology that surrounds DOS memory management causes some users to shy away from using these tools. The PC has been around for more than a decade, and for much of that time, extending DOS addressing beyond the 1M byte boundary has been a topic of discussion. During that decade, the terminology of memory management has evolved so that several terms mean almost the same thing. Commonly used terms are:

User Memory/Conventional Memory/DOS Memory

This is the first 640K bytes of memory. This is the memory that is used by DOS applications. It is fully addressable by DOS without any memory manager.

System Memory/Upper Memory/High Memory

This is the 384K bytes of memory that immediately follows the user memory; i.e., the memory between 640K and 1M. This memory is reserved for use by the system. Memory managers are necessary to make effective use of this memory.

Though these terms are used interchangeably, there are subtle distinctions between them. *Upper memory* refers to the unused portions of system memory that are called *upper memory blocks* (UMB). These are the areas of system memory used by the memory manager to replicate software and data from user memory. The distinction between system memory and upper memory is shown below in the sample MEM reports.

The term *high memory* is sometimes used to refer to system memory, but it really has a different meaning. See the box *21-bit Address?* for details about high memory.

Extended Memory

This is the memory above the 1M byte boundary. This memory is accessed by using a memory manager that complies with the Extended Memory Standard (XMS). XMS memory is available on 80386, 80486, and Pentium systems.

Expanded Memory

This is *paged* memory that can be used in any PC, even 8088 and 8086 systems, by adding an expanded memory board. This term is sometimes confused with Extended Memory, but the Expanded Memory Standard (EMS) is an older standard. Most XMS memory managers will emulate EMS memory for old programs that still use EMS. TCP/IP software does not use it.

21-bit Address?

The box *8088 Addressing* in Chapter 1 describes how 20-bit *real mode* addresses are constructed from two 16-bit address registers: the *segment register* and the *offset register*. The largest segment register address defines a location that is 16 bytes below the 1M byte boundary. The largest offset register value is 64K bytes. The two registers are added together to create an address, so it is possible to define an address that is greater than the 1M byte address limit of a standard 8088 system. Normally addresses that exceed 20-bits are truncated at 20-bits, in effect causing large addresses to "wrap around" and address areas in low memory. The 80286 changed that.

The 80286 has 24 address bits that allow it to address 16M bytes of memory, but that address range is not available when the CPU uses real mode addresses. Even on 80286, 80386, and 80486 CPUs, real mode addressing works just like it does on the 8088. And real mode addressing is the only kind supported by DOS. However, some enterprising genius discovered that even in real mode the twenty-first address line can be selectively enabled to give the system a 21-bit real mode address. When the twenty-first address line is enabled, the address produced by adding the largest segment value and the largest offset value doesn't wrap around to low memory. Instead it points to a location that is equal to 1M+64K-16. The 64K-16 byte area above the 1M byte boundary that this technique makes addressable is called *high memory*.

High memory is addressable by DOS, and it is frequently used to relocate the resident portion of DOS from user memory. A high memory driver, such as the HIMEM driver that comes with DOS 6.x, is necessary to enable this feature. If you use the standard DOS memory management software, the following lines appear in CONFIG.SYS when DOS is running in high memory:

```
DEVICE=C:\DOS\HIMEM.SYS
DOS=HIGH
```

A general understanding of these terms is useful for plowing through the documentation that comes with a memory manager, but beyond that, a network administrator does not need a detailed knowledge of memory management. Your goal is limited; all you want to do is get the network running reliably. Most memory managers accomplish this with almost no input from you.

A full-featured memory manager, such as Quarterdeck's Extended Memory Manager (QEMM), can be purchased as a DOS add-on. However DOS 6.x includes a memory manager that is usually all you need for installing TCP/IP on a PC. DOS 6.x has four key components used for memory management. Two are device drivers: HIMEM and EMM386 manage upper memory and extended memory. They load at boot time via CONFIG.SYS. Two are user commands, MEM and MEM-MAKER, that run from the DOS command line.

You really don't need to think about HIMEM and EMM386. Each is automatically installed in CONFIG.SYS when you execute some other command. HIMEM is installed by default when the SETUP program is run to install DOS 6.x. SETUP uses HIMEM to run DOS in the first 64K beyond the 1M byte boundary (see the box earlier in this section). So you should already have HIMEM installed in your system. The EMM386 driver is installed when you run the MEMMAKER command.

MEMMAKER is the command that optimizes the memory on your system. Run MEMMAKER after installing the TCP/IP software, or for that matter, after installing any new memory resident programs or drivers. It frees up as much user memory as possible by relocating software and drivers to system memory and by making use of extended memory. This reduces the possibility of conflicts between memory resident software, such as TCP/IP, and the user's application programs.

The MEM command displays a report of current memory usage. Start with the MEM command to get a picture of the computer's memory. A sample MEM report is shown below.

```
Memory Type        Total =  Used  +  Free
----------------   ------   ------   ------
Conventional         640K     231K     409K
Upper                  0K       0K       0K
Adapter RAM/ROM      384K     384K       0K
Extended (XMS)     19456K    2112K   17344K
----------------   ------   ------   ------
Total memory       20480K    2727K   17753K

Total under 1 MB     640K     231K     409K

Largest executable program size        409K   (419168 bytes)
Largest free upper memory block          0K      (0 bytes)
MS-DOS is resident in the high memory area.
```

This report shows the memory usage on a PC before MEMMAKER is run. The system, which has several memory resident programs installed, is a 486 with 20M bytes of RAM. Yet even with all that RAM, some DOS programs (the AMI ECU program CFG is an example) fail to run because there is not enough memory! The MEM report helps you figure out why.

A few things in the report worth noting:

- There are over 17M bytes of free memory but only 409K bytes of conventional (user) memory is available. 231K of conventional memory is used by resident programs, device drivers, buffers, tables, data, and the other paraphernalia of a DOS system. The lack of conventional memory is the reason CFG won't run on our sample system.

- The HIMEM driver is running. The message "MS-DOS is resident in the high memory area" indicates that SETUP installed HIMEM in the CONFIG.SYS file and that it is being used to relocate DOS to high memory each time the system boots.

- No upper memory (0K) is available because the upper memory manager EMM386 is not running. EMM386 is started by MEMMAKER, which has not yet been run.

Running MEMMAKER is very simple. Type MEMMAKER at the DOS command-line prompt. Select the **Express Setup** option. (The SPACEBAR changes options; the ENTER key selects an option.) Select **No** when asked if you use expanded memory unless you're positive that you have some old programs that still use EMS memory. Press ENTER to reboot the computer when MEMMAKER asks you to. MEMMAKER analyzes the memory requirements of the drivers and programs started during this boot. It displays a series of messages about the process, and if everything goes well, MEMMAKER again prompts you to restart the computer. The second boot brings the system up with the new memory configuration. That's all there is to it!

MEM was run a second time using the same 486 as in the sample MEM report shown above. This time it was run after MEMMAKER was executed with the **Express Setup** option. The second report is shown below:

```
Memory Type         Total =  Used  +  Free
----------------    ------   ------    ------
Conventional         640K     146K     494K
Upper                163K      89K      74K
Adapter RAM/ROM      384K     384K       0K
Extended (XMS)     19293K    2289K   17004K
----------------    ------   ------    ------
Total memory       20480K    2908K   17572K

Total under 1 MB     803K     235K     568K

Largest executable program size      494K   (505872 bytes)
Largest free upper memory block       74K   (75744 bytes)
MS-DOS is resident in the high memory area.
```

In this report we see that 163K of upper memory is now available. 89K of this new-found memory is being used for programs and drivers that were relocated from conventional memory. Even with the addition of the EMM386 driver, which uses about 5K of conventional memory, the amount of conventional memory in use has dropped from 231K to 146K. Notice that XMS usage has increased. We actually have less free extended memory available than we did before. EMM386 maps extended memory to the available upper memory addresses, which uses up as much extended memory as there is available upper memory. However, DOS does not need more extended memory. It needs more conventional memory, and the available upper memory is used to relocate programs, data, and drivers from conventional memory. As a result, we now have 494K bytes of free conventional memory, which is enough to run CFG without a problem. Our goal was to install the network and not have it interfere with any other programs. We've met that goal with very little effort.

Most of the time running MEMMAKER with the **Express Setup** option is all that is required, but not always. Sometimes MEMMAKER doesn't free enough memory. Some things you can do to help are:

- Remove all unused drivers and programs from the startup files.

- Reorder the drivers and programs in the startup files so that those with the largest memory requirements are loaded first. Use **MEM /DEBUG** or look in the MEMMAKER.STS file to get an idea of how much memory each driver and resident program uses. Take care reordering the sequence in which the drivers and programs are loaded. In general, network drivers and programs must be loaded in order. Other programs may also be sensitive to the order in which they are loaded.

A problem may occur when MEMMAKER reboots to analyze the system's memory requirements. If the system hangs during this reboot there are two things you can do:

1. Restart MEMMAKER by pressing **CTRL+ALT+DEL**. When MEMMAKER restarts, select the option **Try again with conservative settings**.

2. If the procedure outlined in item 1 doesn't solve the problem, use **F8** as described in the *Configuration Documenters* section to start the drivers from CONFIG.SYS one at a time, watching for the driver that hangs the system. If the boot program does not hang processing the CONFIG.SYS file, try processing the AUTOEXEC.BAT file. Make sure the file does not contain an ECHO OFF command so that you can watch each command execute. When you find the driver or program that is hanging, exit MEMMAKER by selecting the **Cancel and undo all changes** option. Rerun MEMMAKER and select the **Custom Setup** option. From the **Advanced Options** screen select **Specify which drivers and TSRs to include during the optimization?**. Include every driver and program except the one causing MEMMAKER to hang.

This information is more than enough for the average network administrator. If you have other questions about MEMMAKER, please refer to *Making More Memory Available* in the *MS-DOS User's Guide*. Also, carefully read the documentation that comes with your PC and with your TCP/IP software before attempting any memory management. Some hardware vendors supply their own memory managers in the DOS that they bundle with the PC hardware. Some TCP/IP programs may not be compatible with all memory managers. Read your system's documentation before you begin typing in commands.

Maintenance Tools

Proper installation and configuration is a vital ingredient of a reliable, stable network, but even a properly installed network eventually breaks down and requires maintenance. The right maintenance tools reduce downtime and make it easier to restore the network to service. Gather the necessary tools before you actually need them. Then when things go wrong, as they certainly will, you'll look like a hero.

Frequently simple tools are overlooked because it is easier to think of big things than it is to think of small ones. Don't make that mistake. You need enough simple hand tools to maintain the network's equipment and wiring. A pair of needle-nose pliers and a few screw drivers may be sufficient, but it is usually easier to buy a ready made network maintenance toolkit. You may also need specialized tools to maintain your wiring. For example: attaching BNC connectors to thinnet or RJ45 connectors to UTP requires special crimping tools, and tapping a thicknet cable requires a special hand drill. The special hand tools and tool kits are generally available from the same vendor that sold you the network cable.

Special tools are also needed to test the cable. Users always suspect the cable is the cause of the problem. In reality, cable problems are rare, but when you do have a cable problem they are very difficult to diagnose without the right tools. Traditionally cables have been tested using a *time domain reflectometer* (TDR). A TDR sends a signal down the cable. The reflected image of the signal is shown on a small screen, and the user analyzes the cable problem based on the characteristics of the signal displayed by the TDR. Traditionally TDRs were used on coaxial cable. Traditional UTP cable testers, called *pair testers*, are generally limited to *continuity* tests. In a continuity test a voltage is placed on one end of the cable and tested for at the other end to check that the cable carries a signal from end to end. These tools are still useful but have been superceded by smaller, more versatile test equipment.

Several companies make modern cable testers. One example is the Microtest *Pair Scanner*, a small hand-held unit with a keypad and LCD display. The unit tests either thinnet or UTP cable. Tests are selected from the keyboard and results are displayed on the LCD screen. It is not necessary to interpret the results because the unit does that for you and displays the error condition in a simple text message. For example, a cable test might produce the message "Short at 74 feet." This tells you that the cable is shorted 74 feet away from the tester. What could be simpler? The proper test tools make it easier to locate, and therefore fix, cable problems.

Despite their usefulness, small organizations sometimes may feel that they cannot justify the cost of specialized test equipment. I might disagree, but I understand the logic: cable failures are infrequent, and the smaller the network, the less likely they are to occur. Small organizations are afraid the tester will sit on a shelf gathering dust. A laptop PC, however, is one piece of test equipment that every network, large and small, must have.

People don't usually think of a laptop PC as a piece of test equipment, but properly configured, it is one of the most useful. It is also one of the easiest to "sell" to management. Managers may not understand what a cable tester does, but they are familiar with laptop PCs, and they don't think that a laptop will sit around unused. Familiarity with the laptop is its greatest strength. A successful test from a PC generates more confidence in a user than does a successful test from a cable tester. The reason is simply that the user understands PCs and identifies the PC test with actual work that he does himself. To better understand this, let me explain how a laptop is used as a network tester.

Start with a laptop system that runs the same DOS and Windows 3.1 applications used by the network's users. You need a 386 with 4M bytes of RAM and enough hard disk space to hold all of the network applications at a minimum. You may want a system with at least one PCMCIA (Personal Computer Memory Card International Association) slot so that you can connect to the network with a PCMCIA Ethernet card, but it's not absolutely necessary. There are external Ethernet adapters, such as the Xircom adapter, that attach to the system through the parallel printer port. Whatever laptop you choose, configure it to boot exactly like a user system with the same TCP/IP software and the same batch files the users use to connect to network servers.

To use the laptop for a test, take it to the location where the user reports a network problem. Disconnect the Ethernet cable from the back of the user's system and attach it to the laptop. Configure the laptop with an appropriate address for the user's subnet and reboot it. Then PING various systems on the network and attach to one of the user's servers. If everything works, the fault is probably in the user's computer. The user trusts this test because it demonstrates something he does everyday. Unlike an unidentifiable piece of test equipment displaying the message "No faults found," the user has confidence in the PC. If the test fails, the fault is probably in the network equipment or wiring. That's the time to bring out the cable tester to locate the problem.

Another advantage of using a PC as a piece of test equipment is its inherent versatility. PCs run a wide variety of test, diagnostic and management software. The same PC used to test a user's network connection can be used as a protocol analyzer or network monitor.

Protocol Analyzers

A *protocol analyzer* is software that decodes and displays the structure and contents of a network packet. The packet, called a *datagram* in TCP/IP jargon, is a block of information that contains all of the user's data and all of the instructions (the headers) necessary for the network to deliver the data.

Protocol analyzers are sometimes confused with *network analyzers*, but there is a difference. A network analyzer is a combination of hardware and software that usually includes a protocol analyzer and much more. A network analyzer has special network hardware that allows it to "see" everything on the network, even the damaged packets normally discarded by an Ethernet card. If you've got the money, a network analyzer is a good choice because it is able to detect problems that cannot be detected by a "software-only" protocol analyzer. To reduce cost, some network analyzer packages are offered as hardware and software that can be added to an existing 486 or Pentium. Despite this, you should be prepared for a major expense to purchase a high-quality network analyzer.

Protocol analyzers, on the other hand, are relatively low cost. They are usually "software-only" systems that rely on the Ethernet board that exists in the system. Normally an Ethernet board only accepts packets that are addressed to it. Protocol analyzer software places the Ethernet board in *promiscuous mode*, which causes the board to pass every Ethernet packet up to the software for processing. In promiscuous mode, the analyzer can look at packets addressed to any system. This allows the analyzer to capture the traffic of every system on the network, but it places a large burden on the system to process the packets. For this reason, the PC must be dedicated to the task when it acts as a network analyzer. Use a laptop or portable computer. They are easy to move to the network segment that you wish to analyze. Figure 3-3 shows a protocol analyzer display.

```
┌─────────────────────────────────────────────────────────────────────────┐
│ ─                             NEWTTrace                            ▼  ▲  │
│ File   Capture   Display   Settings   Window   Help                     │
│ ┌──┐ ■■□□ ┌──┐ ┌──┐ ┌──┐ ┌──┐  ┌──────────────────────┐                 │
│ │  │      │ Q│ │FF│ │  │ │  │  │ myself               │                 │
│ └──┘      └──┘ └──┘ └──┘ └──┘  └──────────────────────┘                 │
│ Number Length   Time         Source              Destination            │
│   7     60    0.000   00:00:93:18:28:D5   self                  ARP  ▲  │
│   8    106    0.000   self                00:00:93:18:28:D5      ICMP    │
│   9    106    0.000   00:00:93:18:28:D5   self                  ICMP    │
│  10    106   14.445   self                00:00:93:18:28:D5      ICMP  ▒ │
│  11    106    0.000   00:00:93:18:28:D5   self                  ICMP    │
│  12    146    0.439   00:00:93:E0:E0:A4   broadcast             UDP     │
│  13     60    0.000   00:60:8C:F1:12:B3   broadcast             ARP     │
│  14    106    0.604   self                00:00:93:18:28:D5      ICMP    │
│  15    106    0.000   00:00:93:18:28:D5   self                  ICMP    │
│  16    106    1.044   self                00:00:93:18:28:D5      ICMP    │
│  17    106    0.000   00:00:93:18:28:D5   self                  ICMP    │
│  18    106    1.044   self                00:00:93:18:28:D5      ICMP    │
│  19    106    0.000   00:00:93:18:28:D5   self                  ICMP    │
│  20    106    1.043   self                00:00:93:18:28:D5      ICMP  ▼ │
│ ◄ □                                                                ►    │
│ ┌──────────────┐                          ┌────────────┬──────────┐     │
│ │ Ready for capture │                      │            │ Count: 48│     │
│ └──────────────┘                          └────────────┴──────────┘     │
└─────────────────────────────────────────────────────────────────────────┘
```

Figure 3-3: A Packet Trace

The protocol analyzer display,* as seen in Figure 3-3, is the exchange of Ethernet frames between this system (*self*) and another system on the network. It shows little more than the fact that this PC can send and receive packets. Individual Ethernet frames can be examined in greater detail as shown in Figure 3-4.

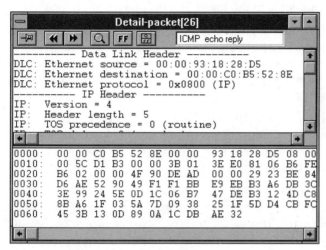

Figure 3–4: Decoding a Single Frame

Figure 3-4 shows a frame containing an ICMP Echo Reply, which is a PING reply. The lower half of the window contains a hexidecimal dump of the frame. The upper half decodes the frame into the Ethernet header, IP header, and ICMP header that it contains.

Use a protocol analyzer to detect protocol problems or simply to verify that data is flowing to a system on the network.

Troubleshooting

Good tools are essential for maintaining a network, but they are only part of the answer. Unlike cable problems and protocol problems, most network problems cannot be diagnosed by a piece of test equipment. Resolving most problems requires a methodical approach and the application of your knowledge of TCP/IP and of your network.

The knowledge needed for troubleshooting is conceptual in nature. You need an understanding of how TCP/IP works and what it needs to work. Detailed knowledge of TCP/IP is not important. Look up the details in a reference when they're

---

* Note that the *NEWTTrace* analyzer used in this example is not a promiscious mode analyzer. It only allows the user to look at broadcast traffic and at traffic that orginates from or is addressed to the system the capture program is running on.

required. They are covered extensively in print, so we won't go over them again here.* We will remind you of a few useful concepts to keep in mind for troubleshooting. They are:

- TCP/IP is a four-layer hierarchy. Problems seen by the user in the *Application Layer* may be caused by problems in the lower layers.

- IP requires that each system have a globally unique, software-defined address. IP uses the address to move data through networks and through the layers of software in a host. Unlike networks that use hardware addresses, IP relies on the system administrator to define the correct address. Problems are frequently caused by configuration errors.

- Routing is required to deliver data between any two systems that are not directly connected by the same physical network. Subnetting divides a network into separate physical networks so that routing may even be required within a single enterprise network.

With these few points in mind, it's clear that the configuration of a TCP/IP system is vitally important to its operation, and that the user only "sees" part of the problem. This suggests a troubleshooting approach for most network problems. It is to verify the TCP/IP configuration and to attempt to locate where in the protocol hierarchy and the network the problem is actually occurring.

The key to solving a problem is knowing what the problem is. That is easier said than done. There are many layers of hardware and software obscuring the real problem. Locating the problem is hard work but it's worth it. When the true nature of a problem is understood, the solution is often obvious. Three steps in tracking down the real problem are:

1. **Gather Information.**

   When the problem is reported, ask the user several questions. What application failed? What is the address and hostname of the remote computer? What is the address and hostname of the user's computer? What error message was displayed? If possible, have the user verify the problem by running the application while you talk through it. If possible, duplicate the problem yourself.

2. **Run Preliminary Tests.**

   Using another application, such as PING, check if the problem occurs in other applications on the user's host. Check if the user's problem occurs with only one remote host, with all remote hosts, or only with hosts off of the user's subnet. Check if the problem occurs on other local systems or just on the user's system. Does it fail from your system? How about from other systems on the user's subnet?

---

* If you want the details, read the first three chapters of *TCP/IP Network Administration*. Want even more? Read Volume One of *Internetworking with TCP/IP*, by Douglas Comer, Prentice-Hall.

3. **Visualize the Problem.**

Visualize each protocol and device that handles the user's data. If the problem occurs on some systems and not others, think about the difference in the path that data takes from those systems. Think about where and how things could go wrong. Visualizing the problem in this manner avoids oversimplifying the problem. It also highlights the areas that are most likely to cause the user's problem. Using your knowledge of TCP/IP and your network, focus on the most likely causes of the problem, but keep an open mind. The problem can be anywhere in the path you visualize.

Properly analyzed, the results of the preliminary tests may point right to the problem. The analysis is where a general knowledge of TCP/IP comes in handy. Some hints on analyzing the test results are:

- If only one application is having a problem, the application may be misconfigured. If the same application fails on different local hosts, but only when connecting to a specific remote host, the application may not be available on the remote host. If the application that fails is from a different source than the TCP/IP protocol stack, e.g., a commercial protocol stack and a freeware application, the application and the stack may not be compatible. This last condition is particularly prevalent in Windows 3.1 when the application is designed for a specific WINSOCK.DLL and a different one is used by the stack.

- If problems occur on all local PCs, regardless of the application or the remote host they are connecting to, the problem is in one of the devices that connects the network to the outside world. If the problem only occurs on systems on a single subnet, the problem is in the device that connects that subnet to the rest of your network. If the problem only occurs on one PC, that PC is probably misconfigured. Check its configuration. If it appears okay, take your laptop over and check the network link.

- Pay attention to the error messages. Error messages are often vague, but they contain valuable pointers to the underlying problem.

  The error "Unknown host" indicates a name server problem. If other computers resolve the name correctly, the user's PC is probably misconfigured. If no system resolves the name correctly, the name the user has may be wrong or the name servers may be misconfigured. Have the user try to connect with the numeric address.

  The error "Network unreachable" indicates a routing problem. It means that there is no route to the remote host. If no system can reach it, the remote site might be down. If only the user's PC has the problem, check the PC's routing configuration.

  The error "Cannot connect" or "No answer" or "Connection timed out" means that the remote system is not responding. Either the remote system is down or a link between the user's PC and the remote system is down. If the user is trying to connect using a numeric address, it could mean that the user has the wrong address. Ask him to use the remote system's hostname.

Not all trouble is caused by systems at your site; it is possible for things to go wrong on other people's networks. If both the local and remote systems are part of the same enterprise, you may know the remote network administrator; on the worldwide Internet, you probably wouldn't. Luckily there is an Internet service that locates the people responsible for a remote network for you. To use it, **telnet rs.internic.net**. At the prompt enter **whois** and enter **help** at the Whois: prompt for information about the service. Some of the TCP/IP implementations we use later in the text have a built-in **whois** command.

This concludes the discussion of troubleshooting techniques. The following chapters include examples of the troubleshooting commands that test basic connectivity and display the basic TCP/IP configuration.

Simple Network Management Protocol

Troubleshooting is necessary to recover from problems, but the ultimate goal of the network administrator is to avoid problems. That is also the goal of network management software. The network management software used on TCP/IP networks is based on the *Simple Network Management Protocol* (SNMP). In the final section of this chapter we take a look at SNMP.

SNMP is a client/server protocol. In SNMP terminology it is described as a *manager/agent protocol*. The *agent* (the server) runs on the device being managed, which is called the *Managed Network Entity*. The agent monitors the status of the device and reports that status to the *manager*.

The *manager* (the client) runs on the *Network Management Station* (NMS), which is usually a UNIX workstation or a powerful PC. The NMS collects information from all of the different devices that are being managed, consolidates it, and presents it to the human network manager. This design places all of the data manipulation tools and most of the human interaction on the NMS. Concentrating the bulk of the work on the manager means that the agent software is small and easy to implement. Correspondingly, most TCP/IP network equipment comes with an SNMP management agent.

SNMP is a request/response protocol. UDP port 161 is its well-known port. SNMP uses UDP as its transport protocol because it has no need for the overhead of TCP. "Reliability" is not required because each request generates a response. If the SNMP application does not receive a response, it simply re-issues the request. "Sequencing" is not needed because each request and each response travels as a single datagram.

The request and response messages that SNMP sends in the datagrams are called *Protocol Data Units* (PDU). The five PDUs used by SNMP are listed in Table 3-1. These message types allow the manager to request management information, and when appropriate, to modify that information. The messages also allow the agent to respond to manager requests and to notify the manager of unusual situations.

Table 3-1: SNMP Protocol Data Units

PDU	Use
GetRequest	Manager requests an update
GetNextRequest	Manager requests the next entry in a table
GetResponse	Agent answers a manager request
SetRequest	Manager modifies data on the managed device
Trap	Agent alerts manager of an unusual event

The NMS periodically requests the status of each managed device (GetRequest) and each agent responds with the status of its device (GetResponse). Making periodic requests is called *polling*. Polling reduces the burden on the agent because the NMS decides when polls are needed, and the agent simply responds. Polling also reduces the burden on the network because the polls originate from a single system at a predictable rate. The shortcoming of polling is that it does not allow for real-time updates. If a problem occurs on a managed device, the manager does not find out until the agent is polled. To handle this, SNMP uses a modified polling system called *trap-directed polling*.

A *trap* is an interrupt signalled by a predefined event. When a trap event occurs, the SNMP agent does not wait for the manager to poll; instead it immediately sends information to the manager. Traps allow the agent to inform the manager of unusual events while allowing the manager to maintain control of polling. SNMP traps are sent on UDP port 162. The manager sends polls on port 161 and listens for traps on port 162. Table 3-2 lists the trap events defined in the RFCs.

Table 3-2: Generic Traps Defined in the RFCs

Trap	Meaning
coldStart	Agent restarted; possible configuration changes
warmStart	Agent reinitialized without configuration changes
enterpriseSpecific	An event significant to this hardware or software
authenticationFailure	Agent received an unauthenticated message
linkDown	Agent detected a network link failure
linkUp	Agent detected a network link coming up
egpNeighborLoss	The device's EGP neighbor is down

The last three entries in this table show the roots of SNMP in *Simple Gateway Management Protocol* (SGMP), which was a tool for tracking the status of network routers. Routers are generally the only devices that have multiple network links to

keep track of and are the only devices that run *Exterior Gateway Protocol* (EGP).[*]
These traps are not significant for PCs.

The most important trap for a PC may be the **enterpriseSpecific** trap. The events
that signal this trap are defined differently by every vendor's SNMP agent software.
Therefore it is possible for the trap to be tuned to events that are significant for a
PC. SNMP uses the term "enterprise" to refer to something that is privately defined
by a vendor or organization as opposed to something that is globally defined by
an RFC.

SNMP has twice as much jargon as the rest of networking—and that's saying
something! Managed Network Entity, NMS, PDU, trap, polling, enterprise—that's
just the beginning! We also need to mention what SMI is, what a MIB is, and what
ANS.1 is used for. Why this bewildering array of acronyms and buzz-words? I think
there are two main reasons:

- First, network management covers a wide range of different devices from
  repeaters to mainframe computers. A "vendor neutral" language is needed to
  define terms for the manufacturers of all of this different equipment.

- Second, SNMP is based on the *Common Management Information Protocol*
  (CMIP) that was created by the *International Standards Organization* (ISO).
  Formal international standards always spend a lot of time defining terms
  because it is important to make terms clear when they will be used by people
  from many different cultures who speak many different languages.

Now that you know why you have to suffer through all of this jargon, let's define
a few more important terms.

The *Structure of Management Information* (SMI) defines how data should be presented in an SNMP environment. The SMI is documented in RFC 1155 and RFC
1065, *Structure and Identification of Management Information for TCP/IP-based
Internets*. The SMI defines how managed objects are named, the syntax in which
they are defined, and how they are encoded for transmission over the network.
The SMI is based on previous ISO work.

Each managed object is given a globally unique name called an *object identifier*.
The object identifier is part of a hierarchical name space that is managed by the
ISO. The hierarchical name structure is used, just like it is in DNS, to guarantee
that each name is globally unique. In an object identifier, each level of the hierarchy is identified by a number.

Figure 3-5 shows an example of some object identifiers displayed by an SNMP
agent. The field called *Enterprise ID* in the figure is actually the object identifier.
Each identifier is a dot-separated list of numbers. Each number represents part of
the naming hierarchy. All SNMP managed objects start with the number 1.3.6.1.

---

[*] EGP is covered in Chapter 7 of *TCP/IP Network Administration*.

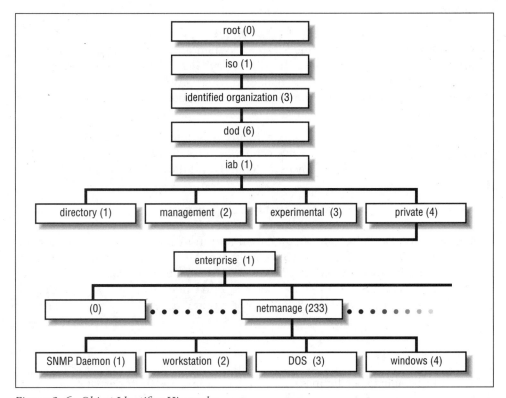

Figure 3-5: *SNMP Object Identifiers*

Figure 3-6: *Object Identifier Hierarchy*

Figure 3-6 shows a map of the hierarchy for the "DOS" object (1.3.6.1.4.1.233.3). The number of the root is not included in the identifier. The first number (1) represents the ISO. The ISO has delegated part of the name space to the U.S. Department of Defense (DOD) that in turn has delegated a part to the Internet Activity Board (IAB). The IAB delegates names to private organizations under the *private* name directory. Hundreds of organizations have delegations in this directory. One of them is NetManage, Inc. (233), which is the vendor of the SNMP agent shown in our example. Within its name space (1.3.6.1.4.1.233), NetManage can define any objects it wishes. One of the objects it has defined is a private "DOS" object.

Objects are defined just as formally as they are named. The syntax used to define managed objects is *Abstract Syntax Notation One (ASN.1)*. ASN.1 is ISO Standard 8824, *Specification of Abstract Syntax Notation One (ASN.1)*. It is a very formal set of language rules for defining data. It makes the data definition independent of incompatibilities between systems and character sets. ASN.1 also includes a set of rules for encoding data for transfer over a network. These rules are defined in ISO Standard 8825, *Specification of Basic Encoding Rules for Abstract Syntax Notation One (ASN.1)*. The *Basic Encoding Rules* (BER) define that bit 8 of an octet is sent first, that 2's complement is used for signed integers, and other nitty-gritty details of data transmission.

Every object managed by SNMP has a unique object identifier defined by the ASN.1 syntax and encoding defined by BER. When all of these unique objects are grouped together, they are called the *Management Information Base* (MIB). The MIB refers to all information that is managed by SNMP. However, we usually refer to "a MIB" or "the MIBs" (plural) meaning the individual databases of management information formally defined by an RFC or privately defined by a vendor.

Refer back to Figure 3-5. MIBII is the standard MIB defined by RFC 1213. Its object identifier is 1.3.6.1.2.1 because it is in the *IAB management* directory. The other MIBs shown in that figure are privately defined, and they all fall in the *IAB private* directory.

All of this detail is necessary to formally define a network management scheme that is independent of the managed systems. But do we need to memorize all this stuff? Not really. Don't be put off by the jargon; most of it is unimportant for the network administrator. You need to know that a MIB is a collection of management information, that an NMS is the network management station, and that an agent runs in each managed device. But you don't need to know a great deal of detail about these things. After all, we're not writing an SNMP monitor; we're just using one.

Installing SNMP

This section contains specific instructions for installing SNMP under DOS and Windows 3.1.[*] It's placed here because it references many of the things that were defined in the previous section. SNMP is an optional part of a TCP/IP installation. You may want to skip this section until you're ready to install SNMP on your system.

Two pieces of software must be installed to use SNMP: the agent and the manager. Only one copy of the manager software is needed for a network. SNMP agents are installed in every system.

---

[*] Installing TCP/IP under DOS and Windows 3.1 is covered in Chapters 4 and 5, respectively.

Most PC TCP/IP packages include an SNMP agent. The agent is installed as part of the default software installation. It either runs by default as part of the TCP/IP stack, a common approach on Windows 3.1 systems, or it requires the user to take some action to run it. DOS systems usually require the user to start the agent explicitly because it runs as a TSR and uses valuable conventional memory. Starting the agent is simple, as this example shows:

```
LSL
3C509
TCPIP
SNMP
```

This example contains the lines from an AUTOEXEC.BAT file that start *LAN Work-Place*. The last line, SNMP, is the command that starts the SNMP agent. The other three lines, which are explained in Chapter 4, start other components of *LAN WorkPlace*. Simply typing **SNMP** is all that is necessary to run the *LAN WorkPlace* SNMP agent; most other agents are just as easy to start.

The SNMP agent will run without any further configuration, but it does have some optional configuration parameters. These are:

Community names

SNMP has a rudimentary security mechanism based on community names. A community name is a group name known only to the members of the group. Every system in the community must use the same community name. The SNMP agent compares the community name contained in each request it receives against its own community name. If they match, it honors the request. If they don't match, the agent discards the request and generates an *authenticationFailure* trap. Two community names are configured: one for get requests and one for set requests.

Optional MIB values

Every agent supports MIBI or MIBII. MIBII is a superset of MIBI, and is the standard MIB for monitoring TCP/IP. It includes optional objects for identifying the managed device. These optional objects are the system name, the name of the person in charge of the system (the system contact), and the location of the system.

The SNMP section of the NET.CFG file on a DOS system running *LAN WorkPlace* shows examples of all of these values:

```
Protocol SNMP
    sysName          pistachio
    sysContact       Tyler McCafferty
    sysLocation      Baltimore Office, Room A27
    monitorCommunity public
    controlCommunity Sd,Itily!
```

The computer name is provided for sysName. The value for sysContact is the name of the person who uses this PC, and the value for sysLocation is the physical location of the PC. The system does not check the contents of these fields, which are designed to provide information to the human manager. Enter any values in these fields that you find meaningful. You could, for example, enter a person's name in the sysName field and a telephone number in the sysContact field. What is important is that the information is meaningful to the manager and is consistent across all of the managed devices. If you decide to use these fields in a special way, make sure that your users know how you want to use them.

The value provided for monitorCommunity is the community name that must be used by systems that request information from this PC. The community name *public* is the default value most systems use for **Get** requests if no value is configured. The controlCommunity name is the name that must be used by systems that want to set object values on this PC. The sample system will only accept set requests from systems that use the community name *Sd,Itily!*. If the controlCommunity line is not included in the file, *LAN Workplace* rejects all set requests.

Configuring the SNMP agent on a Windows 3.1 system looks different, but the configuration values are the same as those used on a DOS system. To configure SNMP on a Windows system running *Chameleon*, run the *Custom* application and select **Settings** from the **SNMP** submenu of the **Services** menu. **Settings** has several selections. Choose **Host Administration**, and the dialogue box shown in Figure 3-7 appears.

Figure 3–7: SNMP Agent Configuration

Use this box to enter the same type of information as is entered with the sysName, sysContact, and sysLocation commands. The community names are provided to the *Chameleon* system by selecting **Community** from the **Settings** menu. Figure 3-8 shows the dialogue box into which the community names are entered.

Figure 3–8: SNMP Community Names

Enter the community name for get requests in the Get box and the community name for set requests in the Set box. These are equivalent to the *LAN WorkPlace* `monitorCommunity` and `controlCommunity` configuration parameters.

These few values are all that is needed to configure an SNMP agent and all that is avaliable on many systems. Some systems provide even more configuration control. For example, it is possible to configure traps on the *Chameleon* system. Notice the first dialogue box shown in Figure 3-7. It has a checkbox for generating traps when the SNMP agent starts. These are the `coldStart` and `warmStart` traps mentioned in Table 3-1. Additional trap settings are available by selecting **Trap Administration** from the **Settings** menu, which opens the following dialogue box shown in Figure 3-9.

Figure 3-9: SNMP Trap Administration

Enter the system name of the network monitoring station in the Default Destination box. Select the traps you want to enable in the Preferences box. The **authenticationFailure** trap and the **enterpriseSpecific** trap are clearly marked. The other checkbox tells the system to process traps coming in from other systems. Unless you are running a manager on this PC, leave the box unchecked.

Another feature of the *Chameleon* agent is that it provides a few private MIBs in addition to the standard MIBII. MIBII is designed for TCP/IP monitoring. It provides such information as the number of packets transmitted into and out of an interface, and the number of errors that occurred sending and receiving those packets—useful information for spotting usage trends and potential troublespots. Private MIBs add to this monitoring capability by providing PC-specific information, such as the applications that are currently running on a managed device. Figure 3-10 is the display of a network management station that shows this type of private MIB information.

Most PC SNMP agents do not provide private MIBs, and those that do may provide information that you're not interested in. Evaluate the network management features when you are buying your TCP/IP software. Determine how important this is

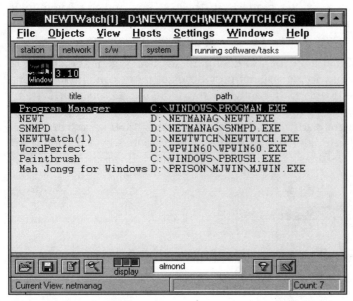

Figure 3-10: An SNMP Monitor

to you in light of all the other features. Remember, almost every system will provide at least MIBII.

No matter what MIBs are provided by the agents, it is the monitoring software that displays the information for the system administrator. A private MIB won't do you any good unless your network monitoring software also supports that MIB. A monitor that includes a *MIB compiler* provides the most flexibility. A MIB compiler reads in the ASN.1 description of a MIB and adds the MIB to the monitor. A MIB compiler makes the monitor *extensible* because if you can get the ASN.1 source from the PC software vendor, you can add the vendor's private MIB to your monitor.

MIB compilers are only part of the advanced features offered by some monitors. Some of the features offered are:

Network maps

> Some monitors automatically draw a map of the network. Colors are used to indicate the state (up, down, etc.) of the devices on the network. At a glance, the network manager sees the overall state of the network.

Tabular data displays

> Data displayed in tables or rendered into charts is used to make comparisons between different devices. Some monitors output data that can then be read into a standard spreadsheet or graphing program.

Filters

Filters sift the data coming in from the agents in order to detect certain conditions. For example, given the private MIB shown above, a filter can be set to look for every system that is still running WordPerfect 5.0.

Alarms

Alarms indicate when "thresholds" are exceeded or special events occur. For example, you may want an alarm to trigger when your server exceeds some specified number of transmit errors. The features available in network monitors vary widely; so does the price. *LAN WorkPlace* includes limited SNMP monitoring in its LWPCON console utility at no additional cost. NetManage sells a low cost monitor for PCs called *NEWTWatch* that has a few of these features, and Castle Rock Computing sells a full-featured PC monitor called *SNMPc*. There are many more products, including many for UNIX workstations. Evaluate as many products as you can in your price range, and if possible, try before you buy.

Installing a monitor is simple. Load the software and set the correct community name. If agents are running on all of your desktop systems, you immediately begin to collect data.

Summary

This concludes the first part of the book. The first three chapters have presented the challenges of networking Personal Computers and a number for strategies for dealing with those challenges. The techniques and tools we have discussed apply to the broad category of systems we call PCs. Unlike most other computers, PCs have many different personalities because they run many different operating systems. The next part of the book covers specific PC operating systems and the configuration of TCP/IP implementations for those operating systems. The material in the next three chapters does not replace the detailed installation documentation provided by the TCP/IP vendors. It does give you insight into TCP/IP configuration and troubleshooting so that you're better able to support the wide variety of PC operating systems.

4

DOS TCP/IP

DOS is probably the most widely-used operating system in the entire world—despite repeated attempts by other operating systems to invade its market. Even its creators, IBM and Microsoft, push alternatives OS/2 and Windows NT, so far to little effect. DOS remains the market leader. There are good reasons why it has been a success.

Disk Operating System has real strengths. DOS is designed for the 8088, and it is a good match. It is small and fast, which makes good use of the limited resources of the original PC. No CPU cycles are consumed by unnecessary operating system overhead, so an application running on DOS has the entire system dedicated to its needs. Correspondingly, applications run very fast under DOS. However, along with its strengths, come many weaknesses.

DOS does not support multitasking or a large amount of memory. There was no need for these when the PC was an 8088 with 1M bytes of memory. However improved processors with large memories make multitasking and other advanced features possible. Soon after improved PC hardware became available, IBM and Microsoft teamed up to produce a successor to DOS, called OS/2, that provides multitasking. However, OS/2 and other contenders for the DOS throne have not been an overwhelming success.

One cause for this lack of success is the lack of application software written specifically for the new operating systems. The new systems usually are able to run DOS applications, but frequently the applications run slower than they do under DOS. This slower application speed is not surprising because the applications are designed for DOS, and DOS is a fast, lightweight operating system. Nonetheless, poor performance on DOS applications is often perceived as a "problem" with the new OS, and acceptance of the system suffers from this perception. Even when the performance of a new system improves over time, the initial impression of poor performance lingers on in PC mythology, limiting acceptance of the system. Recently there has been extensive applications development for the new operating systems. The improved features and user interfaces of the new systems actually help developers make better user applications. Eventually these improved applications will help the new operating systems replace DOS, but the lack of applications in the past has hobbled their growth for years.

Another cause for DOS's continued success is its low cost. Adding features such as networking, which are included in some other operating systems, increase its total cost, but the initial cost of DOS is very low. Frequently DOS is *bundled* with PC hardware. Bundling the software means that the PC includes a copy of DOS installed on the hard drive, and no charge for DOS is listed on the bill. In this case, DOS appears to be "free" while other operating systems have to be purchased separately. Of course the hardware vendor buys DOS and passes the cost on to the customer, but the illusion of "free" software lingers.

DOS has another cost advantage. It runs on the very smallest PC systems. Multitasking operating systems require powerful processors and large amounts of memory, which push up the price of the systems they run on. Most people think of the extra equipment costs as part of the cost of acquiring the new operating system. Unless these higher-cost operating systems exhibit clear advantages, most users don't bother to buy them.

Microsoft Windows, which depends on DOS, has extended its useful life and its market share. Every PC that has a copy of Windows 3.1 also has a copy of DOS. The new Windows 95 operating system may succeed in supplanting DOS, but DOS will continue to be popular for quite some time. Even as its popularity fades, it is needed to support older PCs until those systems are retired. Therefore we start our discussion of various operating systems with Disk Operating System.

Getting Started

If you're a brave soul who jumped over the first three chapters, please read *PC Installation Planning* in Chapter 2, and refer to the *Installation Planning Form* in Appendix A. A substantial amount of information is needed to install a network, and it is best to have the information on hand before you start. This chapter assumes that you have already gathered the information. Furthermore, we assume that you have followed the advice in Chapter 2 and standardized on a particular network interface card and a specific TCP/IP implementation.

There are many implementations of TCP/IP for DOS. I'm familiar with products from Novell, FTP Software, SunSoft, Beame & Whiteside, Wollongong, and DEC. I'm sure there are many more. Appendix B has contact information for these vendors, and you can probably locate more by talking to a software distributor in your area.

DOS implementations of TCP/IP have been around for quite awhile and are well developed. Most of the examples in this section are based on FTP Software's *PC/TCP*, SunSoft's *PCNFS*, and Novell's *LAN Workplace*, but that's not really significant. All of the DOS TCP/IP packages work in pretty much the same way and provide the same basic services. You'll choose a package based on its reputation, a recommendation from a friend, the special features you require, or any of a dozen other reasons. Regardless of the one you choose, the general concepts covered here apply to it just like they do to the implementations used in these examples.

Implementing TCP/IP Under DOS

DOS was designed to run one task at a time, but a network can't always wait around for the current task to complete. There are times that the network needs immediate service: data are arriving from the network or the user's application and must be processed right away. The network software must be installed and ready to process the data when it's needed. Most DOS TCP/IP packages meet this need by using interrupt-driven device drivers and TSR programs.

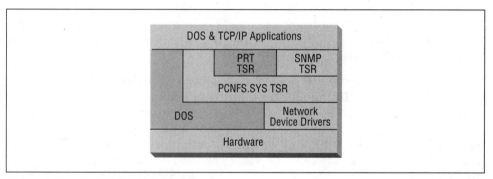

Figure 4-1: PC/NFS Software Modules

Figure 4-1 is a representation of how TCP/IP looks installed in a DOS system. It shows modules that are specific to SunSoft's *PC/NFS.*[*] However, the figure illustrates the structure of device drivers and TSRs common to all DOS implementations of TCP/IP. The names and functions of each module vary from implementation to implementation, but the components used to implement TCP/IP remain the same. The three components are: interrupts, device drivers, and Terminate and Stay Resident programs.

Interrupts

PCs are *interrupt driven*. An interrupt is a signal to the CPU that tells it to suspend the current task and switch to another task. Interrupts allow hardware and software to request immediate service from the CPU. Printing, reading, and writing files, keeping track of time, and a myriad of other functions are made possible by interrupts. Without them DOS would not function.

---

[*] Most *PCNFS* systems don't install every module shown in Figure 4-1.

In Chapter 1 we discussed how hardware interrupts are signaled using the IRQ lines on the bus. Like all hardware, the network interface card uses hardware interrupts to signal the system when it needs service. But IRQs are just the beginning; there are many more interrupts than there are IRQs—256 interrupts to be exact. Some are signaled by hardware, many more are signaled by software, and many others are not used at all. Software interrupts are triggered by the INT (Interrupt) machine language command. Hardware interrupts are electrically signaled to the CPU through its pin-outs. The pins used are:

Non-maskable interrupt (NMI)

> *NMI* is the interrupt reserved for catastrophic problems, such as a power outage. As the name implies, this interrupt cannot be *masked*. Interrupts are masked to allow critical pieces of code to complete. The non-maskable interrupt takes precedence over the critical code and is serviced no matter what mask is set.

INTR

> *INTR* is the standard hardware interrupt. This is the interrupt line used by the 8259 PIC[*] to signal the CPU that an IRQ request needs to be processed. IRQs are discussed in detail in Chapter 1.

The CPU processes interupts as quickly as possible and passes control to the specific interrupt handler. The CPU saves the system context and then jumps to the appropriate interrupt handler by using the vector stored in the *interrupt table*. An 8-bit value passed by the PIC via the bus (in the case of a hardware interrupt) or passed as the argument of the INT command (in the case of a software interrupt) determines which vector is used. The value is used as an index into the interrupt table to retrieve the correct vector address. An excerpt from an interrupt table is shown below:

```
...
1C   F000:FF53
1D   F000:F0A4
1E   0000:0522
1F   C000:3560
20   0116:1094
21   0116:109E
22   093F:02B1
...
5D   F000:EA97
5E   F000:EA97
5F   F000:EA97
60   0000:0000
61   0000:0000
62   0000:0000
63   0EE3:02B1
...
```

---

* The 8259 PIC is a single chip Peripheral Interface Controller (PIC).

The sample shows the contents of a typical interrupt table displayed as a list of interrupt numbers followed by the four byte table entry associated with that interrupt. This is not a complete table; there are 256 possible interrupts, and each interrupt vector is four bytes long. The full table consumes the first 1K bytes of a PC's memory and is much too long to display here. Each ellipsis indicates an area of the table that has been deleted. This excerpt shows examples of the three values commonly found in the table:

Interrupt vector

A table entry that is used as an interrupt vector contains the address of an interrupt-handling routine's entry point in the form of a segment register/offset register (S:O) pair. Interrupt 21 in the example shows this. The address register pair value is 0116:109E. The bytes of the address are actually stored in memory in reverse order, so this entry is really stored in memory as 9E101601.

Reserved vector

Some vectors are reserved for future use. Interrupt 5E is an example of this. Reserved vectors contain an address that points to an IRET (Interrupt Return) instruction in DOS or ROM. The IRET command restores the system context that was saved by the CPU before it jumped to the interrupt handler. This returns the system to processing the suspended task and is an effective way of disabling a vector without leaving it empty. As we discuss next, empty (null) vectors are available for use by any software.

Null vector

An unused vector contains the value 0000:0000. All of these empty table entries are available for use, but the vectors recommended for use by user programs are 60h to 66h.

Many vector table entries have recommended uses. Table 4-1 shows the common interrupt table assignments. These vectors can be overwritten by software; these are only recommended uses. Nothing in the PC hardware limits how the vectors are actually used, so the values in your PC may be different.

Table 4-1: Common Interrupts

Interrupt	Usage	Interrupt	Usage
00h	Divide by Zero	26h	DOS Absolute Disk Write
01h	Single Step	27h	DOS TSR
02h	NMI	28h	DOS Idle
03h	Breakpoint	29h	DOS PUTCHAR
04h	Overflow	2Ah	DOS Network Redirector
05h	Print Screen	2Bh-2Dh	Reserved for DOS
06h	Reserved	2Eh	DOS Execute Command
07h	Reserved	2Fh	Multiplex Interrupt
08h	IRQ 0	30h-32h	Reserved for DOS

Table 4–1: Common Interrupts (continued)

Interrupt	Usage	Interrupt	Usage
09h	IRQ 1	33h	Microsoft Mouse Driver
0Ah	IRQ 2	34h-3Eh	Reserved for DOS
0Bh	IRQ 3	3Fh	Overlay Manager
0Ch	IRQ 4	40h	Floppy Driver
0Dh	IRQ 5	41h	Fixed Disk Parameters
0Eh	IRQ 6	42h	Video Driver
0Fh	IRQ 7	43h	VGA Character Table
10h	Video	44h	Novell NetWare API
11h	Equipment Check	45h	Reserved
12h	Memory Size Check	46h	Fixed Disk Parameters
13h	Disk Driver	47h-49h	Reserved
14h	Asynchronous Communication	4Ah	Alarm Handler
15h	I/O System Services	4Bh-5Fh	Reserved
16h	Keyboard	60h-66h	User Program Interrupts
17h	Printer	67h	Expanded Memory
18h	ROM BASIC	68h-6Fh	Unassigned
19h	Bootstrap Loader	70h	IRQ 8
1Ah	Real-Time Clock	71h	IRQ 9
1Bh	CTRL-Break	72h	IRQ 10
1Ch	Timer	73h	IRQ 11
1Dh	Video Parameters	74h	IRQ 12
1Eh	Diskette Parameters	75h	IRQ 13
1Fh	Video Graphics Characters	76h	IRQ 14
20h	DOS Program Terminate	77h	IRQ 15
21h	General DOS Functions	78h-79h	Unassigned
22h	DOS Terminate Address	7Ah	Novell NetWare (API)
23h	DOS CTRL-Break Handler	7Bh-7Fh	Unassigned
24h	DOS Critical Error Handler	80h-F0h	Reserved for BASIC
25h	DOS Absolute Disk Read	F1h-FFh	Available

Table 4-1 shows that interrupts 60h through 66h are suggested for user programs. Note the entry for vector 63h at the end of the sample interrupt table shown earlier. The vector was inserted by the *PC/TCP* software when it was installed. DOS TCP/IP software works by adding new interrupts that can be invoked by applications software and by intercepting interrupts bound for other processes. The interrupts are "intercepted" by modifying vectors in the interrupt table so that they point to the TCP/IP TSR instead of the original handlers for those interrupts. The next section takes a closer look at TSRs.

Terminate and Stay Resident

Terminate and Stay Resident (TSR) programs are simply programs that stay in memory after they return control to DOS. TCP/IP TSRs are normally loaded into the system at boot time by the AUTOEXEC.BAT file. The TSR executes a short initialization routine that sets its interrupt vectors, reserves the memory it needs, and returns control to DOS using the special 31h function of the standard DOS interrupt 21h. This special function exists because TSRs are a standard part of the DOS system designed to provide a limited form of background processing. The classic TSR example is the DOS **print** command, which allows printing to take place in the background while DOS continues to process other user commands.

Once the TSR is resident in memory, it is called via interrupts. It either shares the *multiplexed interrupt* (2Fh) with other TSRs, installs its own vectors in the interrupt table, or intercepts interrupts that would normally be processed by other TSRs or DOS itself. Network TSRs that intercept requests for DOS I/O services are called *redirectors*. The module PCNFS.SYS in Figure 4-1 works in exactly this way. It intercepts requests for DOS file services and examines them to determine if the requests should be serviced over the network using NFS.

The big advantage of implementing TCP/IP as a TSR is speed. The software is always in memory and is able to service requests in real time. The disadvantage is that the network software uses up valuable DOS memory. For this reason, it is very important to use a memory manager when you install TCP/IP on a DOS system.

Device Drivers

TCP/IP runs over a wide variety of networks because it is designed to be independent of any particular physical network. While it does not require a *specific* underlying network, it does of course require *some* physical network to move the bits from one point to another. To run TCP/IP on a DOS system we must install a device driver for the network interface. Physical devices, such as network interface cards, communicate with DOS and application programs through *installable device drivers*. The physical network hardware and its device driver is not really a part of the TCP/IP protocol stack, but it is a necessary part of any TCP/IP installation.

Installable device drivers are a powerful feature of DOS that make it very easy to add new hardware devices without modifying the operating system kernel. Simply add the proper DEVICE statement to the CONFIG.SYS file and there it is! Of course the driver has to follow certain rules to communicate properly with DOS, and it must know the details of the hardware in order to control it. But the DOS rules are clearly defined, and the work of writing the device driver is handled by the hardware vendor. The driver is different for every manufacturer; therefore, appropriate software is delivered with the network adapter card. The only thing the network administrator needs to do is install it.

DOS defines how drivers talk to the operating system and how upper layer protocols talk to the drivers. Each vendor is free to define its own driver within these guidelines. In the PC world, where there are several different network protocols and dozens of different network card manufacturers, this could lead to a multitude of different, incompatible device drivers. For this reason, two of the leading PC network software developers, Microsoft and Novell, defined standard interfaces for network adapters. Adapter manufacturers that adhere to these interfaces can be sure that their hardware will work with the network software from these major companies.

The standard defined by Microsoft is the *Network Device Interface Specification* (NDIS). The standard from Novell is the *Open Datalink Interface* (ODI). These are different and incompatible specifications, though both work very well. Most implementations of TCP/IP support both NDIS and ODI drivers, and most network interface cards are delivered with both types of drivers. Both of these driver interface standards allow *multiple protocol stacks* to be run on the same PC. This means that TCP/IP can share a single network interface with another protocol, such as NetWare, when an NDIS or ODI driver is used. Figure 4-2 shows a multiple protocol stack installation.

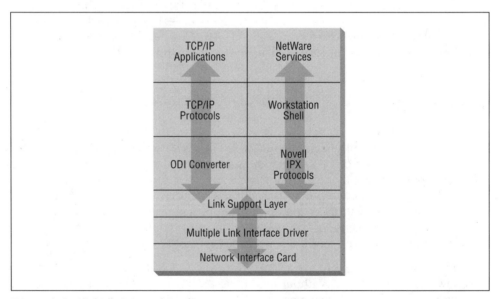

Figure 4-2: Multiple Protocol Stacks

It shows the TCP/IP protocol stack sharing a single network interface card with the IPX protocols using an ODI device driver. The ability to run more than one protocol stack over a single network interface is an important feature. TCP/IP frequently needs to co-exist with NetWare or some other PC networking protocol.

Given that both types of drivers work very well, which one should you choose for your installation? Well, it depends. (Don't you hate it when somebody says that!) It depends on what driver types are supported by the TCP/IP software and network interface hardware that you have. You may not have a choice. If you haven't yet purchased software and hardware, make sure the stuff you choose supports a variety of drivers including both NDIS and ODI.

If your system can use either NDIS or ODI, think about what other protocols besides TCP/IP you might want to run on your network. Do you run Windows for Workgroups (WfW) or LAN Manager? If you do, NDIS is probably your best bet. If you run NetWare on your network, ODI is the natural choice. However, don't worry so much about your choice that you drown in this alphabet soup. Choose based on your best estimate of the protocols you'll be using on your network and then move on. If things change in the future, you can always make adjustments. Novell supports NDIS services on the ODI driver using the ODINSUP (ODI NDIS Support) software, and Microsoft offers an NDIS-compliant version of IPX. Novell dominates the PC networking market because it makes sure that NetWare works with everything, and your Windows for Workgroups clients can run NetWare over an NDIS driver if necessary. So relax! It's not as bad as it might seem.

Not all device drivers are installed using the DEVICE statement in the CONFIG.SYS file. There are *resident device drivers* for such devices as the console (CON) and the printer (PRN) that are a permanent part of DOS. Some networks embed the device driver functions in a TSR started from the AUTOEXEC.BAT file so that no modifications of the CONFIG.SYS file are necessary. ODI device drivers are installed in this manner. The effect is the same: a driver for the hardware interface is installed at boot time and remains resident in memory while the system is running.

Now that we understand the background of interrupts, TSRs, and device drivers, let's look at an example of installing TCP/IP under DOS.

Installing DOS TCP/IP

Installing TCP/IP on a DOS system can be reduced to two basic steps: copying the software onto the hard disk, and configuring the software for a specific system. The two tasks are sometimes combined by a special installation program called **INSTALL** or **SETUP**. Though occasionally the installation program is required to decompress software that is stored on the floppies in compressed format, DOS installation programs are generally optional because DOS users are an independent bunch who like to do it themselves. For the independent minded, the software can usually be copied from the floppy disks to the hard disk using the DOS **COPY** command. Whatever technique is used, the **COPY** command or an **INSTALL** program, copying the software into the PC is a very simple process.

Once the executable files are copied into the system, modify the startup files (CONFIG.SYS and AUTOEXEC.BAT) so that the network is restarted at each boot.

Installation programs modify these files automatically. If you don't use one, edit the files yourself. The modifications are usually small but they do vary slightly from system to system.

One reason for these variations is that the device drivers installed via the startup files vary depending on the network interface card installed in the system. The example below shows the modifications made to the AUTOEXEC.BAT file to install Novell's *LAN Workplace* on a system using a 3COM 3C509 card. The **REM** statements are comments that identify the three TSRs: **LSL**, **3C509**, and **TCPIP**.

```
REM Install Novell Link Support Layer
LSL
REM Install 3COM 3C509 ODI Driver
3C509
REM Install LAN Workplace TCP/IP
TCPIP
```

Another *LAN WorkPlace* installation on a system using a Novell NE2000 Ethernet card would look exactly like this one except the **3C509** command would be replaced with an **NE2000** command.

This same type of variation occurs with other DOS TCP/IP implementations. For example, an installation of FTP Software's *PC/TCP* on a system with a Western Digital Ethernet card has the following command in the AUTOEXEC.BAT file:

```
WD8003
```

Because the configuration varies based on the hardware, it is particularly helpful to standardize on one type of network interface. The variation makes it difficult for DOS users who are unfamiliar with PC hardware to install their own TCP/IP software. The task is simple enough if you know which command to use, but if you don't know what hardware is installed in the system, you don't know which command is correct.

Configuring DOS TCP/IP is challenging. Unlike UNIX, which uses the same TCP/IP configuration commands for both BSD and System V, there are no consistent configuration commands between DOS implementations. We use configuration examples from a few different implementations, but the only way to get a handle on this subject is to keep a copy of the software vendor's documentation on hand and to standardize your network on one specific implementation.

Basic Configuration

Planning and preparation are the most important part of configuring TCP/IP. The TCP/IP installation program prompts for the basic configuration information. If you have the information on hand before the installation program starts, the actual installation involves little more than "filling in the blanks." Even if you don't use the install program, you need to have your configuration planning information on hand when you edit the TCP/IP configuration files.

Chapter 2 explains that all TCP/IP installations require certain basic values: a unique IP address, a valid subnet mask, properly configured routing, and a way to resolve hostnames to IP addresses. This section provides examples of how these values are passed to the TCP/IP software on a DOS system. These are the only values required by TCP/IP to get a system running, but a particular DOS implementation may require more. Your vendor may provide a planning sheet for preparing the additional information required to install its software. Don't forget to fill it out in addition to the planning sheet we provide in Appendix A. The vendor's sheet may have values not included in our planning section.

In the same way that AUTOEXEC.BAT and CONFIG.SYS are modified to pass information to the boot process to start the network, the configuration file is modified to pass information to the TCP/IP process to configure the network. Every implementation of TCP/IP has its own configuration file and its own configuration command syntax. The information required is the same for every implementation, but the commands used to communicate that information vary from system to system. We'll see this as we examine the configuration files for two different TCP/IP implementations: FTP Software's *PC/TCP* and Novell's *LAN WorkPlace*.

First, we'll look at the PCTCP.INI file, which is the file used to configure *PC/TCP*. The sample below is a minimal PCTCP.INI file:

```
[pctcp kernel]
serial-number=1111-2222-3333
authentication-key=4444-5555-6666
interface=wd8003 0

[pctcp wd8003 0]
ip-address=128.66.12.3
broadcast-address=128.66.12.255
router=128.66.12.6
subnet-mask=255.255.255.0
irq=3
ram-addr=0xD000
io-addr=0x300
```

The PCTCP.INI file can be built from scratch or created from a copy of the TEMPLATE.INI file that is delivered with the *PC/TCP* software. The sample clearly shows where the standard values are stored. The meaning of ip-address, broadcast-address, and subnet-mask is obvious. Even the meaning of router, which in this case is used to define the default gateway, is clear once you stop to think about it. It is easy to understand and modify these values. However, the file also includes values that are specific to *PC/TCP*. Each line of the file is explained below:

[pctcp kernel]

This section contains kernel configuration information. Section headings are enclosed in square brackets.

serial-number
> The serial number of this copy of the software.

authentication-key
> A key used with the serial number to validate the software license. The serial number and the authentication key are provided by the vendor along with the documentation and floppies.

interface
> The network interface. The first field identifies the brand of interface hardware, in this case a Western Digital WD8003. The second field identifies the interface number. The interfaces are numbered from 0 to 5 with 0 indicating that this is the first interface. In our example, it is the only interface.

[pctcp wd8003 0]
> This section contains configuration information for a specific interface card. If the interface name and number in the section header match the name and number used on an interface statement in the kernel configuration, this is an interface being used by the kernel.

ip-address
> The IP address assigned to this interface.

broadcast-address
> The broadcast address used on this network.

router
> The IP address of the router used as the default gateway.

subnet-mask
> The subnet mask used on this network.

irq
> The IRQ number used by this network adapter card. This is not a TCP/IP configuration value. This and the following values are PC hardware configuration parameters necessary to configure the network interface. The meaning and use of these values is covered in Chapter 1.

ram-addr
> The Adapter Memory Address used by this network adapter card.

io-addr
> The I/O Port Address used by this network adapter card.

A similar configuration for another DOS implementation of TCP/IP uses different files and different configuration commands. This in itself is a good reason to standardize on a limited number of TCP/IP implementations. The sample file we'll examine next is clearly different from the configuration file shown above, yet it provides the same basic configuration values.

Our second example is the NET.CFG file used to configure Novell's *LAN Workplace* software.

```
Link Support
        Buffers 8 1500
        MemPool 4096
Link Driver NE2000
        Int 5
        Port 320
        Frame ETHERNET_II
Protocol TCPIP
        PATH TCP_CFG    C:\TCP
        ip_address      128.66.12.3
        ip_router       128.66.12.6
        ip_netmask      255.255.255.0
```

Again the standard values for the IP address (`ip_address`), the subnet mask (`ip_netmask`), and the default gateway (`ip_router`) are obvious.[*] But several other vendor-specific fields also exist. The meaning of each entry is as follows:

Link Support

This is the Link Support section, which defines parameters for the Link Support Layer (LSL) driver. The LSL driver is a *LAN Workplace* TSR that provides *buffer management* for Novell's TCP/IP.[†] The sections in the NET.CFG file parallel the TSRs started in the AUTOEXEC.BAT file with one section for each TSR.

Buffers

The number and size of buffers used to receive packets. The example defines 8 buffers of 1500 bytes each, which is enough to hold eight of the largest possible Ethernet frames.

MemPool

The number of bytes allocated for the send buffer. The example sets aside 4K bytes for buffering packets waiting for acknowledgement.

Link Driver

This section contains the network adapter configuration. The name provided on the Link Driver command line is the name of the ODI device driver installed from the AUTOEXEC.BAT file. In this example it is NE2000.

Int

The IRQ number used by this interface.

Port

The I/O Port Address used by this interface.

---

[*] *LAN Workplace* uses the standard broadcast address and does not provide a parameter to change it.

[†] Novell's IPX/SPX protocol does not require buffer management because each packet is individually acknowledged. IPX/SPX do not support the TCP/IP concept of transmission windows.

Frame
> The type of media framing used on this Ethernet. This specific configuration parameter really has nothing to do with TCP/IP, but it has to be configured correctly for the network to work. In our example, we specify Ethernet II framing. Most TCP/IP networks, and particularly those with UNIX systems, use Ethernet II (DIX) framing. Because of this, most DOS TCP/IP implementations default to it. Novell is one of the exceptions because Novell's NetWare protocols default to IEEE 802.3 framing, and they use the same default for their TCP/IP software. See the box *When is Ethernet Ethernet?* for more details.

Protocol TCPIP
> This section contains the TCP/IP configuration parameters.

PATH TCP_CFG
> The path to the directory that contains various *LAN Workplace* configuration files. The files located in this directory are: HOSTS, RESOLV.CFG, NETWORKS, PROTOCOLS and SERVICES.

ip_address
> The IP address assigned to this PC.

ip_router
> The address of the router used as the default gateway.

ip_netmask
> The subnet mask for this network.

Both samples are minimal files that only cover the things required to boot a TCP/IP configuration. There are many more configuration commands that could be put in the NET.CFG file and the PCTCP.INI file. Luckily the default values for optional configuration commands are usually correct. Most installation problems come from incorrectly modified configuration values, not from the values provided by the vendors. Configuration mistakes are most common when PC users are required to edit their own configuration files. Central control of the PC's network configuration helps reduce these problems.

Bootstrap Protocol

It is possible to centralize some TCP/IP configuration values by using BOOTP (Bootstrap Protocol). The protocol allows the PC client to learn its IP address and other configuration parameters from a central server. The advantages and disadvantages of central configuration control and the details of how the service is setup are examined in Chapter 8. That's the hard part; the PC part is easy.

To set up the client (PC) side of Bootp on a DOS system running *PC/TCP*, simply put the BOOTP command into the AUTOEXEC.BAT file after the commands that start the *PC/TCP* kernel. A PC running *LAN Workplace* doesn't even need a BOOTP command. It uses Bootp automatically if the NET.CFG file doesn't contain the ip-address, ip-router, and ip-netmask parameters. Simple! And the same configuration file can be used for every PC on a physical network because the real configuration work is done on the central server. PC users don't have to get involved in the details of addressing, routing, and the rest of it.

When is Ethernet Ethernet?

Ethernet is not Ethernet when it's really IEEE 802.3! 10M bps Ethernet was specified by Xerox, Digital Equipment Corporation, and Intel (DIX). IEEE 802.3 is a networking standard that was specified by the Institute of Electrical and Electronic Engineers. Ethernet and IEEE 802.3 are almost identical, but not quite. One big difference is that they use different frame headers. Frames are the packets of data transmitted over the physical network. Two computers connected to the same network cannot successfully exchange information if they use incompatible frame headers.

Most TCP/IP local area networks use Ethernet frames. TCP/IP and Ethernet grew up together and have a very close association. Running TCP/IP over IEEE 802.3 requires a little help. To help TCP/IP and 802.3 be friends, a third protocol, *Sub-Network Access Protocol* (SNAP), was defined in RFC 1042, *A Standard for the Transmission of IP Datagrams Over IEEE 802 Networks*. If you use IEEE 802.3 on your TCP/IP network, you should use it with SNAP.

In our *LAN Workplace* example, we use either `Ethernet_II` or `Ethernet_SNAP`, but not `Ethernet_802.3`, as the frame type for a TCP/IP network.

Domain Name Service

We have seen configuration examples of everything in our basic configuration list—IP address, subnet mask, default route, and broadcast address—everything except name service. Name service is a client/server system. DOS PCs run only the client side of name service, which is called the *resolver*. The resolver configuration only requires a default domain name and the address of at least one name server. Again, we'll use FTP Software's *PC/TCP* and Novell's *LAN WorkPlace* for sample resolver configurations.

First we'll look at the *PC/TCP* configuration. Adding the following statements to the PCTCP.INI file configures the resolver on a *PC/TCP* system to use *nuts.com* as the default domain name and to use the name server at address 128.66.12.1.

```
[pctcp general]
domain-name=nuts.com

[pctcp addresses]
domain-name-server=128.66.12.1
```

Our second resolver configuration example is for Novell's *LAN WorkPlace*. *LAN Workplace* provides a pleasantly familiar way to configure its resolver. It uses a file

called RESOLV.CFG that has the same syntax as the *resolv.conf* file used to configure the resolver on a UNIX system. Look at the name server section of any UNIX
reference book, and you'll know how to configure the *LAN Workplace* resolver.
Here's a sample RESOLV.CFG file.

```
; our local domain name
domain nuts.com
; try almond first
nameserver 128.66.12.1
; try pecan second
nameserver 128.66.12.6
; try filbert last
nameserver 128.66.3.1
```

The RESOLV.CFG file is located in the directory pointed to by the PATH TCP_CFG
command in the NET.CFG file. This directory contains several configuration files
that exactly parallel the syntax and function of like-named files used on UNIX systems. The HOSTS file is of particular interest since we are talking about name service.

It is possible to resolve names without using a name server by maintaining a host
table on each PC. If you decide to use a host table under *LAN Workplace*, it is configured exactly as it is under UNIX. Here's a sample table:

```
128.66.12.2      peanut.nuts.com peanut
128.66.12.1      almond.nuts.com almond
128.66.12.6      pecan.nuts.com pecan
128.66.3.1       filbert.nuts.com filbert
```

PC/TCP also uses a host table that looks exactly like the UNIX */etc/hosts* file. The
only difference between the *LAN Workplace* host table and the one used by
PC/TCP is the command used to point to the file containing the table. For *LAN
Workplace*, it was the PATH TCP_CFG command. On a *PC/TCP* system a host-
table entry is added to the [pctcp kernel] section of the PCTCP.INI file as in
this example:

```
host-table=C:\PCTCP\HOSTS
```

Most sites, however, should rely on name service. If it is used at all, the host table
is generally limited to a few entries.

This completes the basic DOS TCP/IP configuration, which includes addressing,
routing, and name service. After completing the configuration, run a few quick
tests to ensure that everything is running properly.

Debugging a DOS Configuration

Two types of commands are used to debug a new configuration: commands that
display the current configuration and commands that test the network connection.
Check the connection first and let the results of that test guide subsequent testing.

The classic TCP/IP test command is **PING**. It sends an *ICMP Echo Request* to a remote system's IP protocol. If the system responds, the link is operational. If it fails to respond to repeated pings, something is wrong. Most DOS TCP/IP packages include a **PING** command. There are slight variations in syntax, so check your documentation, but a simple **PING** *hostname* should work on any implementation. For example, using the *LAN WorkPlace* implementation of ping:

```
C:\> ping almond.nuts.com
almond.nuts.com is alive
```

In the example, the reply `almond.nuts.com is alive` means that this PC can communicate with the remote system. If **PING** returns an error message, refer to the *Troubleshooting* section of Chapter 3 for some help in interpreting what it means. Remember, each implementation is different and displays slightly different messages. Use your judgement and the vendor documentation to interpret the messages. When you have an idea of what you're looking for, examine the PC's configuration to see if anything is wrong.

DOS systems have a variety of commands for displaying the TCP/IP configuration. *PC/TCP* uses its own **PCTCPCFG** command. Check the values set in a section of the *PC/TCP* configuration by putting the section name followed by a pair of quotation marks on the **PCTCPCFG** command line. The section heading for a network interface includes the interface name and number, and both values are used to check the interface settings. For example, assuming that the interface is a Western Digital WD8003, the settings for the wd8003 0 section are displayed in the following manner:

```
C:\> pctcpcfg wd8003 -s 0 ""
[pctcp wd8003 0] - ip-address=128.66.12.3
[pctcp wd8003 0] - broadcast-address=128.66.12.255
[pctcp wd8003 0] - router=128.66.12.6
[pctcp wd8003 0] - subnet-mask=255.255.255.0
[pctcp wd8003 0] - irq=3
[pctcp wd8003 0] - ram-addr=0xD000
[pctcp wd8003 0] - io-addr=0x300
```

The system you work with may not have a special command that displays the configuration, or if it does you may not remember its syntax. As long as you remember the name of the configuration file, you can always look inside of it for the configuration information. If you're sitting at the PC keyboard, start a text editor and browse through the configuration file. If you're talking the user through a test over the phone, the **FIND** filter is helpful for displaying the values in the configuration file.

In the following example, we check the configuration values in the *LAN Workplace* NET.CFG file using **FIND**.[*]

```
C:\> FIND "ip_" < NET.CFG
ip_address      128.66.12.2
ip_router       128.66.12.6
ip_netmask      255.255.255.0
```

This example is a simple one because *LAN Workplace* has a consistent search parameter that can be used with **FIND**. Every TCP/IP configuration line in NET.CFG contains the string `ip_`. Other implementations can be harder to check. Here's another more complex check on the PCTCP.INI file:

```
C:\> FIND "128.66" < PCTCP.INI
ip-address=128.66.12.3
broadcast-address=128.66.12.255
router=128.66.12.6
domain-name-server=128.66.12.1
C:\> FIND "mask" < PCTCP.INI
subnet-mask=255.255.255.0
```

Even in this more complicated example, the network address (128.66) is a common feature of all of the configuration parameters except the subnet mask. Using **FIND** is generally easier than talking a user through an editor session, especially over the phone. And one goal you should have in all of your interactions with your users is to keep it simple.

Summary

A general book about TCP/IP on PCs cannot possibly give all of the details of all the different TCP/IP implementations. Each implementation is different; each has its own commands and syntax. You must rely on the vendor documentation for the details. However, the underlying structure is the same. All implementations are built on interrupts, TSRs, and device drivers. All need the same IP configuration values; all are debugged in a similar manner. This chapter supplements the details of the vendor documentation with concepts that can apply to all DOS systems. In the next chapter we take a similar look at Windows.

---

[*] **FIND** is a standard DOS filter. There are DOS implementations of **grep**, but they are not a standard part of DOS. When you talk a user though a test, be positive that the user has the command you want him to use on his system.

5

Windows on the Network

Microsoft Windows is one reason for the continued success of DOS. Windows is not an operating system, despite the fact that this chapter treats it as one. It is a *graphical user interface* (GUI) that runs on top of DOS as an application. To use Windows, you must first install DOS. Millions of copies of DOS are really being used to host Windows.

Windows programs provide a more consistent user interface than DOS applications. Windows *is* a user interface. You can sit down in front of an unfamiliar application and immediately begin to do productive work because the pulldown menus and popup windows (called *dialogue boxes*) provide a graphic interface that many people find simple to use. If you're used to the direct access that a DOS command gives you, working through the menus and dialogue boxes can be frustrating. However, most people find the Windows interface simple to learn.[*]

Windows extended the life of DOS by overcoming its two big weaknesses: lack of multitasking and limited memory support. You need at least a 386 processor with 4M bytes of memory to run Windows effectively, but if you have adequate hardware, Windows is one way to put that hardware to good use. Windows provides support for a full 16M bytes of memory and a limited form of multitasking.

Windows uses a scheme called *cooperative multitasking* that relies on "well-behaved" applications to permit the operating system to share resources among multiple programs. An application program can "hang" Windows, and the operating system cannot forcibly take back control. You may be required to do it manually by pressing the Ctrl-Alt-Del keys and cleaning things up with the *Task Manager*. The form of multitasking that most of us are familiar with is called *preemptive multitasking*. A preemptive multitasking operating system is able to take control away from the application at will.

---

[*] Even DOS emulates this interface. See the DOS **edit** command or the ECU programs illustrated in Chapter 3 for examples of programs that use a "pseudo-windows" interface.

Tasks running under Windows are not completely protected from each other. Even the operating system is unable to protect itself from an application that is running amuck because Windows 3.1 does not have a memory protection scheme. The lack of memory protection has been exploited in the past by some DOS programs. Those same programs running under Windows can be a major headache.

Because of these weaknesses, Windows has a reputation for being unreliable. Most of this reputation comes from running DOS programs that were never designed for Windows. It is possible to avoid DOS applications by running the large selection of programs that are specifically written for Windows. Running only Windows programs greatly increases the reliability of the system. To provide a wider variety of examples, this chapter only uses TCP/IP products that are specifically written for Windows, although the programs used in the Chapter 4 examples also have Windows versions.

Some people argue that multitasking is not needed on a single user system. Well, it is for networking! People want to know that mail has arrived even when they are busy with a spreadsheet. They want to be able to do word processing while a large file is being transmitted in the background. Windows does a better job of multitasking than DOS, so Windows is better for TCP/IP networking. TCP/IP developers have made good use of Windows multitasking abilities. They have used it to support a number of server functions that are surprising to see on single-user PC systems.

Implementing TCP/IP for Windows

All implementations of TCP/IP for DOS are constructed from TSRs, but the configuration and command syntax of DOS implementations vary widely. For Windows it is just the opposite. The consistent user interface reduces the differences in configuring and using various implementations, but Windows developers have multiple choices of how to build the software. Our discussion of TCP/IP for Windows starts with these implementation choices.

Three techniques are used to implement TCP/IP for Windows systems. It can be implemented as a TSR, DLL or VxD.

Terminate and Stay Resident (TSR)

TSRs are discussed on Chapter 4. Because Windows runs on top of DOS, the same TSR structure used for DOS can be used for Windows. The advantages and disadvantages are almost the same as they are for DOS. A TSR is very fast. It operates in real time in response to an interrupt. However, it uses precious, limited DOS memory, and one of the reasons for using Windows is to get away from the DOS memory limit. A special advantage for Windows is that a TSR provides service to all windows—even DOS windows—and the same TSR can be used by DOS even when Windows is not running.

Dynamic Link Library (DLL)

A DLL is a library that can be called from a program without having been statically linked to the program at compile time. In the context of this discussion the term is used to refer to programs that are implemented using Windows dynamic link libraries. These are "true" Windows programs. They run as windows inside of the Windows environment and are not available in DOS or even in a DOS window running under Windows. DLLs use very little memory, and the memory they use is abundant Windows memory; they don't use any DOS memory at all. DLL-based TCP/IP implementations depend on Windows for service. They are not interrupt-driven, real-time processes.

Virtual Device Driver (VxD)

The VxD is the newest approach to implementing TCP/IP for Windows. A VxD is a device driver created inside of the Windows *virtual machine*. Like a DOS device driver, a VxD can be designed to respond to interrupts in real time. A VxD does not use any DOS memory. It is available to DOS windows, though not to DOS when Windows is not running.

Does any of this matter to you? Maybe. TSR-based systems run under both DOS and Windows. A TSR system is desirable if it is important to standardize support on a single TCP/IP implementation that runs in both environments. The problem with this approach is that it is essentially backward-looking. Where will your PC users be in the near future? Will most of them be Windows users, or Windows 95 users? If so, select a package because of how well it supports those environments and not because of backward compatibility with DOS.

DLL and VxD implementations are both native Windows systems. VxD systems have a performance edge over DLL systems because they are interrupt driven. Several vendors have announced VxD implementations for their next generation of Windows software, so it is the future direction of TCP/IP software. Speed is important for systems such as servers that are heavily loaded, and a PC can be used as a server when it runs Windows 3.1. However, most PCs are not heavily loaded and most network administrators use robust operating systems like UNIX on their servers. VxD performance is desirable, but probably not the most important feature for selecting an implementation.

Regardless of how it is implemented, the most important thing when choosing a TCP/IP package for Windows is the applications that the package supports and the quality of those applications. Most PC users don't notice the difference between 200K bps and 240K bps file transfers, but they all notice if the email system won't deliver their mail!

There are several Windows TCP/IP packages to choose from. I'm personally familiar with software from SPRY, Distinct, Frontier Technology, NetManage and Microsoft, and there are several other packages that I have never worked with. In addition to these, all of the major DOS TCP/IP packages run under Windows. You have many choices. It is even possible to choose more than one package. For example, the Microsoft package is a TCP/IP protocol stack without many applications, and the SPRY package is a comprehensive set of applications without a protocol stack. The SPRY package can be combined with a package that includes a stack, such as the software from Distinct or Microsoft, to create a full TCP/IP implementation. At first SPRY's unique "applications-only" approach seems odd. How can they offer applications that run on TCP/IP protocol stacks from companies as diverse as Distinct and Microsoft? The answer is the *Winsock* standard.

Winsock is a standard *Application Programming Interface* (API) defined to run TCP/IP over Windows. Winsock stands for *Windows Sockets*, and it is an implementation of a Berkeley-style TCP/IP sockets interface for Microsoft Windows. Applications and protocol stacks that comply with the Winsock standard should be able to interoperate. There are some problems, but how well this standard works and how widely it is accepted are surprising.

All of the packages listed above state that they are Winsock compliant. As the Winsock standard improves, you may be able to pick and choose the stack and applications you want from various vendors and run them together on a single system—assuming you have enough money to buy all of these different packages!

In this chapter we look at applications from several vendors, but the bulk of the examples are based on NetManage's *Chameleon/NFS* and Frontier Technology's *SuperTCP* because those are the packages I know best. We begin with examples of installing TCP/IP on a Windows system.

Installing TCP/IP

The same two steps, copying the software from floppies and modifying the configuration files, that were required to install TCP/IP on DOS are required to install it on Windows. The difference is that the Windows system always uses an installation program.

It is extremely important to have all of the installation information on hand *before* you start the installation program. (See Chapter 2 and Appendix A for advice on preparing for the installation.) If you have the information on hand, the installation is simple. You merely fill in the blanks on several dialogue boxes. On the other hand, a user attempting to wade through several dialogue boxes without any instructions as to what information should be provided can become confused and frustrated. If the frustration ends with the user turning off his computer in the middle of the installation, you might have a mess to clean up. Bottom line: prepare before you install.

All Windows TCP/IP packages use an installation program with a name like **install** or **setup**. The installation program is located on one of the floppies delivered with the software and is run from within Windows by selecting **Run** from the **File** menu in the *Program Manager*. Then enter the pathname of the installation program in the Command Line dialogue box.

Each vendor imprints his own style on the setup program, so the details of the program vary between implementations. Despite this, most installations follow a similar pattern. Generally the setup program walks through a series of dialogue boxes that create a minimal configuration. The installation steps you'll encounter might not occur in the same order as our example, but the same general tasks will be performed.

For example, a minimal installation of Frontier Technology's *SuperTCP* follows these steps:

1. The setup program begins by displaying a dialogue box that requests the license information. After this information is correctly entered, a screen appears that allows you to choose a custom configuration or a default configuration. This option permits you to select only those applications that you actually plan to use so that you don't waste disk storage on unused programs. For many users, saving disk space is not as important as the convenience of having all of the applications on hand. You never know what program might be needed in the future, and most newer PCs have large disk drives. Therefore, most users want a full installation. If your implementation defaults to a full installation, select the default installation. If it doesn't, or you're not sure what it does default to, choose the custom installation and select the applications you want installed.

2. The system then copies the selected applications from floppy disks to the hard drive. Various informational dialogue boxes appear, the icons are initialized, and you're warned about modifications to the DOS boot files. The AUTOEXEC.BAT file and the CONFIG.SYS file are modified by the TCP/IP installation because some of the groundwork for a Windows network must be laid during the DOS boot. The Windows startup files are also modified, and the installation may warn you of this. The Windows initialization files are covered in the box *INI Files*.

   Most TCP/IP implementations make backup copies of the DOS boot files and the Windows initialization files before modifying them. But to be safe, make your own copies before beginning the installation. You should also have a bootable floppy disk ready for drive A: in case the installation corrupts the DOS boot.*

3. Next the setup program attempts to find out if a network device driver has been installed. The adapter hardware must be installed before installing TCP/IP. However, it is possible, particularly if no other network software has been installed, that no device driver was installed with the hardware. If no driver is found, the setup program asks what type of network driver you want (NDIS, ODI, Packet, etc.) and what type of adapter hardware is installed. The TCP/IP package includes a selection of common adapter drivers; however, it may not have the exact driver you need. In that case, select **Other** from the

---

* To create a bootable floppy insert a blank disk in the A: drive and type **format a: /s**.

adapter menu and use the floppy disk provided by the adapter vendor to load the driver.

Driver configuration is the trickiest part of setting up TCP/IP on a PC. You must know the details of the hardware installation to know the adapter's configuration parameters. You'll be prompted for vendor-specific configuration information. Make sure you have the adapter documentation and any installation notes on hand to answer these question. Use a utility program or the configuration program that came with the network adapter card to find out the correct values for this adapter before beginning the TCP/IP installation. If you find yourself in the middle of the installation and realize that you don't know the correct configuration values, use the default values presented by the TCP/IP implementation and go on to complete the installation. The correct values can be input later.

4. A minimal configuration dialogue box appears that asks for the PC's IP address, hostname, domain name, and the address of the domain name server. Other implementations may ask other questions, but you will certainly be asked to provide at least the hostname and IP address of the PC. With this basic information, the adapter information, and the software and driver data read from the floppy disks, the system has the minimal information it needs to connect to the TCP/IP network.

5. Once the minimal configuration is done, a configuration program is called from which some applications can be configured and from which the interface configuration can be modified. This configuration program can be started anytime from within Windows. You don't need to configure all of the applications completely during the initial installation, and it may not be desirable to do so. Attempting to configure everything at once makes the configuration more complex and offers more opportunities for mistakes. Stop and reboot the system after finishing the minimal configuration. You'll then be able to test the network connection before the lower layers of TCP/IP are obscured by the added confusion and complexity of the applications.

The type of information entered during the initial setup is the same from system to system—the same IP address, subnet mask, hostname, domain name, license information, routing information, and adapter configuration information discussed in Chapter 4. It is possible that not all of this essential information is entered through the minimal configuration dialogue box. If it isn't, it's easy to add.

Finishing the Basic Configuration

After completing the minimal installation and rebooting the system, the Windows *Program Manager* contains an icon for the TCP/IP programs. Double-clicking this icon opens a window that contains icons for several different programs. One of these allows you to customize your TCP/IP configuration.

INI Files

Windows reads its configuration from five standard *INI files*:

SYSTEM.INI   Stores the hardware configuration.

WIN.INI   A catch-all file that stores a wide variety of Windows information. This file is also used by some applications to store their configurations.

PROGMAN.INI Holds the configuration information for the *Program Manager* groups.

CONTROL.INI Stores some user-defined *Control Panel* values, such as the color scheme, screen saver, user-installed drivers, and MIDI multimedia information.

MOUSE.INI   Stores information about the mouse.

SYSTEM.INI, WIN.INI, and PROGMAN.INI are the most important of these files. Appendix D covers the modifications made to them by a sample TCP/IP installation.

INI files have a standard structure and command syntax. The files are divided into sections that begin with a label enclosed in square brackets. For example, the network section of the WIN.INI file begins with the label [network]. Each configuration command is written as a keyword, an equal sign and some variable value, e.g., network.drv=C:\DRIVERS\MULTI400.DRV.

Windows applications also use INI files to retain their configurations. As noted, some applications store information in WIN.INI. Others create private INI files. An example is the SLIP.INI file, which is *Chameleon's* SLIP configuration file.

Not every application uses the extension INI on its configuration file. Many vendors follow Novell's lead and use the extension CFG for configuration files. For example *Chameleon*, which used INI for SLIP, uses CFG for the FTP.CFG file. Look for both extensions when looking for a configuration file.

On a *SuperTCP* system this icon is labeled SetupTCP. Selecting the icon opens the window shown in Figure 5-1. From the scrolling window shown on the left of the Figure, select the Interfaces icon to modify the PC's IP address and subnet mask.[*] Select the IP Setup icon to define a default gateway or to enable RIP routing. Make the necessary modifications to the subnet mask and the routing. Close the configuration program and restart Windows to allow the changes to take effect. **PING** local and remote systems to verify that the interface is properly configured.

---

[*] Checking the **Bootp** box in the Interfaces window loads the address and mask from the boot server. Boot servers are covered in Chapter 8.

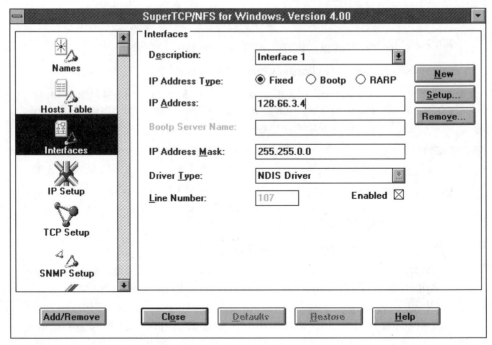

Figure 5–1: SuperTCP Setup Window

This basic configuration process is really very simple. Confusion often arises because on the surface each vendor's configuration program looks different. However, all of these programs can be used to set the necessary configuration values. Don't panic when presented with a new configuration program. Stop and think. The facilities for entering configuration information exist somewhere in that program. You may have to look through multiple levels of dialogue boxes to find them, but if you're patient you'll succeed.

Chameleon's Custom Program

Chameleon provides another example of a configuration program. The *Chameleon* program is named *Custom*. It is shown in Figure 5-2. Select the network interface from the listbox at the bottom of the window and pull down the **Setup** menu for selections that set the IP address and subnet mask. The default gateway is set through the **Default Gateway** item in the **Services** pulldown menu.[*] This is only superficially different from the *SuperTCP* program, and it is just as easy to use.

Defining multiple network interfaces is simple using these configuration programs, and switching between interfaces once they are defined is easy. A laptop

---

[*] The meanings of the **Default Gateway, Domain Servers,** and **Host Table** menu items are obvious. Use the **Frequent Destinations** selection to make manual ARP table entries, and the **SNMP** entry to configure the SNMP agent. SNMP is covered in Chapter 3.

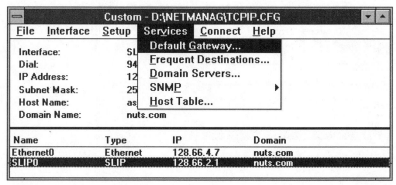

Figure 5–2: Chameleon Custom Program

computer is the classic example of a PC that needs more than one interface; in the office it attaches to the network through an Ethernet interface, and on the road it attaches to the network through a COM port running *Serial Line IP* (SLIP) or *Point to Point Protocol* (PPP). Many network administrators dread SLIP and PPP configuration, but with Windows it's easy.

Configuring SLIP

The details vary, but most Windows TCP/IP implementations provide a simple, straightforward technique for configuring SLIP. If you have experience with configuring SLIP for UNIX, Windows configuration should be a pleasant surprise. The *Chameleon Custom* program demonstrates just how easy it is. In the Custom window, select the **Add** item from the **Interface** menu.

Figure 5-3 shows the Add Interface box. Select the type of interface from the listbox. SLIP (Serial Line IP), PPP (Point to Point Protocol), and CSLIP (Compressed SLIP) are all serial line protocols. SLIP is the most commonly used. CSLIP is a version of SLIP with header compression to improve performance. PPP is a standard TCP/IP protocol that has several advanced features.[*]

These protocols perform similar functions, but they are different and incompatible. Your PC must run the same protocol as the server, so choose a protocol type that matches the server's offerings. In the example we choose SLIP.

The system generates the interface name based on the type of the interface. The first SLIP interface is named *SLIP0*, the second is *SLIP1*, and so on. Click the **Add** button, hidden in our example by the listbox, to add the new interface.

The interface is installed, but it is far from configured. Some configuration parameters are given default values and some are not given any value at all. In the example, COM2 is the default serial port, and 9600 baud is the default line speed, but no IP address, hostname, domain name, or subnet mask are assigned. To provide

---

* SLIP and PPP are covered in *TCP/IP Network Administration.*

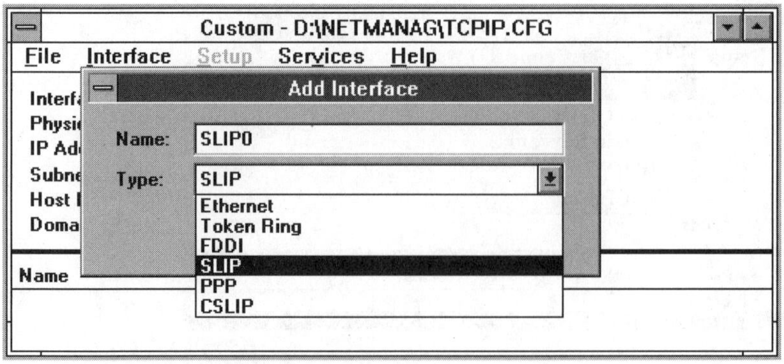

Figure 5-3: Adding a SLIP Interface

these necessary values, select the **Setup** menu. As shown in Figure 5-4, it has menu selections for most of the important configuration values.

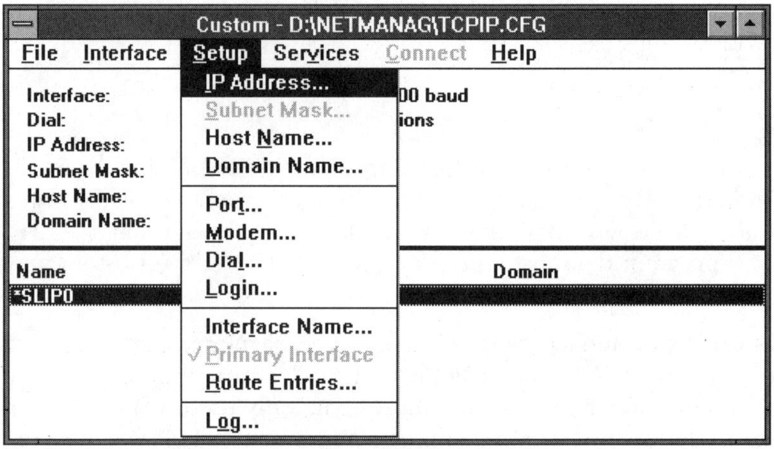

Figure 5-4: Chameleon Custom Setup Menu

The menu selections used to set basic TCP/IP configuration values require no explanation. By now we all know what an IP address and a hostname are, but some other menu items are not as familiar. A few of the selections are specific to serial line communications. These are:

Port

> Defines the characteristics of the serial port. In the *Chameleon* example, it is used to select the port (COM1 to COM4) and to set the baud rate, number of data bits, number of stop bits, parity, and flow control. These settings should match the settings on the modem, and they should be compatible with SLIP.

Standard SLIP settings are 8-bit data with no parity. Never use software flow-control (XON/XOFF) on a SLIP line. If you need to use flow control, use hardware (RTS/CTS) flow control.

Modem

Defines the commands used by the modem. The command strings used to initialize the modem, dial a number, and hangup the line are the key commands. *Chameleon* provides defaults for Hayes, Telebit, and MultiTech modems. It is important that you know your modem's command set to be able to set and troubleshoot these values. Another SLIP implementation may have a different interface for gathering this information, but all implementations need to know the correct modem commands.

Dial

Defines the telephone number of the remote SLIP server.

Login

Defines the username and password used to log in to the remote SLIP server. It also allows you to define a startup command to be passed to the remote server. A general purpose terminal server that supports terminal logins, SLIP logins, CSLIP logins, and PPP logins requires a command to set the receiving port to the correct mode. That is generally what the startup command is used for. A sample Login Settings dialogue box is shown in Figure 5-5.

Figure 5–5: SLIP Login Settings

After setting all of the values, we're ready to test the interface. Open a window to watch the progress of the connection by clicking on **Log** in the **Setup** menu, and then click **Connect** to start the connection process. If everything works, that's great! If it doesn't we have to do some debugging. The area that probably requires debugging when the initial connection fails is the login script.

Chameleon puts the login script in a file called SLIP.INI. The file contains login scripts for several popular dial-in service providers. If you're using one of these providers, the configuration of the SLIP interface is almost automatic. But we're not. We're using the private SLIP server at *nuts.com*. We have to custom configure our own login script.

All login scripts follow a similar pattern. The script expects a string from the server and responds with its own string. The syntax is different for every implementation, so there is no point in trying to learn the *Chameleon* syntax in detail. However, by looking at a *Chameleon* and a *SuperTCP* example we'll see how similar the logic of these scripts can be. First let's look at a *Chameleon* SLIP login script.

Each login script in the SLIP.INI file begins with an identifying name. The name of the script we want to modify is the same as the name of the SLIP interface we just installed—SLIP0. In the SLIP.INI file we find the following entry:

```
[SLIP0]
SCRIPT=login: $u$r word: $p$r
TYPE=SLIP
```

The script expects the string "login:" and responds with the username ($u) and a carriage-return ($r). It then expects the string "word:" and responds with the password ($p) and a carriage-return ($r). This works if the remote SLIP server is a UNIX host, but *nuts.com* uses a general purpose terminal server. Our terminal server prompts for "Username>" not "login:" and for "Password>" not "password:". Additionally it requires a carriage-return before it will send either prompt, and it requires a startup command to setup the port for SLIP. We have to rewrite the script for SLIP0. Here's the result:

```
[SLIP0]
SCRIPT=-n $1$r name> $u$r word> $p$r > $c$r
TYPE=SLIP
```

Without waiting for any string (–n means expect nothing) this script delays for one second ($1) after the connection and then sends a carriage-return ($r). It waits for the string "name>" and responds with the username ($u) and a carriage-return ($r). It then expects the string "word>" and responds with the password ($p) and a carriage-return ($r). When the server is ready for input, it sends a variable port number followed by the ">" character, so the script waits for the ">" and sends the startup command ($c) and a carriage-return ($r). $u, $p, and $c are macros that use the values entered into the Login Settings dialogue box. This syntax is unique to *Chameleon*.

SuperTCP FTCMODEM.INI File

On a *SuperTCP* system, the equivalent login script looks very different but performs the exact same functions. The script is stored in a file named FTCMODEM.INI and is entered through the a dialogue box.

Figure 5-6 shows the window used to enter a SLIP/PPP login script on a *SuperTCP* system. The strings expected from the remote server and the responses to those strings are clearly shown. The differences between *SuperTCP* and *Chameleon* configuration are purely cosmetic. The dial, modem, and login settings entered into different dialogue boxes on the *Chameleon* system are all entered here through one dialogue box.

The *SuperTCP* script starts by dialing the server's phone line. When the "Connect" message is received it sends a carriage-return (\r). When prompted for the user

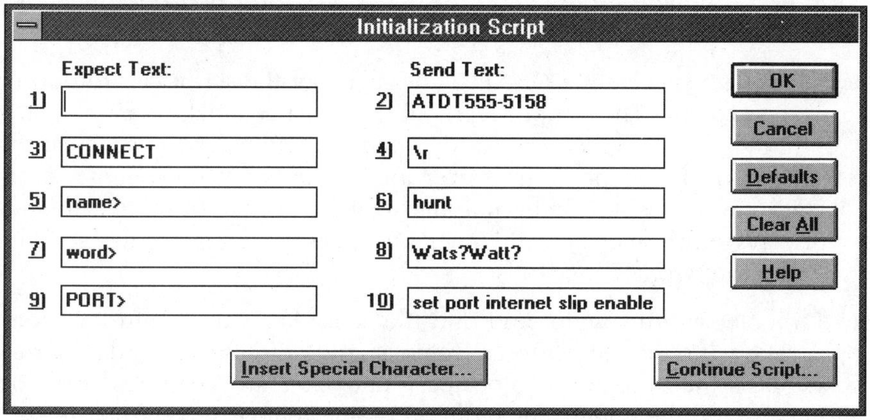

Figure 5–6: SuperTCP Dialing Script

name it sends the username *hunt*, and when prompted for the password it sends
the password *Wats?Watt?*.[*] The server displays a variable port number and a ">"
when the system is successfully logged in and the script responds with the startup
command.

Troubleshooting SLIP/PPP

Configuring the modem correctly and creating the login script are the most difficult
parts of setting up a serial interface, but even they are really not as difficult as they
first appear. The syntax of login scripts is often arcane, but the scripts are surprisingly easy to debug. Login scripts can usually be monitored in real time—through
the **Log** menu selection on a *Chameleon* system, and in the Master-Services window on a *SuperTCP* system. When a new script is tested, it is simple to see and
correct any errors. A script only needs to be developed and debugged once. After
that it is simply copied onto other PCs with minor variations (e.g., username and
password).

Watching the SLIP or PPP connection process through a real-time logging window
provides important debugging clues. These are some of the things to look out for.

The modem dials but fails to connect with the remote system. If the connection
fails with a message such as "ring no answer" or "ring busy," the problem is at the
remote server—it might be down or extremely busy. If the connection fails after
the modems begin negotiating the connection parameters, indicated by the high-
pitched tone heard through the modem speaker, your modem may not be properly configured for the remote server. You need to know exactly what the remote
modem expects from your modem. The source of that information is the

---

[*] To avoid storing the password in a file, *SuperTCP* provides a command (\w) that prompts
the user to type in the password.

administrator of the remote server, and the source of information on configuring your modem is your modem documentation.

The modem displays a successful CONNECT message, but the script fails to start or hangs during processing. The script is probably to blame. Make sure that the responses from the remote server are exactly what the script expects and that the commands sent from the script to the server are exactly what the remote server requires. If the script hangs, it is expecting the wrong response from the server. If the server displays errors messages or other unexpected responses, the script is probably sending the wrong commands.

If you have trouble with the script and find the script language confusing, don't use a script. Make your connection to the remote server through a standard terminal window. Make the connection repeatedly until you are confident that you completely understand the commands required by the remote server and are sure that the modem and everything else is working. Once you have confidence in all of these things, you can concentrate on developing and debugging the script.

The modem connects, the login script runs, but the PC cannot successfully pass TCP/IP data over the SLIP/PPP link. There are several possible causes for this:

- Make sure your system only requests features that are supported by the remote server. You cannot use features such as header compression (CSLIP) or PPP *Link Control Protocol* (LCP) extensions unless they are supported by both systems. This type of problem is likely if the system cannot pass any data at all.

- Make sure that your modem is properly configured. Accidentally setting software flow control (XON/XOFF) can cause the system to hang during data transmission.

- Make sure the serial port is properly configured. Do not set the port to a speed that is greater than the speed at which it can properly run. Older PCs have low performance serial ports that have a maximum speed of 19.2K bps. Some of these systems only run at 9600 bps. If your system appears to run fine for awhile, then slows down and finally stops, you should try reducing the port speed on the PC to 9600 bps. If that doesn't work, you can go even lower (4800 bps) or try reducing the SLIP frame size from 1006 bytes to 512 bytes. If that doesn't work, try using a high-speed serial card in the PC.

- Make sure the PC modem is compatible with the server modem. If all else fails get a loaner modem from the computer center and see if it helps. Old modems may need to be replaced to obtain adequate SLIP/PPP performance. High-speed modems can be finicky; you're least likely to have trouble if the PC and the server use the same brand.

If you're responsible for the SLIP server, document the exact modem configuration it requires and provide that information to your remote users along with a list of recommended, fully supported modems. Limit the list to those modems that you can intelligently answer questions about, but include some low cost modems that home users can reasonably be expected to purchase. Serial communications are often used to connect home computer users into the network, and the network administrator has very little control over a user's home system. The user could have an old modem with no documentation at all and still expect you to support it!

Configuring PPP

Because PPP is a different protocol from SLIP, you may assume that it is configured differently. In general that is not true. To use PPP instead of SLIP in the Chameleon example shown above, select PPP in the Interface dialogue box and change the login command as shown in Figure 5-7.

Figure 5-7: PPP Login Command

The command shown in Figure 5-7 is specific to one type of PPP terminal server. The command is not important; use whatever is correct for your server. The point is that PPP configuration is only slightly different from SLIP configuration. If you can do one, you can do the other as long as you make sure that the TCP/IP software you select for your PC includes PPP.

This concludes our discussion of basic interface configuration for Windows TCP/IP systems. The basic information is important because it is vital to configuring an operational network interface. But TCP/IP applications are what make Windows a desirable networking environment, so configuring the applications is also important. One unique aspect of configuring Windows TCP/IP applications is that some of them require user accounts.

User Accounts on a PC?

Most Windows TCP/IP implementations require user accounts to keep track of the different users who are accessing network services. User accounts may seem out of place on a single-user PC system, but they are useful for two reasons:

- As a network client, the PC is sometimes required to provide the user's name and password to a remote server.

- As a server, the PC may need to verify the username and password of a remote user. Windows runs server applications as easily as it runs client applications.

PC user accounts are not as unusual as you might think, and they are not unique to TCP/IP. Other network systems, such as Windows for Workgroups (WfW), place the same requirement on the system. A PC is a *peer* of the other systems on a WfW network, meaning it is both a client and a server to the other systems. TCP/IP provides both client/server and peer-to-peer communications—even for a PC. A PC running TCP/IP needs user accounts just as it does when running WfW.

To enter usernames and passwords on a *SuperTCP* system, start the *SetupTCP* program and select the Users icon. Figure 5-8 shows the window used to enter user accounts. Select the **New** button and enter the username to add a new user. The UserID field is significant to the system because it is the login username. The rest of the information is personal data about each user. Clicking on the pulldown arrow in the UserID field provides a list of users. Double-clicking on a username in the list brings up the personal information for that user. Whether or not this information is useful is up to you. You certainly want to know the real name of a user and how to reach them, but the specific fields may not be what you want.

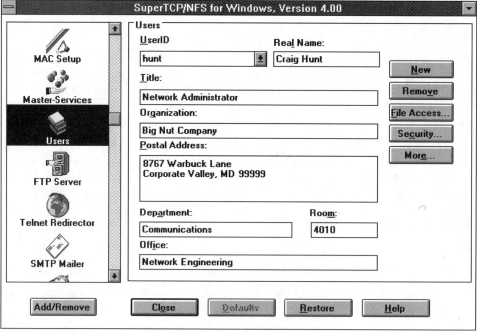

Figure 5-8: Adding User Accounts

Additional personal information can be entered by clicking the **More..** button. The Additional User Information dialogue box displays the path to the user's mailbox file, and it permits you to enter the user's Internet and X.400 email addresses, and the user's voice and FAX telephone numbers. Personal information is useful to the network administrator, but of all the information entered into these two dialogue boxes, only the username is needed by TCP/IP.

In addition to the login username, the system needs a password for the user. Good passwords are necessary to prevent the system from being misused.[*] Click the **Security** button to open the dialogue box into which the password is typed. That box also allows you to set a numeric UID (user ID) and GID (group ID) for the user.

The UID and GID are used for UNIX file permissions and are essential for *Network File System* (NFS) servers. Every user accessing a file server must have a unique UID, and only users who are in the same group should have the same GID. It is only necessary to assign a valid UID and GID on the PC if the PC is an NFS file server or if the PC provides **pcnfsd** authentication for this user. Normally the UID and GID values are assigned on the file server and ignored on the PC. UIDs, GIDs, NFS, and **pcnfsd** are covered in Chapter 10.

SuperTCP allows the PC to act as an NFS server. The file permissions granted an NFS user are set through the dialogue box shown in Figure 5-9, which is started by selecting the **File Access** button. The path of the directory to which access is being granted is typed in the Full Path box at the top of the screen. The access being granted is defined in the Access Rights box. Individual access rights, such as *Read* and *Create*, can be checked off or all forms of access can be granted by checking *Full Access*. Define the access you wish to grant and press the **Add Access** button. The specific access rights and the directory to which those rights are granted are then displayed in the listbox at the bottom of the screen. To delete or change access permissions, highlight an entry in the listbox and select the appropriate button. Just like the UID and GID, these permissions only need to be set if the PC is an NFS server.

The user account setup on *SuperTCP* is unique. Other implementations set up user accounts differently, and most do not provide for this much personal information. Configuring the mail application on a *Chameleon* system provides a good example of this difference.

Email Accounts

Electronic mail is another application that needs user accounts. Most PCs have only one mail user account, though it is possible to have a shared PC with several mail users. The mail application uses the account to:

- Create a local user mailbox. Each mail user has a private mailbox, which is identified by the user's account name.

---

[*] Guidelines for creating good passwords are defined in *TCP/IP Network Administration* and in *Practical UNIX Security*.

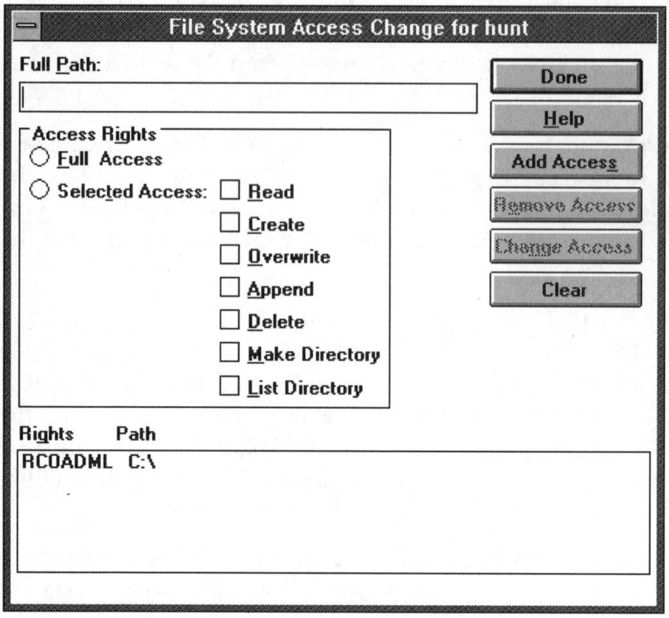

```
┌─────────────────────────────────────────────────────────┐
│ ─   ▓▓▓▓▓File System Access Change for hunt▓▓▓▓▓▓        │
│ Full Path:                        ┌──────────────┐       │
│ ┌─────────────────────────┐       │    Done      │       │
│ ││                        │       └──────────────┘       │
│ └─────────────────────────┘       ┌──────────────┐       │
│ ┌Access Rights──────────────────┐ │    Help      │       │
│ │ ○ Full Access                 │ └──────────────┘       │
│ │                               │ ┌──────────────┐       │
│ │ ○ Selected Access: ☐ Read     │ │  Add Access  │       │
│ │                    ☐ Create   │ └──────────────┘       │
│ │                    ☐ Overwrite│ ┌──────────────┐       │
│ │                    ☐ Append   │ │Remove Access │       │
│ │                    ☐ Delete   │ └──────────────┘       │
│ │                    ☐ Make Directory                    │
│ │                    ☐ List Directory                    │
│ └───────────────────────────────┘                        │
│ Rights    Path                                           │
│ ┌─────────────────────────────────────────────────┐     │
│ │ RCOADML  C:\                                     │     │
│ │                                                 │     │
│ └─────────────────────────────────────────────────┘     │
└─────────────────────────────────────────────────────────┘
```

Figure 5–9: Defining NFS File Permissions

- Create a default From: address for outbound mail.

- Provide a username with which to access the mail server. It is possible to have a different username and password on the PC than the one used to gain access to the mail server, but normally they are the same.

To create a mail user account on a *Chameleon* system start the *Mail* application and log in as *postmaster*.[*] Figure 5-10 shows the postmaster's email window. Select **Mailboxes** from the **Services** menu. Type the new username in the dialogue box that appears and press the **Add** button.

The window shown in Figure 5-11 appears. In it, enter the user's password and real name. The value for the mail directory is generated by the system. It uses a standard directory name with the username (*hunt* in the example) added. Click **OK** when the values are what you want and click **Yes** when asked to create the mailbox. Save your new creation, and you're done.

---

[*] The postmaster account exists on all *Chameleon* systems.

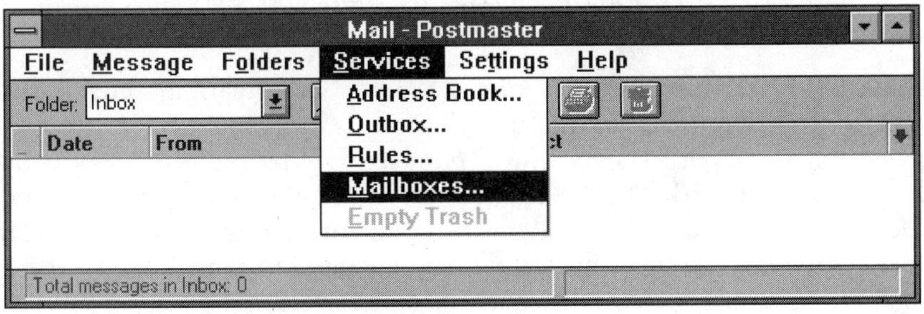

Figure 5–10: Chameleon Postmaster Account

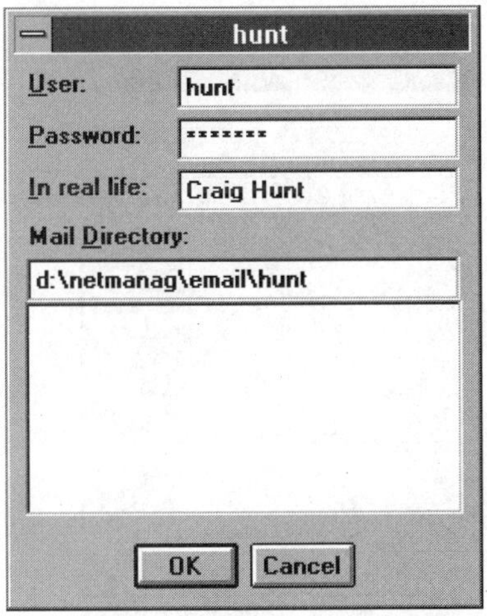

Figure 5–11: Creating a New Mailbox

Electronic mail is not the only application that needs user accounts. Any application relying on a remote server that demands user authentication needs them. Network File System (NFS), which is used for file sharing, and Line Printer Daemon (LPD), which is used for printer sharing, are two prime examples of such applications. All of these applications, email, NFS, and LPD, are covered extensively later in this text because most of the configuration of these applications takes place on the server.

Windows Applications

Windows TCP/IP applications require little or no configuration. The little configuration that is required is limited to creating user accounts, identifying servers, and performing some personal customization. As the network administrator it is not your responsibility to customize the user's desktop system; however, you are the user's main source of advice and information. It's possible that your server systems require that applications be customized in order to function smoothly. If this is true, tell the users exactly what is required.

A good example of this type of customization is the keyboard mapping in a Telnet terminal emulator. Figure 5-12 shows the keyboard mapping screen from a *Chameleon* system. The figure shows how *Chameleon* maps the VT100 terminal keyboard to the PC keyboard. The Backspace key sends the ASCII BS character, and the Delete key sends the VT200 **Remove** command string.[*] Depending on how you have configured the login host, the user may need to remap one of these keys. A user that expects the PC's Backspace key or Delete key to erase the last character typed might be surprised if the remote host requires the DEL character for this function.

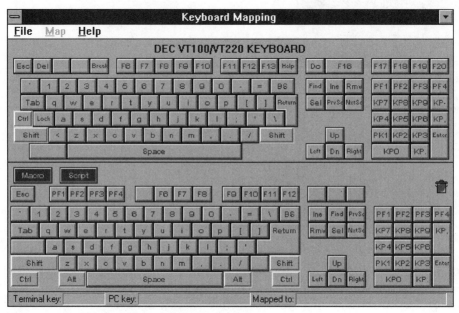

Figure 5-12: Telnet Keyboard Mapping

To remap the PC's Backspace key to send the ASCII DEL character, drag the Del key from the VT100 keyboard and drop it on the Backspace key on the PC keyboard. Now pressing Backspace on the PC sends the DEL character. Remapping keys is easy for most users to do. The network administrator's role is to ease things along by warning users about situations in which user customization is helpful.

FTP running under Windows also benefits from customization. The changes that make FTP work better take place on the server. The Windows FTP application displays a graphic representation of the remote directory. To do this, the application

---

* This is the same character string as the VT100 **Cut** command string.

downloads a full directory listing every time the user changes directories. Performance is poor if the server has directories with large numbers of files. It works best with servers that have small directories. If you plan to service Windows users, design your FTP server accordingly. Avoid a broad, flat directory structure in favor of a deep, hierarchical structure. See Figure 5-13 for a comparison of these structures. If you already have large servers that can not be redesigned, tell the users to disable the automatic directory listing feature.

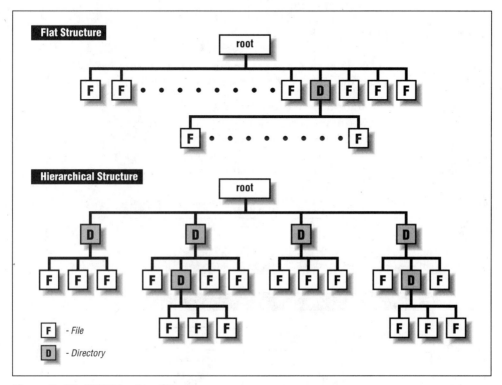

Figure 5-13: FTP Directory Structures

Personal customization occurs in all applications. While helpful, it is not usually essential for proper operation—identifying the correct server is. A Gopher client is an example of an application for which the server is vital. As a client it must connect to a server to obtain the information it displays. On a *Chameleon* Gopher client, identify the server by selecting **Add Gopher Server** from the **Item** menu and typing the server name in the dialogue box that appears. See the example in Figure 5-14.

We added the server *gopher.ora.com,* but there are many other servers to choose from. One of the other servers is run by NetManage, the company that sells *Chameleon* software. Some vendors ship Gopher client software pre-configured to point to the vendor's own server, and it is possible to use the vendor's server as a

Figure 5–14: Identifying the Gopher Server

starting point if you don't have a server of your own. This only works if you have an Internet connection that allows you to communicate with the remote server.

Newsreaders also require a connection to a server. For most news readers you must identify your own news server during a connection process, much like the way you connect to a TELNET or FTP server. Figure 5-15 shows this. Some need to be preconfigured with a default server; one vendor, SPRY, even preconfigures their newsreader software to point to a vendor supplied news server.

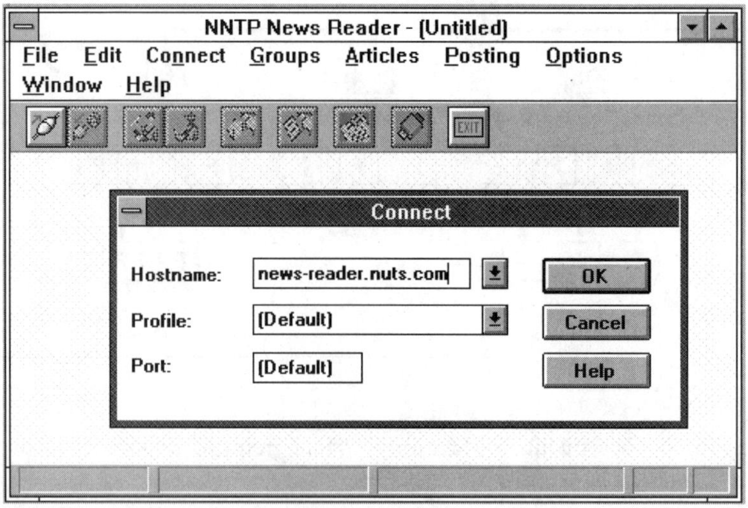

Figure 5–15: Defining the News Server

The biggest part of configuring a Windows news reader, however, is selecting the news groups. The initial connection downloads the full list of news groups supported by your server. This could be thousands of groups. Select just those groups that you want from a newsgroup subscription menu; *SuperTCP*'s subscription menu is shown in Figure 5-16. Save the configuration by selecting **Save** from the files menu to avoid downloading the full hierarchy and resubscribing the next time you reboot the system.

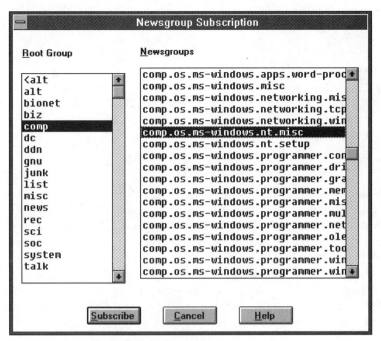

Figure 5–16: Selecting Newgroups

Web Browsers

Mosaic has rapidly become one of the most important Internet tools, and the premier Web browser. A Web browser is a tool for accessing the servers in the *World Wide Web* (WWW). Detailed instructions for using WWW and Mosaic have been covered in several books.* As network administrators, we're more interested in installing a browser than in using it.

The most detailed information about installing a Mosaic client on a Windows system is *The Mosaic Handbook for Microsoft Windows.* This book contains over 200 pages of detailed information specifically about Mosaic for Windows and includes *Enhanced NCSA Mosaic* from Spyglass on two floppy disks tucked into the back cover. *Enhanced NSCA Mosaic* is extremely easy to install and can be used to download the optional viewers.

Optional viewers are very important. Without them a user cannot play an audio file, view a graphic image and play a video file. Many users assume that Mosaic is "broken" if it doesn't have these capabilities. You should select a standard set of viewers and install them on every system. *The Mosaic Handbook* suggests certain viewers to handle certain types of files and provides detailed information for setting up those viewers. Table 5-1 lists the viewers it suggests.

---

* The classic book on this subject is *The Whole Internet User's Guide and Catalogue.*

Table 5-1: Mosaic Viewers

File Format	Viewer
JPEG image	LView
GIF image	LView
TIFF image	Paint Shop Pro
Sound files	WHAM
MPEG video	MPEGPlay
QuickTime video	QuickTime viewer
PostScript	GhostView

The *Mosaic Handbook* provides instructions for installing all of these viewers, but of course they are under constant development. Revision levels change, as do the installation instructions. In the final analysis, you must rely on the documentation that comes with the system and on your own intelligence to resolve problems. You will probably have to provide direct installation support to your users even when they are installing something as simple as Enhanced Mosaic. If you have a small network, you may be able to provide one-on-one support. In a larger network you may find it easier to install Mosaic on a central system directory that can then be mounted and copied onto the PC systems.

No matter how you handle it, you can encounter problems installing software. I installed Enhanced NCSA Mosaic on a *Chameleon* system that was running in a special mode where *Newt*, the DLL that contains the TCP/IP stack, was not continually running. On this system, *Newt* is launched by the *Chameleon* applications when they are invoked and terminates when the applications terminate. Because Enhanced NCSA Mosaic is not a standard *Chameleon* application, it doesn't launch *Newt* and therefore fails to run if you try to start it when *Newt* is not running. This problem is simple to resolve, but it is indicative of the type of problems that are encountered when you try to integrate software from several different sources.

The simplest way to avoid these problems is to buy an integrated commercial software package. SPRY offers a TCP/IP package that includes a version of Mosaic designed to work with their other applications.

There are many Web browsers besides Mosaic. *SuperTCP* provides a browser called WinTapestry that is designed to work with the other *SuperTCP* applications. Frontier Technologies includes the browser in their *SuperTCP Pro* and *SuperHighway Access* packages. The popular Netscape browser is available free for noncommercial use. All of these packages are simple to install. The biggest problem with an alternate browser is that people familiar with Mosaic may take a while to get used to the slight differences in the interface. For example, the Mosaic command for accessing a remote Web server is **Open URL** located in the **File** menu; the WinTapestry command is **Connect To** located in its **File** menu.

Select a browser that you feel comfortable with and that integrates well with your standard TCP/IP package. Test your selection thoroughly before recommending it to your users.

Windows Servers

In addition to applications, Windows makes it possible to run server software. This section discusses some servers that run under Windows.

A Windows PC becomes a file server by running NFS and the **pcnfsd** user authentication program. The PC can also be a print server. PC servers share printers through NFS-based printer sharing and through the Line Printer Daemon (LPD) program. File servers and print servers are the basic services upon which most PC LANs are built. These Windows servers are covered in Chapter 10.

A PC can even be used as a boot server to configure the other PCs on the network. Boot servers, also called configuration servers, are covered in Chapter 8. That chapter describes a *Bootstrap Protocol* (BOOTP) server that runs under Windows.

Another service that runs on a PC is DNS (*Domain Name Service*). Although UNIX systems are commonly used as name servers,[*] there is no reason a PC can't be used. We'll now look at how to get a DNS server running under Windows.

BIND

The *Berkeley Internet Name Domain* (BIND) program is the most popular DNS name server implementation in the world. Originally developed as part of the BSD UNIX operating system, it is now available on many different systems, including Windows.

Chameleon provides a version of BIND bundled in with its other applications. Configuring this DNS server is very different from configuring a UNIX server, but it works remarkably well.

To start the name server, double-click on the BIND icon in the Chameleon window. When first run, the server contains no host information. Create a domain by selecting the **Add** button in the BIND window and typing the name of the domain in the dialogue box that appears. For our imaginary network the domain name is *nuts.com*. Figure 5-17 shows the server after the *nuts.com* domain has been added.

Initially the domain is empty. To add host address records to the domain, select **Modify** in the BIND window and then **Add** in the domain window that appears. A dialogue box pops up; type the hostname and address that you want to add into this box. Repeatedly select the **Add** button until you have added all the hosts in

---

* For information about configuring a UNIX name server, see *TCP/IP Network Administration* and *DNS and BIND*.

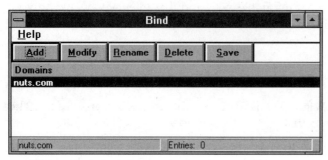

Figure 5-17: Chameleon BIND Server

the domain, one at a time. After a few hosts have been defined, the domain window looks like Figure 5-18.

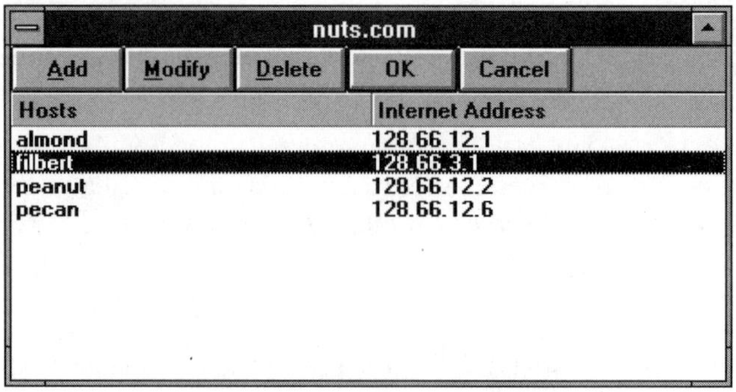

Figure 5-18: Adding Hostnames to the Domain

Naturally the PC only acts as a DNS server when the BIND program is running. Make sure that the BIND program starts every time Windows is rebooted by copying BIND to the Startup program group. Modify the **Properties** of that copy of BIND so that it runs minimized. All finished!

But does it work? Yes, but only address record information is available. This is not intended to be a full service DNS server for a large network. Within its limitations, it works well. Below is a query from a UNIX system to the PC server:

```
% nslookup
Default Server:  almond.nuts.com
Address:  128.66.12.1

> server  acorn.nuts.com
Default Server:  acorn.nuts.com
Address:  128.66.3.2

> pecan.nuts.com
Server:  acorn.nuts.com
Address:  128.66.3.2
```

```
Name:     pecan.nuts.com
Address:  128.66.12.6

> exit
```

The domain data is stored on the PC in the familiar zone-file format. The data entered for *nuts.com* created a file named NUTS.ZNE. The filename is derived from the first part of the domain name and the extension .ZNE. Therefore creating a domain named *sales.nuts.com* creates a zone file named SALES.ZNE. The NUTS.ZNE file created by the domain windows shown above is:

```
@              IN    SOA    nuts.com.    noname  (
                             1315027968
                             808058880
                             134676480
                             2163095040
                             2152792320)
pecan   IN    A      128.66.12.6
almond  IN    A      128.66.12.1
filbert IN    A      128.66.3.1
peanut  IN    A      128.66.12.2
```

This looks exactly like a standard *named.hosts* file with the exception that the records are limited to address records.

Unless you have *Chameleon* software the specific details of this installation are unimportant. What is important is to note that a Windows PC can act as a TCP/IP network server and do it remarkably well. A TCP/IP network lets you use PCs as servers when appropriate, while retaining the flexibility to install servers based on different hardware and operating systems when needed.

Configuring Windows for Workgroups

Windows for Workgroups 3.11 (WfW) is a variant of Windows 3.1 that recognizes its ability to act as a network client and a server. From a user's perspective, WfW and Windows are almost identical; WfW runs Windows software, and if you aren't interested in networking, WfW could be used in place of Windows 3.1 with no changes.

However, WfW is software for "workgroups," and this means networking. WfW comes with its own network applications based on the NetBIOS protocol. NetBIOS can be run over a TCP/IP network (NBT), but we'll defer that topic until Chapter 7. In this section, we'll cover basic TCP/IP setup under WfW. Note that adding TCP/IP software on top of an existing NetBIOS network can lead to problems; we'll see one example in Appendix E. If you don't understand the basics of Net-Bios, read Chapter 7 before installing WfW, then return here for information about TCP/IP.

WfW adds the PROTOCOL.INI file to the list of Windows initialization files. PRO-TOCOL.INI contains configuration information for the WfW network. It describes the network adapters, transport protocols, drivers, and the bindings between all of these. It is not a file you should edit directly.

The commercial TCP/IP software vendors are aware of the problems of running multiple networks on a single system, and of the difficulties of properly configuring the PROTOCOL.INI file. Many vendors provide tools in the SETUP program to properly install TCP/IP on a WfW system. For example, NetManage provides a booklet called *WorkGroup ChameleonNFS* with their Windows software. The booklet tells you how to install their product under WfW. Basically it says to install WfW, configure and test the WfW NetBIOS network, and then install *Chameleon* as you would on any Windows system. The SETUP program detects the presence of the WfW networks and installs the necessary components and makes the necessary modifications to be compatible with it. If you will be using WfW, you should select a commercial package that is compatible with it and will handle most of the installation problems for you.

Another approach is to install a TCP/IP stack that is known to be compatible with WfW and rely on Winsock to run the applications you want on top of it. Trumpet Winsock, covered in Appendix E, offers a shareware product that is compatible with Windows for Workgroups 3.11, and Microsoft offers a free TCP/IP stack, available via anonymous FTP. The next step is to bundle TCP/IP and WfW networking into the new Windows 95 operating system. While you're waiting for Windows 95, you can download the free version of TCP/IP and use it with WfW.

Download the file WFWT32.EXE from *ftp.microsoft.com*. It is located in the *peropsys/windows/public/tcpip* directory. WFWT32.EXE is a self-exploding file and must be transferred in binary mode. Create a directory to hold the TCP/IP files; change to the directory; copy WFWT32.EXE into it and enter WFWT32 at the system prompt. The file explodes into 33 separate files. Installation instructions are in the MTCPIP32.HLP file, and the release notes are in the README.TXT file. Read both before installing the software.

WfW has a configuration program named *Network Setup* that is located in the Network program group. The Network program group is a group in the *Program Manager.* To install TCP/IP, launch *Network Setup* and select **Drivers** from the window that is displayed. In the Drivers dialogue box, highlight your network adapter and click the **Add Protocol** button. The Add Network Protocol dialogue box that appears does not list TCP/IP,[*] so select **Unlisted or Updated Protocol** and click **OK**. When prompted, provide the path of the directory into which you copied WFWT32.EXE. Click **OK** again to install the software. You then return to the Network Drivers box where you select **Setup** in order to configure TCP/IP. The window shown in Figure 5-19 appears. Highlight your network adapter and provide the IP address, subnet mask, and default router address. Select the DNS button to get the dialogue box in which you enter the domain name and the list of domain servers. Don't be confused by the WINS (Windows Internet Name Servers) boxes;

---

[*] If TCP/IP is already installed it must be removed before Microsoft TCP/IP is installed.

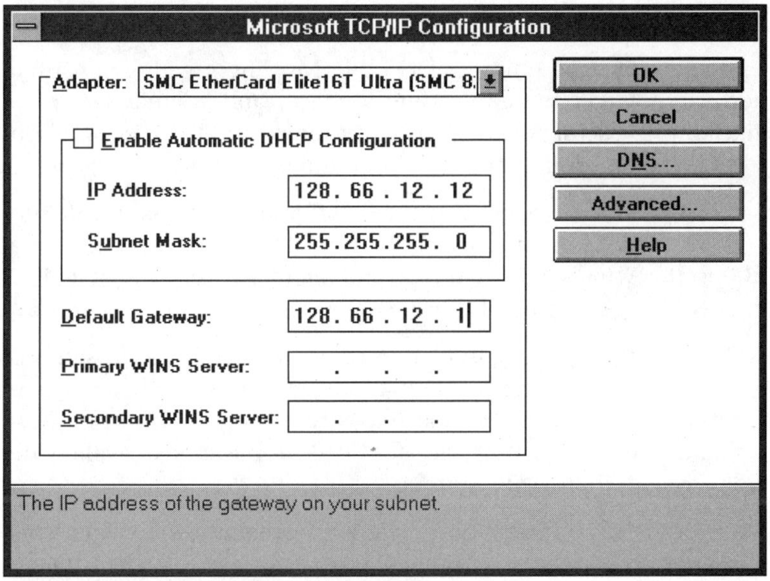

Figure 5-19: WfW TCP/IP Configuration

they are not related to domain name service and can be ignored. WINS servers resolve NetBIOS names into IP addresses; it is covered in Chapter 8. Even if you have a WINS server you need a DNS server. You can ignore the two WINS boxes.

To set the NBT-specific parameters, click on the **Advanced** button. NBT is only used if you run NetBIOS applications over the TCP/IP network. If you just run NetBIOS over your local network segment you don't need it, and if you just run TCP/IP applications, you don't need it. However, if you do use it, NBT can be configured here. The key configuration item is the *Scope ID*. All systems using NBT that want to exchange information should use the same scope ID. The network administrator will assign some value. It is often an arbitrary workgroup name or the DNS domain name. If your network manager gave you a scope ID, click the **Advanced** button and enter it in the dialogue box that appears.

The Microsoft TCP/IP stack comes with very few applications: just a simple Ping, FTP, and Telnet. SPRY offers a suite of TCP/IP designed to run on top of this stack. After installing the stack, it is a very simple procedure to install SPRY's software. The Microsoft stack ensures compatibility with WfW, and the SPRY product provides the applications you expect.

That's it! The differences between WfW and Windows 3.1 configuration are slight, and the similarities are great. WfW is simply Windows 3.1 with integrated NetBIOS networking. The new Windows 95 operating system is a replacement for WfW that offers greater reliabilty features and greatly expanded network capabilities. The next section looks at this new system.

Summary

Windows has extended the life and utility of DOS by providing it with a consistent graphical user interface, a larger memory address space, and a limited form of multitasking. Multitasking is useful for single-user systems in networked environments because the user is often doing more than one thing at a time.

Windows system software is implemented in three different ways: as a TSR running under DOS, as Windows Dynamic Link Library (DLL) code, or as a Virtual Device Driver (VxD) in the Windows virtual machine. Different versions of TCP/IP have been implemented using all three of these techniques.

TCP/IP software is installed through an installation program usually called **setup** or **install**. Most implementations provide a configuration program that makes it easy to add interfaces, but applications are the real reason users favor Windows. Most Windows implementations provide a full set of TCP/IP applications, rivaling the variety of applications available on UNIX systems.

Windows systems can be used as servers and most implementations provide some server code to run on the PC. However, reliability and performance make it inadequate for large server tasks. Micosoft uses the server capabilities of Windows to create a peer-to-peer network in its Windows for Workgroups (WfW) product. The peer-to-peer network does not rely on any one PC to act as the server. The new Windows 95 operating system is a replacement for WfW that offers greater reliabilty and greatly expanded network capabilities. The TCP/IP capabilities of Windows 95 are covered in the next chapter.

Windows 95 TCP/IP

The newest generation of Windows is not dependent on DOS. At this writing, Microsoft has released a beta version of its next operating system—Windows 95. Windows 95 is not simply a new version of Windows; it is an entirely new operating system. Its link to Windows 3.1 is a commitment to be fully compatible with software written for Windows and DOS.

Even though the new system has not yet been finalized, most of its features are known. These are:

- A fully integrated operating system. Windows 95 does not depend on DOS; it replaces it. The PC boots directly into Windows 95. The new operating system provides all its own I/O support. DOS applications are run from Windows 95.

- A completely new user interface. The Windows *Program Manager* and *File Manager* are gone, replaced by a new desktop interface.

- Built-in network support. Windows 95 includes TCP/IP, NetWare, and NetBEUI protocols.

- Extensive use of 32-bit code. The kernel is 32-bit protected mode code, which should greatly improve reliability. Most of the operating system is constructed from 32-bit code. Only modules that require backward compatibility with Windows 3.1 use 16-bit code.

- Preemptive multitasking. 32-bit applications can take advantage of true preemptive multitasking. 16-bit applications are still limited to cooperative multitasking.

- Improved system management. Windows 95 includes new tools for managing systems and users. The tools are accessible over the network so that PCs can be remotely managed. All configuration parameters are centralized in a single "registry" database. Plug-and-Play support is built into the operating system to simplify hardware configuration.

The most noticeable change is the new user interface, but from the perspective of the network administrator it is the least significant change. No matter what the interface, the configuration requirements of TCP/IP remain the same. In the following sections we configure TCP/IP on a Windows 95 system. The example is based on a beta version, so some details might change before the final system is released. Therefore, an updated version of this chapter will be made avaiable via the O'Reilly & Associates Web page after the final version of Windows 95 is released.

Installing Windows 95 TCP/IP

Windows 95 includes TCP/IP. It is installed from the Network applet in the *Control Panel*. Open the *Control Panel* by selecting it from the **Settings** menu of the **Start** menu. (The **Start** menu is a key part of the new user interface. The menu bar is located at the bottom of the screen, and the **Start** button is located to your left on the menu bar. Follow the various submenus from the **Start** menu, and you'll find all of the standard Windows 95 applications.) Open Network by double-clicking on the Network icon in the *Control Panel* window. (Some things are just like Windows 3.1!)

Figure 6-1 shows the Configuration tab of the Network window after several network components have been configured. The first time you see this window on your system, the listbox may be empty. The Network window is used for all network components—it is not specific to TCP/IP:

- On the Configuration tab, the **File and Print Sharing** button brings up a window with checkboxes that allow you to say whether or not you want this system to offer file or printer sharing to other computers.[*] The Primary Network Logon box in this window defines what server should validate the logon for this system. Whenever you boot a Windows 95 system you are asked to provide a username and password. In Figure 6-1, the username and password are validated by the "Microsoft Network" server, which is usually a Windows NT server. If your PC is not a client of a server that requires a login, choose **Windows Logon** from the pulldown list to validate the username and password directly on the local host. Otherwise choose the server that is appropriate for the network client you have installed.

- The Identification tab is used to set the NetBIOS name and the NetBIOS workgroup. (NetBIOS is covered in Chapter 7.)

- The Access Control tab is used to select whether the system should use share-level access control like Windows for Workgroups or user-level access control like Windows NT. Share-level access control sets one type of access for the

---

[*] These checkboxes had no effect on the beta system I tested, but I expect they will be operational in the final release.

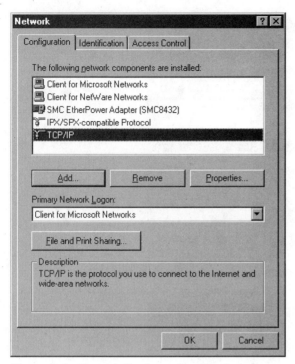

Figure 6–1: Network Configuration Window

entire shared filesystem. User-level access control can set a different type of access for each user of the filesystem. (Access control is covered in Chapter 7.)

To install TCP/IP, click on the **Add** button in the Configuration tab of the Network window. Another window, labeled Select Network Component Type, will appear. Highlight **Protocol** in this new window and click **Add**. The window shown in Figure 6-2 appears.

In the Select Network Protocol window, highlight **Microsoft** in the Manufacturers subwindow. When you do, a list of protocols will appear in the Network Protocols subwindow. One of these is TCP/IP. Highlight it and click **OK**.

If you have not yet configured a network interface, you will be asked to do so now. It is very possible that Windows 95 detected and configured the network interface when the operating system was initially installed. If it did, you can skip the following step. Otherwise, the window shown in Figure 6-3 appears asking you to select a network adapter.

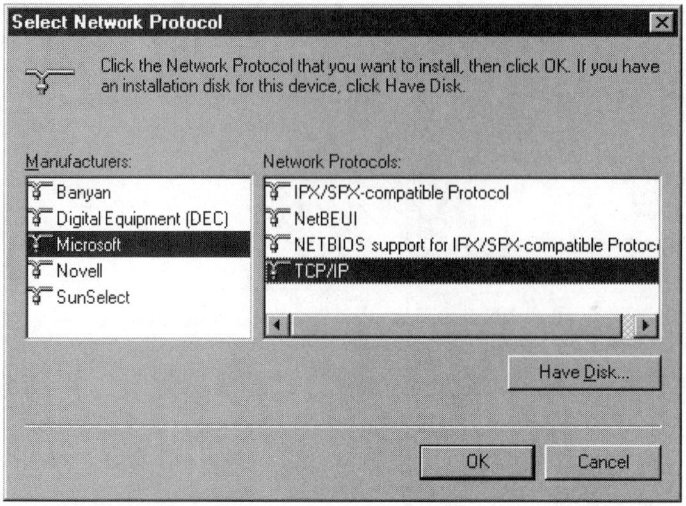

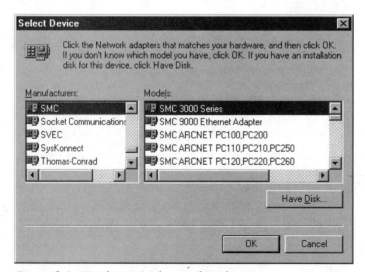

Figure 6–2: Windows 95 Selecting TCP/IP

Figure 6–3: Windows 95 Selecting the Adapter

If your network adapter is listed here, simply highlight it and click **OK**. Each of the adapters listed in this window has a driver included in the Windows 95 distribution. If your interface is not listed here, get the adapter manufacturer's software disk and click **Have Disk**. At this writing, Windows 95 is still in beta test, so most vendors aren't shipping Windows 95 drivers yet, but that doesn't matter. If your adapter has a driver that can be installed under Windows 3.1, it will probably work with Windows 95. Simply provide Windows 95 with a disk that contains the OEMSETUP.INF file and the driver. Once the driver is loaded, you're prompted for the adapter configuration (IRQ, I/O Port, etc.), if one is required.

The system now returns to the Network window shown in Figure 6-1. If you ever need to modify the adapter configuration, highlight the adapter in this window and click **Properties**. Likewise, to configure TCP/IP, highlight it and click **Properties**. The TCP/IP Properties window shown in Figure 6-4 appears.

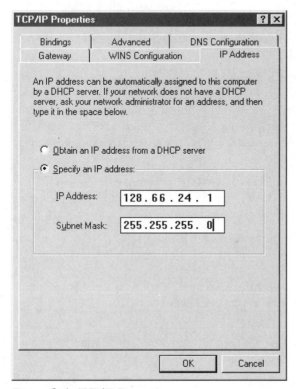

Figure 6–4: TCP/IP Properties

This window contains six tabs. Three of these affect the NetBIOS configuration:

Advanced
> Use this tab to specify that TCP/IP is the default protocol. The tab is only "active" if another protocol, such as NetBEUI, is also installed. If the majority of your traffic is to other TCP/IP systems, select TCP/IP as your default protocol.

Bindings
> Use this tab to identify the network components that communicate over TCP/IP. If you will be encapsulating NetBIOS inside of TCP/IP, make sure that all of the Microsoft network components listed under this tab are selected.

WINS Configuration
> Use this tab to enable or disable WINS. WINS is a name server for NetBIOS names. Generally you want to disable it and use DNS on a TCP/IP network.

The three other tabs, IP Address, Gateway, and DNS Configuration, are critical for the TCP/IP configuration. The IP Address tab is shown in Figure 6-4. Use it to enter the address and the subnet mask.

The Gateway tab is used to enter the default gateway. Select the tab, enter the IP address of the default gateway in the New gateway box, and click **Add**. The tab allows more than one gateway to be entered, but only the first gateway is really used. Don't try to use this tab to build complex static routes. If static routes are required, use the **ROUTE** command.

Before leaving the topic of gateways and routes, I want to digress from the TCP/IP Properties window and talk about the **ROUTE** command. The **ROUTE** command and other important networking tools are available through the Windows 95 command-line interface. To use the command-line interface, open **MS-DOS** from the **Program** menu in the **Start** menu. This opens a window that provides the familiar DOS-style command-line prompt.

The function and syntax of the Windows 95 **ROUTE** command is similar to the UNIX **route** command. The command lets you manually configure the routes in the routing table. Its syntax is:

```
ROUTE [-f] [command [destination] [MASK netmask] [gateway]]
```

The options are used as follows:

-f   Flush all of the routes from the routing tables. If used with one of the commands, the table is flushed before the command is executed.

command

The *command* field specifies the action that the ROUTE command should take. There are four command keywords:

```
ADD         Add a route
DELETE      Delete a route
CHANGE      Modify an existing route
PRINT       Display the routing table
```

destination

This is the network or host that is reached through this route.

MASK *netmask*

The *netmask* is applied to the address provided in the *destination* field to determine the true destination of the route. If a bit in the *netmask* is set to 1, the corresponding bit in the *destination* field is a significant bit in the destination address. For example, a *destination* of 128.66.12.1 with a *netmask* of 255.255.0.0 defines the route to network 128.66.0.0, but the same *destination* with a mask of 255.255.255.255 defines the route to the host 128.66.12.1. If no value is specified for the *netmask*, it defaults to 255.255.255.255.

gateway

This is the IP address of the gateway for this route.

In the following example we add a route to the host 128.66.12.3 and a route to the subnet 128.66.8. In each case, the netmask determines if the route is interpreted as a network route or a host route. After entering the new routes, we display the routing table with the **ROUTE PRINT** command to examine our handiwork.

```
C:\>route add 128.66.12.3 mask 255.255.255.255 128.66.24.5
C:\>route add 128.66.8.0 mask 255.255.255.0 128.66.24.8
C:\>route print
Active Routes:
     Network Address          Netmask  Gateway Address     Interface  Metric
           0.0.0.0          0.0.0.0     128.66.24.254       128.66.24.1      1
         127.0.0.0        255.0.0.0       127.0.0.1         127.0.0.1        1
        128.66.8.0    255.255.255.0      128.66.24.8        128.66.24.1      1
       128.66.12.3  255.255.255.255      128.66.24.5        128.66.24.1      1
       128.66.24.0    255.255.255.0      128.66.24.1        128.66.24.1      1
       128.66.24.1  255.255.255.255       127.0.0.1         127.0.0.1        1
    128.66.255.255  255.255.255.255      128.66.24.1        128.66.24.1      1
         224.0.0.0        224.0.0.0      128.66.24.1        128.66.24.1      1
   255.255.255.255  255.255.255.255      128.66.24.1        128.66.24.1      1
```

As the display shows, there are several more routes than the two we just entered. The default route (destination 0.0.0.0) is the route we entered using the Gateway tab in the TCP/IP Properties window. All of the other routes are part of the minimal routing table that is created by installing TCP/IP. By destination, they are:

127.0.0.0
   The loopback network route. 127.0.0.1 is the address of the loopback interface.

128.66.24.0
   The direct route of the local interface. This is the route this computer uses to reach the network it is directly attached to. The gateway address is the address of this computer's own Ethernet adapter.

128.66.24.1
   The localhost route. This is a special route to this localhost. The address 128.66.24.1 is the address of this host. The route to this host is through the loopback interface.

128.66.255.255
   The broadcast route. Broadcasts to this network are sent through the local Ethernet interface.

224.0.0.0.
   The multicast route. Multicasts are sent through the local Ethernet interface.

255.255.255.255
   The limited broadcast route. Limited broadcasts are sent through the local Ethernet interface.

The routes added by the ROUTE ADD command will not survive a boot. Put the ROUTE ADD commands in a batch file and store the batch file in the

C:\WINDOWS\START MENU\PROGRAMS\STARTUP folder. Programs in the STARTUP directory are executed everytime Windows 95 restarts. It's one way to ensure that the routes are reinstalled after a boot.

By default, the batch file will run and leave an ugly MS-DOS window open. Fix this by setting the correct properties for your new batch file. Assume the file you created is named ROUTES.BAT. To set the file properties, open the C:\WINDOWS\START MENU\PROGRAMS\STARTUP folder. Highlight the ROUTES icon that represents the ROUTES.BAT file (you can highlight the icon with a single click). Then select **Properties** from the **File** menu of the Startup window. A window labeled Routes Properties will appear. Check the **Close on exit** box and select **Minimized** in the **Run** listbox. After these two values are set, click **OK**. You're done. The system automatically creates a ROUTES.PIF file to handle the execution of your new batch file. Your routes will be reinstalled every time Windows 95 is restarted.

You only need to use the **ROUTE** command if your system requires complex static routes. Most PCs use a single default route because most local area networks only have one router to the outside world. Most of the time you can do the complete configuration from the TCP/IP Properties window. Let's return there now and finish the TCP/IP configuration. Figure 6-5 shows the DNS Configuration tab. Click **Enable DNS** and enter the hostname and the domain name. In the DNS Server Search Order subwindow, enter the IP address of each of your name servers in priority order, i.e., enter the most preferred server first, the next most preferred server second, and so on.

The Domain Suffix Search Order box at the bottom of the window is used to define the order in which domains are searched for host information. Normally it is blank. The function of this subwindow is similar to the **domain** and **search** commands in a UNIX */etc/resolv.conf* file. If nothing is entered in the subwindow, the domain name from the Domain box is used as the default search domain and the parents of that domain are also searched. This procedure works in exactly the same way as the **domain** command in a */etc/resolv.conf* file. If domains are specified in the subwindow, those domains, and only those domains, are searched—the same behavior as seen in the **search** command.[*] A Windows 95 example should help make the purpose of the Domain Suffix Search Order subwindow clear.

When a query is made for a hostname that does not end with a dot, the hostname is extended to a fully qualified domain name before the query is passed to the name server. The domain name appended to the host name depends on what is entered in the Domain Suffix Search Order subwindow:

* If nothing is entered, the hostname is extended with the default domain from the Domain box. For example, if the box contains *plant.nuts.com* and the

---

[*] The *resolv.conf* commands are explained in the Nutshell Handbooks *TCP/IP Network Administration* and in *DNS and BIND*.

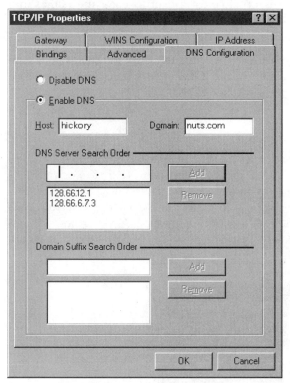

Figure 6–5: DNS Configuration

hostname to be resolved is *almond*, the system creates a query for *almond.plant.nuts.com*. If this name cannot be resolved, the system checks the parent domain by generating a query for *almond.nuts.com*. That is as far as the search goes. The system will not append a parent domain name that contains less than two fields; it will not generate a query for *almond.com* because the top-level domains do not contain host addresses, only pointers to the servers for second-level domains.

- If the subwindow contains the domain entries *plant.nuts.com* and *sales.nuts.com*, a request for the IP address of *acorn* generates a query for *acorn.plant.nuts.com* and then one for *acorn.sales.nuts.com* (assuming the first query was not successful). The system does not, however, search the parent domain *nuts.com*. Even the domain provided in the Domain box is not searched if there are entries in the Domain Suffix Search Order subwindow. When a search list is provided, it must include all of the default domains that you want searched.

A query is also issued for the name exactly as it is typed in by the user. If the user asks for the address of *peanut.nuts.com*, a query for that domain name is sent regardless of what is entered in this subwindow. The default domains are only used to extend hostnames so that it is possible for a user to enter the names in a shorter form. Default domains do not interfere with the normal processing of a query.

When the configuration is the way you want it, click **OK**. Provide the system with the necessary Windows 95 and adapter vendor diskettes when prompted. Then reboot the system, and the TCP/IP network is installed.

Windows 95 PPP

Windows 95 includes *Point-to-Point Protocol* (PPP), which we introduced in Chapter 5. It enables the use of TCP/IP over a dial-up connection (e.g., a modem). PPP configuration is very similar to the configuration of TCP/IP on a LAN adapter. The first step is to install the *Dial-Up Adapter*. Run Network from the *Control Panel* and click the **Add** button. In the Select Network Component Type window, highlight **Adapter** and click **Add**. The Select Network Adapter window shown in Figure 6-6 appears.

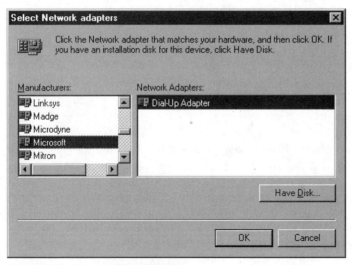

Figure 6–6: Selecting the PPP Adapter

Highlight **Microsoft** in the Manufacturers subwindow and **Dial-Up Adapter** in the Network Adapters box. Click **OK**. The PPP device driver will then be loaded from one of the Windows 95 diskettes. You may be warned that you are only allowed to have one dial-up adapter. You can ignore the warning.

The system returns to the Network window, which shows that two new network components are installed. One of the new components is, of course, the dial-up adapter. The other is TCP/IP, which is automatically installed with the dial-up adapter.

Figure 6-7 shows the Network window after PPP was added to a system. Notice that the TCP/IP associated with the dial-up adapter is clearly labeled as TCP/IP -> Dial-Up Adapter. You are permitted to define a configuration for PPP without interfering with the configuration you have already defined for your Ethernet, which is very useful for laptops that are sometimes docked into a LAN and are at other times used on the road. We saw a similar approach used in Chapter 5 when we configured *Chameleon*'s software, which allowed SLIP and PPP configurations to coexist with a system's Ethernet configuration.

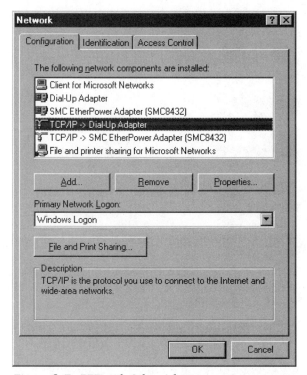

Figure 6–7: PPP with Other Adapters

To configure PPP, highlight **TCP/IP -> Dial-Up Adapter** and click **Properties**. This gives you a set of tabs identical to those used in the previous section to define the IP address, subnet mask, and default gateway. Each interface has its own address, so the values entered here do not interfere with the values entered for the Ethernet interface.[*]

---

[*] There is one exception. If you connect to a remote PPP server while still connected to your Ethernet, it is possible to have two default routes (one from the Ethernet configuration and one from the PPP configuration) installed at the same time. Use the ROUTE command to delete the Ethernet default route if you are just testing PPP. If you normally use PPP and Ethernet at the same time, define only one default route. Use either an Ethernet default route or a PPP default route, but not both. See Chapter 2 for advice on selecting a default route.

Complete the basic PPP configuration by highlighting **Dial-Up Adapter** and clicking **Properties**. The window shown in Figure 6-8 appears. The window contains three tabs: Advanced, Bindings, and Driver Type.

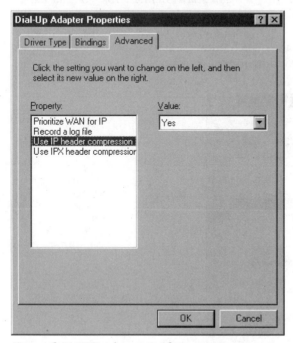

Figure 6–8: PPP Adapter Configuration

The Advanced tab sets the following PPP properties:

Prioritize WAN for IP
Set the value of this property to **Yes**. Windows 95 relies on TCP/IP as its primary WAN protocol. Anyone using TCP/IP should leave this value set to **Yes**. Only use **No** if your primary WAN protocol is some other PPP-compatible protocol.

Record a log file
Set this value to **No**. When you want to create a log of a session for debugging or other purposes you can set this value to **Yes**. But don't forget you have set it to **Yes**. Log files can grow very large.

Use IP header compression
Set this value to **Yes** if your remote server supports header compression. It increases performance. Only set the value to **No** if you are sure the remote system cannot operate with header compression.

Use IPX header compression

You can ignore this parameter on a pure TCP/IP network. However, if you're using NetWare, set the value to **Yes** unless the remote server cannot support IPX header compression.

The Bindings tab associates transport protocols with the dial-up adapter. Make sure that TCP/IP is checked on this tab.

The Driver Type tab defines the type of driver used with the dial-up adapter. The tab offers three choices:[*]

Enhanced mode (32-bit and 16-bit) NDIS driver

This is the default, and it is the one you should probably use.

Real mode (16-bit) NDIS driver

Use this driver for compatibility with older TCP/IP software. If you are using a driver that was designed for Windows 3.1, it may be an NDIS1 driver.

Real mode (16-bit) ODI Driver

Use the ODI driver if you are using NetWare client software that is not compatible with the NDIS driver.

The default values on all of the Dial-Up Adapter Properties tabs are probably just what you need. On most PPP clients, defining the TCP/IP configuration is enough. Usually you can ignore the other tabs. Once everything is set the way you want it, click **OK** and restart the system.

Making the PPP Connection

When the system reboots, it installs the *Dial-Up Networking* folder in *My Computer*.[†] To set up your PPP network connection, open the *Dial-Up Networking* folder. The first time you open it, the modem installation wizard runs if a modem has not yet been installed.[‡] (You can run the modem wizard any time you wish by opening Modems in the *Control Panel*.) The modem wizard automatically detects the type of modem connected to the system and configures it. If the wizard makes a mistake detecting the modem, click the **Change** button and select the correct modem from the modem list.

After the modem driver is properly installed, the *Dial-Up Networking* folder opens to show the Make New Connection icon. Double-click the icon to run the "new connection" wizard. Figure 6-9 shows the opening window of this wizard. Enter a unique name to identify the connection—use something descriptive. Click **Next** and enter the phone number of the remote server in the appropriate boxes of the second window. That's all the wizard will request from you.

---

[*] You may not be given a choice. The system may limit the selection based on the characteristics of the software installed earlier in the dial-up configuration.

[†] *My Computer* is an icon that is normally displayed at the top of the screen to your left. When opened, it provides a high-level view of the devices installed in the computer.

[‡] A *wizard* is a program that simplifies the configuration of hardware and software.

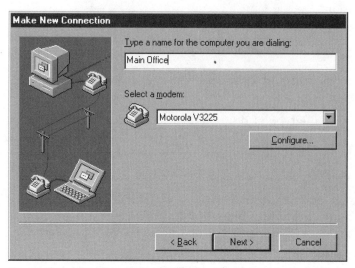

Figure 6-9: New Connection Wizard

You may, however, want to make sure that the modem is properly configured for this connection. To review or modify the modem configuration, click the **Configure** button. (See Figure 6-9.) The modem configuration window shown in Figure 6-10 appears.

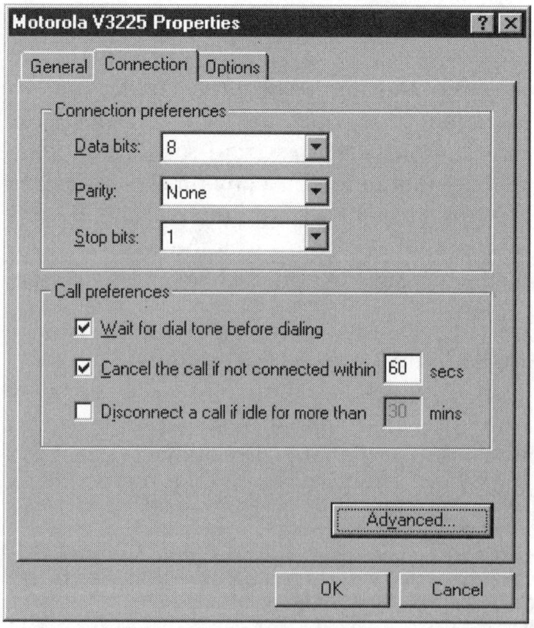

Figure 6-10: Modem Configuration

This configuration window contains three tabs: General, Connection, and Options. The General tab is used to set the baud rate and the COM port. The COM port should be correctly set by the modem wizard. The baud rate, however, may need to be adjusted because of the performance characteristics of the remote server to which you are connecting.

The Connection tab allows you to set the data bits and parity, which should always be *8* and *none* respectively for a PPP connection. Stop bits are usually 1. The **Advanced** button allows you to set the type of flow control, which must be either *Hardware (RTS/CTS)* or none for PPP, and whether or not error control and compression should be used. Error control is a safe bet for PPP connections, but data compression is debatable. Don't use modem data compression unless the serial port speed (the DTE speed) is greater than the modem speed (the DCE speed) at both ends. In other words, if you have a 9600 baud modem and the serial ports at each end are also set at 9600 baud, do not use data compression. It will actually slow things down. Use modem data compression when you have high-speed serial ports, e.g., 38,400 bps, and a low-speed link, e.g., 14,400 baud.

The most important item in the Options tab is labeled Connection control. It contains checkboxes that allow you to bring up a terminal window before or after the computer dials the remote system. Select the **Bring up terminal window after dialing** checkbox if you have a remote system that requires a special login sequence. You must use the terminal window to key in the special instructions during the actual connection sequence, as shown in Figure 6-11, because Windows 95 does not provide a built-in script language for automating SLIP/PPP connections (we hope this will be fixed in a future release).

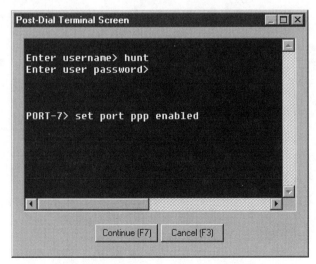

Figure 6-11: PPP Connection Terminal Window

When everything is set up the way you want, exit the new connection wizard. It creates a new icon in the *Dial-Up Networking* folder and labels it with the name you provided. Double-click on this new icon to open the connection to the remote system. You're then prompted for a username and password. Enter them and click **Connect**. The computer will dial the remote system. If you have requested the connection terminal window, enter the login commands for the remote server into this window and click **F7 Continue**. Test your connection with the PING command in the MS-DOS window. If you have problems, see the SLIP section earlier in this chapter for troubleshooting advice.

Summary

The significance of Windows 95 for network administrators is the promise of a more reliable, more easily managed PC operating system that includes support for TCP/IP. The features planned for Windows 95 address many of the problems mentioned in the first chapter of this book. How well the new operating system fulfills these promises remains to be seen. At the very least it shows that the PC market understands the problems of DOS and is working hard to address them.

The next chapter looks at still another Windows operating system, Windows NT, that is designed to provide a reliable multitasking environment for a network server.

7

Windows NT Networking

Network servers need reliable, robust operating systems. DOS and Windows 3.1 are not suitable. Most PC LAN administrators turn to NetWare and most TCP/IP administrators turn to UNIX to create reliable network servers. Naturally Microsoft wants to change this. Its most recent attempt is Windows NT.

Windows NT 3.5 uses the same graphical user interface (GUI) as Windows 3.1, but it is far more than a GUI. NT is a multitasking, multi-user, multithreaded operating system. It comes in a single-user version for high-end PC workstations and in the Windows NT Server version for multiuser network servers.

NT is designed from the ground up to be a "network-capable" operating system. From the earliest versions, Windows NT included TCP/IP software and based its enterprise networking on TCP/IP. However, TCP/IP is not the only, or even the most important, networking protocol on a Windows NT system. Most of the network applications bundled with Windows NT are based on NetBIOS. To understand Windows NT networking, including its TCP/IP, we first must understand NetBIOS.

NetBIOS and the associated protocol NetBEUI (*NetBIOS Extended User Interface*) have long been the basis of Microsoft's networking strategy. Microsoft's earlier LAN Manager product and the current Windows for Workgroups (WfW) and Windows NT products are all based on this protocol. Therefore our discussion of WfW and Windows NT begins with NetBIOS.

NetBIOS

BIOS, the *Basic Input Output System*, is the part of DOS that defines the I/O calls that applications use to request DOS I/O services. NetBIOS extends this to include calls that support I/O over a network. Sytek developed NetBIOS for IBM's short-lived *PC Network* product. It has survived *PC Network* and gone on to be the basis of many other network products including Windows for Workgroups, LAN Manager, and Windows NT.

Originally, NetBIOS was implemented in a ROM on the Sytek network interface card. It was a monolithic protocol that took data all the way from the application to the physical network. Today, NetBIOS is an *application program interface* (API) that defines how an application program requests services from the underlying network.

IBM and Microsoft have added to the basic NetBIOS definition over the years to produce the current version of the *NetBIOS Extended User Interface* (NetBEUI). Don't confuse NetBEUI and NetBIOS. NetBEUI includes the NetBIOS API, the *Service Message Block* (SMB) protocol, and the *NetBIOS Frame* (NBF) protocol. SMB, like NetBIOS, is an API that defines how applications ask for network services, but NetBEUI is not just an API. It also includes the NBF protocol that builds NetBIOS frames for transmission over the network. That said, it should be pointed out that "NetBIOS" is the more generic term. It is not just used to refer to the API. It is frequently used to refer to any network that uses NetBIOS.

NetBIOS requires very little memory and runs on any type of PC equipment, even the oldest PCs. It is a fast, lightweight protocol suitable for small LANs. However, NetBIOS is only suitable for LAN applications. NetBIOS cannot be used by itself for a WAN or an enterprise network because it is a "non-routable" protocol, and it depends on an underlying broadcast medium. What do these two limitations mean?

non-routable
> The protocol cannot be passed through routers. NetBIOS packets can only be passed on a single physical network. It has no routing protocol and no independent address structure. It depends completely on the underlying physical network address, which limits it to a single physical network.

broadcast dependent
> NetBIOS depends on an underlying network that supports physical layer broadcasts. It cannot be used over serial lines, point-to-point networks, or internets built from dissimilar physical networks.

How a new node inserts itself into a Windows for Workgroups network is a good example of how NetBIOS depends on broadcasts and how it operates without a network-independent address structure. When WfW starts, it broadcasts a *name registration request* packet. The packet contains the proposed NetBIOS name that identifies the system. If another computer on the network already uses this name, it responds to the broadcast with a *negative name registration response* packet. If the new node does not receive any negative responses to its broadcast, it uses the name as its identifier.

The name is literally used as the node's "address." The source and destination fields of a NetBIOS frame are each 16 bytes long.[*] The fields contain the names of the source and destination computers. Therefore if a computer named *sunflower* sends a frame to a system named *sesame*, the source address is "sunflower" and the destination address is "sesame".

This naming scheme has some advantages:

- It is intuitive. Most people prefer to identify things by names instead of by numbers, and NetBIOS names can be very descriptive, e.g., *hpprinter*.

- Each system is automatically self-registering. The scheme requires no central name authority or name server.

However, this scheme does not scale well. Each name must be broadcast to every node on the network, which is difficult in a large network, and each name must be unique throughout the network. With no central name authority and no hierarchical name structure, it is difficult to maintain unique names on large networks. This is clearly an inadequate scheme for a large network—let alone a global internet!

The strengths and weaknesses of NetBIOS make it an excellent protocol for small, isolated LANs and inappropriate for large enterprise networks. Microsoft realizes this and provides a solution for enterprise networking by shipping TCP/IP with Windows NT and Windows 95, and by making it freely available for Windows for Workgroups.[†]

NetBIOS Over TCP/IP

NetBIOS has changed over time from a monolithic protocol to a layered protocol. This change causes confusion in the way the term "NetBIOS" is used—sometimes it refers to the entire protocol, and sometimes it refers to the application interface. But the real effect of this change is that in its current form as an applications interface, NetBIOS is not dependent on the underlying NBF protocol. NetBIOS can run over a range of different network protocols, including TCP/IP. Installing TCP/IP does not eliminate the availability of NetBIOS-based applications. Rather, it enables the full array of Internet applications *and* it allows NetBIOS applications to run over large networks that include routers. It does this by encapsulating the NetBIOS messages inside TCP/IP datagrams. The protocol that does this is *NetBIOS over TCP/IP* (NBT).

NetBIOS over TCP/IP is a standard protocol defined in RFCs 1001 and 1002, and Microsoft's version of NBT is based on these RFCs. Microsoft is not the only company that supports NetBIOS over TCP/IP; several companies offer NBT for DOS systems. However, this chapter concentrates on the Microsoft NBT implementation

---

[*] WfW and Windows NT node names cannot exceed 15 bytes.

[†] The VxD version of Microsoft TCP/IP for Windows for Workgroups 3.11 is downloadable from *ftp.microsoft.com* in the file *peropsys/windows/public/tcpip/wfwt32.exe*.

for two reasons. First, it is provided free of charge for users of Windows NT, Windows 95, and WfW. Second, the configuration of this package is remarkably similar for all three systems, so that the information covered about one can largely be applied to the other.

Microsoft's NBT protocol is based on the *b-node* architecture defined in the RFCs. A b-node (broadcast node) is an end node that uses broadcast messages to register its name and to request the names of other systems on the network. The NetBIOS messages are encapsulated in UDP messages and sent using the IP broadcast address. In effect, IP acts as the broadcast medium for the NetBIOS protocol.

The b-node architecture doesn't address the problem of broadcast dependence, so Microsoft uses a *modified b-node* architecture. Microsoft's NBT loads a cache with NetBIOS-name-to-IP-address mappings from the LMHOSTS file.* The cache supplements the use of broadcasts for resolving NetBIOS names.

In the b-node model, broadcasts are only needed for name resolution. Other messages are addressed directly to the remote host. Therefore, broadcasts are only needed for names that cannot be resolved by other means. NBT also uses a name cache to further improve performance. The name cache provides information about computers that cannot respond to a broadcast. These are computers located outside of the "broadcast area," including computers located behind routers or on non-broadcast links. Broadcasts continue to be used to locate local computers, so no entries need to be made for them in the LMHOSTS file. This keeps the file small and permits it to be cached in memory. Each system helps the other do a better job.

There are, of course, complications. Encapsulating NetBIOS inside IP datagrams reduces the performance and increases the complexity of the protocol. Both protocols require some level of configuration, whether it is the address for IP or the LMHOSTS file for NetBIOS. Additionally, computers using NBT can talk to other computers using NBT but not to those using NBF. We'll discuss these things and how they are handled as we walk through the installation of TCP/IP and NBT in the following sections.

TCP/IP for Windows NT

Windows NT is designed to be a network-oriented operating system. It asks you to configure the network adapter and the network software during the initial installation of the operating system. Be prepared with the basic network configuration information before starting the installation. You should know:

---

* Under certain circumstances, DNS can be used to map NetBIOS names to IP addresses; more on this later.

- The adapter card information. The amount of information required varies with different cards, but you should be ready to provide the card manufacturer and model, the IRQ number, the I/O base address, and the ROM address.

- The network software you want to use. NT includes several different network packages. By default, NT installs NetBEUI, but you'll be expected to tell it what other packages you want. From the point of view of this book, the package that you want to use is TCP/IP.

- The TCP/IP-specific configuration information. This is all of the stuff we are so familiar with: IP address, hostname, domain name, default gateway, and the list of name servers.

- The NetBIOS-specific information. Examples of this type of information are the *workgroup* name, the *scope ID*, and the location from which the LMHOSTS file should be imported. This is all new, and is explained later in the chapter.

If you don't know the answers to all of these questions, you can continue with the installation and correct the values later. If your system is not attached to a network, it is possible to skip the entire network installation. The system will still boot correctly, and the network can be added later. If your system is attached to a network, NT detects the network adapter, prompts for any necessary configuration parameters, and installs NetBEUI. TCP/IP is usually added later.

Configuring the Adapter

To add TCP/IP to an existing system, open the *Control Panel* and select **Network**. The box shown in Figure 7-1 appears. If the network adapter has not been configured, click on **Add Adapter**. The dialogue box shown in Figure 7-2 appears.

The pulldown list for Network Adapter Card contains a list of popular adapters for which Windows NT has a driver.[*]

These drivers were "frozen" when the CD-ROM was created. New drivers and new adapter cards are being created all the time. The adapter manufacturers are the best source of up-to-date drivers. Check with the manufacturer to make sure you are using the latest driver.

If your card is not listed, select **Other** and use the driver that you obtained from the vendor. Unfortunately, some vendors do not ship an NT driver on the disk provided with their hardware, and you cannot use a DOS or Windows 3.1 driver.[†] You may have to make a special request to the vendor for the NT driver.

---

[*] Don't look for a dial-up SLIP or PPP adapter here. Windows NT 3.5 provides PPP support through the *Remote Access Software* (RAS). See the PPP section at the end of this chapter for more details.

[†] This is not a problem for WfW or Windows 95, which can use Windows 3.1 drivers.

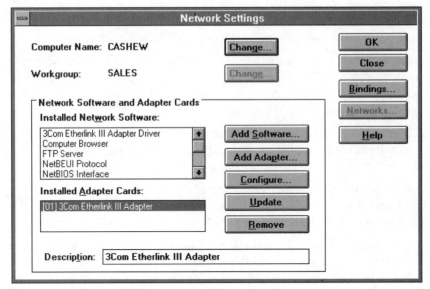

Figure 7-1: Windows NT Network Settings

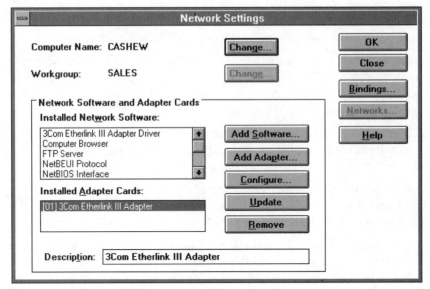

Figure 7-2: Adding a Network Adapter to Windows NT

Make sure you can get a driver for your specific adapter card before you try to use it with NT. Ask the vendor if a driver is available before you buy. You can find out what hardware NT supports by calling Microsoft and requesting a Windows NT hardware compatibility list, or by downloading the list from the directory *advsys/winnt/winnt-doc/hcl* on *ftp.microsoft.com*.

After selecting a card from the Adapter list, you're prompted for the adapter configuration information as in Figure 7-3. Here we are only asked to provide the IRQ and the I/O Port Address. Every card and driver is different. Some request less information; some request more. Fill in the requested values and click **OK**.

You may be prompted for the path to the driver. If the adapter is in the Adapter listbox, the driver is on the Windows NT installation media, usually a CD-ROM.[*] Otherwise, enter the path to the vendor-supplied driver. Even when you use a

---

[*] Assuming that E: is the CDROM drive and that the PC uses an Intel processor, enter E:\I386 as the path.

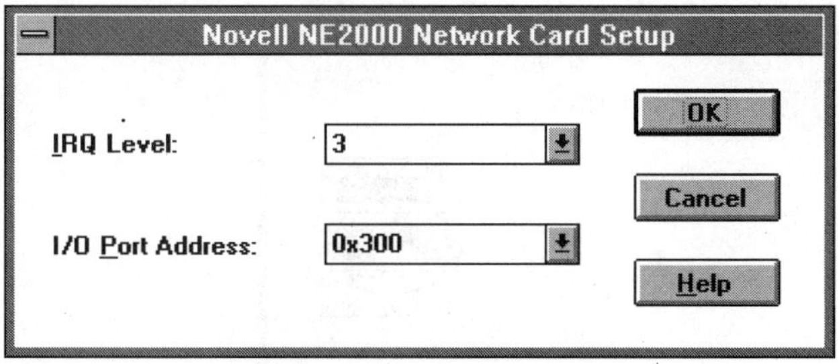

Figure 7–3: Windows NT Network Card Setup

vendor supplied disk, the system asks for "the full path of the Windows NT distribution files" a few times during the installation. Don't enter the path to the NT CD-ROM; enter the path to the vendor disk. The files that NT is looking for are provided by the adapter vendor. The prompt is confusing, but the default path displayed with it is the path you provided for the vendor disk. Accept this default, and you'll be all right.

Configuring the Software

The system then returns to the Network Settings window. Select **Add Software** and then select **TCP/IP Protocol and related components** from the listbox that pops up. Selecting TCP/IP opens the window shown in Figure 7-4.

This window lists all of the TCP/IP software components that are available on your system. The window in Figure 7-4 is from an NT server system—an NT workstation lists fewer components. By default, the system installs TCP/IP Internetworking when you click **Continue**. This will give you a fully functional TCP/IP stack. To install a basic system with tools such as Ping, Telnet and FTP, also check **Connectivity Utilities** before pressing **Continue**. All of the other items are optional. They are:

SNMP Service
    An SNMP agent

TCP/IP Network Printing Service
    LPD/LPR print software

FTP Server Service
    FTP server software

Simple TCP/IP Services
    Servers, such as the echo server, that are used for simple connectivity tests

DHCP Server Service
    A Dynamic Host Configuration Protocol server. DHCP is covered in Chapter 8.

WINS Server Service
    A Windows Internet Name Server

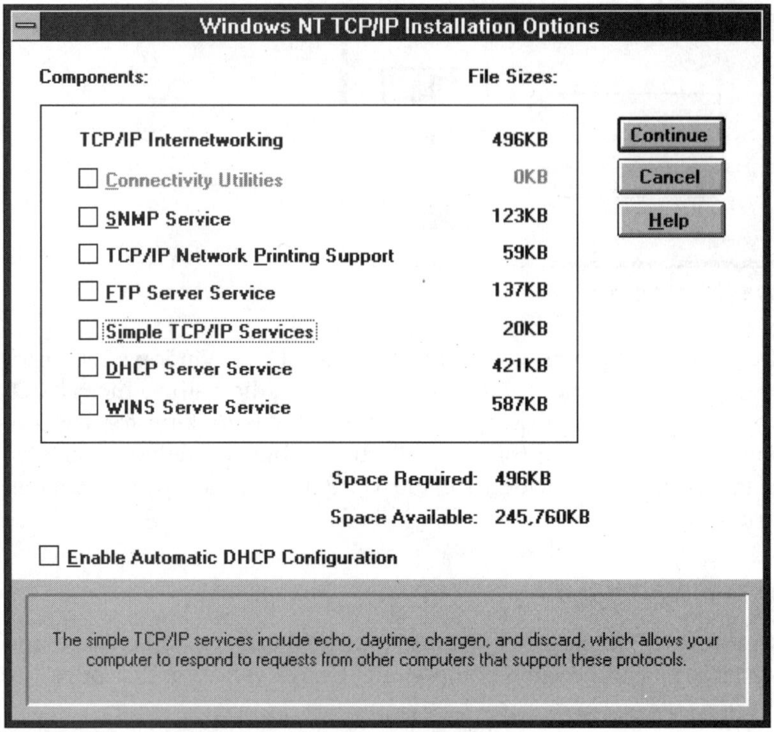

```
┌─────────────────────────────────────────────────────────────┐
│ ▬         Windows NT TCP/IP Installation Options              │
├─────────────────────────────────────────────────────────────┤
│  Components:                        File Sizes:               │
│  ┌──────────────────────────────────────────┐  ┌───────────┐ │
│  │ TCP/IP Internetworking          496KB     │  │ Continue  │ │
│  │ ☐ Connectivity Utilities          0KB     │  └───────────┘ │
│  │ ☐ SNMP Service                  123KB     │  ┌───────────┐ │
│  │ ☐ TCP/IP Network Printing Support 59KB    │  │  Cancel   │ │
│  │ ☐ FTP Server Service            137KB     │  └───────────┘ │
│  │ ☐ Simple TCP/IP Services         20KB     │  ┌───────────┐ │
│  │ ☐ DHCP Server Service           421KB     │  │   Help    │ │
│  │ ☐ WINS Server Service           587KB     │  └───────────┘ │
│  └──────────────────────────────────────────┘                │
│                                                               │
│            Space Required:  496KB                             │
│            Space Available:  245,760KB                        │
│                                                               │
│  ☐ Enable Automatic DHCP Configuration                        │
├─────────────────────────────────────────────────────────────┤
│   The simple TCP/IP services include echo, daytime, chargen,  │
│   and discard, which allows your computer to respond to       │
│   requests from other computers that support these protocols. │
└─────────────────────────────────────────────────────────────┘
```

Figure 7-4: Windows NT TCP/IP Software Options

After you select the item you want and click **Continue**, you're prompted for the path to the Windows NT distribution files. The system copies in the selected software and returns to the Network Settings window (see Figure 7-1).

Click the **OK** button to configure the TCP/IP software. Intuition might tell you to highlight **TCP/IP Protocol** and select **Configure** to configure TCP/IP. However, that procedure is for reconfiguring TCP/IP. The first time, the protocol must be configured by selecting the **OK** button because some preliminary processing, such as binding the protocol to the adapter, must be done before TCP/IP is configured. After this initial processing, the window shown in Figure 7-5 appears.

This is familiar ground. The boxes for the IP address, subnet mask, and default gateway are clearly marked. Only two items on this window, DHCP and WINS, require any explanation. A *Dynamic Host Configuration Protocol* (DHCP) server can provide all of the TCP/IP configuration for a PC client. If you have one on your network and you wish to use it to configure this system, check **Enable Automatic DHCP Configuration** and click **OK**. That is all that is required. DHCP servers are covered in Chapter 8.

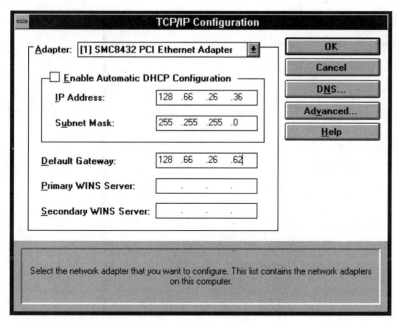

Figure 7–5: Windows NT TCP/IP Configuration

The *Windows Internet Name Server* (WINS) is a server for resolving NetBIOS host-names to IP addresses. WINS is a NetBIOS service, and the WINS server only runs under Windows NT. On a TCP/IP network, use DNS instead of WINS.

To configure the DNS name resolver, click the **DNS** button to open the window shown in Figure 7-6. The computer's hostname is displayed near the top of the screen. Enter the domain name, *nuts.com* in the example, in the Domain Name box.

Enter the names of the DNS servers in the box in the Domain Name Service (DNS) Search Order subwindow and click on **Add**. Each entry will be added to the list-box on the right. Most people enter the most important server first and work down from there, entering two or three servers. The list of servers is searched from top to bottom. To change the position of a server in the list, highlight it and click on the "up arrow" or "down arrow" button to move it up or down in the list. This subwindow performs the same function as the **nameserver** commands in a *resolv.conf* file.

The Domain Suffix Search Order subwindow is identical to the Domain Suffix Search Order subwindow used in Windows 95. If nothing is entered in this window, the domain name from the Domain Name box is used as the default search domain, and the parents of that domain are also searched. If domains are specified in this window, those domains, and only those domains, are searched. See the section on the Domain Suffix Search Order subwindow in Chapter 5 for a detailed description of how values in this window affect DNS queries.

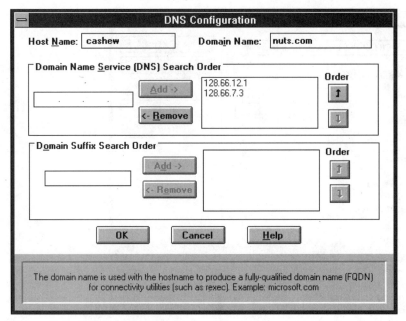

Figure 7-6: Windows NT DNS Configuration

So far this procedure is very similar to the UNIX and DOS configurations we have discussed before. Things become unfamiliar when we consider the NetBIOS-specific configuration parameters. The Network Settings window defines the host-name and the workgroup name. The **Advanced** button in the TCP/IP Configuration window (see Figure 7-5) opens a window for defining the Scope ID and for defining the technique used to map NetBIOS names to IP addresses. All of these things are used to configure NetBIOS. But before you configure it, you should decide whether you need NetBIOS or any of the other optional network protocols.

Selecting Optional Software

How do you decide what optional software should be installed? It's a good question for which there is no good answer. This is one of those questions for which the dreadful answer "it depends" is correct, because it depends on what you will be doing with the computer. Think about the other computers you need to communicate with and the protocols those computers use. If you're not sure, ask your network administrator for advice. And don't panic! If you overlook a protocol, you can add it later. Table 7-1 lists the various pieces of network software provided with NT and what each is used for.

Table 7-1: NT 3.5 Network Software

Software Item	Usage
Computer Browser	Locates NetBIOS services
DLC Protocol	An IBM mainframe protocol
Gateway Service for NetWare	SMB to NCP translator
NetBEUI Protocol	NT's native LAN protocol
NetBIOS Interface	An applications interface
Network Monitor Agent	Collects statistics
NWLink IPX/SPX	Novell NetWare protocols
Remote Access Service	Dial-in access for NetBIOS
Remoteboot Service	Boot service for diskless PCs
RPC Configuration	A server for remote procedure calls
Server	Supports the various server functions
SAP Agent	Agent for Novell's SAP protocol
Server	Supports various NT server functions
Services for Macintosh	Appletalk services
SNMP Service	An SNMP agent
Streams Environment	Streams (TLI) support for TCP/IP
TCP/IP Protocols	The good stuff
Workstation	Supports various client functions
Other	Third-party protocols

A simple approach to the problem of selecting software is to add TCP/IP to the protocols installed by NT during the initial installation, which is exactly what we have done. This covers most TCP/IP networks, and additional protocols can be added later if necessary. Having all of this software installed does consume some system resources, but it saves you from being called in to fix a non-existent "network problem" detected by a user who is trying to use a protocol that is not installed. This advice assumes that NT systems are only one of a variety of different systems that you must support. If you are going to be dedicated to NT support or making extensive use of NT's NetBEUI networking, you may want more details about different network configurations. See *Networking Windows NT,* by John D. Ruley, et al., for a book-length treatment of NT networking.

For our imaginary network, we want TCP/IP to talk to our UNIX servers and to communicate with the Internet. We also want to communicate with the other NetBIOS systems located on our TCP/IP network. NetBIOS was installed automatically, so selecting **TCP/IP Protocol and related components** from the Add Software listbox gives us everything we need.

If you will not be using NetBEUI, it can be removed by highlighting it in the Network Settings window (see Figure 7-1) and clicking **Remove**. Most people, however, do not bother to remove it. They think that it may come in handy later, and personally I agree. Most NT applications are NetBIOS-based. Users may want to work with these applications even if they are not the basic TCP/IP applications from which the network is built. NetBIOS applications can run over TCP/IP, but on a single network segment, NetBEUI is more efficient. For that reason, I recommend leaving NetBEUI installed. If you do remove it and later decide that it's needed, the software can be added back into the system without difficulty.

Now that we've decided that we need NetBIOS, let's look at how it is configured to run over TCP/IP.

Configuring NetBIOS

The configuration of *NetBIOS over TCP/IP* (NBT) combines some aspects of a standard NetBIOS configuration with some things that are unique to NBT. The traditional NetBIOS parameters, hostname and workgroup name, are entered during the initial installation when NT identifies that a network adapter is installed and automatically installs the NetBEUI software.

The NetBIOS hostname is simply a unique name that is 15 characters or less in length. Case is insignificant because the characters you enter are interpreted as uppercase. The name needs to be unique among the NetBIOS hosts with which the system can communicate. That includes the hosts within the system's broadcast area and those listed in its LMHOSTS file. As we previously explained, the hostname is used as the unique "address" of the computer on the NetBIOS network.

The workgroup name has not been previously explained. A workgroup is a hierarchical grouping of hosts much like a directory is a hierarchical grouping of files. Workgroups organize network resources in the same way that directories organize file resources, and they are used for the same reason. Grouping computers into workgroups helps a user locate related systems because the computers in a workgroup are assumed to have a common bond, such as all being part of a single organization.

Workgroups are not used for security. The workgroup does not prevent hosts that are not in the workgroup from sharing the files of systems that are. Security is enforced using username/password authentication. How security and permissions are defined for NetBIOS file sharing is covered later.

Every NetBIOS system is expected to "join" a workgroup. This means you are expected to specify a workgroup name during the initial configuration. The name should be the one defined by the network administrator. If you don't provide one the system defaults to the name *WORKGROUP*. Choose a workgroup name that is 15 characters or less in length and is not already used by some other workgroup or as a hostname. For example, the Government Sales Division at our imaginary company favors *SALES* or *GSD* as possible workgroup names. If another marketing division has already used *SALES*, the newcomers must use *GSD*.

The workgroup name can be modified in the Network Settings window. To change it, click on the **Change** button next to the current Workgroup value. The window shown in Figure 7-7 appears. Make sure the **Workgroup** button is lit and

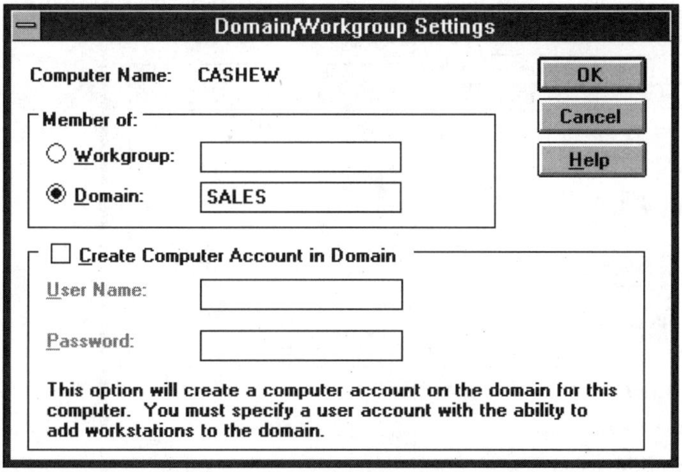

Figure 7–7: Setting Domain/Workgroup

enter the new workgroup name in the proper box. If the **Domain** button is lit, the subwindow for registering the host in the NT server domain is active. You must be an NT server administrator to register a host in an NT server domain. We assume that you're adding a system to a workgroup on a TCP/IP network.

Don't confuse a workgroup with an NT server domain. A workgroup for NT is exactly the same as a workgroup for WfW, simply a way to organize the variety of systems on a NetBIOS network. An NT domain is an administrative domain of an NT server. You cannot just "join" an NT domain. Your system must be put into the domain by the domain administrator, and the NT server domain you belong to is assigned by the administrator. It's also easy to confuse NT domains with DNS domains. However, they are unrelated and defined in different configuration windows. NT domains are beyond the scope of this book because they are specific to NT and are not related to TCP/IP.[*]

Every Windows 95, WfW, and NT system that uses NetBIOS needs a hostname and a workgroup name. The other two parameters, the *Scope ID* and the LMHOSTS file, are specific to NBT. To set these parameters, click on the **Advanced** button in the TCP/IP Configuration window (Figure 7-5). This opens the Advanced Microsoft TCP/IP Configuration window shown in Figure 7-8.

The upper half of the window, labeled Adapter, does not affect NBT configuration. It allows you to define additional default gateways and to define additional addresses and subnet masks for the network adapter. Additional addresses are used when more than one IP network address is used on a single physical network. This is rare, but it does happen. Additional default gateways are not really useful. I suggest you use the **ROUTE** command to handle complex static routing

---

[*] See *Networking Windows NT* by John D. Ruley, et. al., John Wiley & Sons, 1994.

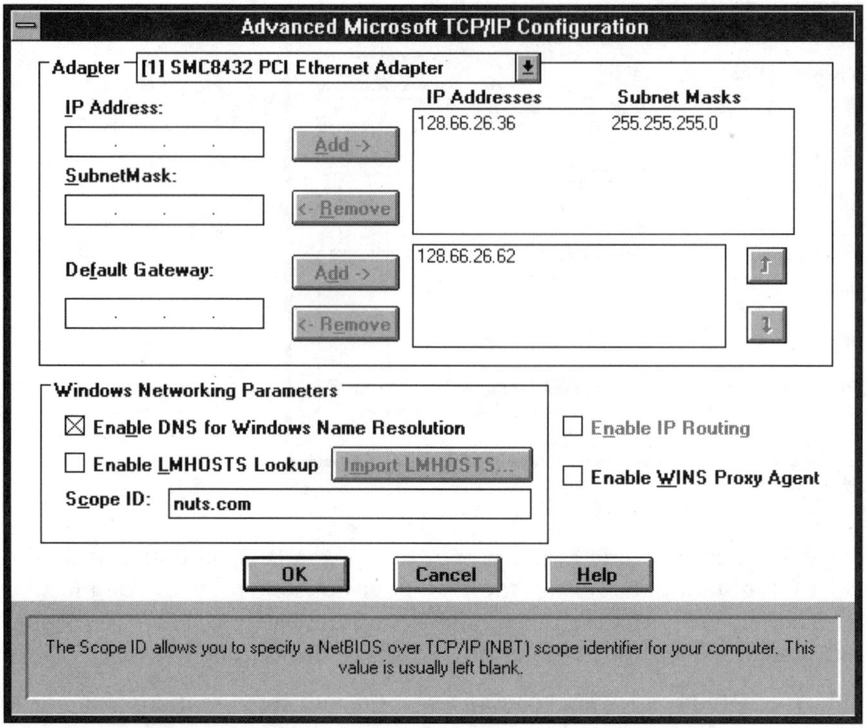

Figure 7–8: Advanced TCP/IP Configuration

situations or **Enable IP Routing** for dynamic routing.* The lower section of the window, labeled Windows Networking Parameters, is used to set the *Scope ID* and to define the technique used to map NetBIOS names to IP addresses.

The *Scope ID* limits communications between NBT hosts. Hosts must have the same scope ID to communicate successfully. Scope IDs create separate logical NetBIOS networks on a single TCP/IP network. Unlike the workgroup name, which provides a hierarchical structure but does not limit access, the scope ID limits access and prevents the resources being offered by a system from being seen by systems with a different scope ID. Its purpose is to reduce clutter and confusion, particularly on a large TCP/IP WAN. If your system is on a network with 200 other NetBIOS systems but only 10 of those systems share its scope ID, you only see 10 systems in the File Manager display. The scope ID filters out unwanted information.

This is not a security mechanism, but it does limit access. If a user attempts to mount a shared directory from a system that has a different scope ID, the mount fails with an error. It is possible to choose an obscure scope ID to enhance

---

* The **ROUTE** command is covered in Chapter 5. NT and Windows 95 use the same **ROUTE** command syntax.

security, but it is not possible to keep it secret. Everyone you want to share data with must know what it is. Therefore few people bother with obscure scope IDs, and most are easily guessed. At best, the scope ID prevents accidental access. It is not designed to deter a determined effort to breach security.

The network administrator should assign the scope ID because it is important that the correct systems have the same ID. The scope ID is a 15-character name similar to a NetBIOS hostname or workgroup name. It is common to use the DNS domain name as the scope ID on TCP/IP networks where all of the systems want to share information, or to use the workgroup name as a scope ID on networks where you want to limit access to a workgroup. However, scope IDs are more flexible. It is possible to group together multiple workgroups within a scope ID while still maintaining a group that is much smaller then a full DNS domain. For example, assume that the marketing department has three workgroups named *DIRECT*, *RESELLERS*, and *GSD*. These are all given the scope ID *SALES*. They are all "visible" to each other but not to another group with a different scope ID.

The last NBT configuration item we have to discuss is the choice of techniques for mapping NetBIOS names to IP addresses. We have already talked about the purpose of address mapping: it provides IP addresses for the NetBIOS names of hosts that exist outside of the local system's broadcast area. In NT 3.5, there are three ways to map the addresses:

- WINS. *Windows Internet Name Service* is a protocol that was developed by Microsoft specifically to provide name service for. NetBIOS names. The advantage of WINS is that it dynamically learns names and addresses from the transmissions on the network, and that it can be dynamically updated by DHCP (see Chapter 8). The disadvantage is that it requires an NT server, and it is primarily a NetBIOS service. It is generally not used on TCP/IP networks.

- DNS Windows Name Resolution. DNS can be used to map a NetBIOS name to an IP address, but only if the NetBIOS name and the internet hostname of the computer are the same. For example, our imaginary computer has the NetBIOS name CASHEW. If its internet hostname is *cashew.nuts.com*, DNS can be used to map the NetBIOS name to the IP address. It is a good idea to always make the NetBIOS name and the hostname the same on every system. If you do, check the **Enable DNS for Windows Name Resolution** box and let DNS do its job.

- LMHOSTS File Lookup. The LMHOSTS file is a simple flat file that associates NetBIOS names with IP addresses. Select the **Enable LMHOSTS Lookup** checkbox to use this file. You can load the LMHOSTS file from an existing file by clicking the **Import LMHOSTS** button and providing the path to the file when prompted. LMHOSTS lookup can be selected with DNS Windows Name Resolution. If both are selected, the system first checks the LMHOSTS file and then issues a DNS query if the NetBIOS name is not found in the file.

Many systems use a small LMHOSTS file to provide the addresses of important servers. The next section describes how to build an LMHOSTS file.

Configuring the LMHOSTS File

The LMHOSTS file looks exactly like a UNIX */etc/hosts* file and functions in a similar way. The difference is that the LMHOSTS file maps NetBIOS names to IP addresses, and the */etc/hosts* file maps TCP/IP hostnames to IP addresses. A sample LMHOSTS file shows how similar these two files look:

```
128.66.3.16      hickory
128.66.3.10      hazel
128.66.3.7       cashew
```

Each entry in an LMHOSTS file contains an IP address that is separated by whitespace from the NetBIOS name associated with that address. An entry must not exceed a single line and comments begin with the pound sign (#).

The LMHOSTS file is stored in the WINDOWS directory on WfW systems and in the WINNT\SYSTEM32\DRIVERS\ETC directory under Windows NT, assuming that NT is installed in WINNT. Change the path accordingly if NT is installed in another directory.

The same LMHOSTS file can be used on a WfW system or an NT system, but the NT version of the LMHOSTS file does have some features that are not supported by WfW. These special commands begin with pound signs (#) so that WfW systems will treat them as comments, allowing the same file to be used on both systems. The NT commands are:

#PRE
> Causes the entry to be pre-loaded into the cache and permanently retained there. Normally entries are only cached when they are used for name resolution and are only retained in the cache for a few minutes. Use #PRE to speed up address resolution for frequently used hostnames.

#DOM:*domain*
> Identifies NT domain controllers. The *domain* variable is the name of the NT domain for which this system is a controller. Every domain controller in the LMHOSTS file should be identified by a #DOM command. If you don't use NT domains, this command is not needed.

#INCLUDE *file*
> Specifies a remote file that should be incorporated in the local LMHOSTS file. This allows a centrally maintained LMHOSTS file to be automatically loaded. To provide redundant sources for LMHOSTS, enclose a group of #INCLUDE commands inside a pair of #BEGIN_ALTERNATE and #END_ALTERNATE statements. The system tries the various sources in order and stops as soon as it successfully downloads one copy of the LMHOSTS file.

The LMHOSTS file shown below contains examples of all of these commands. The #PRE command is combined with #DOM to pre-load the address of the NT domain controller. The two #INCLUDE statements define alternate sources of additional LMHOSTS information. Notice that the address of *cashew*, the system specified in the second #INCLUDE statement, is defined in this file. If a source of LMHOSTS information is not in the local broadcast area, the address of that source must be included in the file.

```
128.66.3.16      hickory    #PRE #DOM:ACCOUNTS
128.66.3.10      hazel
128.66.3.7       cashew     #PRE
#BEGIN_ALTERNATE
#INCLUDE \\acorn\admin\lmhosts
#INCLUDE \\cashew\admin\lmhosts
#END_ALTERNATE
```

The cache is pre-loaded during the system boot. Additional information is added to the cache every time the system references the LMHOSTS file, but only the entry used to resolve an address is added. When you add new #PRE entries to the LMHOSTS file they are not cached unless you reboot the system or flush the existing cache and force it to reload with the **NBTSTAT -R** command. The **NBTSTAT -C** command shows the entries that are currently cached.[*]

NBT Applications

Windows NT and Windows for Workgroups both include a set of NetBIOS applications that provide some of the same services we are familiar with on TCP/IP networks. The important services of file sharing, print sharing, and electronic mail are provided as well as a minor service, *Chat*, that is similar to the UNIX **talk** command.

Two unique NetBIOS applications, *Schedule+* and *ClipBook*, are also provided. *Schedule+* is a network-based calendar. Some TCP/IP systems have network-based calendars; Sun includes one with their operating system. But most TCP/IP packages do not include calendars.

ClipBook is an interesting application. On a Windows system, material from a file or window display is moved to the clipboard using the **Cut** or **Copy** commands from the **Edit** menu. Using the *ClipBook* application, data from the clipboard can be moved to a *ClipBook* "page," and multiple pages can be organized into a "book." The *ClipBook* material can then be viewed or modified by others on the network. No similar application is bundled with TCP/IP, though workgroup software that provides much greater capabilities can be purchased for TCP/IP networks.

---

[*] The **NBTSTAT** command, like most NT commands, is entered in the command window that is launched by selecting the MS-DOS icon in the Main window.

The important NetBIOS applications (file and printer sharing) are the ones that you are most likely to be involved with. They are the applications we concentrate on in this section.

File Sharing

File and printer sharing are the heart of a local area network. Every LAN system includes a facility to provide these services, and Microsoft's networking is no exception. File sharing is integrated directly into the Windows File Manager. Working with File Manager shows some of the power and limitations of running NetBIOS applications over TCP/IP.

In File Manager parlance, offering a local directory to others is called "sharing a directory." This is equivalent to "exporting" a directory under NFS. To share a directory, open the File Manager, highlight the directory you want to offer, and select **Share As** from the **Disk** menu. (There is an icon for this on the toolbar. It looks like a hand offering a file folder.) Type the "share name" in the window that appears. The share name is a logical name that replaces the physical path of the directory when it is referenced by a remote system. How it is used will become clear when we look at an example of connecting to a remote directory.

It's important to set access permissions properly for any directory that you share. Frequently systems default to permissions that allow much more access than you wish. You have to take care to ensure that the proper permissions are set so that your system is not compromised.

Windows for Workgroups offers only two types of shared directory access: *Read-only* and *Full*. These permissions apply to the entire shared directory. Read-only access allows remote users to read any file in the directory and full access allows the users to read, write or delete any file. Access is controlled by passwords. If no password is defined in the Passwords subwindow, anyone with the same scope ID is granted the specified access. Enter a password in the Read-Only Password box to control read-only access or in the Full Access Password box to control full access. Put a password in each box and click the **Depends On Password** button to grant either read-only or full access depending on the password entered by the remote user.

Setting permissions under Windows NT is substantially different. NT understands the concept of user accounts and user groups, and different permissions for different users or groups of users. NT also offers a greater variety of shared directory permissions than WfW does. The NT Shared Directory window has a button labeled **Permissions**. Click on it, and the window shown in Figure 7-9 appears.

Figure 7-9 shows the permissions already applied to this shared directory. The group *Everyone* is granted full control of this directory. We don't want that! To change it, highlight the entry and click the **Remove** button. Add your own permissions by clicking the **Add** button. Figure 7-10 shows the window used to grant permissions to users and groups.

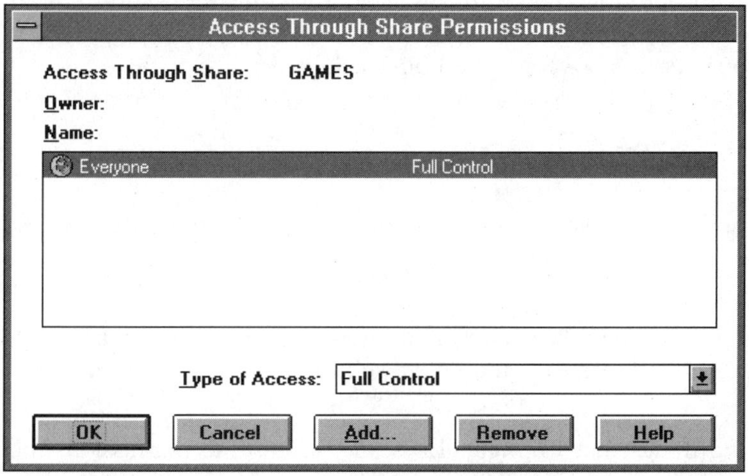

Figure 7-9: Viewing the Permissions on a Shared Directory

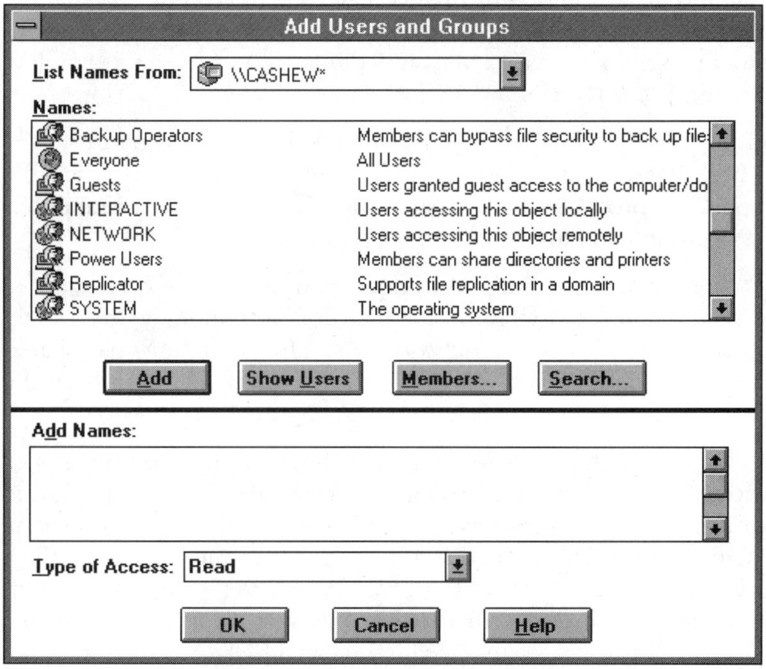

Figure 7-10: Granting File Access Permissions

Figure 7-10 displays the groups known to this host. Select a group and grant an access permission to that group by selecting a permission from the Type of Access listbox. NT offers four permissions for shared directories:

No Access
    Denies all forms of access.

Read
    Permits the remote user to list the directory, read the files in the directory, and execute programs from the directory.

Change
    Permits all of the things that *Read* allows and permits the remote user to write files in the directory and to create and delete sub-directories.

Full Control
    Permits all of the things that *Change* allows and adds some permissions that are specific to NT File System (NTFS) files and directories. NT supports three different filesystems: File Allocation Table (FAT) files that are compatible with DOS, Windows, and WfW; High Performance File System (HPFS) files that are compatible with OS/2; and NTFS files, which are native to NT. *Full Control* allows the remote user to set NTFS file and directory permissions. For FAT files, the *Change* and *Full Control* permissions are equivalent.

Once a group and permission are selected, click the **OK** button. You return to the Access Through Share Permissions window. To add more groups, just click the **Add** button and repeat the procedure. Permissions can be granted to several different groups, and each group can have a different level of permission.

Offering to share a directory is the hard part because you need to be careful about security. Using a shared directory is easy. In Microsoft terminology the mount point for a shared directory is called a *network drive* and mounting that shared directory is called *connecting to a network drive*. Simply select that item from the **Disk** menu of the File Manager. The window shown in Figure 7-11 appears.

The lower part of Figure 7-11 shows the workgroups, hosts, and shared directories that this system knows about. Click on a workgroup to see the hosts under it, and click on a host to see its shared directories. If you see the directory you want, highlight it. The path of the highlighted directory appears in the Path box. Click the **OK** button to mount the directory on the drive shown at the top of the window. The drop-down box associated with Drive allows you to pick any available disk drive. Some people like to associate specific drives with specific shared directories, but by default the drives are simply mounted in alphabetic order. Check the **Reconnect at Logon** box to automatically mount the directory every time the user logs in. If this box is not checked, the directory only remains mounted as long as this user is logged in.

Don't despair if the resource you want is not shown in the Shared Directories subwindow. If you know the network path of the directory you want to mount, you

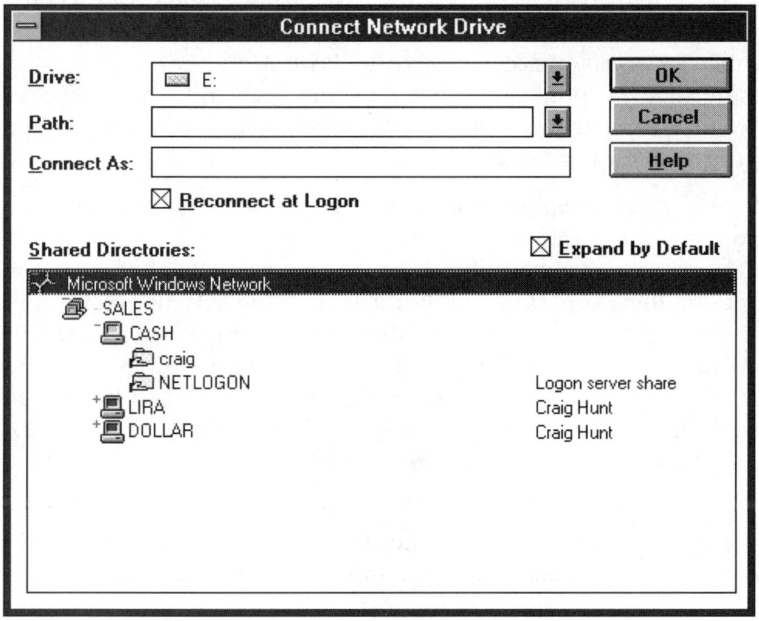

Figure 7–11: Connecting a Network Drive

may be able to reference it by name, even though it isn't shown in the subwindow. The subwindow is built by the Browser, which has difficulty working between WfW and NT, and over TCP/IP. It is very possible that some of the important services on your TCP/IP network are not detected by the Browser.

To minimize the effect of this problem, the paths of important resources should be advertised by the network administrator. The path contains the remote system's NetBIOS hostname and the share name of the remote directory. It starts with two backslashes (\\) followed by the hostname, a single backslash (\), and the share name. This naming format is called the *Universal Naming Convention,* or UNC. Enter the path in the Path box and click **OK**. Even though the Browser does not know about the resource, the system will have no trouble mounting it, and once the directory is mounted, it can be used just like a local filesystem.

Printer Sharing

Sharing a printer is also very easy. On a WfW system, open the *Print Manager* from the *Control Panel* window. Highlight the printer you want to share and select **Share Printer As** from the **Printer** menu.[*] (You can select the **Share Printer As** icon from the toolbar. It looks like a hand offering a printer.) In the dialogue box that

---

[*] Printers are normally installed when WfW is installed. To add a printer to a running system, select **Printer Setup** from the **Options** menu and fill in the appropriate information in the dialogue boxes that appear.

pops up, enter the share name of the printer and, optionally, a password to limit access to the printer. The *Print Manager* must be left running at all times for the printer to be available for remote access. Copy the *Print Manager* to the Startup window to make sure that the printer is available every time the system restarts. You also need to remember that the remote WfW system must locally install the correct Windows printer driver for the shared printer.

NT is slightly different. *Print Manager* does not need to be launched from the Startup window, and it is not necessary for every client to install a local copy of the printer driver. There are also slight differences in how a printer is shared. The printer is still offered via the *Print Manager*, but it is done by selecting **Properties** from the **Printer** menu. In the dialogue box that appears, click the **Share this printer on the network** checkbox and enter the share name of the printer. Sharing a printer requires that the *Server* service is running. *Server* is installed by default when NT installs NetBEUI. If it is not running on your system, start it from the *Services* application that is contained in the *Control Panel*.

Printer security is also different for Windows NT. Printer permissions are set by selecting **Permissions** in the **Security** menu of the Windows NT *Print Manager*. NT allows permissions to be set for users or groups, and it supports four different permissions:

No Access
Denies all forms of access to the printer.

Print
Permits printing.

Manage Documents
Permits limited forms of printer control, but it does not permit printing.

Full Control
Permits printing and all forms of printer control, even deleting the printer.

Connecting to a network printer is extremely easy on an NT system. Select **Connect To Printer** from the **Printers** menu of the *Print Manager*. In the window that appears, highlight the printer you want and click **OK**. Again it is possible that the Browser will not locate all of the printers on a TCP/IP network. If the printer you want isn't displayed in the window, enter the path of the printer in the Printer box using the NetBIOS name of the host that offers the printer and the share name of the printer. Click **OK** to finish.

It is a little more difficult to connect to a network printer using WfW. Make the same menu selections to get to the Connect to Printer window, but be prepared to provide a little extra information. The network printer must be associated with a logical printer port: LPT1, LPT2, LPT3, or LPT4.* Select an unused port and make sure that you have the necessary driver for the printer. If the driver is not already

---

* If necessary, the serial ports COM1 to COM4 can also be used.

installed, you're prompted to insert the diskette that contains the driver. This is one of the diskettes provided with Windows or a diskette provided by the printer vendor.

The NetBIOS file and print services are easy to use over a TCP/IP network, but similar services are already offered by common TCP/IP programs. (The TCP/IP protocols for sharing files and printers are covered in Chapter 10.) In a heterogeneous network with several different kinds of computers and operating systems, the standard TCP/IP applications allow all of the different systems to share data and print services. The NetBIOS services are generally limited to PCs running Microsoft operating systems.

Other Limitations

The Windows NT and WfW NetBIOS applications use NBT to run over a TCP/IP network. The applications work well in that mode, but there are limitations:

- Applications running over NBT can only work with other applications that are also using NBT. They cannot interoperate with applications that are running over NetBEUI. Every system that is expected to communicate via a TCP/IP WAN must run NBT.

- The NetBIOS applications do not interoperate with the standard TCP/IP applications. Even though they perform similar functions, special software is required to make NetBIOS and TCP/IP applications cooperate.

- There are differences between NT and WfW that create some incompatibilities in the same applications when running on these two different systems.

The biggest application disappointment for WfW and NT users on a TCP/IP network is Microsoft *Mail*. The *Mail* application is a very nice LAN email system. The problem for TCP/IP network users is that it cannot be used to send email to anyone except other Microsoft *Mail* users. The package does not come with an SMTP gateway and cannot send mail to remote sites on the Internet or even to UNIX hosts on the local network. To fix this problem, Microsoft offers an add-on SMTP gateway, but it is priced in the thousands of dollars—not an option for many small networks. Most users turn to third-party email systems that support SMTP. This is particularly easy for WfW because all of the Windows TCP/IP applications covered in the last chapter run under WfW.

NT does not have as many third-party TCP/IP applications as WfW does. However, not all NT applications are NetBIOS applications. NT provides a few important TCP/IP applications of its own.

TCP/IP Applications

Windows NT bundles Ping, Telnet, and FTP with its TCP/IP stack. The most interesting of these is FTP because it comes as both a client and a server. We'll cover the FTP server configuration in a minute. First let's take a quick look at the client applications.

NT's **ping**, **telnet**, and **ftp** commands can all be executed in the command window. To get the command window, run *Command Prompt* from the Main program group. **ping** and **ftp** execute as character-oriented applications within the command window, as in the example below:

```
C:\users> ping ruby.ora.com
Pinging host ruby.ora.com : 198.112.208.25
ICMP Echo Reply:TTL 240
ICMP Echo Reply:TTL 240
ICMP Echo Reply:TTL 240
ICMP Echo Reply:TTL 240
Host ruby.ora.com replied to all 4 of the 4 pings
C:\users> ftp ftp.ora.com
Connected to ruby.ora.com.
220 ruby FTP server (Fri Apr 15 1994) ready.
User (ruby.ora.com:): anonymous
331 Guest login ok, send your complete e-mail address as password.
Password:
230-Welcome to O'Reilly & Associates, Inc. FTP Archive.
ftp> quit
221 Goodbye.
```

These character-oriented applications are exactly what you'd expect if you are familiar with UNIX. Telnet is only slightly different. When the **telnet** command is entered in the command window it opens a separate terminal window. The same window is available by running Telnet from the Accessories program group. To connect to a remote host, select **Remote System** from the **Connect** menu in the Telnet window. Enter the DNS hostname of the remote system in the box that appears and click **Connect**. When you logout from the remote host, you return to the Telnet window and can, if you wish, connect to another remote host. To exit the Telnet window, select **Exit** from the **Connect** menu.

FTP Server for Windows NT

NT does not provide a Telnet server as a standard application, but it does provide an FTP server. Install the FTP server software through the Network icon in the *Control Panel*. Open the Network window and select the **Add Software** button. Select **TCP/IP and related components** from the listbox and **FTP Server Service** from the window that appears (see Figure 7-4). When the software is installed it will be listed in the Installed Network Software box of the Network Settings window (see Figure 7-1). Configure the FTP server by highlighting its entry and clicking the **Configure** button. The window shown in Figure 7-12 appears.

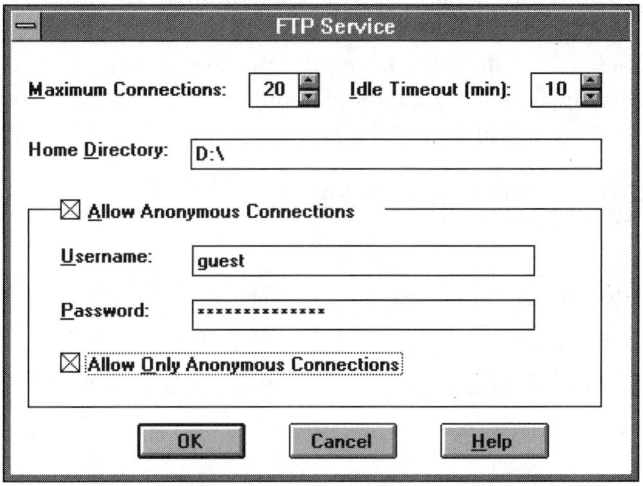

Figure 7–12: FTP Server Configuration

The window shows has several different configuration values, some of which are more important then others. The server configuration lets you define the maximum number of concurrent FTP connections and the number of minutes the system should wait before dropping an idle connection. The defaults are good choices for most systems. Generally you don't need to change these fields.

The configuration also specifies the Home Directory that FTP users start in when they log into the server. This should be a directory in the partition assigned to the FTP server. Usually it is the root directory of that partition. More later on assigning a partition to the FTP server.

To permit anonymous FTP access, click the **Allow Anonymous Connections** box. This enables the subwindow in which you enter the Username and Password of the user account assigned to the anonymous FTP user. Everyone accessing an NT system, even the anonymous FTP user, is assigned a user account that determines the privileges of that user. This is NOT the username and password used to login as the anonymous FTP user; the standard *anonymous* username and *guest* password are used for that. This user account determines the privileges of the anonymous user. By default, this is the standard Windows NT *guest* account, which is used by NetBIOS for default file and printer access. You may want to create another user account[*] specifically for FTP to keep the privileges of these services separate. To restrict the FTP server so that it can only be used for anonymous FTP, click on **Allow Only Anonymous Connections**.

After filling in all of the values, click **OK** in this window and **OK** once again in the Network Setting window. The system will restart, and a new FTP Server icon will

---

[*] User accounts are created through the *User Manager* application found in the Administrative Tools group.

appear in the *Control Panel*. Double click on this icon to open the FTP User Sessions window. The window is used to monitor users connected to the FTP server and, if necessary, to disconnect any or all of the users. For the server configuration we use this window to set some final configuration parameters by clicking the **Security** button to open the box shown in Figure 7-13.

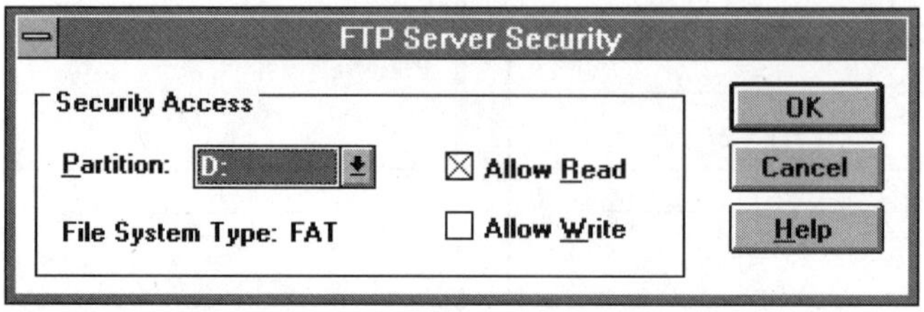

Figure 7–13: Setting the FTP Server Partition

Set the disk partition that you want to assign to the FTP server. This limits FTP users to that partition. Set the access that you will permit FTP users to have to that partition. This can be *Read* or *Write* or both. Finally, click **OK** and then **Close**. The FTP server is now configured.

Third Party Applications

The minimal number of TCP/IP applications that ship with the NT operating system leaves the field wide open for third party application developers. Commercial, shareware and freeware developers have all rushed into this opening.

Most Windows TCP/IP vendors offer a version of their product specifically written for Windows NT. The NT versions do not include a TCP/IP protocol stack, instead using the one that comes with NT. Therefore the installation of these products requires little more than copying the software onto the hard disk. The look and feel of these products is so close to the Windows versions that there is really no need to distinguish between them. But two things do distinguish the commercial products available for NT from their Windows counterparts:

- Expense. TCP/IP applications for NT are very expensive when compared to the same product from the same vendor for Windows. This is inevitable. Compared to the Windows market, the NT market is very small and new. The market does not have the volume to drive down prices. The "newness" of the market means that many products are still trying to recover initial development costs.

- Lack of features. Not all of the features that are available in the Windows versions of a commercial package are ported to NT. One reason is that the size of the Windows market earns it the lion's share of the development effort. The other is that the functions of some traditional TCP/IP applications, such as email, are provided by NetBIOS applications in NT.

For these reasons there is very strong interest in freeware and shareware TCP/IP products in the NT market place. There are Telnet servers, SMTP email packages, NFS packages, even a NetBIOS/SMB package that turns a UNIX server into a NetBIOS file server—all available for little or no cost. This software is of widely varying quality and subject to frequent changes. To keep up with the latest news about these packages, subscribe to the Windows NT newsgroup *comp.os.windows-nt.misc.*

Installing PPP for Windows NT

Windows NT 3.5 provides SLIP and PPP as part of the *Remote Access Service* (RAS). RAS has always been part of Windows NT. But in the past, RAS only provided remote access for NetBEUI networks. NT 3.5 was the first release to add SLIP and PPP to RAS, and it has made RAS a much more useful service.

To install PPP under NT 3.5, run *Network* from the *Control Panel.* In the Network window click the **Add Software** button. Select **Remote Access Service** from the listbox that appears, and click **Continue.** When prompted, provide the path to the Windows NT distribution files.

After the RAS software files are loaded, the Add Port dialogue box appears asking which serial port the modem is attached to. Select the correct port, COM1, COM2, COM3, or COM4, and click **OK.** The RAS software then attempts to detect what type of modem is connected to the port. It displays its best guess of the modem type. Regardless of whether RAS is right or wrong about the modem type, click **OK.** You can correct any mistake RAS may have made in the Configure Port dialogue box show in Figure 7-14. If RAS did not select the correct modem, select it yourself from the Attached Device box at the top of this window.

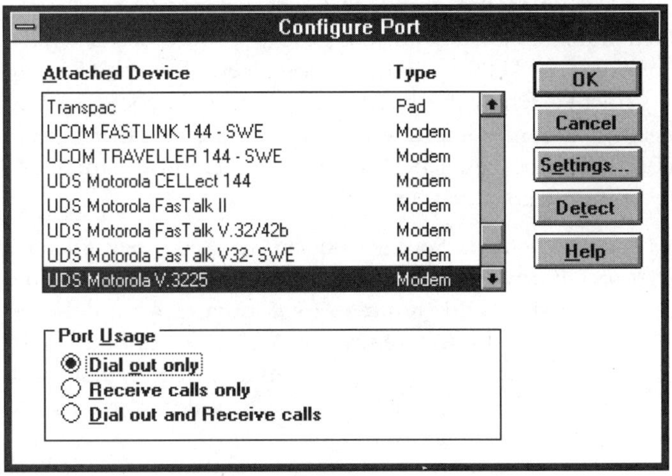

Figure 7–14: NT Modem Selection

Use the Port Usage box to define whether this is an originate only, answer only, or originate and answer port. **Dial out only** is used on a workstation client that connects to a remote PPP server, or on an NT server that connects a local area network into a wide-area network. **Dial out only** is the most secure setting because the connection must originate from your system.

Dial out and Receive calls and **Receive calls only** are used on NT servers that accept inbound, dial-up connections. These settings are used to provide remote access to the NT server or to the local area network behind the NT server. Any substantial dial-in workload should be handled by a separate, dedicated terminal server, and not by an NT server that is also acting as the network's file and print server.

If you select either **Receive calls only** or **Dial out and Receive calls**, click the **Settings** button to define certain modem parmeters. The Settings dialogue box contains the following checkboxes:

Enable Modem Speaker
  Check this box to turn the modem speaker on during the dialup and connection process.

Enable Hardware Flow Control (RTS/CTS)
  Hardware flow control is the only kind of flow control permitted on a SLIP/PPP connection. If the modem cannot handle hardware flow control, "uncheck" this box to disable flow control.

Enable Error Control
  Check this box to turn on the modem's error correction protocol. This setting is not absolutely required for PPP because TCP/IP is designed to run over unreliable links. However, it is normally turned on when available.

Enable Modem Compression
  Modem compression is used when the port speed at both ends of the link is greater than the modem transmission speed, e.g., the ports are set at 19,200 bps, and the modem transmits at 9600 baud. It is most useful for speeding up file transfers and least effective when the bulk of the data is keyboard input, such as in a Telnet session. Modem compression is not used when the modem transmission rate is as great as the serial port speed, e.g., the ports are set to 9600 bps, and the modem transmits at 9600 baud.

If you select **Dial out only**, do not click the **Settings** button. Instead, click **OK** and go to the Remote Access Setup window shown in Figure 7-15. The buttons at the bottom of Figure 7-15 that are used to add, remove, or configure a modem are largely self-explanatory. The **Configure** button returns you to the Configure Port window shown in Figure 7-14. The **Clone** button copies a modem configuration to another serial port, which is only useful if you have identical modems attached to multiple ports.

The **Network** button opens a window that is used to define the protocols that are associated with this dial-up device. The choices are NetBEUI, TCP/IP and IPX. For

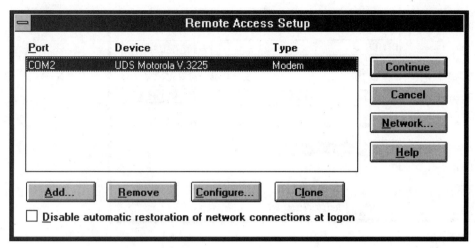

Figure 7–15: Remote Access Setup

PPP on a TCP/IP network, click the **Network** button, check **TCP/IP** in the Network Configuration window, and click **OK**.

To finish up, click **Continue** in the Remote Access Setup window. You may be prompted again for the path to the NT distribution files. A new Remote Access Service group is then added to the Program Manager. Click **OK** in the Network Settings window and restart the computer when prompted to do so. When the system comes back up, RAS is installed.

Configuring PPP

Open the Remote Access Service program group in the *Program Manager*. It contains several different icons related to RAS and PPP. The icon Remote Access and the Internet is an online book about TCP/IP and PPP. There is also online help available through the Remote Access Help icon. The *Remote Access Monitor* program provides a simple graphic display of the modem's status. The heart of all of this is the RAS program. Run it by double-clicking on the Remote Access icon.

The first time that Remote Access is run after the installation, you're warned that the "phone book" is empty, and the system automatically opens the Add Phone Book Entry window. Click **Advanced** to see the full window shown in Figure 7-16. Enter a descriptive name for the new phone book entry and the phone number of the remote server in the appropriate boxes. You can also enter an optional description for this entry. (The optional description is helpful if you have lots of phone book entries.) If you want to use the name and password that you used to login to Windows NT as your username and password on the remote server, check the **Authenticate using current username and password** box. If you don't check this box you will be prompted for the username and password during the connection process.

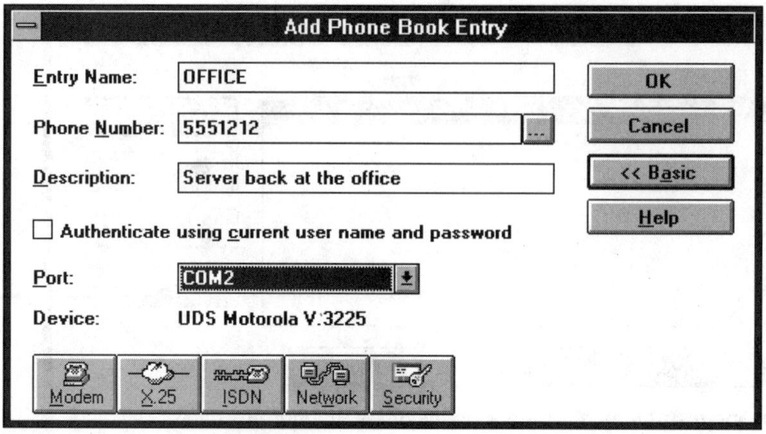

Figure 7-16: PPP Phone Book Entry

The Port and the Device are the serial port and modem that were selected during the RAS installation. These should be correct and should not require any modification. If they are not what you expect, the entire RAS installation may be incorrect. If that is the case, **Cancel** this window and return to the Remote Access Setup window, Figure 7-15, to correct these values. To get back to the Remote Access Setup window, run the *Network* program in the *Control Panel*, and then highlight **Remote Access Service** and click **Configure** in the Network window. It is, however, very unlikely you will need to do this.

The majority of the configuration is done through the buttons at the bottom of the Add Phone Book Entry window. The **X.25** button is used if the port is set to **Any X.25** or the device is a PAD (Packet Assembler/Disassembler). A PAD is used when the PC connects to the remote server through an X.25 Public Data Network (PDN). If your PC is attached to a PDN, select the PAD from the list in the Attached Device box of the Configure Port window (see Figure 7-14). Each PAD is identified by the name of the public network it is designed for, e.g., Tymnet, Transpac, Compuserve, etc.. Use the **X.25** button to set the X.121 address of the remote server and to define the user and facilities commands required by your X.25 service provider. These values are specific to the X.25 service provider and can only be obtained from them.

The **ISDN** button is used only if the port is set to **Any ISDN.**[*] If you have an ISDN card installed in your PC, use this button to set the line speed and the number of channels. Many networks connect to ISDN through an ISDN LAN bridge instead of passing the data through the NT server. If you use an ISDN LAN bridge, do not configure it here because you do not have an ISDN card installed directly in the PC. Instead, the ISDN LAN bridge is connected to the local area network, and the

---

[*] Integrated Services Digital Network (ISDN) is a telephone server that can operate at up to 128K bps.

NT server talks to it directly through the local Ethernet. With a LAN bridge, the only configuration on the NT server is the standard Ethernet configuration. The LAN bridge forwards the correct packets to the ISDN network, and the NT server is not required to act as a router.

Because our device is a modem, we can ignore the **X.25** and the **ISDN** buttons. The buttons that affect our configuration are the **Modem**, **Network**, and **Security** buttons. The **Modem** button opens the Modem Settings window. Use this window to set the baud rate and to enable hardware flow control, modem error correction, and modem data compression. The role of flow control, error correction, and data compression on a PPP link were all explained earlier.

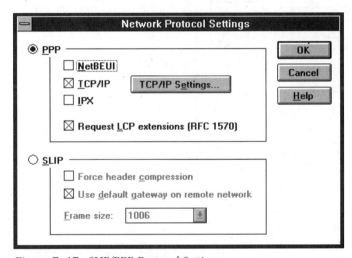

Figure 7–17: SLIP/PPP Protocol Settings

The **Network** button opens the Network Protocol Settings window shown in Figure 7-17. This window contains two subwindows: one for PPP and one for SLIP. In the SLIP subwindow:

- You can choose CSLIP header compression. Header compression improves performance, but will only work if the remote server supports it.

- You can specify that the server at the remote end of the link is your default router, which is usually the case on a SLIP link.

- You can change the size of the SLIP transmission frame. The standard SLIP frame is 1006. If you have a slow serial port (e.g., 8250 UART), you may experience data loss or buffer overruns using the large frame size with modem speeds of 9600 baud or more. If that happens, reduce the frame size and lower the baud rate until the problems disappear. The best solution is to install a high speed serial port (e.g., 16550 UART).

PPP is configured in the PPP subwindow. Check **PPP** and **TCP/IP**. Check **NetBEUI** only if the server at the other end of the serial link is an NT server that uses Net-BEUI as its primary RAS transport protocol. Check **IPX** only if the server at the other end of the link is a NetWare server running PPP. On a TCP/IP network, Net-BIOS and IPX are normally tunneled inside of IP. Therefore, use TCP/IP as the protocol carried over PPP. We'll talk about the Request LCP extensions checkbox later. For now, just select **TCP/IP** and press the **TCP/IP Settings** button.

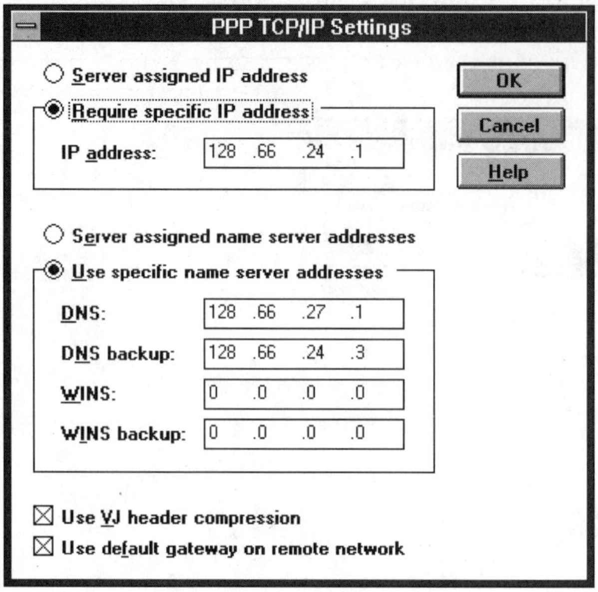

Figure 7-18: PPP TCP/IP Settings

The PPP TCP/IP Settings window shown in Figure 7-18 defines the TCP/IP configuration for the PPP link. It is possible to get the configuration from the remote PPP server, but only if the server supports this feature. Check with the administrator of the remote system to find out if the PPP server supports dynamic configuration and if you are allowed to use it. If the answer to both questions is "yes," you can select **Server assigned IP address** and **Server assigned name server addresses**. Most servers do not provide this information, in which case you must enter the IP address and the DNS server addresses directly into the appropriate boxes in this window.

Select the header compression checkbox if the remote server supports it. Use the remote system as the default gateway unless you have your own local default gateway. If the remote system provides your access to the outside world, use it as the default gateway. If it is merely a client or a peer, do not use it as the default gateway. When everything is set the way you want it, click **OK**.

The last button on the Add Phone Book Entry window is the **Security** button. This opens the Security Settings dialogue box. The upper half of the window sets the type of user authentication that is acceptable to this system: clear text or encrypted. To avoid problems, select **Accept any authentication including clear text**. This setting allows the server and the client to use whatever works. If you force the systems to use encryption, be sure that all of the systems involved support the same type of encryption and that they work together.

Identify the login script, if any is used, in the Terminal or Script box in the lower half of the Security Settings window. Scripts can be invoked before the remote system is dialed and after the dial-up connection is made. There are three choices for handling the connection process: no script (*none*), identifying a script by name, or requesting a terminal window for a manual login (*Terminal*). I highly recommend that you select **Terminal** for the After dialing box in this window when you are first debugging your connection. Creating scripts and using the terminal window are covered in the next section.

Making the Connection

Click **OK** to exit the Add Phone Book Entry window when everything is configured the way you want it. You will see the Remote Access window shown in Figure 7-19. Four of the buttons at the top of the window are for managing phone book entries. You can add new entries or edit existing ones. (The **Add** and **Edit** buttons return you to the Add Phone Book Entry window shown in Figure 7-16.) You can also delete (**Remove**) or copy (**Clone**) existing phone book entries. The remaining buttons are for controlling network connections.

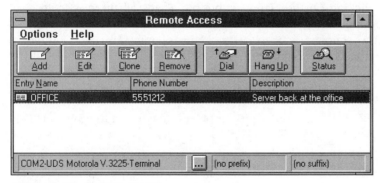

Figure 7–19: Remote Access

To open a PPP connection, highlight the entry of the remote system and press the **Dial** button. The system will display a series of dialogue boxes that report the progress of the connection. If you selected **Terminal** in the Security Settings window, as suggested above, a terminal window opens. Enter the PPP login commands required by your remote server and press the **Done** button. Entering login procedures through the terminal window allows you to debug the connection before you add the complication of debugging a login script. The biggest problems with setting up PPP or SLIP are the modem configuration and the login script. Don't try to debug both at once.

If everything is set up correctly you'll see a "connection complete" message. If not, you'll see an error message. In case of an error:

- Check the modem setup. Make sure that the values you set are compatible with the settings on the remote system. Contact the administrator of the remote system for advice.

- Check the protocol features. Don't request services that the remote system cannot perform, e.g., header compression and encrypted authenication. Find out from the administrator of the remote system exactly what that system will support.

  If the error states that the "PPP negotiation is not converging," make sure that your system is not requesting the *Link Control Protocol* (LCP) extensions. (See the checkbox in the Network Protocol Settings window in Figure 7-17.) Older versions of PPP may not support all of these extensions.

- Don't debug everything at once. Run only TCP/IP over PPP. Don't try to run NetBEUI and IPX until after you have TCP/IP debugged. (See the protocol checkboxes in Figure 7-17.) Also, don't make multiple changes between tests. It is better to methodically make individual changes and test them than try to change everything at once.

If the system connects successfully, press the **Status** button (see Figure 7-9) to view the status of the current connection. When you are finished using the PPP connection, disconnect by clicking on the **Hang Up** button. That's all there is to it. You can, if you wish, continue using the terminal window to make your PPP connections. Actually, it's the simplest way to do it. Many people, however, prefer to automate the connection process with a login script.

The Windows NT SWITCH.INF File

Under Windows NT 3.5, SLIP and PPP login scripts are defined in the SWITCH.INF file, located in the C:\WINNT35\SYSTEM32\RAS directory.* This file contains all of the login scripts.

Each script begins with a section header that provides the name used to invoke the script. (More on how to invoke a script later in this section.) The section header is simply the script's name enclosed in square brackets; for example, a script for logging into your office network with PPP might have the header:

    [OfficePPP]

---

* This assumes that NT is installed in C:\WINNT35.

The body of the script follows the header. It defines what you expect to receive from the remote system using the OK statement, and what the local system sends in response to the expected values using the COMMAND statement. The OK and COMMAND keywords are always entered in upper case, as the following syntax shows:

```
OK=value
```

```
COMMAND=[value]
```

value is the value expected from the remote system, in the case of the OK statement, or the value sent to the remote system in the case of the COMMAND statement. The OK statement requires you to provide a value. If nothing is expected from the remote system, the NoResponse statement should be used instead of OK. (Additional statements, such as **NoResponse**, are covered later.) The *value* is optional for the COMMAND statement. If no *value* is provided, the script simply waits two seconds and then proceeds to the next line in the script.

value contains an arbitrary mixture of literals and macros. A literal is a character string. The macros used in a SWITCH.INF script are listed in Table 7-2.

Table 7–2: SWITCH.INF Script Macros

Macro	Usage
<cr>	A carriage-return.
<lf>	A line-feed.
<match>"*string*"	Waits for a match to the literal *string*.
<ignore>	Ignores the rest of the response.
<?>	A wildcard character.
<h*XX*>	A byte containing the hexadecimal digits *XX*.
<diagnostics>	Displays a diagnostic message box.

A few examples will clarify how the macros and literals are used in SWITCH.INF script statements. The following statement sends the command "enable ppp" to the remote system:

```
COMMAND=enable ppp<cr>
```

Because the string is followed by a <cr> macro, the entire string and the carriage-return are sent immediately to the remote system. This is the most common way commands are sent. If the remote system is so slow that it has trouble processing the characters as fast as the PC sends them, you can send the string without the <cr> macro.[*] When the macro is not used, the string is sent, and there is a slight delay before the script proceeds to the next statement. It is then possible to send small pieces of the string with several COMMAND statements, concluding the last

---

[*] This information is provided for the sake of completeness. It is unlikely that a remote system providing adequate PPP or SLIP service will not be able to process the string in a timely manner.

statement in the series with the <cr> macro. The script expects a response to every command, so if you do use multiple COMMAND statements to send a single command, separate the statements with NoResponse statements.

In the same way that most COMMAND statements end with a <cr> macro, most OK statements start with a <match> macro. The <match> macro matches its associated string against the data received from the remote system. If the string is found anywhere in that data, the script considers that it has made a successful match and moves on to the next statement. The following example shows how the <match> macro is used:

```
OK=<match>"user"
COMMAND=craig<cr>
```

The OK statement will match any reponse from the remote system that contains the string user. The match is case sensitive, so Enter username> would match, but Enter Username> would not. If the OK statement detects a match, the script moves to the next statement, which in this case sends the username *craig* to the remote server.

The <ignore> macro is used to ignore data coming from the remote system. Its most common use is to ignore complete lines of data, such as a welcome banner, that do not require a response from the local system. The following statements skip two lines of data received from the PPP server:

```
COMMAND=
OK=<ignore>
COMMAND=
OK=<ignore>
```

The other macros are less-frequently used. The <lf> macro is used to send a line-feed or to check for a line-feed in data received from the remote system. The wild-card macro is used to replace an individual character in a string. For example, PORT-<?> will match PORT-1 or PORT-2. The hexadecimal character macro is used when sending or receiving non-printable characters. For example, <h00> represents the ASCII NULL character. Finally, the <diagnostics> macro is used with the ERROR_DIAGNOSTICS statement to display an error message received by the script.

We have mentioned the NoResponse and ERROR_DIAGNOSTICS statements, but we have not really explained them. There are only two types of statements in a SWITCH.INF script: command statements and response statements. All command statements begin with the keyword COMMAND and are used to send a string to the remote system. All response statements handle data sent from the remote system to the local system, but there are multiple response statements and each one begins with a different keyword. The most important one is OK, which we have already discussed. The response statements are listed in Table 7-3.

Table 7–3: SWITCH.INF Script Response Statements

Statement	Meaning
OK=*value*	The expected response
NoResponse	No response expected
CONNECT=*value*	The response in the script
ERROR_NO_CARRIER=*value*	Checks for loss of carrier
ERROR_DIAGNOSTICS=*value*	Checks for diagnostic messages
LOOP=*value*	Loop waiting for a match

The NoResponse statement is used only when you don't expect the remote host to respond to a command. The CONNECT statement is used only for the last response in the script, and even there it is not required. The script will terminate properly without a closing CONNECT statement, but CONNECT should be used if the script terminates with a response. For example, assume that the last command in the script sends the command **ppp** to the remote server, and that when it executes on the remote system it returns the message "PPP enabled". The last command/response pair in the script would be:

```
COMMAND=ppp<cr>
CONNECT=<match>"PPP"
```

If the remote server does not return a response to the final command, for example, if the server jumps immediately from terminal mode into SLIP/PPP mode, the script might not end with a CONNECT statement. Here is an example of the last two lines in a script that ends with a command instead of a response:

```
COMMAND=ppp<cr>
NoResponse
```

Response statements can be clustered together after a single command. It's a stretch, but a cluster of response statements can be thought of as a primative case statement. The script passes the data received from the remote server through each of the response commands until a match is found. When the data matches, the script takes the action appropriate to that response statement. In the case of an OK statement, a match drops the script down to the next command. In the case of both error response statements, the system performs the error processing appropriate to the error condition. An example should help:

```
COMMAND=ppp<cr>
CONNECT=<match>"PPP"
ERROR_NO_CARRIER=<match>"NO CARRIER"
ERROR_DIAGNOSTICS=<cr><diagnostics>
```

This script ends with the same command/response pair we saw earlier. If everything works, we get the response "PPP enabled", which matches the CONNECT statement and terminates the script. However, if things go wrong, we have two possible failure modes. In the first case, the remote system drops the line and the modem sends us a "NO CARRIER" message. If that happens, the NT user is informed through a standard error window. In the second case, the remote system does not drop the line but instead sends some error message. All messages from this remote system end with a carriage-return, so we look for that character and use the <diagnostics> macro to display the error message to the NT user.

The LOOP statement is always clustered with at least an OK statement. LOOP is used to walk through several lines of unwanted data until a match is found for the value defined in the OK statement. Because the data is unwanted, the LOOP statement always contains the <ignore> macro. Here's an example:

```
COMMAND=
OK=<match>"user"
LOOP=<ignore>
COMMAND=craig<cr>
```

The remote system sends a banner before the username prompt, and there is no way to tell exactly how many lines are in the banner. The first COMMAND statement delays up to two seconds waiting for data from the remote server. The OK statement checks for the username prompt. If OK finds a match, the script moves to the next COMMAND statement, which sends the username *craig* to the server. If a match is not found, the script drops through to the LOOP=<ignore> statement, which ignores any response from the server until a match is found for the string in the OK statement.

Putting the statements together, let's construct a login script. The lines that begin with a semicolon (;) are comments:

```
;
; A login script for the office PPP server
;
[OfficePPP]
;
; Send a carriage-return and wait for the username prompt
;
COMMAND=<cr>
OK=<match>"username"
;
; Send my username and wait for the password prompt
;
COMMAND=craig<cr>
OK=<match>"password"
;
; Send my password and look for the command-line prompt,
; which contains the string "PORT".
;
COMMAND=Wats?Watt?<cr>
OK=<match>"PORT"
;
; Send the command that starts PPP. We don't expect any response.
; If we do get a response, it's trouble!
;
COMMAND=set port ppp enabled<cr>
```

```
NoResponse
ERROR_NO_CARRIER=<match>"NO CARRIER"
ERROR_DIAGNOSTICS=<cr><diagnostics>
```

Now that the script is added to the SWITCH.INF file, it needs to be tested.

Troubleshooting a SWITCH.INF Script

There is no need to reboot the system to use a new script, but you will need to re-run RAS. Close *Remote Access* if it is running, and re-run it from the RAS Services program group.

To invoke the new script, highlight the phone book entry in the Remote Access window and click **Edit**. In the Edit Phone Book Entry window, click the **Security** button; the Security Settings window, shown in Figure 7-20, appears.

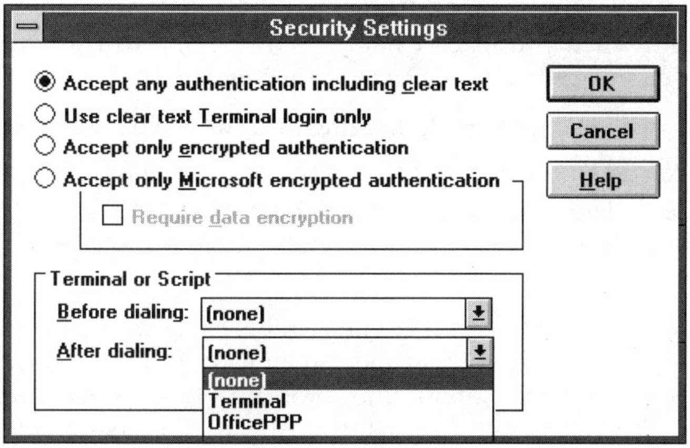

Figure 7-20: Invoking a Login Script

In addition to the standard *(none)* and *Terminal* entries, the Before dialing and After dialing listboxes contain an entry for the new script. A script that is invoked before dialing is used only to initialize intermediate equipment such as the local modem or a local telephone switch. A login script, such as the one we just wrote, is always invoked after the modems have successfully connected. Therefore, choose **OfficePPP** from the After dialing listbox and click **OK**.

Now you are ready to run the script. Return to the Remote Access window and click the **Dial** button. The system displays a series of dialogue boxes tracking the progress of the connection. One of these tells you when the OfficePPP script is being used. If everything works properly, the process ends with a message telling you that the system is successfully connected, and your work is done. In all likelihood, the script will fail and will need to be debugged. If it does fail, terminate *Remote Access* and follow the steps written below.

Login scripts are debugged by logging the interaction of the script with the remote host. We saw two examples of that in Chapter 5, because both *Chameleon* and

SuperTCP provide built-in logging capabilities. Well, it's not so easy with Windows NT 3.5. To turn on logging we will have to edit the registry.

The registry is a database of key values used to configure Windows NT. Modifying the registry is like modifying the UNIX kernel—it must be done carefully or it can lead to big problems.[*] The following steps detail what must be done to enable logging of a SWITCH.INF script:

1. Run the registry editor REGEDT32.EXE.

2. When the registry editor opens it will contain several subwindows. Select the window labeled HKEY_LOCAL_MACHINE.

3. The HKEY_LOCAL_MACHINE window describes a tree-structured database. The branch of the tree that we want to reach is SYSTEM\CurrentControl-Set\Services\RasMan\Parameters. A double-click on each element in this path—SYSTEM CurrentControlSet, Services, RasMan, and finally Parameters—walks you down the tree. When you reach Parameters, the values that we are interested in are displayed in a listbox to the right of the window.

4. To change the logging value, double-click **Logging:REG_WORD:0x0**. In the box that appears enter the value 0x1 and click **OK**.

Figure 7-21 shows the registry editor after the logging parameter has been set to 1. Exit the editor and restart *Remote Access* to begin logging. There is no need to reboot.

Retest your script by highlighting the phone book entry and clicking the dial button. When the script fails, take a careful look at the error message displayed by RAS to see if it gives you any clues about the problem. Next, open the C:\WINNT35\SYSTEM32\RAS\DEVICE.LOG file, which contains the log of the interactions between the script and the remote system. The log shows approximately where in the script the login process failed. A sample log might contain the following:

```
Remote Access Service Device Log  05/06/1995  19:59:34
-------------------------------------------------------
Port:COM2 Command to Device:AT&F&C1&D2 V1 S0=0 S2=128 S7=55
Port:COM2 Echo from Device :AT&F&C1&D2 V1 S0=0 S2=128 S7=55
Port:COM2 Response from Device:
OK
Port:COM2 Command to Device:ATDT5551212
Port:COM2 Echo from Device :ATDT5551212
Port:COM2 Response from Device:
CONNECT 9600
Port:COM2 Connect BPS:9600
Port:COM2 Carrier BPS:2400
Port:COM2 Command to Device:
```

---

[*] A mistaken entry in the registry can cause booting problems. If you have booting problems after modifying the registry, press the spacebar when the "Press spacebar for previous menu" message is displayed during the boot.

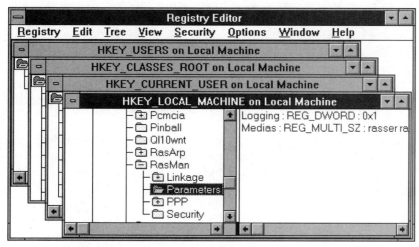

Figure 7–21: Enable Logging with the Registry Editor

```
Port:COM2 Echo from Device :
Port:COM2 Response from Device:Enter Username>
```

The log shows the initialization command sent to the modem, the modem dialing, and the connect message from the modem. After the modem connects, the commands come from our script, and the "device" that the commands are being sent to is the remote server. A command is sent to the remote server that appears to be blank lines. This is the carriage-return at the start of the script.

The last line in this log is a response from the server prompting for the username. The script, however, did not send the username; instead, it timed out with an error. In this case, the script is probably looking for the wrong username prompt. Correct the script, restart *Remote Access*, and try again. The script may fail several times. Each time correct the problem and move on to the next test. You should note that every time the script runs it appends its log to anything that already exists in the DEVICE.LOG file. To keep the log small, delete the old file before running the test. You must terminate *Remote Access* to delete the file, but you should terminate and restart it between every test anyway.

Once you have a script that works with your server, make a copy of it without your username and password, and distribute it to the other NT systems in your organization that connect through the same server. No one else should have to go through this pain!

Summary

Windows NT is an operating system with built-in networking. It uses NetBEUI for local area networking and TCP/IP for wide area networking. NetBEUI cannot be used for enterprise network applications. It depends on physical layer broadcasts and it has no independent, hierarchical address structure. NetBEUI is a "non-routable" protocol. To overcome this limitation and allow the applications bundled with NT to run over a wide area network, Microsoft provides *NetBIOS over TCP/IP* (NBT). NBT uses the LMHOSTS file to reduce dependence on broadcasts and a *scope ID* to filter out unwanted traffic in the larger WAN network. In addition to these two special parameters, configuring TCP/IP for NT requires the same values as any other TCP/IP installation. *Remote Access Server* (RAS) provides dial-up communications for Windows NT. RAS includes both PPP and SLIP.

Windows NT comes with several applications that depend on the NetBIOS application interface. The NetBIOS applications duplicate many of the functions provided by standard TCP/IP applications, which are covered in the following chapters.

8

Configuration Control

I'm sure you've already figured it out, so I might as well admit it: TCP/IP is not as easy to configure as some other networking systems. Take a look at what TCP/IP provides:

• Open protocol standards that are freely available and not dependent on any one operating system or computer hardware platform

• Independence from specific network hardware

• A globally unique addressing scheme

• Support for internetworking and routing

These powerful features add to the utility and flexibility of TCP/IP. They also add to its complexity.

TCP/IP requires the configuration to provide information on hardware, addressing, and routing. Since it is designed to be independent of any specific underlying network hardware, information that can be built into the hardware in some network systems cannot be built in for TCP/IP. The information must be provided by the person responsible for the configuration. This assumes that every system is run by people who are knowledgeable enough to provide the proper information to configure the system. Unfortunately, this assumption is not always true.

TCP/IP was originally designed to provide a robust network for professionally run mainframes and mini-computers. The computers on a TCP/IP network are regarded as *peers*—equals that are fully capable of acting as servers for one application while acting as clients for another. TCP/IP doesn't make a distinction between a PC and a mainframe. To TCP/IP they are all *hosts*, and all hosts have the same basic configuration requirements.

Networking protocols designed specifically for PCs often take a different approach. Some peer-to-peer networks, such as Windows for Workgroups, lighten the configuration load by using the physical addressing available in the hardware and by not supporting routing. Two fewer things to configure! NetWare simplifies the configuration of PC clients by placing most of the intelligence and all of the knowledge of the network configuration in the server.

Of course, TCP/IP has not been standing still while PCs and PC LAN software has evolved. TCP/IP has tools that simplify the task of configuring a PC. The chapters on installing TCP/IP under DOS and Windows mention two of these, RARP and BOOTP. A third protocol, DHCP, expands on BOOTP's capabilities. Like NetWare, these tools simplify configuration by moving the configuration information to a well maintained server. In this chapter, we use these tools to create a server that simplifies TCP/IP configuration for networked PC users. We begin with the oldest and most basic of these configuration tools—RARP.

Reverse Address Resolution Protocol

RARP, defined in RFC 903, is a protocol that converts a physical network address into an IP address. This is the reverse of what Address Resolution Protocol (ARP) does. Address Resolution Protocol, defined in RFC 826, maps an IP address to a physical address so that data can be delivered over a physical network. It does this by broadcasting an ARP packet that contains the IP address in question. When a system receives an ARP packet that contains its IP address, it responds with a packet that contains its physical network address, e.g., its Ethernet address.

Reverse Address Resolution Protocol maps a physical address to an IP address for a system that doesn't know its own IP address. The client uses the broadcast services of the physical network[*] to send out a packet that contains the client's physical network address, and asks if any system on the network knows what IP address is associated with the address. The RARP server responds with a packet that contains the client's IP address.

But how do you discover the physical network addresses, which you'll need to configure the RARP server? Physical addresses, such as Ethernet addresses, are encoded in the network interface hardware. On most systems you can easily check the value with a command. For example, on a SunOS system the superuser can type:

```
# ifconfig le0
le0: flags=63<UP,BROADCAST,NOTRAILERS,RUNNING>
        inet 128.66.12.1 netmask ffffff00 broadcast 128.66.12.255
        ether 8:0:20:e:12:37
```

The **ifconfig** command can set or display the configuration values for a network interface. *le0* is the device of the Ethernet interface. The Ethernet address is displayed after the ether label. In the example, the address is 8:0:20:e:12:37.

---

* Like ARP, RARP is a *Network Access Layer* protocol that uses physical network services residing below the *Internet Layer.* See the discussion of TCP/IP protocol layers in *TCP/IP Network Administration.*

On a Windows system running Chameleon, double-clicking on the *Custom* icon brings up the window shown in Figure 8-1. It clearly displays the Ethernet address and several other interface values.

```
┌─────────────────────────────────────────────────────┐
│ ─      Custom - D:\NETMANAG\TCPIP.CFG        ▼  ▲    │
│  File   Interface   Setup   Services   Help          │
├─────────────────────────────────────────────────────┤
│  Interface:          Ethernet0                       │
│  Physical Address:   00:20:AF:33:7A:E5               │
│  IP Address:         128.66.3.4                      │
│  Subnet Mask:        255.255.255.0                   │
│  Host Name:          acorn                           │
│  Domain Name:        nuts.com                        │
├─────────────────────────────────────────────────────┤
│  Name            Type        IP            Domain    │
│  *Ethernet0      Ethernet    128.66.3.4    nuts.com  │
│  PPP0            PPP         128.66.8.6    nuts.com   │
│  SLIP0           SLIP        128.66.8.6    nuts.com   │
└─────────────────────────────────────────────────────┘
```

Figure 8-1: Displaying the Ethernet Address

However, both of these examples depend on TCP/IP software to obtain the Ethernet address. To create an RARP server that can help with the initial installation of the TCP/IP software, you need a way to discover the Ethernet address that doesn't depend on TCP/IP. There are a few ways to do this.

Sometimes an Ethernet board has the Ethernet address printed in its documentation or on the board itself. Pick a brand that does. You can waste more time and money trying to figure out the Ethernet address of an unfamiliar Ethernet board than the board is worth. This is another reason to standardize on one PC Ethernet adapter.

Some boards report their Ethernet address during the driver installation. Figure 8-2 shows the configuration utility for the 3C509 card. The utility is started by running **menu** from the 3COM configuration diskette. The configuration window shown in Figure 8-2 contains the Ethernet address.

These examples show how the client gets the physical address, but how does the UNIX server get the IP address that it uses in its response to the client? As usual, it gets it from you. The RARP server looks up the necessary information in the */etc/ethers* file. This file contains the PC's Ethernet address followed by the PC's hostname. Sample *ethers* file entries are shown below:

```
2:60:8c:48:84:49        hazel
0:0:c0:a1:5e:10         hickory
0:80:c7:aa:a8:04        acorn
8:0:5a:1d:c0:7e         cashew
8:0:69:4:6:31           pistachio
```

To respond to a RARP request, the server must also resolve the hostname found in the */etc/ethers* file into an IP address. Domain name service or the *hosts* file is used

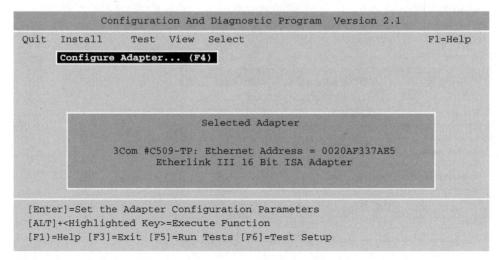

```
        Configuration And Diagnostic Program   Version 2.1

    Quit   Install      Test   View   Select                      F1=Help
    ┌─────────────────────────────┐
    │ Configure Adapter... (F4)   │
    └─────────────────────────────┘



              ┌──────────────────────────────────────────────┐
              │              Selected Adapter                │
              │                                              │
              │   3Com #C509-TP: Ethernet Address = 0020AF337AE5 │
              │        Etherlink III 16 Bit ISA Adapter      │
              │                                              │
              └──────────────────────────────────────────────┘

    [Enter]=Set the Adapter Configuration Parameters
    [ALT]+<Highlighted Key>=Execute Function
    [F1}=Help [F3]=Exit [F5]=Run Tests [F6]=Test Setup
```

Figure 8-2: Adapter Configuration Program

for this task. The following *hosts* file entries could be used with the *ethers* file shown above.

```
    hazel        128.66.3.10
    hickory      128.66.3.16
    acorn        128.66.3.4
    cashew       128.66.3.7
    pistachio    128.66.3.21
```

Because Sun systems that use NIS first look in the NIS map, the hostnames and IP addresses of RARP clients are traditionally put in the */etc/hosts* file, even when DNS is used. This is not required, but it is common practice. If you use NIS, build new maps whenever changes are made to the *ethers* file and to the *hosts* file, as in this example:

```
    # cd /var/yp
    # make ethers
    updated ethers
    pushed ethers
    # make hosts
    updated hosts
    pushed hosts
```

Given these sample configuration files, if *acorn* broadcasts an RARP request that contains its Ethernet address, 0:80:c7:aa:a8:0, the server finds the Ethernet address in the *ethers.byname* map. The server uses the name returned from that map to look up the IP address in the *hosts.byname* map. It then sends the IP address returned from that query back to *acorn*. Now *acorn* knows that its IP address is 128.66.3.4.

These examples show a Sun system being used as an RARP server. This is not necessary; any UNIX system can be used. In fact, a DOS PC can be used as an RARP
server. In the executable file RARPD.EXE, Novell's *LAN Workplace* provides RARP
server software that is very similar to the UNIX RARP server. RARPD.EXE reads
Ethernet address information from the file ETHERS found in the directory pointed
to by the PATH TCP_CFG command in the NET.CFG configuration file.[*] The
ETHERS file has the same format as the */etc/ethers* file shown above. RARPD.EXE
uses the HOSTS file or DNS to get the IP address just as the UNIX system did. Of
course, a DOS PC running as an RARP server is dedicated to that purpose and
can't be used for anything else. However, a PC can be a very inexpensive RARP
server for a small subnet.

RARP is a useful tool, but it only provides the IP address. There are still several
other values that need to be manually configured. One way to make RARP more
effective is to "pre-configure" the TCP/IP software for your PC users. This is possible because many of the configuration values are the same for every PC on a network. The IP address, which varies from system to system, is handled by RARP.
The values for the subnet mask, the default gateway, the list of name servers, and
the broadcast address can be defined in a configuration file on a disk you give to
the user. The user copies all of the files from the vendor installation disks, copies
this configuration file, and reboots the system without having to do any custom
configuration.

The following is a TCP/IP protocol section for a *LAN Workplace* NET.CFG file. It is
an example of a "pre-configuration" file that could be given to every PC user on
subnet 128.66.3.0:

```
Protocol TCPIP
     PATH TCP_CFG     C:\ETC
     ip_address       0.0.0.0
     ip_router        128.66.3.25
     ip_netmask       255.255.255.0
```

The section contains the information needed to configure a system on subnet
128.66.3.0 except for the IP address. Setting the IP address to 0.0.0.0 tells *LAN
Workplace* that the real address is provided via RARP. Other TCP/IP implementations have different ways to indicate that the IP address is to be obtained from a
configuration server. See Chapters 4 and 5 for additional examples.

This is great stuff, but even pre-configuration has its limits. Not every TCP/IP
implementation can be pre-configured. Many Windows implementations use setup
scripts that are not easy to alter. Another obvious limitation is that pre-
configuration is subnet specific. Each subnet has a different default gateway. Also,
the pre-configuration file must be written on a disk and delivered to each user.
This is no problem when only a small number of systems are involved but can be
troublesome for large networks. Large networks need a more flexible configuration

---

[*] The PATH TCP_CFG command is covered in Chapter 4.

tool that provides more values than just the IP address and can deliver those values via the network. BOOTP is the tool we need.

Bootstrap Protocol

Bootstrap Protocol (BOOTP) is defined in RFC 951. The RFC describes BOOTP as an alternative to RARP, and when BOOTP is used, RARP is not needed. BOOTP, however, is a more comprehensive configuration protocol than RARP. It provides much more configuration information, and it continues to evolve to provide ever more comprehensive information. The original specification allowed vendor extensions that have been a vehicle for the protocol's evolution. RFC 1048 formalized the definition of these extensions. Over time they have expanded to become the Dynamic Host Configuration Protocol (DHCP). More on DHCP later.

The BOOTP client broadcasts a single packet called a *BOOTREQUEST* packet that contains, at a minimum, the client's physical network address. The client sends the broadcast using the address 255.255.255.255, which is a special address called the *limited broadcast address.*[*] The client waits for a response from the server, and if one is not received within a specified time interval, the client retransmits the request. The server responds to the client's request with a *BOOTREPLY* packet.

BOOTP uses UDP as a transport protocol and, unlike RARP, it does not require any special *Network Access Layer* protocols. It uses two different well-known port numbers: UDP port number 67 is used for the server, and UDP port number 68 is used for the client. This is very unusual. Most software uses a well-known port on the server side and a randomly generated port on the client side.[†] The random port number ensures that each pair of source/destination ports identifies a unique path for exchanging information. A BOOTP client, however, is still in the process of booting; it may not know its IP address. Even if the client generates a source port for the *BOOTREQUEST* packet, a server response addressed to that port and the client's IP address won't be read by a client that doesn't recognize the address. Therefore BOOTP sends the response to a specific port on all hosts. A broadcast sent to UDP port 68 is read by all hosts, even by a system that doesn't know its specific address. The system then determines if it is the intended recipient by checking the physical network address embedded in the response.

The server fills in all of the fields in the packet for which it has data. There are many different values a server can provide. One of these is the location of a boot file, as BOOTP is designed to support diskless workstations. This function is not useful for PCs because they all have their own local disks, but many of the other values provided by BOOTP are very useful for configuring a PC. In the next section we look at how these configuration values are defined on a BOOTP server.

---

* This address is useful because, unlike the normal broadcast address, it doesn't require the system to know the address of the network it is on.
† How and why random source port numbers are used is described in *TCP/IP Network Administration.*

Creating a BOOTP Server

A UNIX system becomes a BOOTP server when it runs the BOOTP daemon (**bootpd**). Several versions of **bootpd** are available from many different sources on the Internet. The software used in this section is *bootp-2.4.0*. It was downloaded from the *usenet/comp.sources.unix/volume28/bootp-2.4.0* directory of *ftp.uu.net*. The source code is stored there as a collection of self-exploding shell scripts. Create a directory to receive them and download the scripts as binary files.

```
% mkdir bootp
% cd bootp
% ftp ftp.uu.net
Connected to ftp.uu.net.
220 ftp.UU.NET FTP server (Version wu-2.4(3) Fri Nov 25 1994) ready.
Name (ftp.uu.net:craig): anonymous
331 Guest login ok, send your complete e-mail address as password.
Password:
ftp> cd usenet/comp.sources.unix/volume28/bootp-2.4.0
250 CWD command successful.
ftp> binary
200 Type set to I.
ftp> prompt
Interactive mode off.
ftp> mget *.Z
200 PORT command successful.
...
226 Transfer complete.
ftp> quit
221 Goodbye.
```

Uncompress the scripts. Edit the files *part01*, *part02*, *part03*, and *part04*, removing all of the lines before the beginning of the shell script. Change the file permissions to make the scripts executable, and then run them to extract all of the BOOTP files.

```
% uncompress *.Z
% chmod 744 pa*
% vi part01
  Remove everything before #! /bin/sh
% vi part02
  Remove everything before #! /bin/sh
% vi part03
  Remove everything before #! /bin/sh
% vi part04
  Remove everything before #! /bin/sh
% part01
  shar: Extracting "Announce" (2382 characters)
...
shar: End of archive 1 (of 4).
You still need to unpack the following archives:
      2 3 4
% part02
shar: Extracting "Changes" (8535 characters)
```

```
...
shar: End of archive 2 (of 4).
You still need to unpack the following archives:
        3 4
% part03
shar: Extracting "bootpd.c" (33311 characters)
...
You still need to unpack the following archives:
        4
% part04
shar: Extracting "readfile.c" (47888 characters)
...
shar: End of archive 4 (of 4).
You have unpacked all 4 archives.
```

su to *root* and compile the server software with **make**. The *Makefile* has entry
points for several different UNIX architectures. (We use the *sunos4* entry point in
the example.) If the software compiles without errors, do a **make install** to install
the executable daemon in the */usr/etc* directory. Copy *bootpd.8* to the directory for
manual pages—usually */usr/man/man8*.

```
% su
Password:
# make sunos4
make SYSDEFS="-DSUNOS -DETC_ETHERS" ...
    .
    .
    .
# make install
for f in bootpd bootpef bootpgw bootptest ;\
do \
        /usr/bin/install -c -s $f /usr/etc ;\
done
# cp bootpd.8 /usr/man/man8
```

All network services should be defined in the */etc/services* file. Since you're adding
BOOTP to your system, you'll probably need to add an entry to */etc/services*. Add
the following lines if they are not already there:

```
bootps          67/udp                          # bootp server
bootpc          68/udp                          # bootp client
```

If you use yellow-pages, rebuild the map created by the */etc/services* file, as in this
Sun-specific example:

```
# cd /var/yp
# make services
updated services
pushed services
```

bootpd is now ready to run. There are two ways to run the BOOTP daemon: it
can be started at boot time from a startup script, or it can be started by the *Internet daemon*, **inetd**. If the server has a large number of clients that are frequently
rebooted, run **bootpd** from a startup file. Starting **bootpd** in this manner reduces

the amount of "startup" overhead because the daemon is only started once. These are sample lines for starting **bootpd** from the *rc.local* file on a Berkeley UNIX system:

```
if [ -f /usr/etc/bootpd -a -f /etc/bootptab ]; then
     bootpd -s;           echo -n ' bootpd'
fi
```

The code checks to make sure that the daemon and its configuration file are available. **bootpd** is then started with the **–s** switch. This switch tells **bootpd** not to time out if there is no activity on its port. The disadvantage of starting **bootpd** in this manner is that it continues to use system resources even when it is not needed. On most servers, **bootpd** is not started at boot time. It is started from **inetd**.

Instead of having a unique process running on every well-known port, one process, **inetd**, runs and listens to many ports. It starts the other daemons only when they are needed to process data. To start a daemon from **inetd**, place an entry for that daemon in the *inetd.conf* file. The *inetd.conf* file is explained in *TCP/IP Network Administration*, so we won't go into too much detail here. Basically the entry in the *inetd.conf* file tells **inetd** what port to listen to and what process to start if data arrives on that port. The entry for **bootpd** is:

```
bootps    dgram    udp wait root /usr/etc/bootpd    bootpd
```

This entry tells **inetd** to listen on the UDP port that is identified as bootps in the */etc/services* file, and if it hears data on that port, to run */usr/etc/bootpd* as user *root*. Once the line is added to the *inetd.conf* file, send a SIGHUP to **inetd** to force it to read the new configuration, as in this example:

```
# ps -acx | grep inetd
  200 ?  IW    0:00 inetd
# kill -HUP 200
```

The daemon is now installed, but that is only the beginning. The real challenge of managing a BOOTP server is providing the configuration information that the PCs need. The package we have installed is the BOOTP daemon from Carnegie Mellon University (CMU), which has its own unique configuration commands. Another BOOTP server implementation probably uses another command syntax for its configuration. However, the type of information provided by BOOTP is the same regardless of the implementation.

The CMU server reads its configuration from the */etc/bootptab* file. The syntax used in this file is very similar to the syntax of the */etc/termcap* and */etc/printcap* files. Each **bootpd** configuration parameter is two characters long and is separated from the other parameters by a colon. The general format of a *bootptab* entry is:

```
hostname:pa=value:pa=value:pa=value...
```

where *hostname* is the hostname of the PC client, *pa* is the two character parameter name, and *value* is the value assigned to that parameter for this client.

Newline characters separate each client's entry. If an entry spans multiple lines, the newline character at the end of each line must be escaped with a backslash (\). Comments in the *bootptab* file begin with a pound-sign (#). Table 8-1 contains a full list of the *bootptab* configuration parameters.

Table 8–1: bootptab Configuration Parameters

Parameter	Description	Example
bf	Bootfile	:bf=null
bs	Bootfile size	:bs=22050
cs	Cookie servers list	:cs=128.66.3.7
ds	Domain name servers list	:ds=128.66.35.5
gw	Gateways list	:gw=128.2.13.1
ha	Hardware address	:ha=7FF8100000AF
hd	Bootfile directory	:hd=/usr/boot
hn	Send hostname boolean	:hn
ht	Hardware type	:ht=ethernet
im	Impress servers list	:im=128.66.8.12
ip	Host IP address	:ip=128.66.11.1
lg	Log servers list	:lg=128.66.12.1
lp	LPR servers list	:lp=128.66.6.6
ns	IEN-116 name servers list	:ns=128.66.12.6
rl	Resource location servers	:rl=128.66.99.31
sm	Subnet mask	:sm=255.255.255.0
tc	Template continuation	:tc=default1
to	Time offset	:to=18000
ts	Time servers list	:ts=128.66.12.1
vm	Vendor magic cookie selector	:vm=auto
Tn	Vendor extension n	:T132="12345927AD3B"

Every parameter in Table 8-1 that has the word "list" in its description accepts a list of whitespace-separated values. For example, the name server list is defined using the ds parameter in this format: :ds=128.66.12.1 128.66.7.3:. One parameter in the table, hn, is a boolean. If it is specified, the server sends the *hostname* from the *bootptab* entry to the client. As a boolean, hn does not take any values, but all the other parameters do.

Use these parameters to configure TCP/IP for each PC on your network. The following sample *bootptab* file defines the domain name servers, the default routers, the Ethernet addresses, the hostnames, the IP addresses, the print servers, and the subnet masks for three different PCs. (Don't worry about the details yet; each command will be explained later.)

```
#  /etc/bootptab file for nuts.com
acorn:\
      :hd=/usr/boot:bf=null:\
```

```
        :ds=128.66.12.1 128.66.3.5:\
        :sm=255.255.255.0:\
        :lp=128.66.12.1:\
        :gw=128.66.3.25:\
        :ht=1:ha=0080c7aaa804:\
        :hn:ip=128.66.3.4:
peanut:\
        :hd=/usr/boot:bf=null:\
        :ds=128.66.12.1 128.66.3.5:\
        :sm=255.255.255.0:\
        :lp=128.66.12.1:\
        :gw=128.66.12.1:\
        :ht=1:ha=0800200159C3:\
        :hn:ip=128.66.12.2:
hickory:\
        :hd=/usr/boot:bf=null:\
        :ds=128.66.12.1 128.66.3.5:\
        :sm=255.255.255.0:\
        :lp=128.66.12.1:\
        :gw=128.66.3.25:\
        :ht=1:ha=0000c0a15e10:\
        :hn:ip=128.66.3.16:
```

Notice that much of the information is repetitive. All of the PCs use the same name servers, subnet masks, and print servers. PCs on the same subnets also use the same default routers. It is possible to define repetitive information in templates that are then referenced in individual client configurations. The following example uses a global template that defines the name servers, subnet masks, and print servers. The template is then referenced in each of the PC configurations by using the tc parameter.

```
#   /etc/bootptab file for nuts.com
defaults:\
        :hd=/usr/boot:bf=null:\
        :ds=128.66.12.1 128.66.3.5:\
        :sm=255.255.255.0:\
        :lp=128.66.12.1:\
        :hn:
acorn:\
        :tc=defaults:\
        :gw=128.66.3.25:\
        :ht=1:ha=0080c7aaa804:\
        :ip=128.66.3.4:
peanut:\
        :tc=defaults:\
        :gw=128.66.12.1:\
        :ht=1:ha=0800200159C3:\
        :ip=128.66.12.2:
hickory:\
        :tc=defaults:\
        :gw=128.66.3.25:\
        :ht=1:ha=0000c0a15e10:\
        :ip=128.66.3.16:
```

The first entry, defaults, is the template. The remaining entries are client entries. The template defines information used by all of the hosts, and the specific client entries define information unique to each host. Looking at the template and at one of the host entries shows a full configuration. The meaning of each parameter is described below:

defaults: \

> The name by which this template is referenced is defaults. A template can be assigned any name as long as it doesn't conflict with any hostname in the *bootptab* file.

:hd=/usr/boot:bf=null: \

> The first line of the defaults template defines the bootfile (bf) and the boot directory (hd). BOOTP clients can be diskless systems that boot from the server. The values provided by hd and bf are used by a diskless system to retrieve the boot image via Trivial File Transfer Protocol (TFTP). These are not used by PC clients but traditionally are defined to prevent any confusion. In the sample, the parameters intentionally point to a directory and file that do not exist.

:ds=128.66.12.1 128.66.3.5: \

> The ds parameter defines the IP addresses of the name servers used on this network.

:sm=255.255.255.0: \

> The sm parameter defines this network's subnet mask.

:lp=128.66.12.1: \

> This parameter defines the IP address of an **lpr** server that is available to every system on the network.

:hn:

> The hn parameter tells the server to send the hostname to the client. When this parameter is incorporated in the *peanut* entry as part of this template, the server sends the name *peanut* to the client. When it is incorporated in the entry for *acorn*, then the name *acorn* is sent. Because this is the last line in the defaults template it does not end with a backslash.

acorn: \

> The hostname associated with this client entry is *acorn*.

:tc=defaults: \

> This tc parameter tells **bootpd** to incorporate all of the information defined in the defaults template into this client entry. To use multiple templates in a client entry, include multiple tc parameters. Exclude an individual parameter from a template by specifying the parameter preceded by an at-sign (@). For example, to exclude the **lpr** server parameter provided by the defaults template from inclusion in the *acorn* configuration, add :@lp: to the *acorn* entry.

`:gw=128.66.3.25:\`

> The default gateway for this subnet is 128.66.3.25.

`:ht=1:ha=0080c7aaa804:\`

> The ht parameter identifies the type of hardware used for the client's network interface. The hardware type is identified by a number or by a keyword. Table 8-2 lists the acceptable hardware type numbers and keywords, and their meanings. The numbers used to identify the different types of network hardware are taken from the *Address Resolution Protocol Parameters* section of the *Assigned Numbers* RFC.

> The ha parameter defines the physical hardware address associated with the client's network interface. The example shows an Ethernet address. The type of address provided must be consistent with the hardware type defined by the ht parameter. These two parameters always appear together in a *bootptab* file.

`:ip=128.66.3.4:\`

> The IP address for this client is 128.66.3.4.

Table 8-2: Valid Hardware Types

Description	Number	Keyword
10Mb Ethernet	1	ethernet or ether
3Mb Ethernet	2	ethernet3 or ether3
AX.25 Amateur Radio	3	ax.25
ProNET Token Ring	4	pronet
Chaos	5	chaos
IEEE 802 Token Ring	6	token-ring or ieee802
ARCNET	7	arcnet

With only three PCs in the example, the benefit of using templates may not be immediately clear. The benefits of saving time, reducing typing, and avoiding errors are clearer when a large number of PCs are involved.

It is possible to configure a BOOTP server to handle a very large number of clients. However, when a large number of PCs rely on a single boot server, the server can be overwhelmed if all of the PCs attempt to boot at one time, as they might do in the case of a power outage. Most PC clients cache the configuration provided by the server in a local disk file, so they are not completely dependent on the server. And the BOOTP protocol includes back-off algorithms that avoid contention problems, but it is still possible for an overloaded server to cause a significant delay when booting its clients. One way to avoid problems is to have several boot servers. One server for each subnet is a good design because it eliminates the need to pass BOOTP information through a router, which requires a special router configuration. Low-cost boot servers can be built from PCs using products such as the BOOTP server from Distinct.

A PC-based Boot Server

Distinct sells a TCP/IP implementation for Windows, and their Windows orientation is very evident when configuring their BOOTP server. The server is easily configured using two dialogue boxes, but this ease of configuration has a price: you cannot control the configuration as completely as you can with the CMU server, and you cannot define an unlimited set of vendor extensions. However, the Distinct server works well for configuring PC clients.

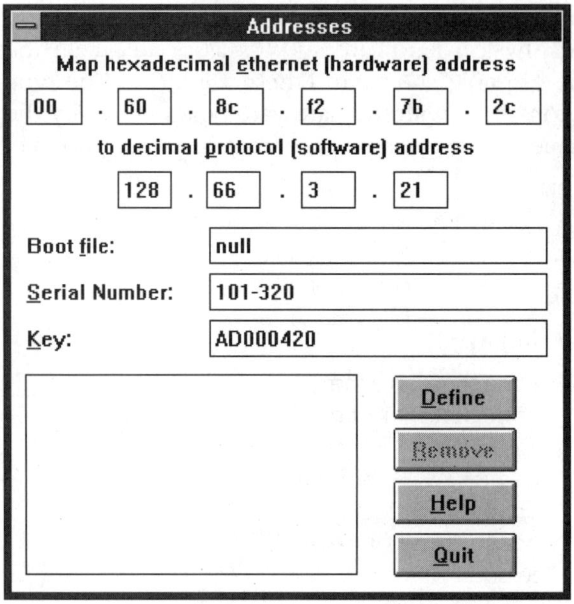

Figure 8-3: Distinct BOOTP: Assigning Addresses

To configure the Distinct server, select **Addresses** from the **Setup** menu in the BOOTP server window. The Addresses configuration window is shown in Figure 8-3. It handles the Ethernet to IP address mapping. It also has fields for identifying the boot file, the serial number, and authentication key. The boot file is not used by PCs, of course, and can be left blank or filled in with the name of a dummy file. The serial number and authentication key are used for license management. Unfortunately, these only work with clients that run Distinct TCP/IP.

The Networks box, which is also started from the **Setup** menu in the BOOTP server window, provides most of the information used to configure the clients. This box, shown in Figure 8-4, provides the network address, the subnet mask, the default router's address, and the name server's address.

BOOTP in all of its implementations provides an adequate set of configuration parameters, but the developers of TCP/IP protocols are not resting on their laurels. New protocols are being defined that provide even more configuration control.

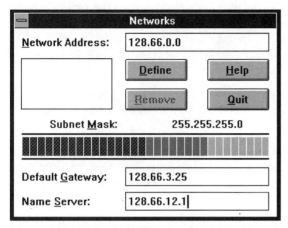

Figure 8–4: Distinct BOOTP: Configuration Parameters

DHCP

Dynamic Host Configuration Protocol (DHCP), defined in RFC 1541, is the latest generation of BOOTP. It is designed to be compatible with earlier versions; interactions between BOOTP clients and DHCP servers and between DHCP clients and BOOTP servers are outlined in RFC 1534. DHCP is only a proposed standard. Interoperability problems are possible, so it's best to use DHCP clients with DHCP servers.

DHCP uses the same UDP ports, 67 and 68, as BOOTP, and the same *BOOTREQUEST* and *BOOTREPLY* packet format. But DHCP is more than just an update of BOOTP. The new protocol expands the function of BOOTP in two areas:

- The configuration parameters provided by a DHCP server include everything defined in the *Requirements for Internet Hosts* RFC. DHCP provides a client with a complete set of TCP/IP configuration values.

- DHCP permits automated allocation of IP addresses.

DHCP uses the portion of the BOOTP packet originally set aside for vendor extensions to indicate the DHCP packet type and to carry a complete set of configuration information. DHCP calls the values in this part of the packet *options* instead of vendor extensions. This is a more accurate description because DHCP defines how the options are used and does not leave their definition up to the vendors. To handle the full set of configuration values from the *Requirements for Internet Hosts* RFC, the *options* field is expanded to 312 bytes from the original 64 bytes of the BOOTP *vendor extensions* field.

You don't usually need to use this full set of values to configure a PC. Don't get me wrong—the parameters are needed for a complete TCP/IP configuration; it's just that you don't need to define values for them. Default values are provided in most TCP/IP implementations, and the defaults only need to be changed in special circumstances. Frankly, you don't need most of the parameters defined by BOOTP (see Table 8-1), let alone any additional parameters. The expanded configuration parameters of DHCP make it a more complete protocol than BOOTP, but they are of only marginal value for configuring PCs.

For most network administrators automatic allocation of IP addresses is a more interesting feature. DHCP allows addresses to be assigned in three ways:

Manual allocation

> The network administrator keeps complete control over addresses by specifi- cally assigning them to clients. This is exactly the same way that addresses are handled under BOOTP.

Automatic allocation

> The DHCP server permanently assigns an address from a pool of addresses. The administrator is not involved in the details of assigning a client an address.

Dynamic allocation

> The server assigns an address to a DHCP client for a limited period of time. The client can return the address to the server at any time, but the client must request an extension from the server to retain the address longer than the time permitted. The server automatically reclaims the address after the lease expires if the client has not requested an extension.

Dynamic allocation is useful in a large distributed network where many PCs are being added and deleted. Unused addresses are returned to the pool of addresses without relying on users or system administrators to take action to return them. Addresses are only used when and where they're needed. Dynamic allocation allows a network to make the maximum use of a limited set of addresses.

DHCP servers can support BOOTP clients; however, a DHCP client is needed to take full advantage of the services offered by DHCP. At this writing, most TCP/IP implementations for PCs offer only RARP and BOOTP, but that is changing. The Microsoft version of TCP/IP used in Chapter 6 includes a DHCP client. Microsoft also provides a DHCP server for Windows NT 3.5, FTP Software provides one that runs under Windows, and Sun sells one as part of its SolarNet product. In the next section we configure the DHCP server that comes with Windows NT Server 3.5.

DHCP Server Configuration

DHCP is included in Windows NT Server 3.5. It is not installed during an *Express* installation, and for good reason. Dynamic address assignment makes it possible for multiple DHCP servers to assign the same IP address to different hosts. Care must be taken to ensure that the servers help each other and don't interfere with each other. The network administrator should control all DHCP server installations to avoid problems.

To install DHCP on an NT system, run *Network* from the *Control Panel* and then click the **Add Software** button. Select **TCP/IP Protocol And Related Components** from the Network Software listbox and click the **Continue** button. The window shown in Figure 8-5 appears.

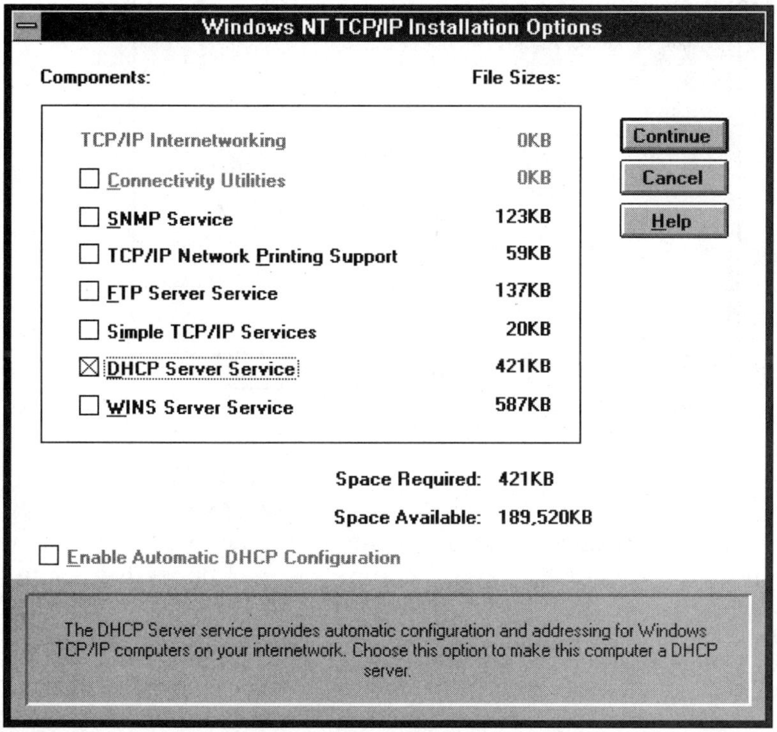

Figure 8-5: Installing DHCP Server Software

All of the items listed in Figure 8-5 in bold black type have not yet been installed. Check **DHCP Server Service** and click **Continue**. You'll be prompted for the correct path to the Windows NT distribution files, e.g., E:\I386. Click **OK** when the path is correct and the server software will load. To complete the installation, reboot the system when prompted. DHCP is now ready to be configured.

Start the *DHCP Manager* from the Network Administration group. A window similar to the one in Figure 8-6 is displayed.* The left side of the window lists all of the servers that the *DHCP Manager* knows about. It is possible to use the manager program to control remote servers. If the DHCP server you want to work with is not listed here, choose **Add** from the **Server** menu, and enter the remote server's IP address to add it to the DHCP Servers group box. In our example, however, we are interested in configuring the local server.

---

* Figure 8-6 shows the window after the manager has been configured. The first time you see this window, it may have much less information in it.

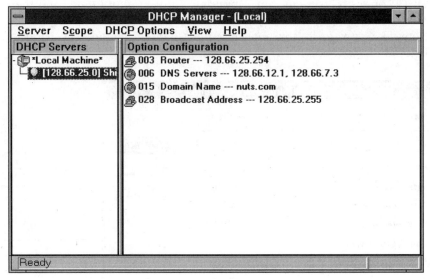

Figure 8-6: Windows NT DHCP Manager

The first configuration step is to define the range of addresses over which the server has configuration control. Microsoft calls this address group a *scope*. Highlight **Local Machine** and select **Create** from the **Scope** menu to pop up the configuration window shown in Figure 8-7. Use the boxes in the upper half of the window to define the pool of IP addresses controlled by this server. The range of addresses is defined by the Start Address and the End Address. In our example, it is an entire subnet (128.66.25.0) of the *nuts.com* network.

Define addresses that fall within this range, but are not included in the configuration control of this server, using the various boxes under the Exclusion Range section of the window. A few reasons to exclude addresses from configuration management are:

- *The addresses are already assigned.* You may be adding DHCP to an existing network where many addresses are already assigned. Excluding these addresses allows you to start using DHCP for new systems without having to wait until you get all of the older systems reconfigured. If you're lucky, addresses were assigned sequentially and are easy to exclude. In Figure 8-7, most previously-assigned addresses fall in the range 128.66.25.1 to 128.66.25.30. Individual addresses can also be excluded, as the Figure shows for 128.66.25.50 and 128.66.25.99.

- *The addresses are being used by another server.* To provide redundancy, it is useful to have some of the subnet's addresses available from a second server. That way, if the primary server is down when a PC requests an address assignment, the PC gets a valid address from the backup server. It's important to make sure, however, that the two servers cannot assign the same address. This

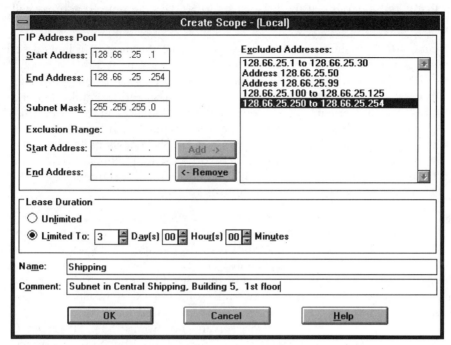

Figure 8-7: Creating the DHCP Scope

is done by creating a scope on the secondary server that is limited to a range of addresses excluded from the scope of the primary server. In Figure 8-7, addresses 128.66.25.100 to 128.66.25.125 are excluded for this reason.

- *The addresses are saved for future use.* You may wish to save some addresses for a special purpose. For example, you may want to save numbers for network equipment that you plan to purchase in the future. In the example, addresses 128.66.25.250 to 128.66.25.254 are excluded for future use.

To illustrate our point, the exclusions in Figure 8-7 are somewhat exaggerated. On your server, one contiguous block of excluded addresses may serve all of these purposes.

The *Lease Duration* block is used for automatic and dynamic address assignments. The DHCP server assigns a permanent address to any client that requests an address if *Unlimited* is checked. For dynamic address assignment, check *Limited To* and enter the length of time that the client may keep the address. Use a short lease duration if you have high demand for a limited set of addresses. Use a long lease if you have an abundance of addresses.

One reason to use dynamic addressing, even if you have an abundance of addresses, is to simplify moving equipment. When a PC moves to a new subnet it is dynamically assigned a new IP address by the server on that subnet. Its old address is returned to the pool of available addresses on its old server once the lease on that address expires. If the lease is set to 30 days, an unused address will not be out of circulation for more than a month.

In some circumstances, short duration leases help make the most of a limited set of addresses. Assume that you run the server for a sales group and that you set a short lease duration of 12 hours. This particular sales group has about half of its people out on the road at any one time. The address assigned to Frank's PC one day might be used by Norman's PC the next day when Frank is on the road. This, of course, assumes that Frank turns off his desktop system when he is out of the office. If the PC is left running on the network, it simply renews its lease on the address every 12 hours. Short duration leases work best if systems are frequently removed from the network (e.g., laptops that frequently dock and undock), or systems are shutdown whenever they are not in use.

It is easy to exaggerate the importance of dynamic address assignment because it is one of the most interesting features of DHCP. But dynamic addressing is not useful for all systems. It is generally useful only for systems that do not offer any services to remote users. Never use dynamic addressing to assign the address for a computer that users access by name. This includes file servers, print servers, domain name servers, login hosts, and even some UNIX workstations. Users access these systems by name, and the name is converted to an IP address by DNS. DNS gets the address from the DNS server—not from the DHCP server. If DHCP dynamically changes the address, the address returned by DNS is incorrect, and the users are not able to access the computer.* For that reason, all server systems are manually assigned premanent addresses that are placed in the DNS database. For most networks, manual address assignment is still the best solution.

To assign an address manually, highlight the scope from which the address will be taken and choose **Add Reservations** from the **Scope** menu. In the dialogue box that appears, enter the IP address, the client's MAC address (e.g., Ethernet address), the client's hostname, and optionally, a comment. Then click **Add**, followed by **Close**. Figure 8-8 shows the address reservation for a system named *boxes*.

It is not necessary to assign manual addresses in this manner; the address can simply be excluded from the server's scope to avoid address conflicts. However, reserving addresses, which is what the *DHCP Manager* calls manually assigning addresses, is useful. It avoids address conflicts as effectively as excluding the address, and it includes the address in the various management displays available through the *DHCP Manager*. DHCP is useful for networks that use manually assigned addresses because it allows the network manager to centralize that configuration task.

We have seen how addresses are assigned manually, automatically, and dynamically using the *DHCP Manager*, but address assignment is only part of the story.

---

* Proposals for a "dynamic DNS" that automatically learns of address changes are under consideration. Currently, there is no standard for a dynamic DNS.

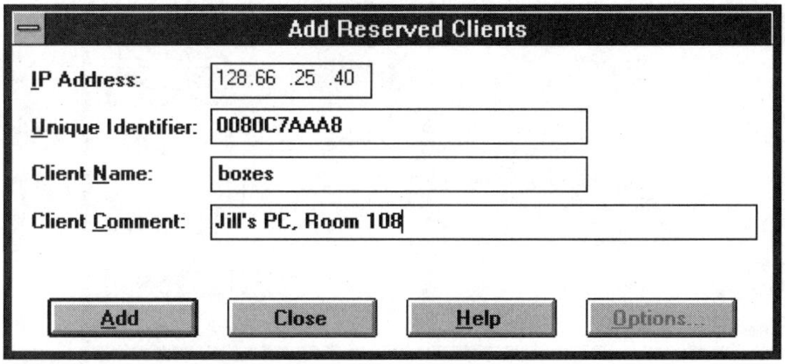

Figure 8-8: DHCP Address Reservations

We also want to be able to provide other TCP/IP configuration parameters. In DHCP terminology, these configuration parameters are called options.

DHCP Options

DHCP supports a large number of configuration parameters. The specific configuration values that are available are defined in RFC 1533. Most of these you'll never use, but they can all be set by the *DHCP Manager.** Configuration values can be set for:

- Global options that affect every system on the network

- Scope options that affect a group of systems (a scope)

- Options for individual systems that are identified by individual reserved IP addresses

To define global configuration parameters, select **Global** from the **Options** menu in the DHCP Managers window. Figure 8-9 shows the DHCP Options dialogue box. The Unused Options listbox contains a full list of DHCP configuration parameters. Highlight the parameter you want to configure and click the **Add** button. The selected option moves to the Active Options listbox. In Figure 8-9 we have selected the **DNS Servers** and the **Domain Name** options.

To set the value for an option, highlight the option in the Active Options listbox and click the **Value** button. A box for entering the value of the selected option will appear at the bottom of the DHCP Options window. A single IP address or a string value can be entered directly into the box. An option, such as DNS Servers, that requires a list of IP addresses causes the **Edit Array** button to appear. Click this button, and a dialogue box similar to the one shown in Figure 8-10 appears. Enter an IP address in the New IP Address box and click **Add**. When all addresses are entered, click **OK**.

---

* RFC 1533 is a only a proposed standard. Not every DHCP client or server supports all of these options.

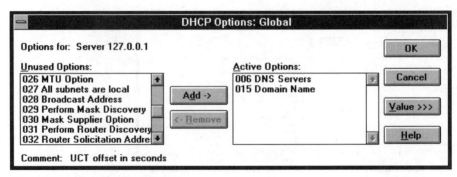

Figure 8-9: Defining DHCP Options

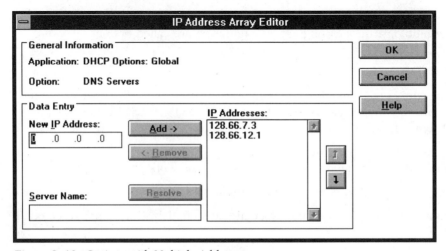

Figure 8-10: Options with Multiple Addresses

To define options for every host within an address scope, highlight the scope and select **Scope** from the **Options** menu. You'll see the same DHCP Option window that we used for global options. Setting values for scope options is identical to setting values for global options.

Setting configuration values for a reserved address is slightly more complicated. Highlight the scope that contains the reserved address and select **Active Leases** from the **Scope** menu in the DHCP Manager window. In the Active Leases window, highlight the individual address and click on **Properties**. In the Properties window, select the **Options** button. You'll then see the familiar DHCP Options window where you define values for these options in the same way as you did for global options.

Global options apply to every host, scope options apply to every host within the scope, and reserved address options apply to a single host using a specific address. The narrower the scope of an option, the higher its precedence. In other words, if the same option is defined for a reserved address and for the scope to which that address belongs, the value defined for the reserved address has precedence over the value defined for the scope. Additionally, if an option is defined for a scope and globally, the scope value takes precedence over the global value for addresses within the scope.

Once the options are defined they appear in the Option Configuration section of the DHCP Manager window (refer back to Figure 8-6). They are then available to the clients. Every value needed to configure a TCP/IP host can be defined in the DHCP server. Nothing needs to be done on the client except to indicate that it wishes to takes its configuration from the server. Examples in Chapter 6 show that this is simply a matter of checking the DHCP box in the IP address configuration window. The user is freed from the responsibility of configuring TCP/IP for his PC.

Managing Servers

Large networks have multiple configuration servers. As noted earlier, the servers are often distributed around the network with a server on every subnet. This improves booting efficiency, but it conflicts with the goal of central configuration control. The more servers, the more dispersed the control, and the more likely that a configuration error will occur. Implementing distributed servers requires a technique for maintaining central control and coordinating configuration information among the servers. TCP/IP offers several techniques for doing this.

Any file transfer protocol can be used to move configuration data, or any other kind of data, from a central system to a group of distributed systems. Either FTP or TFTP will work, but both of these protocols present difficulties when used in this way. FTP and TFTP are *interactive* protocols; both require multiple commands to retrieve a file, making them difficult to script. Additionally, FTP requires password authentication before it grants access to a file, and most security experts frown on storing passwords inside of scripts. For these reasons we don't concentrate on using these protocols to distribute the configuration file. Besides, if you know how to use FTP (and you should!), you know how to use it to send a configuration file.

Another possibility is to use *Network File System* (NFS) to distribute the information. NFS is a TCP/IP *file sharing* protocol that allows a server to *export* files that are then *mounted* by clients and used as if they are local files.[*] It is a powerful tool, but it does have limitations when used to distribute configuration information to boot servers. The same power outage that affects the distributed servers can cause the central server to crash. The distributed servers and their clients can be delayed in booting while they wait for the central server to come back online. Sharing a single copy of the configuration file conflicts with the effort to distribute boot services by putting too much reliance on the central server.

---

* NFS server configuration is discussed in Chapter 10.

One way to avoid this problem is for the distributed servers to periodically copy the configuration file from the mounted filesystem to a local disk. This is very simple to script, but it creates the possibility that the servers will be "out of synch." This may happen at times because the distributed servers copy the configuration file on a periodic schedule without knowing if the master file has been updated in the interim. Of course it is possible for all of the remote servers to export filesystems that the central server mounts. It is then possible for the central server to copy the configuration file directly to the remote filesystems whenever the master file is updated. However, there are easier ways to do this.

The UNIX **r**-commands provide the most popular methods for distributing the configuration file. Two different commands are used: **rcp** and **rdist**. The biggest problem with these commands is that they are not included in all TCP/IP implementations. However, if your server is a UNIX system, it will probably have the **r**-commands.

Remote copy (**rcp**) is simply a file transfer protocol. It has two advantages over FTP for this particular application: it is easy to script and it does not require a password. **rcp** is easy to script because only a single line is needed to complete a transfer. Here is an example of transferring the file *bootptab* from the master server to a remote server named *pistachio.nuts.com*:

```
# rcp /etc/bootptab pistachio.nuts.com:/etc/bootptab
```

For every remote server that the file is sent to, add a line like the one shown above to the procedure that updates the master configuration file. Using **rcp** is the easy part. Setting up the proper security for the **r**-commands takes a little more thought.

Instead of passwords, the UNIX **r**-commands use *trusted hosts* and *trusted users* for security. Trusted hosts are listed in the */etc/hosts.equiv* file. The users of any host listed in that file have "password-free" access to "like-named" accounts on the local host. For example, on *pistachio* the */etc/hosts.equiv* file contains the following lines:

```
almond.nuts.com
pecan.nuts.com
```

Assume that *pistachio* has a user account named *tyler*. These entries in the *hosts.equiv* file say that if someone is logged into *almond* or *pecan* under the username *tyler*, that person is granted the same access to *pistachio* as the local user *tyler*.* Furthermore, because *almond* and *pecan* are trusted hosts, the remote user is granted access without being required to provide a password. This works for every user account except *root*. Having an entry in the *hosts.equiv* file is not enough to grant a remote user root access, even if the user is logged into a trusted system as *root*. Root access requires an entry in the */.rhosts* file.

---

* This is the *same* access. If the local user *tyler* cannot write a file to the */etc* directory, a remote user *tyler* cannot **rcp** a file to that directory.

Entries in the */.rhosts* file look exactly the same as those in the *hosts.equiv* file. The difference is that entries in */.rhosts* explicitly grant remote users root access to the local host. If *pistachio* has the following entries in */.rhosts*, it grants root access to any person logged into *almond* as *root* and to anyone logged into *pecan* as *craig.*

```
almond.nuts.com
pecan.nuts.com craig
```

Most security experts discourage the use of the **r**-commands because they do not trust this form of security. One problem with *trusted host* security is that it is often set up incorrectly. A few guidelines may help you avoid mistakes:

- Never grant a host "trusted" status unless it is absolutely necessary. Start with empty *hosts.equiv* and */.rhosts* files, and add hosts to those files only when you're sure there is a good reason to do it.

- Never have a line in either file that contains only a plus-sign (+). A plus-sign grants trusted status to all remote systems. If you're on the Internet, this grants password-free access into your system from every system on that worldwide network. Not a good idea!

- Only grant trusted status to systems when you personally know the people who are responsible for the security of those systems. Make sure you really do have a reason to "trust" the remote system.

If you have more questions about this topic see *TCP/IP Network Administration* for a detailed description of **r**-command security.

The security implications of the **r**-commands are not all negative. Intruders stealing passwords from the network is a large and growing problem. Intruders steal passwords by using protocol analyzer software to capture login sequences. Most TCP/IP login sequences send the password across the network as clear text. The intruder captures the packet that contains the password and uses it later to break into the target system. The **r**-commands, however, do not send passwords across the network. Password authentication takes place on the trusted system, so it is not necessary to revalidate the password on the target system. For this reason, the **r**-commands are currently experiencing something of a renaissance among network administrators.

After *hosts.equiv* and */.rhosts* are configured, any **r**-command can be used. **rcp** is only one choice for distributing the central configuration file. **rdist**, while a little harder to use, is often a better choice because it has several features that make it particularly well suited for this application.

rdist

The *Remote File Distribution Program* (**rdist**) is designed to maintain identical copies of files on multiple hosts. A single **rdist** command can distribute several different files to many different hosts. It does this by following the instructions stored in an **rdist** configuration file called a *Distfile*.

The function of a *Distfile* is similar to that of the *Makefile* used by the **make** command, and it has a similar syntax and structure. Now don't panic! It's not that bad. The initial configuration of an **rdist** command is more difficult than the straightforward syntax of an **rcp** command, but the **rdist** command provides much more control and is much easier to maintain in the long run.

A *Distfile* is composed of *macros* and *primitives*. Macros can be assigned a single value or a list of values. If a list of values is used, the list is enclosed in parenthesis, e.g., *macro = (value value)*. Once assigned a value, the macro is referenced using the syntax ${*macro*}, where *macro* is the name of the macro. The other components of a *Distfile*, the primitives, are explained in Table 8-3.[*]

Table 8–3: rdist Primitives

Primitive	Description
install	Recursively updates files and directories
notify *address*	Sends error/status mail messages to *address*
except *file*	Omits *file* from the update
except_pat *pattern*	Omits filenames that match the pattern
special "*command*"	Executes *command* after each file update

The simpliest way to understand how the primitives and macros are combined to make a functioning *Distfile* is to look at a sample. The following configuration file distributes the current version of **bootpd** and the latest *bootptab* configuration file to the remote boot servers *pecan*, *pistachio*, and *cashew*:

```
HOSTS = ( pecan root@cashew pistachio )
FILES = ( /usr/etc/bootpd /etc/bootptab )

${FILES} -> ${HOSTS}
        install ;
        notify craig@almond.nuts.com
```

Let's look at each line of the file:

HOSTS = (pecan root@cashew pistachio)
:   This line defines a macro called HOSTS, that contains the hostname of each of the remote servers. Notice the entry for *cashew*; it tells **rdist** to login as *root* on *cashew* to perform the update. On *pecan* and *pistachio*, **rdist** will use the username under which it is running on the local host.

FILES = (/usr/etc/bootpd /etc/bootptab)
:   This macro defines the two files that will be sent.

${FILES} -> ${HOSTS}
:   The -> symbol has a special meaning to **rdist**. It tells **rdist** to copy the files named at the left of the symbol to the hosts named at the right. In this case,

---

[*] For more details, see the **rdist** man page.

FILES contains the filenames */usr/etc/bootpd* and */etc/bootptab*, and HOSTS contains the hostnames *pecan*, *cashew*, and *pistachio*. This command tells *rdist* to copy two files to three different hosts. Any primitives that follow apply to this file-to-host mapping.

`install ;`

> The `install` primitive explicitly tells **rdist** to copy the specified files to the specified hosts if the corresponding file is "out-of-date" on the remote host. A file is considered to be "out-of-date" if the creation date or the size is not the same as the master file. The semicolon at the end of this line indicates that another primitive follows.

`notify craig@almond.nuts.com`

> Status and error messages are to be mailed to *craig@almond.nuts.com*.

Additional files and hosts can be easily added to this file. In the long run, most people find **rdist** the simplest way to distribute multiple files to multiple hosts.

One final note: the configuration file does not have to be called *Distfile*. Any filename can be specified on the **rdist** command line using the **−f** option. For example, the *Distfile* shown above could be saved under the name *bootp.dist* and invoked with the following command:

```
% rdist -f bootp.dist
```

Summary

Many configuration values are needed to install TCP/IP on a PC. These values can be provided by a configuration server. Two protocols are popular for distributing configuration information to PCs:

RARP

> *Reverse Address Resolution Protocol* tells a client its IP address. The RARP server does this by mapping the client's Ethernet address to its IP address. The Ethernet-to-IP address mappings are stored on the server in the */etc/ethers* file.

BOOTP

> *Bootstrap Protocol* provides a wide range of configuration values to the PC client. Each implementation of BOOTP has a different configuration file and command syntax. The CMU BOOTP server stores configuration parameters in the */etc/bootptab* file and uses a syntax very similar to the */etc/printcap* syntax covered in Chapter 10.

New configuration protocols are being developed. *Dynamic Host Configuration Protocol* (DHCP) extends BOOTP to provide the full set of configuration parameters defined in the *Requirements for Internet Hosts* RFC. It also provides for *dynamic address* allocation, which allows a network to make maximum use of a limited set of addresses.

Large networks use distributed boot servers to avoid overloading a single server and to avoid sending boot parameters through IP routers. The configuration files on distributed boot servers are kept synchronized through file transfer, NFS file sharing, or the *Remote File Distribution Program* (**rdist**).

Boot servers provide basic configuration information such as hostnames, IP addresses, subnet masks, default routes, etc. Basic TCP/IP configuration is just the beginning. Users are more interested in the applications that run on the network than they are in the basic network software. In the next chapter we move from configuring the underlying TCP/IP protocols to configuring the most important network application—electronic mail.

9

Personal Email

Most users consider electronic mail the most important network application because it is crucial to their daily communications. Some applications are newer and fancier. Other applications consume more network bandwidth. Others are more important for the continued operation of the network. But mail is the application people use to communicate with each other. Like the telephone, email isn't very fancy, but it's vital. Also like the telephone, people expect it to work.

You must plan a reliable, flexible email system that meets the needs of your users if you want a happy user community. To plan effectively you need some background information about how mail works and how mail systems are designed.

Internet Mail Protocols

Only a few protocols are commonly used to build a TCP/IP electronic mail network: *Simple Mail Transfer Protocol* (SMTP), *Post Office Protocol* (POP), and *Multipurpose Internet Mail Extensions* (MIME). These aren't the only mail protocols around. *Interactive Mail Access Protocol*, defined in RFC 1176, is an experimental protocol designed to supplant POP. It provides remote text searchs and message parsing features not found in POP. *PCMAIL*, defined in RFC 1056, is a protocol designed to create a PC-based distributed mail system. These and other protocols have some very interesting features, but they are not yet widely implemented. Our coverage sticks to the three protocols you are most likely to use building your network: SMTP, POP, and MIME. We start with SMTP, which is the foundation of all TCP/IP email systems.

Simple Mail Transfer Protocol

SMTP is the TCP/IP mail delivery protocol. It moves mail across the Internet and across your local network.[*] It runs over the reliable, connection-oriented service provided by *Transmission Control Protocol* (TCP), and it uses *well known port number 25.*[†] Table 9-1 lists some of the simple, human readable commands used by SMTP.

Table 9-1: SMTP Commands

Command	Syntax	Function
Hello	**HELO** <*sending-host*>	Identify sending SMTP
From	**MAIL FROM:**<*from-address*>	Sender address
Recipient	**RCPT TO:**<*to-address*>	Recipient address
Data	**DATA**	Begin a message
Reset	**RSET**	Abort a message
Verify	**VRFY** <*string*>	Verify a username
Expand	**EXPN** <*string*>	Expand a mailing list
Help	**HELP** [*string*]	Request online help
Quit	**QUIT**	End the SMTP session

SMTP is such a simple protocol you can literally do it yourself. **telnet** to port 25 on a remote host and type mail in from the command line using the SMTP commands. This technique is sometimes used to test a remote system's SMTP server, and is convenient for illustrating how mail is delivered between systems. The example below shows mail manually input from Daniel on *peanut.nuts.com* to Tyler on *almond.nuts.com.*

```
% telnet almond.nuts.com 25
Trying 128.66.12.1 ...
Connected to almond.nuts.com.
Escape character is '^]'.
220 almond Sendmail 4.1/1.41 ready at Tue, 29 Mar 94 17:21:26 EST
helo peanut.nuts.com
250 almond Hello peanut.nuts.com, pleased to meet you
mail from:<daniel@peanut.nuts.com>
250 <daniel@peanut.nuts.com>... Sender ok
rcpt to:<tyler@almond.nuts.com>
250 <tyler@almond.nuts.com>... Recipient ok
data
354 Enter mail, end with "." on a line by itself
Hi Tyler!
.
250 Mail accepted
```

---

[*] SMTP is defined in RFC 821, *A Simple Mail Transfer Protocol.*
[†] Most standard TCP/IP applications are assigned a *well known port* in the *Assigned Numbers* RFC, so that remote systems know how to connect the service.

```
quit
221 almond delivering mail
Connection closed by foreign host.
```

The user input is shown in bold type; all of the other lines are output from the system. Given the fear that email configuration inspires, it's surprising how simple the protocol is. A TCP connection is opened. The sending system identifies itself. The *From* address and the *To* address are provided. The message transmission begins with the **DATA** command and ends with a line that contains only a period (.). The session terminates with a **QUIT** command. Very simple and very few commands are used. (Unfortunately, this simple exchange isn't the whole story.)

There are other commands (**SEND**, **SOML**, **SAML**, and **TURN**) defined in RFC 821 that are optional and not widely implemented. Even some of the commands that are implemented are not commonly used. The commands **HELP**, **VRFY**, and **EXPN** are designed more for interactive use than for the normal machine-to-machine interaction used by SMTP. The following excerpt from an SMTP session shows how these odd commands work.

```
HELP
214-Commands:
214-   HELO    MAIL    RCPT    DATA    RSET
214-   NOOP    QUIT    HELP    VRFY    EXPN
214-For more info use "HELP <topic>".
214-For local information contact postmaster at this site.
214 End of HELP info
HELP RSET
214-RSET
214-    Resets the system.
214 End of HELP info
VRFY <jane>
250 <jane@brazil.nuts.com>
VRFY <mac>
250 Kathy McCafferty <<mac>>
EXPN <admin>
250-<sara@pecan.nuts.com>
250 David Craig <<david>>
250-<tyler@nuts.com>
```

The **HELP** command prints out a summary of the commands implemented on the system. The **HELP RSET** command specifically requests information about the RSET command. Frankly, this help system isn't very helpful!

The **VRFY** and **EXPN** commands are more useful, but are often disabled for security reasons because they provide user account information that might be exploited by network intruders. The **EXPN <admin>** command asks for a listing of the email addresses in the mailing list *admin*, which the system provides. The **VRFY** command asks for information about an individual instead of a mailing list. In the case of the **VRFY <mac>** command, *mac* is a local user account, and the user's account information is returned. In the case of **VRFY <jane>**, *jane* is an alias in the */etc/aliases* file. The value returned is the email address for *jane* found in that file. **HELP**, **VRFY**, and **EXPN** are interesting but rarely used. SMTP depends on the other commands to get the real work done.

SMTP provides direct end-to-end mail delivery. This is unusual. Most mail systems use *store and forward* protocols like UUCP and X.400 that move mail toward its destination one hop at a time, storing the complete message at each hop and then forwarding it on to the next system until final delivery is made. Figure 9-1 illustrates both store and forward and direct delivery mail systems. The UUCP address clearly shows the path that the mail takes to its destination, while the SMTP mail address implies direct delivery.[*]

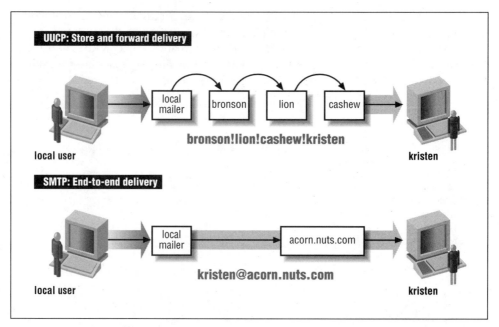

Figure 9–1: Mail Delivery Systems

Direct delivery allows SMTP to deliver mail without relying on intermediate hosts. If the delivery fails, the local system knows it right away. It may inform the user that sent the mail, or queue the mail for later delivery without relying on remote systems. The disadvantage of direct delivery is that it requires both systems to be fully capable of handling mail. Sometimes that's not true, particularly in the case of small systems such as PCs. PCs are usually shut down at the end of the day. Mail directed from a remote host to a PC will fail with a "cannot connect" error when the PC is turned off. To handle these cases, mail can be routed to a mail server in lieu of direct delivery. When a mail server is used, a protocol is needed to move mail from the server to the PC desktop system. Most TCP/IP networks use POP.

---

* The address doesn't have anything to do with whether or not a system is store and forward or direct delivery. It just happens that UUCP provides an address that helps to illustrate this point.

Post Office Protocol

A PC user can connect to the mail server via Telnet, and read mail using the PC as a terminal. This is a very common technique, particularly for DOS systems. However, it is often desirable to move the mail from the server to the desktop where it can be read using full-featured, user-friendly PC software. The *Post Office Protocol* is used to transfer the contents of the user's mailbox from the server to the users desktop.

There are two versions of POP in widespread use: POP2 and POP3. POP2 is defined in RFC 937; it uses port 109. POP3 is defined in RFC 1725; it uses port 110. These are incompatible protocols that use different commands, but they perform the same basic functions. The POP protocols verify the PC user's login name and password, and move the user's mail from the server to the PC where it is read using a local PC mail reader.

A sample POP2 session illustrates how a POP protocol works. POP2 is a simple protocol, and just as with SMTP, you can type POP2 commands directly into its well known port (109) and observe their effect. Here's an example with the user input shown in bold type:

```
% telnet almond.nuts.com 109
Trying 128.66.12.1 ...
Connected to almond.nuts.com.
Escape character is '^]'.
+ POP2 almond POP2 Server at Wed 30-Mar-94 3:48PM-EST
HELO hunt WatsWatt
#3   ...(From folder 'NEWMAIL')
READ
=496
RETR
   The full text of message 1
ACKD
=929
RETR
   The full text of message 2
ACKD
=624
RETR
   The full text of message 3
ACKD
=0
QUIT
+OK POP2 Server exiting (0 NEWMAIL messages left)
Connection closed by foreign host.
```

The **HELO** command provides the username and password for the account of the mailbox that is being retrieved. (This is the same username and password used to log into the mail server.) In response to the **HELO** command, the server sends a count of the number of messages in the mailbox, three (#3) in our example. The **READ** command begins reading the mail. **RETR** retrieves the full text of the current message. **ACKD** acknowledges receipt of the message and deletes it from the server. After each acknowledgement the server sends a count of the number of bytes in the new message. If the byte count is zero (=0), there are no more messages to be retrieved, and the PC ends the session with the **QUIT** command. Table 9-2 lists the full set of POP2 commands.

Table 9–2: POP2 Commands

Command	Syntax	Function
Hello	**HELO** *user password*	Identify user account
Folder	**FOLD** *mail-folder*	Select mail folder
Read	**READ** [*n*]	Read mail, optionally start with message *n*
Retrieve	**RETR**	Retrieve message
Save	**ACKS**	Acknowledge and save
Delete	**ACKD**	Acknowledge and delete
Failed	**NACK**	Negative acknowledgement
Quit	**QUIT**	End the POP2 session

The commands for POP3 are completely different than the commands used for POP2. Table 9-3 shows the set of POP3 commands defined in RFC 1725.

Table 9–3: POP3 Commands

Command	Function
USER *username*	The user's account name
PASS *password*	The user's password
STAT	Display the number of unread messages/bytes
RETR *n*	Retrieve message number *n*
DELE *n*	Delete message number *n*
LAST	Display the number of the last message accessed
LIST [*n*]	Display the size of message *n* or of all messages
RSET	Undelete all messages; reset message number to 1
TOP *n l*	Print the headers and *l* lines of message *n*
NOOP	Do nothing
QUIT	End the POP3 session

Despite the fact that these commands are different from those used by POP2, they can be used to perform similar functions. In the POP2 example we logged into the server and read and deleted three mail messages. Here's a similar session using POP3:

```
% telnet almond 110
Trying 128.66.12.1 ...
Connected to almond.nuts.com.
Escape character is '^]'.
```

```
+OK almond POP3 Server Process 3.3(1) at Mon 15-May-95 4:48PM-EDT
user hunt
+OK User name (hunt) ok. Password, please.
pass Watts?Watt?
+OK 3 messages in folder NEWMAIL (V3.3 Rev B04)
stat
+OK 3 459
retr 1
+OK 146 octets
   The full text of message 1
dele 1
+OK message # 1 deleted
retr 2
+OK 155 octets
   The full text of message 2
dele 2
+OK message # 2 deleted
retr 3
+OK 158 octets
   The full text of message 3
dele 3
+OK message # 3 deleted
quit
+OK POP3 almond Server exiting (0 NEWMAIL messages left)
Connection closed by foreign host.
```

Naturally you don't type these commands in yourself; your PC mail program sends the server a string of commands very similar to the ones shown in the example above when processing your mail. Experiencing hands-on interaction with SMTP and POP gives you a clearer understanding of what these programs do and why you need them.

Multipurpose Internet Mail Extensions

The last protocol on our quick tour is MIME. As its name implies, *Multipurpose Internet Mail Extensions* is an extension of the existing TCP/IP mail system, not a replacement for it. MIME is more concerned with what the mail system delivers than it is with the mechanics of delivery. It doesn't attempt to replace SMTP or TCP; it extends the definition of what constitutes "mail."

The structure of the mail message carried by SMTP is defined in RFC 822, *Standard for the Format of ARPA Internet Text Messages*. RFC 822 defines a set of mail headers that are widely accepted and used by many non-SMTP mail systems. RFC 822 thus provides a common ground for mail translation and delivery between different mail networks. MIME extends RFC 822 into two areas:

• Support for various data types. The mail system defined by RFC 821 and RFC 822 can only transfer 7-bit ASCII data. This is suitable for carrying text data composed of US ASCII characters, but it does not support several languages that have different character sets, and it does not support binary data transfer.

- Support for complex message bodies. RFC 822 does not provide a detailed description of the body of an electronic message; it concentrates on the mail headers.

MIME addresses these two weaknesses by defining encoding techniques for carrying various forms of data and by defining a structure for the message body that allows multiple objects to be carried in a single message. The RFC 1521, *MIME (Multipurpose Internet Mail Extensions) Part One: Mechanisms for Specifying and Describing the Format of Internet Message Bodies*, defines two headers that give structure to the mail message body and allow it to carry various forms of data. These are the *Content-Type* header and the *Content-Transfer-Encoding* header.

As the name implies, the Content-Type header defines the type of data being carried in the message. The header has a *subtype* field that refines the definition. The number of supported data types is expected to grow as new data formats appear and are used in message transmissions. The RFC defines seven initial content types:

text

> Text data. The only subtype defined for text is *plain*. Plain text is simply unformatted text data.

application

> Binary data. The primary subtype is *octet-stream*, which indicates the data is a stream of 8-bit binary bytes. One other subtype, *PostScript*, is also defined in RFC 1521. Other subtypes will probably be defined in the future.

image

> Still graphic images. Two subtypes are defined: *jpeg* and *gif*. Both of these subtypes are widely used image data standards.

video

> Moving graphic images. The initially defined subtype is *mpeg*, which is a widely used standard for computer video data.

audio

> Audio data. The only subtype defined for audio is *basic*, which means the sounds are encoded using pulse code modulation (PCM).

multipart

> Data composed of multiple independent sections. A multipart message body is made up of several independent parts. The primary subtype is *mixed*, which means that each part of the message can be data of any content type. Other subtypes are: *alternative*, meaning that the same data is repeated in each section in different formats; *parallel*, meaning that the data in the various parts is to be viewed simultaneously; and *digest*, meaning that each section is data of the type *message*.

message

> Data that is an encapsulated mail message. The primary subtype, *rfc822*, indicates that the data is a complete RFC 822 mail message. The other subtypes, *partial* and *External-body*, are both designed to handle large messages. *partial* allows large encapsulated messages to be split among multiple MIME messages. *External-body* points to an external source (like an FTP archive) for the contents of a large message body, so that only the pointer, not the message itself, is contained in the MIME message

The Content-Transfer-Encoding header identifies the type of encoding used on the data. Traditional SMTP systems only forward 7-bit ASCII data with a line length of less than 1000 bytes. To ensure that the data from a MIME system is forwarded through gateways that may only support 7-bit ASCII, the data can be encoded. RFC 1521 defines six types of encoding. Some types are used to identify the encoding inherent in the data. Only two types are actual encoding techniques defined in the RFC. The six encoding types are:

7bit

> US ASCII data. No encoding is performed on 7-bit ASCII data.

8bit

> Octet data. No encoding is performed. The data is binary, but the lines of data are short enough for SMTP transport, i.e., the lines are less than 1000 bytes long.

binary

> Binary data. No encoding is performed. The data is binary, and the lines may be longer than 1000 bytes. There is no difference between *binary* and *8bit* data except the line length restriction; both types of data are unencoded byte (octet) streams. MIME does not handle unencoded bit stream data.

quoted-printable

> Encoded text data. This encoding technique handles data that is largely composed of printable ASCII text. The ASCII text is sent unencoded while bytes with a decimal value greater than 127 or less than 33 are sent encoded as strings made up of an equal sign followed by the hexadecimal value of the byte. For example, the ASCII form-feed character, which has the hexadecimal value of 0C, is sent as =0C. Naturally there's more to it than this—the literal equal sign is sent as =3D; the newline at the end of each line is not encoded; etc.—but this is the general idea of how *quoted-printable* data is sent.

base64

> Encoded binary data. This encoding technique can be used on any byte stream data. Three octets of data are encoded as four 6-bit characters, which increases the size of the file by one-third. The 6-bit characters are a subset of US ASCII chosen because they can be handled by any type of mail system. The maximum line length for *base64* data is 76 characters. Figure 9-2 illustrates this 3-to-4 encoding technique.

x-token

> Specially encoded data. It is possible for software developers to define their own private encoding techniques. If they do so, the name of the encoding technique must begin with' X–. Private encodings are strongly discouraged because they limit interoperability between mail systems.

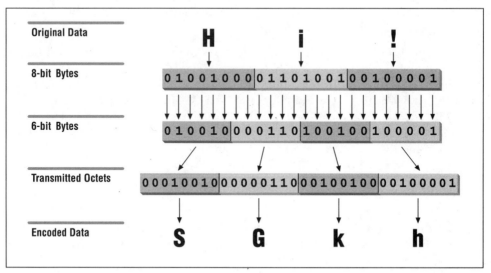

Figure 9–2: BASE64 Encoding

MIME defines data types that SMTP was not designed to carry. To handle these and other future requirements, RFC 1425, *SMTP Service Extensions*, defines a technique for making SMTP *extensible*. The RFC does not define new services for SMTP; in fact the only service extensions mentioned in the RFC are the optional services such as SOML and TURN that are defined in RFC 821. What this RFC does define is a simple mechanism for systems to negotiate which SMTP extensions are supported. The RFC defines a new *hello* command (**EHLO**) and the legal responses to that command. One response is for the receiving system to return a list of the SMTP extensions it supports. This response allows the sending system to know what extended services can be used, and to avoid those that are not implemented on the remote system. SMTP implementations that support the **EHLO** command are call Extended SMTP (ESMTP).

Two ESMTP service extensions have been defined for MIME mailers: **8BITMIME**, defined in RFC 1652, and **SIZE**, defined in RFC 1653. The **SIZE** extension allows the sending system to find out, before attempting delivery, how large a message the remote system can accept. This is not a MIME-specific service, but the potentially enormous size of a video image or other binary message is the major motivation for this service. The other service extension, **8BITMIME**, is obviously a MIME-specific extension. It indicates that the receiving system can accept MIME data whose Content-Transfer-Encoding type is *8bit*, which is unencoded binary data. If the receiving system cannot accept 8-bit data, the MIME data should be encoded before it is sent. These two service extensions are just the beginning. Undoubtedly more will be defined to support MIME and other SMTP enhancements.

MIME is important for a PC network because it provides a standard way to transfer non-ASCII data through email. PC users share lots of application-specific data, such as Lotus spreadsheets and Word Perfect documents, that are not 7-bit ASCII. PC users depend on email as a file transfer mechanism more than UNIX users, who are more likely to use FTP, **rcp**, or some other service. An example of how MIME is used to transfer a binary file is shown later in this chapter.

SMTP, POP, and MIME will be a part of the mail system you design, but other protocols will also be needed in the future. The one thing that is certain is that the network will continue to change. You need to track the current developments and include helpful technologies into your planning. In the next section we plan a TCP/IP email network using SMTP, POP, and MIME.

Planning Your Mail System

Our goal is to create a reliable, flexible electronic mail system. The system should provide service to everyone inside the organization and the ability to reach the people outside that the users need to contact. Users shouldn't have to change the email address on their business cards every time they change offices or PCs. They should have full mail access even when on travel or working at home. Reality may fall short of these goals, but this is what we work toward.

Most PC email networks are server-based systems, because servers improve reliability. It is possible to create a peer-to-peer email network in which every PC directly sends and receives its own mail. However, relying on each user's PC to deliver and collect the mail only works if the number of PCs is small enough for you to administer them personally, or the users are technically skilled enough to administer the systems on their own. Most networks use a server so that only one system needs to be properly configured for the mail to go through.

The terminology that describes email servers is vague. In part this is because all of the server functions usually occur in one computer, and all of the terms are used interchangeably to refer to that system. For the purposes of organizing this text we need to differentiate between these functions, but we expect you will do all of these tasks on one machine. We use these terms in the following manner:

mail server
> The mail server, sometimes called a mailbox server, is a system that collects incoming mail for other computers on the network. It is usually a multi-user system that supports logins as well as POP so that the widest range of PC users can read their mail as they see fit. A UNIX system is the most popular server choice for a TCP/IP email network. All of our examples assume that a UNIX system running *sendmail* is used.

mail relay

A mail relay is a host that forwards mail between internal systems and from internal systems to remote hosts. Mail relays allow internal systems to have simple mail configurations because only the relay host needs to have software to handle special mail-addressing schemes and aliases.

mail gateway

A mail gateway is a system that forwards email between dissimilar systems. You don't need a gateway to go from one Internet host to another because both systems use SMTP. You do need a gateway to go from SMTP to X.400 or to a proprietary mailer, like *cc:mail* or Microsoft *Mail*.

The mail server is the most important component of a reliable system because it eliminates reliance on the user's PC. A centrally controlled, professionally operated server collects the mail regardless of whether or not the user's PC is operational.

The relay host also contributes to the reliability of the email system. If mail cannot be immediately delivered by the relay host it is queued and processed later. PC systems also queue mail, but if the PC is shut down for the night, no attempts can be made to deliver queued mail until the PC is restarted in the morning. The mail server and the mail relay are operated 24 hours a day.

Mail gateways are only needed to communicate with systems that don't use SMTP. Occasionally you may be responsible for converting mail to a format that a remote non-SMTP system can accept, but generally this is not your problem. Most remote systems are able to convert their mail into SMTP for you. SMTP is the *lingua franca* of electronic mail. Therefore, most proprietary mail systems offer tools to convert to SMTP, and most public networks have gateways to the Internet that perform the conversion.

A more common problem is dealing with local systems that don't speak SMTP. The best approach for a local network is to standardize on one mail system, but that is not always possible. The network administrator usually doesn't have enough influence to get the organization to standardize on SMTP, even if it is the best idea. Sometimes you have to deal with a department that uses a proprietary mail system and will not change to be compatible with the rest of the network. In that case, a simple choice is to buy the SMTP gateway from the proprietary mail system vendor. All of the major email vendors have SMTP gateways.

The design of most TCP/IP email networks is based on the following guidelines:

- Use a mail server to collect mail for all PC users. Promote the use of POP for delivering mail to the desktop.

- Use a mail relay host to forward mail from the PCs. Implement a simplified email address scheme on the relay host.

- Standardize on TCP/IP and SMTP. Users who insist on using a proprietary email system should be responsible for obtaining and configuring an SMTP mail gateway for that system in order to connect to your TCP/IP email network.

- Standardize on MIME for binary attachments. Avoid proprietary attachment schemes; they just cause confusion when the users of Brand X email cannot read attachments received from Brand Y.

Our sample design is based on these guidelines. Figure 9-3 illustrates the structure and shows how it differs from the configuration of a network based on UNIX workstations. The solid lines connecting the PCs show their reliance on the server while the dotted line between the workstation and the server shows that it is less dependent on the server. In a UNIX environment, the mail server plays a more limited role. It is not needed as a mailbox server for these systems; the UNIX workstations are fully capable of handling their own mail delivery. But it does simplify the configuration of UNIX clients by handling complex addressing and mail forwarding for them. PCs, on the other hand, rely on the mail server. They read mail from the server and pass outgoing mail through it. In most networks, PCs do not act as standalone mail systems.

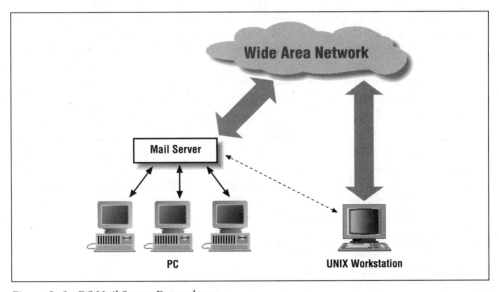

Figure 9-3: PC Mail Server Dependence

The following sections contain examples of implementing a TCP/IP email system based on these principles. We start by configuring the mail server.

Configuring a Mail Server

Two things are necessary for a mail server to operate effectively. First, the server must be known to the world as the place where mail bound for the user is actually delivered. Second, the server and the PC must be properly configured to move mail to the PC when the user is ready to read it. For users who login to the server directly, these two elements occur as a matter of course. The login user's advertised email address is the server, so naturally mail is sent to the server without any special configuration. Also, because the login user reads the mail directly on the server, no extra protocol is needed to move the mail to the user's PC. This scheme works, but takes no advantage of the user's PC. We won't consider this type of user in our discussion. Any book on UNIX system administration tells you how to create all of the things necessary for a login user account.[*] Our interest is in setting up a system that advertises itself as the mail server, collects incoming mail, and sends it to the PC when the user wants it.

The MX Record

A *Mail Exchange* (MX) record is used to advertise the mail server to the outside world. The MX record is a standard part of domain name service that redirects mail addressed to one host to another host.[†] That is exactly what we want to do: redirect mail that is addressed to a PC to a mail server. Every system that wishes to route its mail to the mail server should have an explicit MX record associated with its name in the DNS database.

While every host in the domain database should have its own MX record, an MX record should also be assigned to the entire domain. The MX record assigned to the domain permits simplified addressing in the form of *user@domain*. Simplified addressing depends heavily on the use of email aliases, which are covered in the section on mail relays. The MX record used for simplified addressing is also covered there. This section concentrates on the general configuration of a server to receive mail that is addressed to another host.

The sample below shows an MX entry:

```
peanut.nuts.com.   IN  MX  10 almond.nuts.com.
```

This record says to redirect mail addressed to *peanut.nuts.com* to *almond.nuts.com*. The numeric value in the MX record, 10 in the example, indicates the "preference" of the mail server. Preference numbers are arbitrary values usually numbered by fives or tens. The lower the number, the more preferred the server. The preference number allows you to have more then one mail server and

---

[*] Two excellent books on system administration are *Essential System Administration*, by Æleen Frisch, and *UNIX System Administration Handbook*, by Nemeth, Snyder, and Seebass.
[†] Domain Name Service is covered in *TCP/IP Network Administration* and in great detail in *DNS and BIND*.

to tell the remote host which server to try first. If the remote system cannot deliver mail to the most preferred server, it tries the other servers in preference order until it finds one that accepts the mail. The example has only one server, but it still requires an explicit preference number.

To deliver mail, the remote system queries the name server for any DNS records available for the destination system. If the name server returns any MX records, they are used to deliver the mail. If no MX record is returned, the remote system sends the mail directly to the address returned in the A record. In our example, a remote system's query for information about *peanut* returns an MX record. The remote system then knows to send the mail to *almond* instead of sending it to *peanut.*

The server *almond* is also defined in the DNS database:

```
almond.nuts.com.    IN  A   128.66.12.1
                    IN  MX  10 almond.nuts.com.
```

The A record assigns the address 128.66.12.1 to *almond.nuts.com.* The second line is the MX record for *almond.* The name of the server identified on an MX record must resolve to an address, as it does in our example. The MX record for *almond* is not really required because it tells remote systems to send mail bound for *almond* to *almond.* Having an MX record that points back to the system itself improves the efficiency of the name server lookup for the remote system, and thus helps the remote system run more effectively.

Now that we have MX records to route mail to the server, the server must be configured to accept the mail and deliver it to the correct recipient.

Host Aliases

The server needs to know that it should accept mail that is addressed to other hosts. The server understands MX records, but despite this, it is possible for mail to arrive that the system believes is addressed to the wrong host. Some systems try to forward the unrecognized mail, and others reject it with an error like the following one.

```
Connected to almond.nuts.com:
>>> HELO almond.nuts.com
<<< 553 almond.nuts.com host name configuration error
554 <andy@peanut.nuts.com>... Service unavailable
```

The MX record directs mail addressed to *peanut* to *almond.* In the example, a remote system connects to *almond* and passes it mail addressed to *andy@peanut.nuts.com.* However, *almond* rejects the mail.

To avoid this problem, configure the names of the hosts for which the server receives mail as aliases for the server. This is usually done on *sendmail* systems by configuring *w* as a class value. If there are many hostnames, *w* can be loaded from a file. Here's an example of setting the values with class (**C**) statements in the *sendmail.cf* file:

```
# define our internet aliases
#Fw/usr/lib/sendmail.cw
Cwalmond.nuts.com
Cwpeanut.nuts.com peanut
```

The **F** command that is commented out in the example loads the names from a file called */etc/sendmail.cw*. It could be used instead of the **C** commands, but not in addition to those commands. The **F** command has some advantages. First, host aliases can be added without editing *sendmail.cf*—a file in which many system administrators fear to tread. Second, the external host alias file can often be built using a simple shell script or program. A sample script that builds a *sendmail.cw* file from the MX records in a DNS zone file is shown in Appendix C.

Once the aliases are defined, the server treats mail addressed to these systems as local mail. Test the hostname aliases using the **sendmail −bt** command-line option that allows you to test addresses through the *sendmail.cf* configuration file. Send an email address that uses one of the hostname aliases through ruleset 0, which is the ruleset that decides how mail is delivered. If ruleset 0 decides to deliver it through the *local* mailer, the system recognizes the alias as a valid nickname. This means the alias is setup correctly.

The example below assumes that the *sendmail.cf* modifications above have been made on the host *almond*. Running the local address *craig@almond.nuts.com* through ruleset 0 naturally invokes the *local* mailer because *almond.nuts.com* is the name of the local host. Running the remote address *hunt@peanut.nuts.com* through ruleset 0 also invokes the *local* mailer. This shows that the modifications are working and that *peanut* is recognized as another name for *almond*.

```
# sendmail -bt
ADDRESS TEST MODE
Enter <ruleset> <address>
> 0 craig@almond.nuts.com
rewrite: ruleset  3   input: "craig" "@" "almond" "." "nuts" "." "com"
 .
 .
 .
rewrite: ruleset  0 returns: $# "local" $: "craig"
> 0 hunt@peanut.nuts.com
rewrite: ruleset  3   input: "hunt" "@" "peanut" "." "nuts" "." "com"
 .
 .
 .
rewrite: ruleset  0 returns: $# "local" $: "hunt"
> ^D
#
```

Notice that ruleset 0 is not the first, or only, ruleset through which the test address is processed. Many systems send the address through ruleset 3 first, even though it is not explicitly requested on the command line. Ruleset 3 processes every address during normal operations, so many systems assume it should do the same for a test. First try the test specifying just ruleset 0 (**0 hunt@peanut.nuts.com**). If your system doesn't automatically invoke ruleset 3, add it to the command line (**3,0 hunt@peanut.nuts.com**).

The MX record redirects mail to the server, and the host aliases make sure that the server accepts the redirected mail. Once it accepts the mail, the system needs to store it for later retrieval. Storing mail on the server is the same for a PC user as it is for any local user. Create a standard login account for the PC user with a home directory, secure password, and a mailbox. The mailbox holds the mail on the server until it is moved to the PC using POP. .

Configuring POP

A UNIX host turns into a POP mail server when it runs a POP daemon. Check your system's documentation to see if a POP daemon is included in the system software. If it isn't, don't worry; POP software is available from the Internet. The software used in these examples was downloaded from *ftp.ftp.com* where it is stored in the *support/pubdom* directory under the filename *PC802.ZIP.*[*] Among other things, *PC802.ZIP* contains source for both POP2 and POP3. Use **PKUNZIP**, a PC program, to unpack the *PC802.ZIP* file into its constituent **tar** files.

The POP2 source code is found in the *pop2d.tar* file. Extract it using the UNIX **tar** command, which creates a directory called *pop2d* under the current directory. Change to this new directory and **su** to *root*. Do a **make** to compile the POP daemon. If it compiles without errors, do a **make install** to install the daemon in */etc*. These steps are shown in the following example.

```
% tar -xvf pop2d.tar
x pop2d/Makefile, 479 bytes, 1 tape blocks
.
.
.
x pop2d/util.c, 10638 bytes, 21 tape blocks
% cd pop2d
% su
Password:
# make
cc -O  -target sun4 -c  main.c
cc -O  -target sun4 -c  tables.c
cc -O  -target sun4 -c  server.c
cc -O  -target sun4 -c  folder.c
cc -O  -target sun4 -c  util.c
cc -o pop2d main.o tables.o server.o folder.o util.o
# make install
install -c -m 711 pop2d /etc/pop2d
```

---

[*] PC802.ZIP is the same name that was used in Chapter 8.

Most network daemons are started by the Internet Daemon, **inetd**; POP2 is no exception. There are two advantages to starting daemons from **inetd**. First, **inetd** only runs daemons when they are needed. Second, daemons started by **inetd** have a security advantage because they can be protected using the *TCP Wrapper* program.[*] For these reasons, start POP from **inetd** by placing the following entry in the *inetd.conf* file:

```
pop-2   stream  tcp     nowait  root    /etc/pop2d              pop2d
```

This entry tells **inetd** to listen on the TCP port identified as *pop-2* in the */etc/services* file, and if it hears data on that port, to run */etc/pop2d* as user *root*. Once the line is added to the *inetd.conf* file, send a SIGHUP to **inetd** to force it to read the new configuration, as in this example:

```
# ps -acx | grep inetd
  200 ? IW    0:00 inetd
# kill -HUP 200
```

Test your new POP server with **telnet**. If the server responds, it is ready to run.

```
% telnet localhost pop-2
Trying 127.0.0.1 .,.
Connected to localhost.
Escape character is '^]'.
+ POP2 almond Server (Version 1.001   February, 1989)
quit
+ Bye POP2 almond Server (Version 1.001) shutdown
Connection closed by foreign host.
```

POP3 is almost as easy to install as POP2. It is found in the *pop3d.tar* file from the same zip file, *PC802.ZIP*. Follow the same basic steps to extract the **tar** file, **make**, and **make install** the daemon. Add an entry to *inetd.conf* that is identical to the POP2 entry except that the port name is *pop-3*, the server path is */etc/pop3d*, and the command argument is *pop3d*. But before you reload **inetd** with a SIGHUP, make sure that *pop-3* is actually defined in */etc/services*. POP3 is newer than POP2, so some systems do not have it in the */etc/services* file. If yours doesn't, add the following line to that file:

```
pop-3           110/tcp     ·           # Post Office Version 3
```

Don't forget about NIS. If your system uses yellow-pages, you need to rebuild the map created by the */etc/services* file, as in this Sun-specific example:

```
# cd /var/yp
# make services
updated services
pushed services
```

Now that *pop-3* is defined, pass **inetd** the SIGHUP and test the new server using **telnet localhost pop-3**. If the POP3 daemon answers, you're in business.

---

[*] *TCP Wrapper* is covered in the *Network Security* chapter of *TCP/IP Network Administration*.

POP Clients

After POP is installed on the server, configure the POP client software on the PC. The PC configuration is a simple two-step process. The first step is to create the mailbox. The mailbox is simply a file used to hold the mail that is associated with some user account. Mailboxes are usually created automatically when user accounts are created. Chapter 5 has examples of this.

Next, identify the host that acts as the mail server, and the username and password necessary to retrieve mail from that host. These are not necessarily the same usernames and passwords used to create the PC mailbox; that username and that password provide controlled access to the mailbox on the PC. The information entered in the dialogue box in Figure 9-4 is used by the POP protocol to access the remote mailbox. Figure 9-4 is from a Windows system running *SuperTCP*.

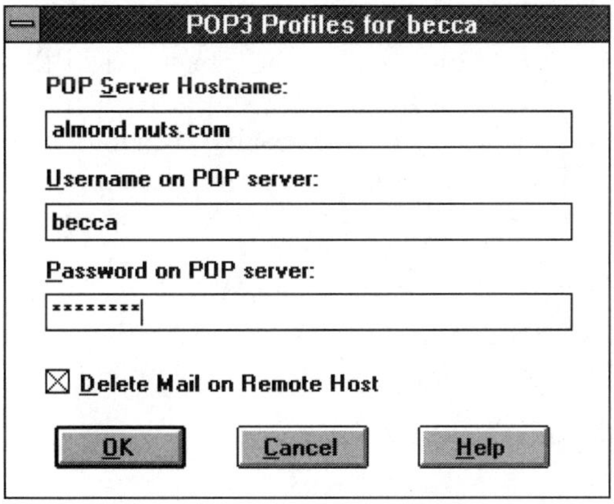

Figure 9-4: POP User Profile

Most PCs offer more than one TCP/IP mail delivery protocol. Both POP2 and POP3 are supported. Select the version of the protocol that is installed on your server.

Some PCs can even act as SMTP servers that send and receive mail directly, although most PC networks use a mail relay host to handle SMTP mail delivery. The relay handles mail for any systems that want to take advantage of its services.

Configuring a Mail Relay

A mail relay is an important part of a reliable PC email network. The mail relay simplifies the PC's configuration by handling a variety of email address formats so that the PC doesn't have to. It also relieves the PC of the obligation of processing errors and queued messages that comes with the responsibility of direct mail delivery. A UNIX system is the most common choice for a mail relay host, and at most sites, the mail server and the mail relay are the same computer.

Simplified Addressing

One function of the mail relay host is to provide simple email addresses for the systems on its network. Simplified addressing requires properly configured MX records, aliases, and sometimes special sendmail re-write rules. In the previous section we saw the MX records and *sendmail.cf* modifications that are necessary to route mail addressed to *user@host.domain* to a mail server. Simplified addressing is different. We want to address mail to *name@domain* and have the mail forwarded to the real email address, which can be the address of a mail server or the address of a desktop system. The point of routing mail to the mail server is to make the PC's job easier; the point of simplified addressing is to make the user's job easier. Email addresses that are independent of hostnames and of login usernames are easier for users to remember, and users are able to change systems and account names without printing new business cards—two benefits most users appreciate!

The MX record used for simplified addressing is identical to the one used in the previous section. The difference is not the syntax of the record, but what it references. For the mail server, an MX record is associated with each hostname. For simplified addressing, one MX record is associated with the entire domain. For example:

```
nuts.com.   IN   MX    10 almond.nuts.com.
```

Normally the domain's MX record is positioned near the beginning of the zone file, among other records that apply to the entire domain, as in this example:

```
nuts.com.   IN   SOA   almond.nuts.com. hunt.almond.nuts.com. (
                       94040501    ; Serial
                       43200       ; Refresh
                       3600        ; Retry
                       3600000     ; Expire  - 41 days
                       604800 )    ; Minimum - 7 days
            IN   NS    big.oil.com.
            IN   NS    almond.nuts.com.
            IN   MX    10  almond.nuts.com.
```

This sample shows the beginning of a domain database file. All DNS zone files begin with a *Start Of Authority* (SOA) record that defines certain characteristics of the domain. It is usually followed by some *Name Server* (NS) records.[*] These records apply to the entire domain, and it is at this point at the beginning of the file that we insert the MX record. The MX record in our sample file redirects mail addressed to *user*@**nuts**.com to *user*@**almond.nuts.com**. It is now possible to address mail without using a specific hostname.

---

[*] A detailed discussion of DNS is beyond the scope of this book. DNS configuration is covered in *TCP/IP Network Administration*; however, the most complete treatment of this topic is in *DNS and BIND*.

Username Aliases

We're getting close, but we also want to use the user's real name in his email address. This second step requires aliases that understand how to forward mail that is addressed to the user's real name to the users login account. The aliases are placed in the */etc/aliases* file of the system pointed to by the MX record, *almond* in our example. Examples of this type of alias are shown below:

```
rebecca.hunt: becca
kathy.mccafferty: mac@filbert.nuts.com
david.craig: david
jane.resnick: jane@brazil.nuts.com
christy.wright: christy
daniel.scribner: dan
```

These examples show a *Firstname.Lastname* scheme. Mail addressed to *Rebecca.Hunt@nuts.com* is sent to *almond.nuts.com* based on the MX record for the domain name *nuts.com*. On *almond* the aliases file is used to direct the mail to user account *becca*. Once the mail is delivered to that local account, it can be retrieved via POP or read locally via a login just like any other mail. The advantage is that remote users don't need to know that Rebecca's real email address is *becca@almond.nuts.com*; all they need to know is her name. This reduces the need to maintain a large email address book on each PC, and it makes the email address independent of the username and the hostname.

Firstname.Lastname aliases can be created from the information in the */etc/passwd* file with a simple shell script. The *passwd* file usually contains the user's first and last names in the *gcos* field, which is a free-form field specifically set aside for this type of information. The file also contains the username. These are the two values we need to create the alias. It is a simple process to extract this information for each user, as long as the structure of the *gcos* field is consistent for each record in the *passwd* file. Here is a sample */etc/passwd* file that could be used:

```
root:NKmu48bsNK:0:1:System Administrator:/:/bin/csh
daemon:*:1:1::/:
sys:*:2:2::/:/bin/csh
bin:*:3:3::/bin:
uucp:*:4:8::/var/spool/uucppublic:
diag:*:0:1:System Diagnostic:/usr/diag:/usr/diag/diag
craig:niYTH65CFni98:198:102:Craig Winslow:/home/craig:/bin/csh
becca:MKOFTRvjk49hds:199:102:Rebecca Hunt:/home/becca:/bin/csh
david:niohGFNb656vsjhv:188:102:David Craig:/home/david:/bin/csh
christy:BIUFD567nmdiHGub:203:101:Christy Wright:/home/christy:/bin/csh
dan:buVBUYGYT68sb87s:201:101:Daniel Scribner:/home/dan:/bin/csh
```

Notice that every "real" user has a *gcos* field that contains the user's first and last names. The following script converts this data into records that are suitable for the */etc/aliases* file.

```
#! /bin/sh
#
# Eliminate "non-login" accounts
#
grep -v '*' /etc/passwd | \
#
# Replace delimiting colons with whitespace
#
sed 's/:/ /g' | \
#
# Output first.last: username to local.aliases
#
awk '{ print $5"."$6":", $1 }' > /etc/local.aliases
```

A cat of the */etc/local.aliases* file produced by this script shows the following aliases:

```
% cat /etc/local.aliases
System.Administrator: root
Craig.Winslow: craig
Rebecca.Hunt: becca
David.Craig: david
Christy.Wright: christy
Daniel.Scribner: dan
```

This file contains aliases only for users with accounts on this system. For example, *Jane.Resnick*, whose real address is *jane@brazil.nuts.com*, is not contained in this file, nor does it contain the mailing lists or other aliases usually found in the full */etc/aliases* file. All of the alias information must be added together before **newaliases** is executed in order to have a complete aliases database.

Defining an alias may not be enough to get *Firstname.Lastname* addresses working on your system. This form of addressing can have other problems. Some systems treat *Firstname.Lastname* as an old-style address of the form *host.user*.[*] Those systems rewrite *Rebecca.Hunt* into *Hunt@Rebecca*. The address is *only* rewritten if it does not include the domain part, therefore it happens only to people who are directly logged into the mail relay, or to systems that route "local" mail to the relay. (We discuss what we mean by routing "local" mail later). Either way, this is an uncommon problem, but we want to eliminate all potential problems. Run **sendmail −bt** to test your mail relay system before you tell the users about your fancy new addressing scheme. The example below shows a test of a server that does not handle *Firstname.Lastname* correctly:

```
# sendmail -bt
ADDRESS TEST MODE
Enter <ruleset> <address>
> 0 Rebecca.Hunt
rewrite: ruleset  3    input: "Rebecca" "." "Hunt"
rewrite: ruleset  8    input: "Rebecca" "." "Hunt"
```

---

[*] Some sites avoid this problem by using an underscore or dash instead of a dot; e.g. *Rebecca_Hunt@nuts.com*. Despite its problems, the dot is still more popular.

```
rewrite: ruleset  8 returns: "Rebecca" "." "Hunt"
rewrite: ruleset  6   input: "Hunt" "<" "@" "Rebecca" ">"
rewrite: ruleset  6 returns: "Hunt" "<" "@" "Rebecca" ">"
rewrite: ruleset  3 returns: "Hunt" "<" "@" "Rebecca" ">"
rewrite: ruleset  0   input: "Hunt" "<" "@" "Rebecca" ">"
rewrite: ruleset  3   input: "Hunt" "@" "Rebecca"
rewrite: ruleset  8   input: "Hunt" "@" "Rebecca"
rewrite: ruleset  8 returns: "Hunt" "@" "Rebecca"
rewrite: ruleset  6   input: "Hunt" "<" "@" "Rebecca" ">"
rewrite: ruleset  6 returns: "Hunt" "<" "@" "Rebecca" ">"
rewrite: ruleset  3 returns: "Hunt" "<" "@" "Rebecca" ">"
rewrite: ruleset  6   input: "Hunt" "<" "@" "Rebecca" ">"
rewrite: ruleset  6 returns: "Hunt" "<" "@" "Rebecca" ">"
rewrite: ruleset  0 returns: $# "tcpld" $@ "Rebecca" "." "nuts" "."
           "com" $: "Hunt" "<" "@" "Rebecca" "." "nuts" "." "com" ">"
>
```

This example tests the address *Rebecca.Hunt* through ruleset 0. As we noted before, most systems first send the address through ruleset 3, which is just what we want. The address is fine when it enters ruleset 3 and when it returns from ruleset 8. However, before ruleset 6 is called, ruleset 3 converts the address to the incorrect format. We know that ruleset 3 makes the mistake by looking at the *input* and *returns* values. *input* is the value passed to a ruleset, and *returns* is the value that comes out of a ruleset when it is finished processing. We have an *input* value for ruleset 3, but there is no *returns* value from ruleset 3 until after ruleset 6 is called. Therefore, ruleset 6 must be called from within ruleset 3, and ruleset 3 must still be in operation when the address gets clobbered. From this we know to look in the *sendmail.cf* file for ruleset 3, and luckily the comment "host.user" points us right to the troublesome rule. We comment out the culprit with a pound-sign (#) as shown below:

```
#R$-.$+          $@$>6$2<@$1>            host.user
```

Rerunning the test shows that the fix did just what we wanted. *Rebecca.Hunt* is now treated as a username and processed by the *local* mailer. Aliases must be "local." If an alias isn't local, an error like the following one is displayed when **newaliases** is run:

```
SYSERR: /etc/aliases: line 52: cannot alias non-local names
```

If you get this error, look at the line indicated by the error message and run that alias through ruleset 0 using the **sendmail −bt** test procedure discussed above.

NOTE

The rewrite rules in your *sendmail.cf* may not be the same as those shown in our examples. The important thing in this example is the logic used to find the problem, not the specific change made to the sample configuration.

The *Firstname.Lastname* scheme is not the only simplified address scheme used. Some organizations use "first-initial lastname" (*rhunt@nuts.com*); others use "last-name first-initial" (*huntr@nuts.com*). Each approach has advantages and disadvantages. *Firstname.Lastname* reduces the number of duplicate names for large organizations especially if users can register nicknames on a first-come first-served basis. For example, if two people are named Rebecca Hunt and one is allowed to register the name Becky Hunt, you have a happy user, and you eliminate the duplicate name problem. However, as mentioned above, this format is more trouble to implement. The "first-initial lastname" format is short and easy to type; small organizations often use it. The "lastname first-initial" format is also short and easy to type, and it is easy for machines to sort in lastname sequence, which is helpful for some mailers. All of these formats are in widespread use, and all work well, so the choice is yours.

Rewriting Sender Addresses

To get the most from simplified addresses, they should be used on outbound mail. Mailers should rewrite the *Sender:* and *Reply-To:* addresses to the simplified format. Mail sent from *jane* on the PC *brazil.nuts.com* should go out as mail from *Jane.Resnick@nuts.com*, not as mail from *jane@brazil.nuts.com*. This is very easy to do on most PC mailers. Their design assumes that you want to show the relay host as the mail's origination point, so they provide a simple way to do this. The dialogue box in Figure 9-5 is from the *Chameleon* mailer. The *From:* value entered in this box is used as the sender address.

Figure 9–5: Defining a From Address

It is not usually that simple when the mail originates from a UNIX system instead of from a PC. To provide a flexible mail system it should be possible for the user to read and send mail directly from her PC or directly from the UNIX mail server. It should be her choice to use POP or login access whenever she chooses. Therefore, we want mail sent from the PC and/or the mail server to look like it originated from the same place. Jane's mail should always go out with the same simplified address regardless of its origin.

One technique for achieving a simplified address is to create a user account name that is identical to the username portion of the simplified email address, and to standardize this account name on every system on the network. Standardizing usernames is not technically difficult, and it facilitates use of the **r**-commands such as **rlogin**. But it is easier if the network is fairly small, and if the "first-initial last-name" or "lastname first-initial" address formats are used. Usernames are commonly limited to a length of eight characters or less. Therefore *Jane.Resnick* is not a valid username but *jresnick* is.

If you standardize usernames on email names, you don't have to rewrite the username portion of an address. Rewriting the hostname part is very easy.[*] Here are the steps:

1. Locate the *sendmail.cf* mailer used to send mail to remote hosts. If you don't know which one it is, use **sendmail –bt** to test a remote address such as *craigh@ora.com* though ruleset 0. This command will return, among other things, the mailer name. For the sake of this discussion, let's say the mailer name is *tcpld*.

2. Find out what ruleset is used to rewrite sender addresses for the mailer. This is the ruleset pointed to by the S= argument on the mailer command line. **grep** the *sendmail.cf* file for the mailer name discovered in step 1 to see the ruleset number assigned to S=. For example, **grep** ´^Mtcpld´ **sendmail.cf**.

3. In that ruleset modify the rules that handle mail from the system itself or its POP clients. If the sender address has only a username part with no hostname or domain name portion, the mail is from a local user. If the host part of the sender address is the local host or one of its host aliases, the mail is from this system or one of its clients. Mail that meets any of these criteria is rewritten so that the portion of the address after the at-sign (@) is the mail domain name. For example, *jresnick* is rewritten as *jresnick@nuts.com*.

The sample *sendmail.cf* file shown in Appendix C is based on the configuration file developed in *TCP/IP Network Administration*. Ruleset 17 in the sample file handles sender addresses for remote mail.[†] Assuming the macros defined in the sample, the rules modified to rewrite the address to a domain name are:

```
R$-             $1<@$A>           user w/o host => user@domain
R$+<@$=w>       $1<@$A>           user@host => user@domain
```

The first rule checks for a sender address that contains only one token ($-). It assumes that token is the username. It rewrites the address to add an at-sign and the domain name, which is stored in the *A* macro. The second rule checks to see if the sender address contains a host alias of this system ($=w). If it does, the hostname is replaced by the domain name when the address is rewritten. In both cases, the sender address is rewritten to the *user@domain* format.

For some organizations, rewriting the host part of the email address is not enough. There are any number of reasons why: they can't, or won't, standardize login names; they want to hide login names for security reasons; they want to use *Firstname.Lastname* addresses. Regardless of the reason, they want to rewrite the

---

[*] The sample *sendmail.cf* in *TCP/IP Network Administration* has a detailed example of how to rewrite the hostname part. See the discussion of the *A* macro in that example.

[†] Traditionally rulesets for sender addresses start with a 1, and rulesets that handle recipient addresses start with a 2.

username portion of the email address as well as the hostname portion. Rewriting both portions is more difficult and requires a system that runs either *sendmail with NIS, IDA sendmail,* or *V8 sendmail.*

IDA sendmail, V8 sendmail, and *sendmail with NIS* have a few additional meta-symbols for rewriting addresses. These metasymbols take a token from the input email address and use it as the key to look up information in a database file. The metasymbols vary slightly, but are almost identical in syntax and use. Detailed descriptions of the syntax of these commands in the various sendmail implementations are given in Chapter 2 of *sendmail,* by Costales, Allman, and Rickert. The examples used in this text are based on *sendmail with NIS,* but the general steps required for this type of address rewrite are the same regardless of the implementation of *sendmail* that is used. These steps are:

1. Identify the database to *sendmail.* If you use *sendmail with NIS,* define a macro that contains the name of the map you wish to use. Take care not to use a macro that is used for any other purpose. If you use *IDA sendmail* or *V8 sendmail,* use the **K** option to identify the pathname of the database file.

2. Locate the ruleset that rewrites the sender address of mail bound for a remote host.

3. Locate the rules in that ruleset that add the domain name to the sender address for mail from the local host and its host aliases. Modify those rules to call the new ruleset you create in the next step.

4. Define a new ruleset that uses the username portion of the sender address as a key to a database that returns the user's real name, and that uses the real name to rewrite the sender address. Take care not to use a ruleset number used elsewhere in the *sendmail.cf* file.

Our sample code uses *gcos* information from the */etc/passwd* file to rewrite the user portion of the sender address into the *Firstname.Lastname* format. */etc/passwd* is not the only file that could be used for this, and it is possible to create a database solely for this purpose. However, the *passwd.byname* map already exists and is a standard part of NIS, so we'll take advantage of it. This, of course, requires that the format of the gcos information for every entry in the */etc/passwd* file is exactly the same. The *gcos* field in the sample *passwd* file used in the previous section contains the user's first and last names. We use the same */etc/passwd* file for this example.

The first step is to associate the name of the database with a *sendmail* macro. We're using gcos data, so for want of a something better, we use the *G* macro to store the name of the NIS map. **grep´^.G´ sendmail.cf** checks that *G* is not already in use.[*]

---

[*] If *G* is already in use, use *P* for password, *N* for NIS, *M* for map, or anything that makes sense to you and is not already used.

Once we're sure that there is no conflict, the following lines are added near the beginning of the *sendmail.cf* file:

```
# Define passwd map for GCOS information
DGpasswd.byname
```

Assuming the sample *sendmail.cf* file from Appendix C, modify ruleset 17 to call the new ruleset to process the *gcos* data. The rules affected by this change are the same ones we modified to rewrite the host portion of the address. Because this change modifies both the user portion and the host portion, it is done instead of—not in addition to—that earlier change.

grep S18 sendmail.cf shows that ruleset 18 is not in use, so we use that ruleset number for our new ruleset. The modifications to ruleset 17 to call ruleset 18 are:

```
R$-             $@$>18$1<@$A>           user w/o host
R$+<@$w>        $@$>18$1<@$A>           this host
R$+<@$=w>       $@$>18$1<@$2>           or an alias
```

The first rule sends mail to be processed in ruleset 18 that has only a username in the sender address with no hostname or domain name. It's assumed that the mail is from someone directly logged into the system. The second rule calls ruleset 18 if the sender address contains the name of this host because that mail is clearly from a user on this system. The third rule sends mail to be processed if it has one of the server's hostname aliases in the sender address. Again, it's assumed that mail from a PC POP client should be processed in case the PC has not properly rewritten the address.

Finally, we add the new ruleset:

```
# Convert username to firstname.lastname
S18
R$!G<@$+>       $@$1<@$2>               return, not in passwd
R$-<@$+>        $:${G$1$}<@$A>          user=>passwd entry
R$+:$+:$+:$+:$+ $2                      align on gcos data
R$-$-$+<@$+>    $:$1.$2<@$4>            gcos=>first.last@mxdomain
```

The first rule in ruleset 18 checks if the username portion of the email address is found in the *passwd.byname* map. If it isn't, exit the ruleset without modifying the sender address. The second rule uses the username as the key to look up data in the *passwd* file. It replaces the hostname portion of the sender address with the domain name and the username portion with the entire string returned by the query. This is more information than we want, so the last two rules clean up the address. The third rule throws away everything before the *gcos* data, and the fourth rule uses the first two tokens in the *gcos* data as the user's first and last names. Obviously, this will work only if the *gcos* data is in the expected format.

This is really a fairly simple process. We have added less than ten lines to the *sendmail.cf* file to accomplish this task. However, the arcane syntax of *sendmail* configuration commands causes confusion for system administrators and often leads to typing errors during the configuration. If the servers are not the only

UNIX systems on your network and users are responsible for their own *sendmail* configurations, there is a potential for configuration errors. Reduce potential problems by maintaining the *passwd.byname* file on a central NIS server and by making a centrally maintained *sendmail.cf* file available to every UNIX system on the network.

Relaying Local Mail

If your PC can route "local" mail to the mail relay, it is possible to address users known to the relay host using only their usernames. Some PC mailers support this and others don't. For example, using the Chameleon mailer, we define *almond.nuts.com* as the *Mail Gateway* (the name Chameleon uses for the mail relay host). To do this, select **Mail Gateway** from the **Networks** item of the **Settings** menu in the mail window. Figure 9-6 shows the Mail Gateway dialogue box.

Figure 9–6: Defining the Chameleon Mail Gateway

Once this selection is made, mail written on the PC and addressed to any username or alias on *almond.nuts.com* is handled as if it were addressed to a local user. Given the alias file shown above, mail addressed to *Rebecca.Hunt*, without any host address, would be delivered. The PC relies on *almond* to handle the actual delivery. It just passes the address to *almond* without modifications. This is simplified addressing taken to the max!

We noted that *Chameleon* calls the mail relay host *Mail Gateway*, which is a common usage of the term. However, in this text we have a special meaning for mail gateway. We reserve that term for systems that translate mail between dissimilar protocols.

Mail Gateways

Not every network uses TCP/IP and SMTP. There are many other network transport and mail delivery protocols. To provide your users with the widest range of service you need to be able to exchange mail with non-SMTP systems. The following suggestions are ways to do this with the least effort:

*   Standardize your network on TCP/IP and SMTP. Make using SMTP as easy as possible by providing high-quality SMTP email software, full installation, training, and support for all PC users. Users who insist on using a proprietary mail system should be responsible for buying and configuring their own gateway to attach that system to your SMTP mail network.

- Don't reinvent the wheel. Use the gateways that already exist on the Internet. Tell your users to ask for a remote user's Internet address. Most remote users on X.400, Bitnet, or UUCP networks have Internet "domain-style" addresses that route mail through the remote network's gateway. These domain-style addresses can be handled on your system without any configuration changes on your part. If the remote user doesn't know his domain-style address, ask for the name of his network administrator and deal directly with that person.

Simple modifications can be made to *sendmail.cf* to handle non-SMTP networks that have well-known gateway systems. The configuration in Appendix C has examples for Bitnet and UUCP. The modifications define the remote gateways:

```
# UUCP relay host
DRuunet.uu.net
# Bitnet relay host
DBcunyvm.cuny.edu
```

The modifications also define internal pseudo-domains used to simplify processing mail bound for the remote gateways:

```
# Internal "fake" domains used in re-writing
CIUUCP BITNET
```

Several rulesets are modified to handle the internal domains but the key modifications are made to ruleset 0 to handle the mail delivery:

```
R$*<@$+.BITNET>$*    $#tcp$@$B$:$1<@$2.BITNET>$3    user@host.BITNET
R$*<@$*.UUCP>$*      $#tcpld$@$R$:$1<@$2.UUCP>      uucp mail
```

The first rule checks for the pseudo-domain BITNET in the address. If it is found, the mail is relayed through the gateway defined in the *B* macro. The second rule checks for UUCP and relays through the gateway defined in the *R* macro. Combined with the other modifications, these rules will properly handle Bitnet and UUCP mail.

These changes are only of marginal importance, because almost all Bitnet and UUCP sites have registered domain names. The stickier problem is handling proprietary mail systems that may be installed on subnets within your own network. This problem is particularly acute at sites that have lots of PCs. There are many different proprietary email packages for PCs, and each subnet seems to select its own unique package.

All proprietary PC email packages use an architecture that is very different from SMTP. SMTP is a command/response protocol that transfers mail from one system to another; PC email packages don't use mail transfer protocols at all. Instead they use a shared database file. Mail is written to and read from that shared file using the file sharing protocol of the PC network. In the case of a TCP/IP network, NFS is used to read and write mail. This type of architecture is called a *mailbox* or *post office* system because there is one shared post office file for all of the mail clients. Figure 9-7 illustrates this architecture.

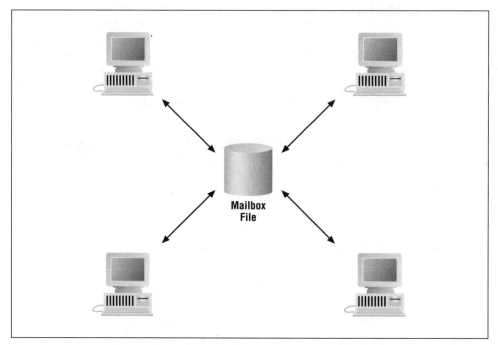

Figure 9–7: PC Mailbox Architecture

This architectural model has some distinct advantages. The architecture is inherently server-based, bringing with it all the reliability advantages of a server system. Using the existing file sharing protocol relieves the PC of the need to support a separate mail transfer protocol. But there are also disadvantages. Security is one. The mailbox is encrypted to prevent unauthorized snooping, but it is designed to be writable by all clients. On a UNIX server "writable" can also mean "deletable" by all clients. Additionally, proprietary email systems may require more servers for the same number of clients than a SMTP/POP system does, because the proprietary server is responsible for the long-term storage of all of the mail. And finally, proprietary solutions limit your choices. There are many vendors of PC mailers for SMTP networks, and all of them work with your UNIX mail server. With proprietary systems, you are often limited to products from one vendor.

Attempting to support more than one email system dilutes the effectiveness of your system support staff. For that reason we have strongly recommended that you standardize on SMTP and require users who select other mail systems to support those systems themselves. This self-support requires users to obtain and maintain an SMTP gateway on the mailbox server of their proprietary system. For compatibility reasons, they should probably select the SMTP gateway provided by the vendor of their email system.

Attachments

The last element of our mail architecture is MIME—the tool we use to attach files and data to email. MIME does not require anything special from the mail server. A server that supports ESMTP is helpful, but not absolutely necessary. The real work is done by the MIME mailer right on the desktop PC. The MIME mailer encodes data so that it can be sent through any SMTP server, even one that doesn't support ESMTP.

Systems have been encoding binary data and sending it in mail for a long time. MIME is not really required for this, but it provides a standardized way to accomplish the task. Before MIME was even thought of, non-standard techniques such as **uuencode** were used to encode mail. **uuencode**, borrowed from UUCP, is still more widely used for encoding SMTP mail than MIME. It works fine, and it is an integral part of many different mailers. For example, the *Chameleon* mailer, which is a MIME mailer, includes *uuencode* and *uudecode* items in the **Message** menu of the mail composition window, for compatibility with non-MIME mailers.

We emphasize MIME because it is a standard designed to be extensible enough to deal with changing network requirements. MIME is the future of SMTP mailers, and there are implementations ready for the PC right now. Our examples are based on two: *SuperTCP*'s mailer and *Chameleon*'s mailer.

First we create a MIME message on a system running *SuperTCP* by selecting the **Compose** button in the mail window. We type in the recipient's address, a subject, and a short note telling the remote user about the attachment. We then select the **Attach** button in the composition window. The File Attachment dialogue box is shown in Figure 9-8. Select the **Add** button and enter the name of the file you wish to attach in the dialogue box that appears. The test uses the bitmap file C:\WINDOWS\CARS.BMP. Notice that the file has a MIME type automatically associated with it.

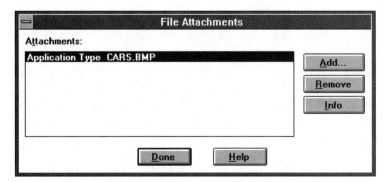

Figure 9–8: Specifying a MIME File Attachment

To change the file type, select the **Info** button, which opens the dialogue box shown in Figure 9-9. This dialogue box has selections for a full range of MIME types; the bitmap file is assigned the *Application Type*. You can change the type assigned to a file but should only do so if you are sure the system made a mistake. The system's selection is correct in this case, so select the **Cancel** button to return to the File Attachments window, and there select **Done**. Now back in the Compose window, select **Send**.

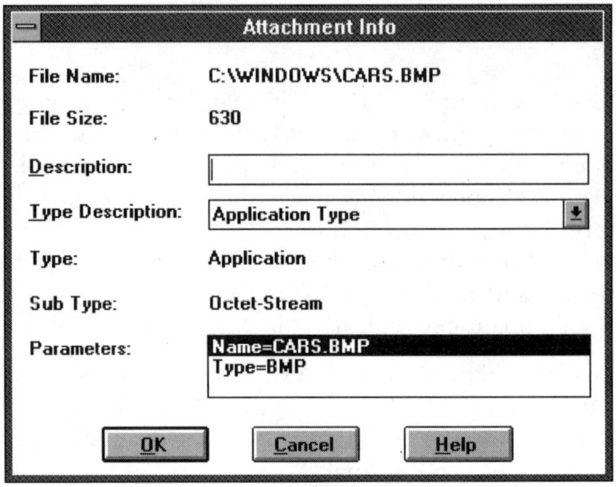

Figure 9-9: MIME Attachment Types

These steps create a multipart MIME message with mixed data types. 7-bit ASCII is used for the introductory text message, and the bitmap is sent as an encoded octet-stream. If we look at the message on a non-MIME system, we see the headers that describe the message:

```
Content-type: Multipart/Mixed; Boundary=EJNGCKDPODRAJHXG-B16ED623
Content-transfer-encoding: 7BIT
--EJNGCKDPODRAJHXG-B16ED623
Content-Type: Text/Plain; Charset=US-ASCII
--EJNGCKDPODRAJHXG-B16ED623
Content-Type: Application/Octet-Stream; Name="CARS.BMP"; Type=BMP
Content-Transfer-Encoding: Base64
```

The first header describes the message as a multipart message and declares that the string *EJNGCKDPODRAJHXG-B16ED623* is used to mark the boundaries between the different parts of the message. (The boundary string is an arbitrary string designed so that it will not be confused with encoded data.) The second header tells us that the message contains 7-bit ASCII data. Since we know that a bitmap is included in the message, we can guess that must be encoded in a format that allows it to be sent as 7-bit ASCII. Next we see a boundary string that marks the first part of the message, described by its header as being plain US ASCII text. This must be the introductory message, which is readable on any system. The next boundary string marks the beginning of the last part of the message. This part is described as being an application octet-stream, which is 8-bit binary data. This binary data is encoded using the Base64 encoding technique. On the non-MIME system, the data that follows this header just appears to be garbage.

Of course, we don't want to read headers; we want to read the content of the message. For that we need another MIME system, and we use a system running Chameleon. We start the mailer, log into the POP server, and start viewing the messages. The MIME message is shown in Figure 9-10.

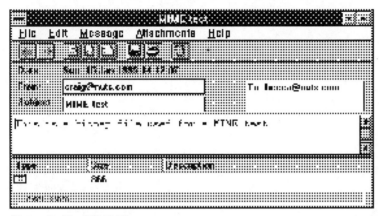

Figure 9–10: MIME Message

Notice that the message in Figure 9-10 is made up of a multipart window. The upper window contains the text of the introductory message and the attachment shows up as a file icon in the lower subwindow. Double-clicking on the icon causes the file in the attachment to be displayed. In this case the file is a bitmap that is displayed by the Window's Paintbrush application. The file is displayed automatically because the file's extension, *.BMP*, is associated with its specific application in the Windows File Manager. Use this standard Windows procedure to launch the application directly from a MIME attachment.

The headers that we saw on a non-MIME system are not apparent here. The MIME system interprets the headers, and properly delivers the mail and the attached files in the form that the user wants. More than that, MIME works between systems from competing vendors. The users are not locked into one vendor. They choose the mailer they like, as long as that mailer is MIME compliant.

Summary

Electronic mail is the most important network application. Simple Mail Transfer Protocol (SMTP), Post Office Protocol (POP), and Multipurpose Internet Mail Extensions (MIME) are the building blocks of a TCP/IP email network. A server-based system provides a reliable, flexible mail network by off-loading mail delivery responsibilities from the PC and by simplifying the PC's configuration. The server collects mail for the PC until the user is ready to read it, and it relays outgoing messages for the PC, handling any special address processing. A simplified email addressing scheme can be implemented in the server that allows users to send mail with no more information than the recipient's name.

Mail is not the only network application. The next chapter covers the configuration of other services that are almost as vital to the operation of a network, including file sharing, printer sharing, and network information services.

10

File and Print Servers

Two network applications, file and print services, are the foundation of PC LANs. In the beginning, cost savings were more of a motivation for PC LANs than convenience or improved service. Not long ago, disk drives and high quality printers were relatively expensive compared to the cost of a PC, but times have changed and so have the motivations for LAN services. Today, every PC has a large hard drive and many have their own laser printers, but the demand for LANs is higher than ever. The reason is that people need to share information even more than they want to economize on hardware resources.

Novell NetWare became the leader in PC LAN software by providing basic file and print services. Over the years many new services grew on top of these basic building blocks, creating the current LAN environment. Most PC email systems are based on a shared mailbox or post office that is accessed via the basic file services of the LAN. Software that is executed on the client PC, but resides on the file server where it can be kept up-to-date, is also accessed using LAN's file sharing software. All of these new network applications are layers added to the basic foundation of file and print services, and all of the PC LAN vendors, Banyan, Novell, Microsoft, etc., provide systems that offer these same basic services.

TCP/IP builds on a different set of basic applications, and the result is a more complete networking environment than the traditional PC LAN. TCP/IP starts from the basic services of remote login, file transfer, and email. To these services it adds file and print service, but TCP/IP has not stopped there. Information services, like Gopher, WWW, and network news are all part of a TCP/IP network.

Why doesn't TCP/IP dominate the PC market? TCP/IP is not really targeted to the PC market nor designed specifically for PCs. It is designed to run on a wide range of hardware and operating systems. NetWare, like DOS, is specifically designed for PCs and runs on even the most primitive PC hardware. The popularity of TCP/IP for PCs is relatively new because it demands more from the hardware and more from the people who configure the software. In return, it provides more features.

Of course, Novell and the other PC LAN vendors are not standing still. Novell bought UNIX from AT&T to add a full-featured application server to its network. All of the network vendors and their customers benefit from competition in the LAN marketplace that pushes constant product improvements. But this book is about TCP/IP, so we confine our discussion to how it provides file and print services.

File Sharing

File sharing is not the same as file transfer, which is simply the ability to move a file from one system to another. A true file sharing system does not require you to move entire files across the network; it allows files to be accessed at the record level. This makes it possible for a client to read a record from a file located on a remote server, update that record, and write it back to the server without moving the full file from the server to the client.

File sharing is transparent to the user and to the application software running on the user's system. Through file sharing, users and programs access files located on remote systems as if they were local. In a perfect file sharing environment, the user neither knows nor cares where the files are actually stored.

File sharing did not exist in the original TCP/IP protocol suite. It was added to support diskless workstations. Unlike a proprietary LAN where one vendor defines the official file sharing protocol, TCP/IP is an open protocol suite, and anyone can propose a new protocol. That is why there are three major TCP/IP protocols for file sharing:

Remote File System
> RFS was defined by AT&T for UNIX System V. It is offered on most UNIX systems, but is not widely implemented for Personal Computers. Even in the UNIX world, RFS never really caught on.

Andrew File System
> AFS is a file sharing system from Carnegie Mellon University. It has several performance enhancements that make it particularly well suited for wide area network (WAN) use. It is not widely implemented for PCs. AFS has evolved into *Distributed File System* (DFS), which is a new file sharing standard. DFS may become important in the future.

Network File System
> NFS was defined by Sun Microsystems to support their diskless workstations. NFS is designed primarily for LAN applications and is implemented for many different operating systems. All of the PC TCP/IP implementations used to prepare this book provide NFS software.

NFS is the only TCP/IP file sharing protocol widely available for PCs. It is the one that we will discuss in detail.

Creating a File Server

NFS is a client/server application. The server makes part of its filesystem available for use by its client, and the client uses the remote filesystem as if it were part of its local filesystem. Attaching a remote directory to the local filesystem (a client function) is called *mounting* a directory. Offering a directory for remote access (a server function) is called *exporting* a directory. Frequently, a system runs both the client and the server NFS software.

This section looks at how to configure a server to export directories. Most networks use UNIX systems for NFS servers, and we use SunOS UNIX in these examples. Even though we already covered this material in *TCP/IP Network Administration*, configuring a file server is so central to the task of creating a PC network that we also describe the procedure in this book.

NFS Daemons

On a UNIX system, the Network File System is run by several daemons, some performing client functions and some performing server functions. PC clients do not use these daemons, as you'll see when we set up a PC client. You only need a basic understanding of these daemons to configure a UNIX NFS server. The daemons are:

nfsd [*nservers*]

The NFS daemon **nfsd** runs on NFS servers. This daemon services the client's NFS requests. The *nservers* option specifies how many daemons should be started. Eight is a commonly used number. Additional NFS daemons may improve performance on a heavily loaded server.

biod [*nservers*]

The block I/O daemon **biod** runs on NFS clients. This daemon handles the client side of the NFS I/O. *nservers* specifies the number of daemons to be run, and again eight is the commonly used number. Because most servers are also clients, you should probably run this daemon on your NFS server.

rpc.lockd

The lock daemon **rpc.lockd** handles file lock requests. Both UNIX clients and servers run the lock daemon. Clients request file locks, and servers grant them.

rpc.statd

The network status monitor daemon **rpc.statd** is required by **rpc.lockd** to provide monitoring services. In particular, it allows locks to be reset properly after a crash. Both UNIX clients and servers run **rpc.statd**.

rpc.mountd

The NFS mount daemon **rpc.mountd** processes the clients' mount requests. NFS servers run the mount daemon.

The daemons necessary to run NFS are started from the boot scripts. The following
sample shows the type of code that is included in the startup file of a UNIX client.
The code checks for the existence of the **biod**, **rpc.statd**, and **rpc.lockd** programs,[*]
and if they are present, starts eight copies of **biod** as well as a copy of **rpc.statd**
and **rpc.lockd**.

```
#       start the NFS client software
#       biod, statd and lockd
#
if [ -f /usr/etc/biod -a -f /usr/etc/rpc.statd
    -a -f /usr/etc/rpc.lockd ]; then
    biod 8;                 echo -n ' biod'
    rpc.statd &             echo -n ' statd'
    rpc.lockd &             echo -n ' lockd'
fi
```

NFS server systems run all of the daemons shown above,[†] plus the NFS server daemon **nfsd** and the mount server daemon **rpc.mountd**. The type of code that starts
the additional daemons necessary for an NFS server is shown below:

```
if [ -f /etc/exports ]; then
        > /etc/xtab
        exportfs -a
        nfsd 8 &                echo -n ' nfsd'
        rpc.mountd
fi
```

This sample code first checks for the existence of */etc/exports*, which is the file that
contains information about the directories the server exports to its NFS clients. If
/etc/exports is found, the code empties */etc/xtab* and runs **exportfs**. **exportfs** reads
/etc/exports, uses the information to export the specified directories, and lists information about the exported directories in the */etc/xtab* file. (The **–a** option tells
exportfs to export *all* directories listed in */etc/exports*.)

Next, the sample code starts eight copies of **nfsd** and a copy of **rpc.mountd**. The
mount daemon determines which directories it should process mount requests for
by reading the */etc/xtab* file created by **exportfs**.

These examples are from a Sun system. Other systems may have different techniques for starting these daemons. If some of the daemons aren't starting, make
sure your startup scripts are correct.

Exporting Filesystems

The first steps in configuring a server are deciding which filesystems to export and
what restrictions to place on their export. Only filesystems that will benefit the

---

[*] These programs may not be in */usr/etc* on your UNIX system, and the "rpc." prefix may
not be used on the daemon names. Check your system's documentation.
[†] It's not really necessary for servers to run **biod**, but many servers also act as clients.

client should be exported. Before exporting a filesystem, think about what purpose it will serve. Some common reasons for exporting filesystems are:

- To provide additional disk space to clients

- To prevent unnecessary duplication of the same data on multiple systems

- To provide centrally supported programs and data

- To share data among users in a group

Most file sharing occurs between similar systems. Similar systems often run the same applications and may share a wide range of data. For example, two PCs running WordPerfect can share a native WordPerfect file. If you want to share this file with a system that doesn't run WordPerfect, it must be converted to a common format such as ASCII. Differences from the original may occur in the conversion. The classic example of this is the difference between the way DOS and UNIX systems terminate lines in a file—DOS uses a carriage-return/line-feed, and UNIX uses only a line-feed.[*]

Another problem can occur in the differences of file-naming conventions. UNIX systems permit names up to 255 characters in length. Windows NT and Windows 95 support long filenames, but DOS limits filenames to eight characters with a three character extension. When a file must be converted and renamed much of the charm of file sharing is lost. Sharing files between similar systems is much easier.

On a PC network, files are generally shared between PCs. The UNIX server is only a repository for the files. Data and programs originate on the PCs, are written to the server, and then retrieved from the server by other PCs. Many times, the filesystem that is exported from the server is just empty space waiting to be filled by the PC clients.

Once you've selected the filesystems to export, define them in the */etc/exports* file.

The /etc/exports File

The */etc/exports* file is the NFS server configuration file. It controls which files and directories are exported, which hosts can access them, and what kinds of access are allowed. The general format of an */etc/exports* entry is:

directory [*−option*][*,option*] . . .

directory names the directory or file that is available for export, while each *option* specifies a condition for the export of that directory. Commonly used options are:

ro   Read-only prevents NFS clients from writing to the directory. Attempts to write to a read-only directory fail with the message "Read-only filesystem" or

---

* Most NFS systems provide conversion programs to handle this condition, like unix2dos and dos2unix. Other common names for these utilities are utod, dtou, and d2u.

"Permission denied." If **ro** is not specified, clients are permitted to write to the directory as well as read from it.

rw[=*hostname*][:*hostname*] . . .

Read-write permits clients to read and write to this directory. When specified without *hostname* as simply **rw**, all clients are granted read-write access. (As noted above, this is the default.) If a *hostname* is specified, only the named host is given read-write permission. All other hosts are limited to read-only permission.

access=*hostname*[:*hostname*] . . .

access limits permission to mount this directory to those hosts specified by *hostname*. No other hosts are permitted to mount this directory. If the **access** option is not used, all hosts are allowed to mount the directory. Servers connected to the Internet should always use the **access** option; otherwise, their filesystems will be exported to everyone on the Internet.

A sample */etc/exports* file might contain these entries:

```
/home/pc/help       -rw=almond:pecan
/home/pc/tools      -ro
/home/pc/public     -access=allofus
/home/pc/research   -access=peanut:brazil:acorn:walnut
```

This sample file says that:

- */home/pc/help* can be mounted by any client, but it can only be written to by *almond* and *pecan*. Other clients have read-only access. This might be a directory where files used by a "help" system are stored. The files can be accessed by the "help" program on any PC but can only be modified by the two systems authorized to write to this directory.

- */home/pc/tools* can be mounted by any client, with read-only access. This might be a directory of freely-distributable public domain PC software.

- */home/pc/public* can be mounted by any client in the netgroup *allofus* and used as if it were that client's local directory. Anyone in the netgroup can put a file in this directory that can then be accessed by all other systems in the group. (Netgroups are discussed in the next section.)

- */home/pc/research* can only be mounted by the PCs *peanut, brazil, acorn,* and *walnut*. These four PCs have read-write access. This is a shared directory that can be used by all of the systems in this workgroup but by no one else.

If your server runs NIS, a netgroup can be used in place of a hostname in any *exports* file entry. Netgroups are defined in the */etc/netgroup* file.

The /etc/netgroup File

The */etc/netgroup* file defines groups of hosts and users that can be referenced wherever hostnames and usernames are used. The */etc/netgroup* file can only be used on systems running NIS, because it is accessed only via its NIS maps *netgroup.byhost* and *netgroup.byuser*. If your UNIX system does not run NIS, skip this section.*

The basic format of an entry in the netgroup file is:

> *groupname member* [*member*] . . .

groupname is any name you wish to assign to the group. *member* is an item included in the group, and it can either be the name of another group (i.e., another *groupname*) or the definition of an individual item. Individual members of the group are defined by their hostname, username, and NIS domain name—a form called a triple. The format of this triple is:

> (*hostname, username, domainname*)

The */etc/netgroup* entry used to define a netgroup called *admin* is shown below. One member contains the host *almond* and the user *kathy*, and the other member contains the host *peanut* and the user *craig*:

```
admin   (almond,kathy,) (peanut,craig,)
```

Notice that the *domainname* field for each member is empty. *domainname* is the name of the NIS domain in which this netgroup is valid. This field either contains your local NIS domain name, or it is empty. An empty field is a wildcard value meaning that every possible value is included. You only need to use your NIS domain name when multiple NIS domains exist on the same network segment, and you need to define which NIS domain owns the netgroup.†

If the sample *admin* netgroup is used in situations that require hostnames, the NIS software accesses the *netgroup.byhost* map and returns the values *almond* and *peanut*. In situations that require usernames, the *admin* netgroup provides the values *kathy* and *craig*, because NIS retrieves the values from the *netgroup.byuser* map. A single reference to the netgroup provides hostnames or usernames, but not both. Which you get depends on the context in which the netgroup is used. Because of this, most administrators prefer to define separate netgroups for hosts and users. For example:

```
adminhosts (almond,-,) (peanut,-,) (pecan,-,)
adminusers (-,kathy,) (-,sara,) (-,david,) (-,rebecca,)
```

---

* The information in this section is very specific to SunOS. Before installing NIS on your system, read your system's documentation.
† NIS domains are specific to NIS. They're not the same as DNS domains or NTAS domains, but they serve the same purpose. An NIS domain indentifies a group of NIS clients and their servers.

These examples have fields that contain dashes (-). A dash means that no values are included in the set. All username fields in our *adminhosts* netgroup contain dashes, and all hostname fields in the *adminusers* netgroup contain dashes. So if the *adminhosts* netgroup is used in a situation where usernames are required, NIS returns a value indicating that no usernames belong to this netgroup. The same null value is returned if the *adminusers* netgroup is used in a situation that calls for hostnames.

As an example of how netgroups are used in configuring NFS, assume the following */etc/netgroup* file:

```
allofus sales research budget
research (acorn,-,) (peanut,-,) (walnut,-,) (brazil,-,)
sales (almond,-,) (pecan,-,) (filbert,-,)
budget (pistachio,-,) (cashew,-,) (hazel,-,)
```

This file defines a netgroup called *allofus* that encompasses all of the other groups: *budget, sales*, and *research*. The *allofus* netgroup is used in the sample */etc/exports* entry that grants access to the */home/pc/public* directory. It grants access to all ten hosts exactly as if each host had been explicitly listed in the access statement. For example, one of the sample */etc/exports* entries is:

```
/home/pc/research  -access=peanut:brazil:acorn:walnut
```

This entry can be rewritten, using the *research* netgroup, as:

```
/home/pc/research  -access=research
```

The hostnames *peanut, acorn, brazil*, and *walnut* are provided by the *research* netgroup. Both of these */etc/exports* statements perform the same function, i.e., they both limit access to the four hosts that are members of the research group. Netgroups are not essential for NFS, but they simplify the job of configuring a UNIX NFS server.

Now, we have defined the filesystems to export and the computers to export them to, and we have started the necessary daemons. Those of you familiar with NFS in a UNIX environment may think the configuration is complete, but one more step is necessary to configure a server to support PC clients.

NFS Authentication Server

The *PC NFS Authentication and Print Server* (**pcnfsd**) is needed to support PC clients on an NFS network. The print services of this daemon are covered later in this chapter. The authentication services are the services needed by NFS.

The reason NFS needs an authentication server for PC clients springs from the difference between *trusted host* security and *password authenticated* security. Trusted host security is discussed in Chapter 8. Essentially, it works this way: we trusted that a remote host has already authenticated its users, and we grant those users equivalent access to our local host. This is more or less how NFS treats UNIX clients. The **−access** option in an */etc/exports* file entry lists trusted hosts that are granted NFS access. A user is allowed to access files through NFS using standard UNIX *user, group,* and *world* file permissions based on the *userid* (UID) and *groupid* (GID) provided by the trusted host. Remember, if the **−access** option is not used, all hosts are trusted to access the exported filesystem.

The trusted host model does not work for traditional PC clients for a couple of reasons. First, PCs traditionally did not perform local user authentication. Anyone who sits at the keyboard of a DOS PC has complete access to the system. Second, DOS PCs do not use user or group IDs. The PC does not provide any value that can be mapped to the UNIX user or group file permissions. At best an unauthenticated PC user can be granted world permissions.[*] Newer PC operating systems do provide authentication, but we need a scheme that will work for all of our PC clients. We need a server that authenticates usernames and passwords and assigns UIDs and GIDs to the authenticated users. That's what the PC NFS authentification server does.

The PC NFS authentication server can run on any system on the network. It is not necessary to run it on the NFS server, but that is the most common configuration.

PCNFSD

The PC NFS authentication server is not included in the software of most UNIX systems, but the source code for **pcnsfd** is available from many anonymous FTP servers on the Internet. The code used in this example came from *ftp.ftp.com* where it is stored as a compressed tar file in *support/pubdom/pcnfsd.taz*. Retrieve the compressed file in binary mode, make a directory to hold the software, and store the file under a standard compressed tar file name, such as *pcnfsd.tar.Z*. The commands used to retrieve this file are shown below:

```
% mkdir pcnfsd
% cd pcnfsd
% ftp ftp.ftp.com
Name (ftp.ftp.com:craigh): anonymous
331 Guest login ok, send your complete e-mail address as password.
Password:
ftp> cd support/pubdom
ftp> binary
ftp> get pcnfsd2.taz pcnfsd2.tar.Z
ftp> quit
221 Goodbye.
```

Uncompress the tar file, and extract the software into the new directory using **tar**.

```
% uncompress pcnfsd2.tar.Z
% tar -xvf pcnfsd2.tar
```

---

[*] PC users who have not been authenticated are assigned the user ID *nobody* and given world permissions.

```
x Makefile, 3953 bytes, 8 tape blocks
...
x pcnfsd.x, 19134 bytes, 38 tape blocks
```

Modify the *Makefile* as necessary for your system and compile the software with
make. Note that **make** creates a directory under the current directory to hold the
compiled programs. The name of the directory varies depending on the value
assigned to TARGET_OS in the *Makefile*. In the example, the TARGET_OS, and
therefore the subdirectory, is *sunos.*[*] If **pcnfsd** compiles without errors, copy the
daemon from the directory created by **make** into some system directory such as
/usr/etc.

```
# make
mkdir sunos
cc  -c  -O -DOSVER_SUNOS41 -o sunos/pcnfsd_svc.o pcnfsd_svc.c
...
cc  -o sunos/clnt.pcnfsd  -O -DOSVER_SUNOS41  sunos/pcnfsd_clnt.o
sunos/pcnfsd_test.o  sunos/pcnfsd_xdr.o -lrpcsvc
# cp sunos/rpc.pcnfsd /usr/etc/rpc.pcnfsd
```

pcnfsd can be started from a boot script in the following manner:

```
if [ -f /usr/etc/rpc.pcnfsd ]; then
      /usr/etc/rpc.pcnfsd; echo -n ' rpc.pcnfsd'
fi
```

Normally, starting a daemon from **inetd** is an alternative to starting it from a boot
script. However, Sun cautions against starting **pcnfsd** from **inetd** because the slow
startup of this daemon can cause time-out errors.

Once the **pcnfsd** daemon is installed and running, the server authenticates usernames and passwords for its PC clients. Here's how. When the user asks to mount
a remote filesystem, the PC NFS software prompts him for a username and password. It sends them to the authentication server, and the server validates them
against its */etc/passwd* file. A user that can successfully login to the server is considered to be a valid NFS user. The server sends the PC client the UID and GID
that are assigned to the user in the *passwd* file, and the client uses them for NFS
access.

The authentication server must have an entry in the */etc/passwd* file for every PC
user who needs NFS access. It is common for a large UNIX server such as the mail
server, which has an account for every PC user, to be used as the authentication
server. However, it is not absolutely necessary to use a large system. A PC can be
used as an authentication server and as an NFS server. The next section looks at
how this is done with a PC running Windows.

---

[*] **pcnfsd** has been ported to many different systems. Check the USENET newsgroup
comp.protocols.nfs for information on various ports.

A PC-based File Server

In many ways it is easier to configure a PC to be an NFS file server than it is to configure a UNIX system for the same job. Also, the authentication server that runs on the PC does not require you to grant login access to users that you really only want to authenticate for NFS access. The reasons that PCs are not used as servers are poor performance and reliability. These limitations are caused by the current weaknesses of Windows multitasking and may be resolved in the next generation of Windows. Meanwhile, a PC running Windows is not a good choice as a server for a large network; at best it is adequate for a very small PC network.

ChameleonNFS from NetManage is used for this section. However, the configuration requirements for a PC-based NFS server are largely the same no matter what implementation of NFS is used.

The first step is to define the users who will be permitted access to the server. The concept of user accounts is foreign to most PC users. PCs are, after all, personal computers—computers dedicated to one person. In a standard PC environment, there is no need for user accounts. As we saw in Chapter 5, TCP/IP for Windows introduces user accounts into the PC environment to authenticate users for such services as POP mail. The same type of authentication is needed for NFS access.

To define NFS users for the *ChameleonNFS* server, select the **Users** button from the NFS Server window. The window in Figure 10-1 appears. To add a new user enter the user name, password, user ID and group ID; then select the **Add** button. To delete or change a user entry, highlight the entry and select the **Delete** or **Modify** button as appropriate.

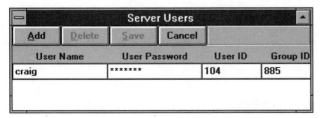

Figure 10–1: Adding NFS Users

After entering the NFS users, select the directories to be exported. Apply the same criteria used for a UNIX server: export only directories that are useful to your clients and export them only to clients that should really have access to your system.

Figure 10-2 shows the window used to define the directories to be exported. Open this window by selecting the **Exports** button in the NFS Server window. The Directory box lists the current directory and all of the disk drives. In the example, the current directory is C:\USERS\CRAIG, and the available disk drives are A: through F:. Select any item from the list or type a DOS pathname in the Directory box and then press the **Add** button. Items added to the export list are displayed in UNIX pathname format in the Exports box. In the example, the DOS directory C:\USERS\CRAIG is listed in the Export box as */c/users/craig*.

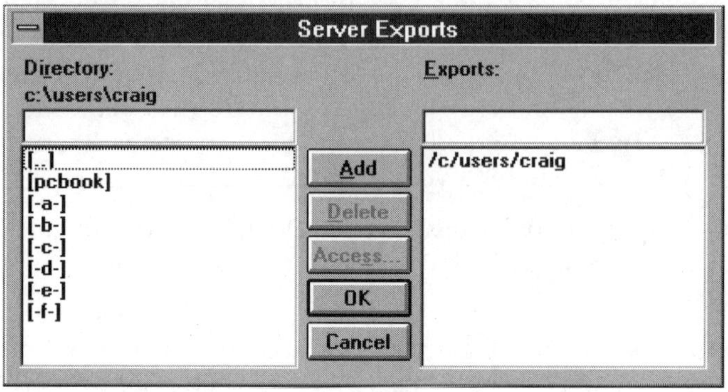

Figure 10-2: Exporting an NFS Filesystem

When a directory is defined for export, the access controls for that directory should also be defined. Highlight the exported directory, */c/users/craig* in Figure 10-2, and click the **Access** button. This opens the dialogue box shown in Figure 10-3. The box in Figure 10-3 shows the list of valid NFS users we defined earlier. Highlight the users you wish to give access to and click the **Add** button. If you do not identify any specific users, the system defaults to granting everyone access.

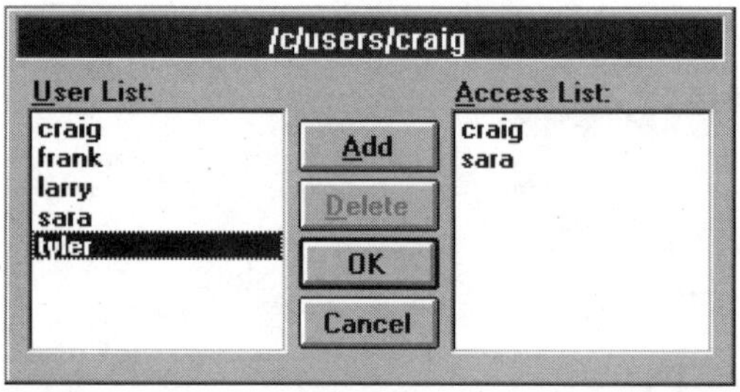

Figure 10-3: NFS File Access

That's it! Define the valid users, define the directories that are to be exported, and define the users to be given access to those directories. That's all there is to creating a PC-based NFS server.

This concludes our discussion of the server side of NFS. If you're responsible for an NFS server for a large site, you should take care in planning and implementing the NFS environment. The short discussion in this chapter tells how to configure a UNIX system or a PC to be an NFS server. You may want more details to design an optimal NFS environment. For a comprehensive treatment, see the Nutshell Handbook *Managing NFS and NIS*, by Hal Stern.

Configuring the Client

Networked PCs are much more likely to be NFS clients than NFS servers. PC users are much more interested in mounting filesystems than they are in exporting them. Users need some basic information in order to decide which NFS directories to mount on their systems: What servers are connected to the network? What directories are available from those servers? How does a user find out what is being exported?

The network administrator is a good source for this information. The administrator tells users what systems are providing NFS service, what directories they are exporting, and what these directories contain. If you are the administrator of an NFS server, you should develop this type of information for your users. This is a laudable goal, but who has time! Documentation is the first thing to suffer when the administrator is too busy.

Luckily, most NFS clients have software that allows the user to obtain information about the exported directories directly from the servers. The NFS servers are often easy to identify because they are usually the same large centrally-supported systems that provide other services such as mail and domain name service. Select a likely server and query it with the software provided by your system.

UNIX clients use the **showmount −e** command to query an NFS server. In response to this command, the server lists the directories that it exports and the conditions applied to their export. For example, a **showmount −e** query to *filbert* produces the following output:

```
% showmount -e filbert
export list for filbert:
/usr/man        (everyone)
/usr/local      (everyone)
```

The export list shows the NFS directories exported by *filbert*, as well as who is allowed to access those directories.

PC clients can also query servers for information about the filesystems they export. *ChameleonNFS* client software provides the Browse Network Connections window shown in Figure 10-4. Enter a server name in the Host box and click the **Directories** button. This displays a list of the directories exported by the server. Figure 10-4 shows the directories exported by *pecan*.

How much you use NFS is a personal choice. Some people prefer the greater personal control you get from keeping files locally, while others prefer the convenience offered by NFS. Your site may have guidelines for how NFS should be used, which directories should be mounted, and which files should be centrally maintained. Check with your network administrator if you're unsure about how NFS is used at your site.

Figure 10–4: Browsing NFS Filesystems

Mounting Directories

A PC client must mount an exported directory before using it. "Mounting" the directory attaches it to the PC's filesystem hierarchy. Any part of the directory exported by the server, such as a subdirectory or a file, can be mounted by the client.

DOS clients use a variety of commands to mount directories. In DOS mode, *SuperTCP V3.0* uses a very UNIX-like **mount** command. *PC-NFS* has a **net use** command reminiscent of *LAN Manager*. *PC/TCP* uses a unique **idrive** command. And each of these packages has a different name for the NFS TSR!

Regardless of the differences, DOS clients are configured in the same basic way. First, start the NFS client TSR in the AUTOEXEC.BAT file and then mount the remote directories assigning each a unique DOS drive letter. *PC/TCP* and *SuperTCP* provide good examples of exactly how this works and how similar different implementations can be.

SuperTCP is really a Windows package. However, the software can be used directly from DOS because it offers an optional TSR-based kernel and a TSR implementation of NFS. Install the NFS TSR by adding the following line to the AUTOEXEC.BAT file and rebooting the system:[*]

```
nfsinit
```

With the **nfsinit** TSR running, mount remote filesystems with the **mount** command. To mount */home/pc/research* from the server *pecan*, the user *kristen* enters the following command:

```
C:\> mount pecan:/home/pc/research r: -n kristen
Password:
```

This command mounts the remote directory on DOS disk drive *R:*. It passes the username *kristen* to the NFS server for authentication and prompts for the password associated with that username. The password can be placed directly on the command line using the **–w** option, but for security reasons most people don't like to put a clear text password on a command line.

---

[*] It's a good idea to test commands by running them from the DOS command-line before putting them in the AUTOEXEC.BAT file.

Once the mount command is executed, Kristen can use the files from */home/pc/research* as if they were files on a local disk drive called *R:*. A DOS **dir** command lists the files as if they were local to the PC:

```
C:\> dir r:
```

There are some differences between local files and files mounted via NFS. First, Kristen's access to NFS files is limited by the file permissions she has on the NFS server. It is possible that there are files on the *R:* drive that Kristen cannot write to or delete because neither the UID nor GID associated with the username *kristen* has write permission for those files. This access limitation could not happen if the files really were on a local disk drive because DOS does not have file permissions. A DOS user has full privileges to all local files.

Second, it is possible that some of the files written to the remote directory were written by non-DOS systems and that they are incompatible with DOS. Even the filenames can be incompatible and may be remapped by the NFS client software into a format that is acceptable to DOS. Most DOS implementations automatically remap incompatible names. This produces some very odd looking names, but at least they can be referenced on a DOS system. We don't see any incompatible names in the sample display because this filesystem is exclusively for the use of DOS clients.

Installing the *PC/TCP* NFS client software has several similarities to installing *SuperTCP*, although on the surface the installations appear quite different. The NFS TSR used by *PC/TCP* is named **idrive**. It is started by including the following command in AUTOEXEC.BAT.

```
idrive -m 8
```

This command starts the NFS client and says that the client will be able to mount up to eight remote filesystems (**–m 8**). The default for **idrive** is to allow two simultaneous mounts. The maximum that *PC/TCP* allows is sixteen, which is the same number of mounts allowed by *SuperTCP's* **nfsinit** TSR. The cost of increasing the number of mounts is memory. PC users that won't be mounting a large number of remote filesystems can reduce TSR memory by setting a low value for **–m**.

To mount directories *PC/TCP* uses the command **idmnt**. On a *PC/TCP* system, *kristen* mounts the */home/pc/research* directory on the R: drive with the following command:

```
C:\> idmnt research pecan /home/pc/research r pcnfs kristen
Mounting filesystem "research"...
Password for kristen:
File system "research" mounted on drive R:
```

Most of the fields on this command line are self explanatory. *pecan* is the name of the NFS server; */home/pc/research* is the remote directory; *r* is the drive the directory is to be mounted on; and *kristen* is the username used for authentication. The other two fields need a little explanation.

pcnfs is the *security keyword* used with **pcnfsd**. **idmnt** requires the security key-word, and the value provided must always be *pcnfs* or *user*. These values are equivalent and interchangeable, though *pcnfs* is the most commonly used.

The first command-line argument, *research*, is an arbitrary symbolic name assigned by the user to this mount. Every filesystem mounted by a *PC/TCP* client is given a unique symbolic name by the user. In the **idmnt** example shown above, all of the mount parameters are provided on the command line, but this is not absolutely necessary. The symbolic name can refer to a set of mount parameters defined in the PCTCP.INI configuration file. Assume that the following lines are included in PCTCP.INI:

```
[pctcp idrive research]
host = pecan
path = /home/pc/research
drive = r
sec-key = pcnfs
sec-arg = kristen
```

With these lines defined in the configuration file, only the symbolic name is required to mount this filesystem. */home/pc/research* can be mounted on *R:* with the following command:

```
C:\> idmnt research
Mounting filesystem "research"...
Password for kristen:
File system "research" mounted on drive R:
```

The point of this discussion is not the details of these commands, because the details vary from implementation to implementation. The key thing to note is that regardless of the command we use, we provide the client software with the name of the NFS server, the path of the remote directory, the name of the local disk drive, and the name of the user to be granted access. All PC clients require this same basic information.

Once a remote directory is mounted, it stays attached to the local filesystem until it is explicitly unmounted or the local system reboots. Naturally, each DOS imple-mentation has its own unique command to unmount a directory: *PC/TCP* uses the command **idumnt**; *SuperTCP* uses **umount**; and other systems use still other com-mands. On the *PC/TCP* system, Kristen unmounts the filesystem mounted on the *R:* drive with:

```
C:\> idumnt r:
Unmounting file system "research" from drive R: ...
Drive R: unmounted
```

To do the same thing on the *SuperTCP* system, she enters:

```
C:\> umount r:
```

Booting also unmounts NFS directories. To mount the same directories every time you boot, put the mount commands in AUTOEXEC.BAT.

Windows Clients

Considering all of the differences in the DOS commands used to configure an NFS client, Windows NFS clients are remarkably similar in appearance. The consistent Windows interface gives them a common look and feel, and most of the NFS clients are directly integrated into the Windows *File Manager*.

The *File Manager* has built-in features that support network file servers. *File Manager's* network support was not specifically developed for TCP/IP; Microsoft probably had Windows for Workgroups and LAN Manager in mind. However, the network support has been put to excellent use by some of the developers of TCP/IP for Windows. The integration of NFS into Windows is much smoother then it is in DOS. We use *ChameleonNFS* in this example, but *SuperTCP* is almost identical in its look and feel.

First, define a username to be used for **pcnfsd** authentication. On a *ChameleonNFS* client, open the **Control Panel** from the Main window. Select the **Network** icon. In the Networks dialogue box, select the **Network . . .** button. Figure 10-5 shows the configuration window that appears. In this window, enter the username in the Username box and the name of the **pcnfsd** server in the Authenticator box. The NFS server is asked to authenticate the user even if there is no Authenticator value entered here. This box gives you a way to identify a central **pcnfsd** server, if the authentication server is a different system than the NFS server.

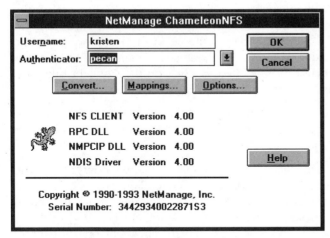

Figure 10–5: ChameleonNFS Client Configuration

On a *SuperTCP* system, the same basic authentication information is entered in a dialogue box started by selecting **NFS/Client** from the SetupTCP listbox. SetupTCP is not found in the Control Panel window; it is started from the SuperTCP window. How the values are entered may vary, but what is entered remains the same. All NFS clients have some way for users to specify their usernames. If a user is having trouble using NFS, make sure he has entered a valid username.

To mount a directory using *ChameleonNFS*, open the *File Manager* and select the
Network Connections ... item from the **Disk** pulldown menu. The window shown
in Figure 10-6 pops up.[*]

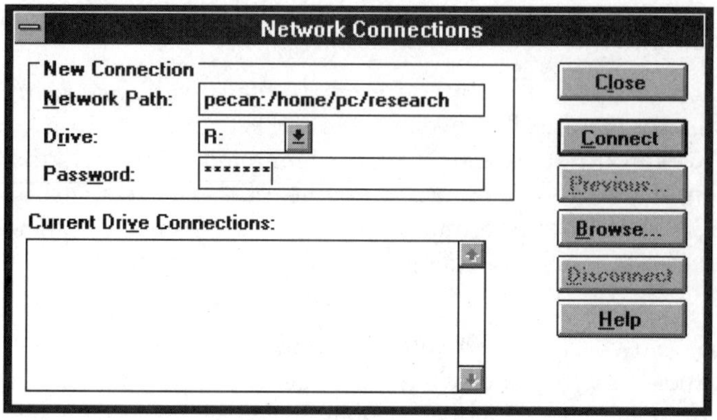

Figure 10–6: Mounting an NFS Filesystem

Use the New Connection box near the top of the window to mount a new directory. In the Network Path box, enter the name of the filesystem you want to
mount as the NFS server name, a colon, and the UNIX path of the remote directory. In Figure 10-6 the server is *pecan* and the directory is */home/pc/research*, so
the entry in this box is *pecan:/home/pc/research*. Use the Drive box to specify the
local drive on which to mount the filesystem. Finally, the password used to
authenticate the user with the **pcnsfd** server is entered in the Password box. The
username used for authentication is the one we entered earlier using the *Control
Panel*. When the New Connection box is filled in, click on the **Connect** button to
mount the filesystem. This is the same information (server, directory, drive letter,
and user) required by the DOS client.

Once a filesystem is mounted, it is listed in the Current Drive Connections box. To
dismount a filesystem, highlight it in that box and click the **Disconnect** button.

Clicking the **Browse** button in the Network Connections window opens the
Browse Network Connections dialogue box discussed earlier. *SuperTCP* has an
almost identical dialogue box for browsing exported directories, and it is used in
almost the same way. Enter a server name in the Hostname box and click on
Mount Info. A list of exported filesystems is displayed. Highlight one and press
Select. This fills in the Network Path value in the Network Connections box. Click
the **Connect** button in that box, and the filesystem is mounted. These steps are
very similar to those used with *ChameleonNFS*. The consistent Windows interface

---

[*] This assumes that TCP/IP is your only network software. If you have installed multiple
network packages, the Select Network box will appear first. If it does, just click on the NFS
button.

makes it possible for a network administrator to apply expertise developed on one Windows package to a competing package.

Network Backup

Without the addition of any other special software, file sharing can be used to backup PC files across the network. The **BACKUP** command that comes with DOS and Windows 3.1 allows one device to be backed up to another. We usually think of backing up a hard drive, C: for example, to a floppy drive, such as A:. But a disk can be backed up to anything that can be identified with a pathname. As we saw in the previous section, a remote filesystem appears to be a local PC disk drive when file sharing protocols are used. It is a simple matter to reference the remote filesystem in the **BACKUP** command.

Figure 10-7 shows the **BACKUP** command on a Windows 3.1 system. In the figure, the C: drive is backed up to the R: drive, and the R: drive is actually a directory on a remote file server.

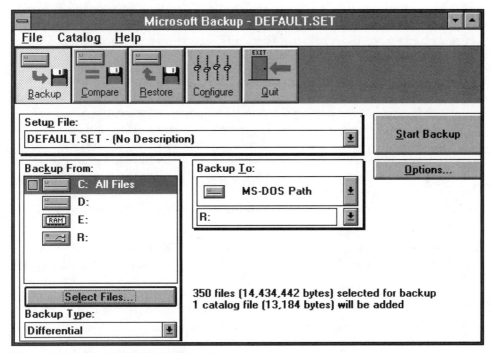

Figure 10–7: The BACKUP Command

This simple use of file sharing with the **BACKUP** command has some advantages. You don't have to play "swap the floppies," so the backup can run unattended once it has started. Additionally, if files on the remote server are periodically backed up to tape, the PC files stored on that server are included in that backup.

Even this simple form of network backup is a real improvement over backing up to floppies, but it does have limitations.

The biggest limitation of using the **BACKUP** command for network backup is that it requires the user to be there to start the backup process. **BACKUP** does not have a delayed start mechanism, and the DOS and Windows 3.1 operating systems do not provide facilities for delayed execution. Of course, users can run **BACKUP** just before going home for the night, but if all of the users on a large network run backups at the same time, it can overload the network and the server. And if network backups are run throughout the workday, they can heavily burden the network during its busiest time. It is best to have a fixed schedule for backups and to schedule them for times when the network is lightly used.

Filling up the remote server's filesystem is another possible problem with backing up to a directory over the network. PC disk drives are getting bigger all the time. If several users do "full" backups to the server at the same time, the server's filesystem may fill up, causing big problems for the server.

There are at least two ways to address these problems. One is to buy special network backup software for the server and the PC. This type of software provides timed execution and remote control for the backup clients. The biggest advantage of custom backup software is that it is usually designed to run on DOS machines as well as Windows 3.1 machines.

Another alternative is to run file server software on the PC so that it can be backed up from a remote computer. An advantage of this approach is that it does not require any special software beyond the PC file sharing software; the timed execution software only needs to be on the remote computer. Take, for example, a TCP/IP network, where a Windows PC runs NFS server software, and the remote computer is a UNIX server. The UNIX server already has built-in timed execution in the form of the **cron** command. Additionally, the administrator of the UNIX server knows the capacity of the server's filesystem. He can backup the PC to the UNIX filesystem or directly to tape, whichever he chooses, because the backup is controlled from the UNIX server.

The first step is to install NFS software on the PC. This was described in "A PC-based File Server" earlier in this chapter. Now, to support network backup of the C: drive:

- Define the UNIX system administrator as a user on the PC. (See Figure 10-1.)

- Export C:\. (See Figure 10-2.)

- Allow only the system administrator access to the newly exported directory. (See Figure 10-3.)

Once the PC is configured, the UNIX administrator can mount the PC filesystem and back it up using UNIX commands. In the following example, the administrator creates a mount point for the PC *peanut*, mounts the C:\ directory from the PC, and backs up the C:\USER subdirectory to tape. The last line in the example

copies a DOS batch file from the UNIX server to the C:\ directory on the PC.*
(More on what the batch file is for in a minute.)

```
# mkdir /mnt/peanut
# mount peanut:/c /mnt/peanut
# tar -cvf /dev/rst0 /mnt/peanut/user
# unix2dos /usr/local/setbits.bat /mnt/peanut
# umount /mnt/peanut
# rmdir /mnt/peanut
```

These steps can be stored in a shell script and executed on a weekly or monthly basis with the **cron** command.

Running the backup from the UNIX system overcomes some of the problems of running the backup from the PC, but it has problems of its own. For example, it provides only a full backup. The Microsoft **BACKUP** command provides three different types of backup:

- *Full*, which backs up every file in the specified path.

- *Incremental*, which backs up every file that has not yet been backed up.

- *Differential*, which backs up every file that was not included in the last full backup.

The different types of backup work by manipulating the *archive* attribute of the files. The full backup does not check the archive bit. It saves every file and clears the archive bit for every file. The incremental backup checks the archive bit and saves only the files that have the archive bit set. It also clears the archive bit of each file that it saves. The differential backup saves every file that has the archive bit set. A differential backup does not clear the archive bit after saving a file, so the file set of a differential backup grows larger with each successive backup until a full backup is run. With differential backups only the last full backup and the last differential backup are needed to fully restore a filesystem. With incremental backups, the last full backup and every incremental backup since the last full backup are needed to restore a filesystem.

As we noted, the UNIX backup example is a full backup. There is no simple way to change this because the UNIX server cannot directly interrogate the archive bit of the files on a remote PC. Additionally, the UNIX commands do not automatically clear the archive bit after saving a PC file. A full backup should save the file and clear the archive bit. To clear the archive bit, the **ATTRIB** (attribute) command needs to be run on the PC. The bit can be changed indirectly from the UNIX server by storing a batch file on the PC that executes the **ATTRIB** command. That's what the last line in the UNIX example does.

For this to work, the batch file must be executed on the PC. One way to do this is to call the batch file from the last line of AUTOEXEC.BAT, so that it is executed every time the PC reboots. In our example, the batch command being run from

---

* The **unix2dos** command converts files from UNIX format to PC format.

AUTOEXEC.BAT is SETBITS.BAT. Therefore, the last line in the AUTOEXEC.BAT file on the PC is `SETBITS`.

The batch file itself clears the archive bit of all the files that were saved and then replaces itself with a "harmless" batch file that is run on most days. The harmless batch file would contain only a REMARK command or a pleasant message to the user such as:

```
ECHO "Don't forget to run your daily differential backup today."
```

Assume that the "harmless" batch file is named DAILY.BAT. The SETBITS.BAT file contains the following lines:

```
ECHO "Please wait while the filesystem is updated."
ATTRIB -a C:\USER\*.*
COPY DAILY.BAT SETBITS.BAT
```

The "real" SETBITS.BAT file is copied from the UNIX server to the PC after the files are backed up. It executes the next time the user reboots the PC and replaces itself with the harmless batch file. That way archive bits are only cleared when the backup is run and are not cleared everytime the system is restarted. If the batch file didn't do this, incremental and differential backups wouldn't work properly because it would appear that a full backup was run every day.

For any of this to work, policies and procedures must be established for when PCs are backed up, when they must be rebooted, and what the directory structure must be on the PC. No one solution is perfect, so you have to decide what is best for you. What you want to back up, how often you want to back it up, and what type of backup is best are all issues that you should think about before putting a policy in place.

The proper use of file backups in a file sharing environment is widely debated. It is possible to design an environment where important data files are kept on the server so that they are backed up as part of the standard operating procedures of the server. Properly used, file sharing not only simplifies file backup, it reduces the need for it.

Print Services

Print services are one of the basic features of a PC LAN. A print server allows printers to be shared by everyone on the network. Printer sharing is not as important as file sharing, but it is a useful network service. The advantages of printer sharing are:

- Fewer printers are needed. It is not necessary for every PC to have a local printer. Less money is spent on printers, and less office space is consumed by computer equipment.

- Reduced maintenance. There are fewer machines to maintain, and fewer people spending time fiddling with printers.

- Access to special printers. Very high quality color printers and very high speed printers are expensive and only needed occasionally. Sharing these printers makes the best use of expensive resources.

There are two techniques commonly used for sharing printers on a TCP/IP network. One technique is the traditional PC LAN approach that uses the network's file sharing services and DOS printer redirection. The other approach is the traditional UNIX network technique that uses the **lpr** command and an **lpd** server. We start with a discussion of how NFS and **pcnfsd** are used to redirect DOS printers across a TCP/IP network.

NFS Print Services

NFS-based print services are easy to understand and simple to configure. The Network File System is used to move the print file to the server, and the server uses standard printer commands to print the file. The NFS server exports a printer spool directory to its clients, and the clients redirect print files into that directory. **pcnfsd** sends files deposited in the directory to printers accessible to the server. Any printer defined in the server's */etc/printcap* file can be used.

NFS-based printing has two advantages:

- Very little code is required on the client. The client doesn't need additional protocols to transfer print files because it uses the file sharing protocol that is already installed as part of the network software.

- DOS printer redirection is supported. DOS uses the logical names LPT1, LPT2, and LPT3 to refer to the printers attached to the PC. These logical names can be redirected to remote printers attached to the print server.

To add NFS print service to a UNIX server, first install **pcnfsd** as described earlier. Next make a print spool directory on the UNIX server for the PC clients. This directory is usually called */usr/spool/pcnfs:*[*]

```
# mkdir /usr/spool/pcnfs
```

Add the spool directory's pathname to the exported filesystems listed in the */etc/exports* file.

```
/usr/spool/pcnfs  -access=allofus
```

Now you've finished! Running **pcnfsd** and exporting the printer spool directory are all that is required to configure the server, assuming that the printers are already properly configured. Check the printers by logging directly into the print server and issuing an **lpr** command for each printer you wish to test. See the following section on **lpr** and **lpd** if a printer is not properly configured.

---

[*] Use the *spool* command in the */etc/pcnfsd.conf* configuration file to define a different directory name. See the **pcnfsd** man page for details.

Setting up the client side of NFS-based printing is just as simple as setting up the server. The client needs NFS software to use the **pcnfsd** printer services, so the first step is to install the NFS client software as detailed earlier in this chapter. It is not necessary to explicitly mount the printer spool directory. That is handled by the NFS client and server software.

After the NFS client is installed, assign a logical printer name to the remote printer you want to use. Each DOS implementation has its own way to do this. The *PC-NFS* command for redirecting DOS printing to a remote printer is **net use**, which has a simple, self-explanatory syntax. The following command redirects LPT2 to the *lw* printer on the server *pecan*:

        C:\> **net use lpt2: pecan:lw**

The same task is done with the **idprint mount** command on a system running *PC/TCP*. This command is used in much the same way as the *PC/TCP* **idmnt** command shown earlier. First define the printer in the PCTCP.INI file, then install it with the **idprint mount** command. Assume that Kristen wants to use the Laser-Writer on *pecan* as LPT2 on her PC. She defines the following entry in PCTCP.INI:

```
[pctcp idprint lw]
host = pecan
printer = lw
user = kristen
device = lpt2
```

She then enters this command:

```
C:\> idprint mount lw
Printer directory initialized: directory = /usr/spool/pcnfs
Password for kristen:
```

Once the printer has been assigned a DOS logical name it is used like any other printer. The following **copy** command, issued from either the system running *PC-NFS* or the one running *PC/TCP*, prints the file *guests.txt* on the *lw* printer attached to *pecan*.

        C:\> **copy guests.txt lpt2:**

Wow! Just like a local printer. Remote printers can even be used from within DOS applications.

Windows Clients

Windows clients have a cleaner, better defined, and better integrated interface for attaching to network printers. Windows TCP/IP systems configure network printers through the standard Windows *Control Panel* in the same way that directly attached printers are configured.

To connect a printer, double-click on the **Printers** icon in the *Control Panel* and then click the **Connect...** button in the Printers dialogue box. In the Connect dialogue box, select the **Network . . .** button. The Network Connection dialogue box shown in Figure 10-8 appears. Select the **Port**, i.e., logical name, to be assigned to the printer and type in the path of the remote printer.

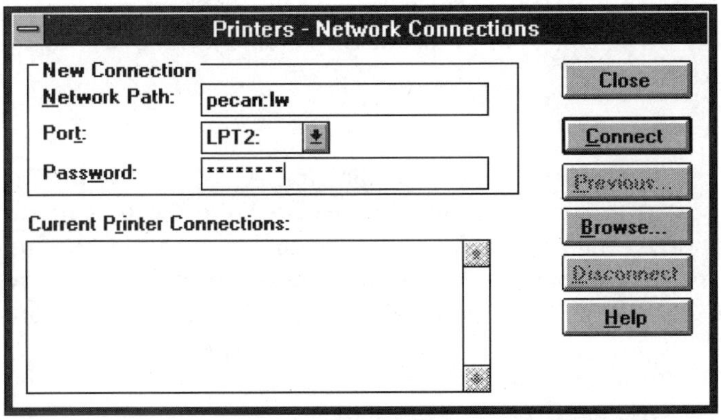

Figure 10–8: Connecting to a Network Printer

If you don't know what printers are offered by the server, use the Windows interface to find out. In the Network Connections dialogue box, select the **Browse** button. The Browse box shown in Figure 10-9 appears. Enter the hostname of the server and press the **PCNFS** button. A list of the printers on that server are displayed in the listbox. Highlight the printer you want to use and click the **OK** button. Enter your password when prompted for **pcnfsd** authentication, then choose **Connect** and **Close**. The printer is installed.

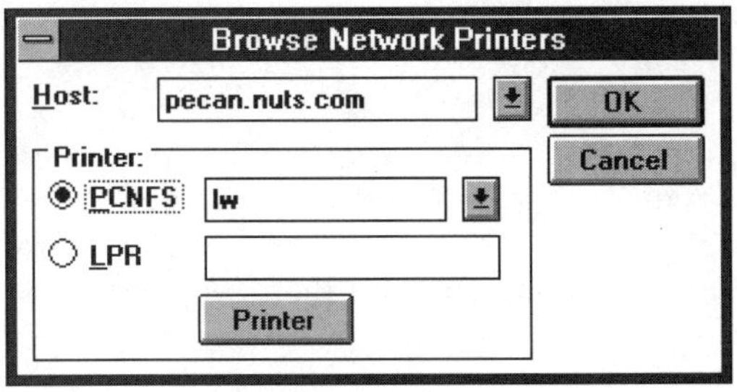

Figure 10–9: Browsing for Network Printers

Believe me, this sounds worse than it is. Because Windows is a visual interface, explaining it with words always makes it sound difficult. Installing a network printer is as easy as installing a directly connected printer, and when it's installed it is as easy to use.

Windows Print Server

Most DOS and Windows NFS implementations allow a PC to act as a print server. This example uses the NFS print server from *ChameleonNFS*. The configuration is very similar to the configuration of a UNIX print server. Again, we begin by defining a printer spool directory. Any name can be used. Let's create a directory called *spool* right under the root of drive *C:*.

```
C:\> mkdir c:\spool
```

Add the new spool directory to the list of exported directories. As we saw in Figure 10-2, directories are added to the export list by selecting the **Exports** menu item in the NFS Server window, entering the name of the directory in the Exports dialogue box, and pressing the **Add** button. In this case the name of the directory being exported is C:\SPOOL. Figure 10-10 shows the export list after the spool directory has been added.

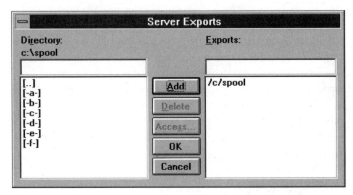

Figure 10-10: Exporting the Printer Spool Directory

Now that the printer spool is exported, enable NFS printing. From the NFS Server window, select the **Printing** menu item, which displays the Printer Server Settings dialogue box shown in Figure 10-11. In this box, enter the printer spool directory in a UNIX pathname format (*/c/spool*), select **Printing On**, and then press **OK**. The PC is now an NFS print server.

Figure 10-11: Enabling NFS Printer Sharing

NFS-based printing is a powerful and popular way to share printers across a TCP/IP network. It is particularly popular with traditional PC users because all implementations support printer redirection. It is not, however, the only way to share printers. We conclude this chapter by looking at how UNIX systems share network printers.

Line Printer Daemon

The *Line Printer Daemon* (**lpd**) provides printer services for local and remote users. **lpd** manages the printer spool area and the print queues. Most **lpd** servers are UNIX systems because **lpd** began as a UNIX program. But now it is widely implemented and is even available for PCs.

On a UNIX server, **lpd** is started at boot time from a startup script. It is generally included in the startup by default, so you probably don't need to add it. If you do, the following code is an example of starting **lpd** from the */etc/rc* script on a Sun system:

```
if [ -f /usr/lib/lpd ]; then
     rm -f /dev/printer /var/spool/lpd.lock
     /usr/lib/lpd;           echo -n ' printer'
fi
```

This code checks that the line printer daemon program is available. If it is, the code removes the internal device and the lockfile left by the last incarnation of the daemon. Only one copy of **lpd** can be running at a time. If multiple copies are allowed to run, the spool area and the printer queues might become unmanageable. The lock file *lpd.lock* prevents this. If **lpd** detects the lock file, it will not start. Therefore, this code needs to remove that file when starting **lpd** at boot time.

The printcap File

When **lpd** starts, it reads the */etc/printcap* file to find out about the printers available. The *printcap* file defines the printers and their characteristics. Configuring a *printcap* file is the scariest part of setting up a UNIX print server. It scares system administrators because the parser that reads the file is very finicky, and the syntax of the parameters in the file is terse and arcane. Most parser problems can be avoided by following these rules:

- Start each entry with a printer name that begins in the first column. No white space should precede the first printer name. Multiple printer names can be used if they are separated by pipe characters (|). One printer must have the name *lp*. If you have more than one printer on the server, assign *lp* to the "default" printer.

- Continue printer entries across multiple lines by escaping the new line character at the end of the line with a backslash (\), and by beginning the following line with a tab. Take care that no blank space comes after the backslash. The character after the backslash must be the newline character.

- Every field other than the printer name begins and ends with a colon. The character before the backslash on a continued line is a colon, and the first character after the tab on the continuation line is a colon.

- Begin comments with a pound-sign (#).

The configuration parameters used in a *printcap* file describe the characteristics of the printer. These characteristics are called "capabilities" in the documentation, but really they are the printer characteristics that **lpd** needs to know in order to communicate with the printer. Parameters are identified by names that are two characters long. The syntax of the parameters varies slightly depending on the type of value they are assigned. Parameters come in three different flavors:

Boolean

All *printcap* boolean values default to false. Specifying a boolean enables its function. Booleans are specified simply by entering the two-character parameter name in the file. For example, `:rs:` enables security for remote users.

Numeric

Some parameters are assigned numeric values. For example, `:br#9600:` sets the baud rate for a serial printer.

String

Some parameters use string values. For example, `:rp=laser:` defines the name of a remote printer.

A glance at the man page shows that there are many *printcap* parameters. Thankfully, you'll never need to use most of them. Most printer definitions are fairly simple, and most *printcap* files are small. Servers usually have only one or two directly attached printers; any other printers defined in the *printcap* are probably remote printers. Below are examples of a serial printer, a parallel printer, and a remote printer entry:

```
#
# Remote LaserWriter
#
lw:\
        :lf=/var/adm/lpd-errs:\
        :lp=:rm=pecan:rp=lw:\
        :sd=/var/spool/lpd-lw:
#
# Entry created by NeWSprint software
#
laser|sp|np:\
        :lp=/dev/lpvi0:\
        :sd=/var/spool/laser:\
        :lf=/var/spool/laser/log:\
        :af=/var/spool/laser/acct:\
        :if=/usr/newsprint/lpd/if:\
        :gf=/usr/newsprint/lpd/gf:\
        :nf=/usr/newsprint/lpd/nf:\
        :tf=/usr/newsprint/lpd/tf:\
```

```
                :rf=/usr/newsprint/lpd/rf:\
                :vf=/usr/newsprint/lpd/vf:\
                :cf=/usr/newsprint/lpd/cf:\
                :df=/usr/newsprint/lpd/df:\
                :of=/usr/newsprint/lpd/of:\
                :mx#0:\
                :sf:\
                :sb:
#
# lp - default line printer
#
lp:\
                :lp=/dev/ttya:br#9600:\
                :ms=-parity,onlcr,ixon:\
                :lf=/var/adm/lpd-errs:\
                :sd=/var/spool/lpd:
```

The first printer in this file (*lw*) is a remote printer. Remote printers are the simplest type to define because most of the real configuration work takes place on the remote system. The remote machine to which the printer is attached is defined by the `:rm=pecan:` parameter, and the name of the remote printer on that machine is defined by the `:rp=lw:` parameter. The `lf` parameter points to the log file used to log status and error messages. Multiple printers can use the same log file. The final parameter, `sd`, defines the spool directory. Each printer has its own unique spool directory.

The second printer is a directly attached parallel printer. In this case, the entry was made by the printer vendor's installation software. The system administrator really didn't have anything to do except install the hardware and insert the floppy disks when the install program asked for them. Printers that are specifically designed for use on UNIX systems sometimes come with predefined *printcap* entries.

The most interesting thing about this entry is the large number of filters defined for this printer. Filters are programs, generally shell scripts, that process the data contained in the print file before it is printed by the printer. The filter programs used in the example were all provided by the printer vendor, but filters can be written by the system administrator when necessary. Specific filters are invoked depending on the type of data in the print file. The filters and the type of data they are used with are:

if   The input filter

gf   The **plot** data filter

nf   The **ditroff** data filter

tf   The **troff** data filter

rf   The FORTRAN text files filter

vf   The raster image filter

cf   The **cifplot** data filter

df   The TeX data filter

of   The output filter

The third printer (*lp*) is a directly connected serial printer. The output device name is defined by the `lp` parameter. In this example it is */dev/ttya*, which is the first serial port on this computer. Care should be taken to prevent the system from attaching a login process to the port used for a printer. The status field in the */etc/ttytab* entry for the serial port, *ttya* in the example, should contain the keyword `off`. Here's a sample *ttytab* entry for *ttya*:

```
ttya  "/usr/etc/getty std.9600"     unknown        off local
```

The baud rate of the printer is defined by the `br` parameter, and the printer's "terminal options" are defined by the `ms` parameter. The terminal options are exactly the same as those used by the **stty** command; see the **stty** man page for details. The `ms` parameter in our example says that the printer uses 8-bit characters with no parity (`-parity`), newline characters should be sent to the printer as carriage-return/line-feed character pairs (`onlcr`), and the printer responds to XON/XOFF flow control characters (`ixon`).

Not every printer is simple to configure. As the serial printer example illustrates, sometimes you must know details of how the printer operates. It is possible to dig these details out of the printer documentation and test various configurations until you get it right, but it may be possible to avoid this. Unless you select a very rare printer, someone has probably already done the work. Writing a *printcap* from scratch is often unnecessary. Ask other system administrators on the newsgroup for your system. You'll be surprised how often others have already solved the problem and how willing they are to help.

LPD Security

The line printer daemon uses trusted host security, and it can use the same security file (*hosts.equiv*) as the r-commands.[*] All users on a host listed in the server's *hosts.equiv* file are permitted to use the server's printers. To restrict access to only those remote users who have accounts on the server, include the `:rs:` boolean in the printer description in the *printcap* file. When `:rs:` is specified, only users who are logged into "like-named" accounts on a trusted host are granted access to the printer. This parameter is applied on a printer-by-printer basis, so it is possible to restrict access to a special printer while permitting access to the other printers on the system.

A problem with using the *hosts.equiv* file for printer access is that the file also grants "password free" login access. It is common to want to share a printer

---

[*] See *TCP/IP Network Administration* for more information about the r-commands and trusted host security.

without wanting to grant any other access to the print server. To accommodate this, **lpd** also uses the */etc/hosts.lpd* file for security. A trusted host defined in that file is only given access to printers, and the `:rs:` parameter works with this host just as it does with a host defined in the *hosts.equiv* file.

The syntax of the *hosts.lpd* file is exactly the same as the syntax of the *hosts.equiv* file. A *hosts.lpd* file might contain:

```
brazil
acorn
+@sales
```

This example shows a file that restricts printer access to the PCs *brazil* and *acorn*, and the hosts defined in the netgroup *sales*.

Windows LPD Server

It is possible to share a printer attached to a PC through LPR and LPD. Many implementations of TCP/IP for both DOS and Windows allow this. This example is based on *SuperTCP*, but the configuration information is essentially the same as the information provided on the UNIX system. No matter what LPD implementation is used, the server needs to know the printer's name, the location of the spool directory, and the hosts that are authorized to use the printer.

The *SuperTCP* LPD print server is configured by selecting **NetPrint Server** in the SetupTCP listbox. Figure 10-12 shows the NetPrint configuration window.

In the NetPrint window, enable the LPD server by clicking the **Enable** checkbox in the LPD Server Settings box. Enter the path for the spool directory, the security file (here called the *Host Access File*), and the log file (called the *Status File*). All three of these files have default values that may be used.

To enter trusted hosts into the security file, click on the **Access** button. This opens the dialogue box shown in Figure 10-13.

In this box, click the **Add ...** button and enter the name of the host to which you want to grant access. The syntax of the entries is the same as it is in the UNIX *hosts.lpd* file, except that netgroups cannot be used. Therefore a plus-sign in this file grants unrestricted access to all hosts just as it does if entered in the *hosts.lpd* file. Checking the **No Access Restrictions** checkbox does the same thing.

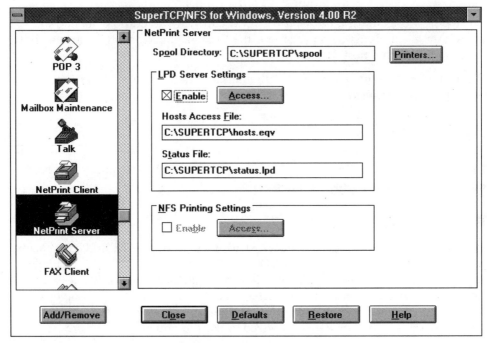

Figure 10–12: SuperTCP LPD Print Server

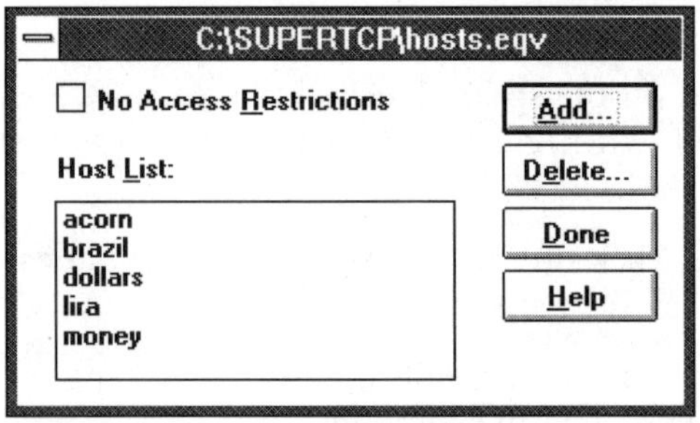

Figure 10–13: SuperTCP Printer Security

To define printers for the LPD server, select **Printers** . . . in the NetPrint Server window (refer to Figure 10-12). In the Network Printers box that appears, select **Add** . . . to get to the dialogue box shown in Figure 10-14. Enter the network name of the printer and select the Windows name of the printer from the dropdown listbox. The network name is the name remote systems use in the **lpr** command. The Windows name is the name of the printer driver that was installed via the *Control Panel* for the physical printer attached to this PC. In Figure 10-14, the network name is *LJ* and the Windows name is *HPLJII*.

That's it. Configuring a Windows-based LPD server is very similar to configuring a UNIX server. If you know how to do one, you can probably do the other.

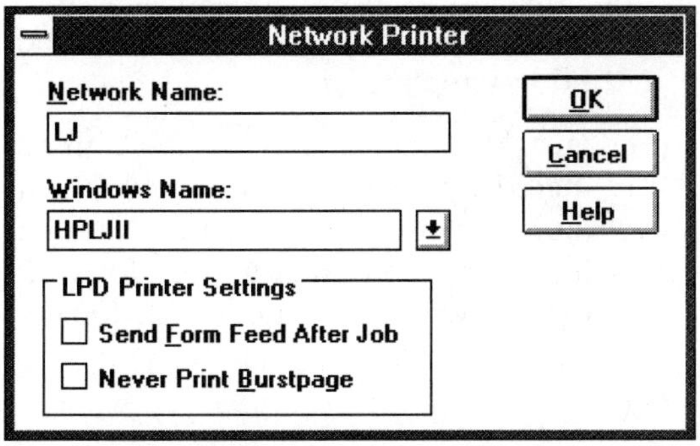

Figure 10–14: Defining the LPD Printer

Using LPD

Print jobs are sent to the line printer daemon using the *Line Printer Remote* (**lpr**) program. The **lpr** program creates a control file and sends it and the print file to **lpd**. On a UNIX system there are many possible **lpr** command-line arguments, but in general the command simply identifies the printer and the file to be printed, as in this example:

```
% lpr -PLJ ch10
```

This command sends a file called *ch10* to a printer called *LJ*. The printer can be local or remote. It doesn't matter as long as the printer is defined in the *printcap* file and therefore known to **lpd**.

Some DOS implementations of the **lpr** program use almost the same command syntax as the UNIX command. On a PC running *PC/TCP*, the command to print the file *guests.txt* on the *LJ* printer attached to the server *pecan* is:

```
C:\> lpr -S pecan -P LJ guests.txt
```

Windows developers have done an excellent job of integrating **lpr** into the system. Under both *Chameleon* and *SuperTCP*, and I'm sure several other implementations, **lpr** printers are configured through the **Printer** icon in the *Control Panel* and used from the Windows *Print Manager* or directly from Windows applications. In the *ChameleonNFS* example we saw in the *NFS Print Services* section of this chapter, selecting the **LPR** checkbox in the Browse window would have allowed us to define an **lpd** server and printer.

SuperTCP provides a special utility named *NetPrint* that works with different types of print servers including **lpd**. Network printers are defined by selecting **NetPrint** from SetupTCP, clicking on **Printers . . .** and then **Add** in the subsequent dialogue boxes, and finally entering the printer and the server names when prompted.

Once a printer is defined in SuperTCP, it is configured for Windows from the *Control Panel*. The Network icon is used to select **LPR** as the network printer driver, and **Printers** is used to bind the network printer to one of the logical printer ports.

When the configuration is complete, the **lpr** printer is used exactly as if it were a local printer; there is no need to issue an **lpr** command. The printer can be used from the *Print Manager* or directly from a Windows application.

We've stated that a remote printer is used just like a local printer. Well, that's almost true. Because the remote printer is shared by several systems, the client software provides additional commands to allow the user to check the status of the print job. That way you don't have to walk over to the printer to look for your job until you know it is done. Other than these additional features, the remote printers are just like local printers.

Managing LPD

The *Line Printer Control* (**lpc**) program is a tool for controlling the printers and administering the print queue on UNIX print servers. It provides a few commands for the user to query the status of a printer, but most of its commands are for the administrator to manage the printers and the print queues. Table 10-1 lists the **lpc** commands, their syntax, and their meaning.

Table 10-1: lpc Commands

Command	Usage
abort [*printer*...]	Kills a printer daemon
clean [*printer*...]	Removes all files from a print queue
disable [*printer*...]	Turns off spooling to a print queue
down [*printer*...] [*message*]	Ends spooling, printing; outputs a message
enable [*printer*...]	Enables spooling to a print queue
exit	Exits from **lpc**
help [*command*...]	Displays a description of each command
restart [*printer*...]	Starts a new printer daemon
start [*printer*...]	Enables printing and spooling
status [*printer*...]	Displays the status of printers and queues
stop [*printer*...]	Stops a printer after the current job ends
topq *printer* [*job#*...] [*user*...]	Moves print jobs to the top of the queue
up [*printer*...]	Enables spooling and printing

lpc can be invoked interactively. The following example shows the printer *laser* being restarted:

```
% lpc
lpc> status all
lp:
        queuing is enabled
        printing is enabled
        no entries
        no daemon present
lw:
```

```
                     queuing is enabled
                     printing is enabled
                     no entries
                     no daemon present
        laser:
                     queuing is enabled
                     printing is enabled
                     2 entries in spool area
                     no daemon present
        lpc> restart laser
        laser:
                     no daemon to abort
        laser:
                     daemon started
        lpc> exit
```

Note that the keyword `all` is used in place of a printer name in the sample **status** command. `all` can be used to refer to all printers in any **lpc** command that accepts a printer name as an optional parameter.

The **status** and **restart** commands used in the example can be used by anyone. Most other **lpc** commands can only be used by the superuser. For example, the following command moves the print jobs belonging to user *tyler* to the top of the queue for printer *laser*:

```
# lpc topq laser tyler
laser:
        moved cfA405acorn
```

While **lpc** is primarily for the system administrator, there are other commands primarily for the users. The UNIX **lpq** command displays a list of jobs queued for a printer. Command-line arguments permit the user to select which printer queue is displayed and limit the display from that queue to a specific user's jobs or even to a specific job. Here's an example of displaying the queue for the printer *laser*:

```
% lpq -Plaser
Rank    Owner      Job  Files                         Total Size
1st     tyler      405  ...                           5876 bytes
2nd     daniel     401  ...                          12118 bytes
3rd     daniel     404  ...                          12118 bytes
```

A queued print job can be removed by the owner of the job with the **lprm** command. Assume that *daniel* wants to remove print job number 404 shown in the example above. He enters the following command:

```
% lprm -Plaser 404
dfA404acorn dequeued
cfA404acorn dequeued
```

PC users have commands that provide very similar capabilities. For example, on a Windows system running *Chameleon*, the user can display the print queue and remove a print job using the LPR Control window. Open the window shown in

Figure 10-15 by selecting the **LPR/LPD** icon from the Chameleon window and then selecting the **Control** menu item.

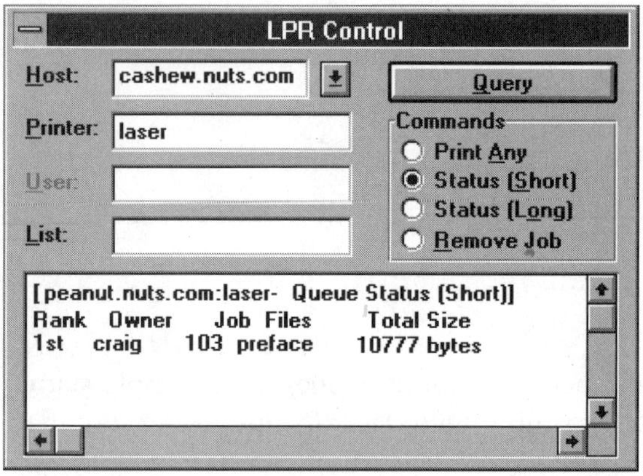

Figure 10–15: Checking LPR Status

In the window shown in Figure 10-15, enter the name of the print server in the Host box and the name of the printer on that server. Check the **Status (Short)** button and press **Query** to display the queue in a form similar to the one shown above in the **lpq** example. The **Status (Long)** button produces a verbose listing similar to the one produced by the **lpq** command with the **–l** option. To remove an entry from the queue, enter your username in the User box, check the **Remove Job** button, and press **Query**. The List box allows you to enter a list of one or more jobs that you want to query the status of, or that you want to delete.

PC clients have all of the capabilities of UNIX clients, and there is no need for PC users to learn UNIX commands to use them.

Summary

File sharing and printer sharing are the heart of traditional PC networks. TCP/IP provides these same network services and provides them on a variety of hardware platforms from PCs to minicomputers.

Network File System (NFS) is the leading TCP/IP file sharing protocol. It allows server systems to export directories that are then mounted by PC clients and used as if they were local disk drives. A special NFS program called **pcnsfd** is used to support PC clients. **pcnsfd** provides password-based user authentication and NFS-based printer sharing. NFS-based printer sharing most closely parallels traditional PC LAN printer sharing. It uses the file sharing protocol to move print files to the printer and supports DOS printer redirection.

NFS-based printer sharing is not the only type of printer sharing available on a TCP/IP network. It is also possible to use the UNIX LPD/LPR protocol. This software is widely available for PCs and some implementations support DOS printer redirection.

File and printer sharing are the foundation of traditional PC LANs but they are only a small part of the applications available on a TCP/IP network. As we have seen, a TCP/IP network is a complex and application-rich environment. This chapter concludes our coverage of TCP/IP applications. In the remaining chapter, we take a closer look at a traditional PC LAN operating system, and at how it is integrated into a TCP/IP internet.

11

NetWare and TCP/IP

No book on networking Personal Computers would be complete without a discussion of NetWare. Novell's NetWare is the leading choice for PC LAN software. Anyone involved in networking PCs will eventually have to deal with NetWare.

Sometimes the task of administering NetWare networks does not get the respect it deserves. NetWare has been so tightly linked to the DOS marketplace that some people believe that knowledge and skill with DOS provides all the necessary knowledge and skill to run a NetWare network. Don't believe it! NetWare is a full network operating system. It requires no more or less network administration skill than any other server-based network.

This chapter focuses on integrating NetWare into a TCP/IP network. This is a complex topic because there are many alternative ways to accomplish this task. For a full treatment of these alternatives see *Novell's Guide to Integrating UNIX and NetWare Networks*, by James E. Gaskin, Novell Press, 1994.

To sharpen our focus, we assume that TCP/IP is your primary enterprise network technology and that you only use NetWare as a LAN technology at some locations within the enterprise. We focus on adding a NetWare LAN to an existing TCP/IP network in such a way that users on the LAN can access the enterprise network services provided by TCP/IP. We examine three ways to do this: Novell's IP gateway software, IP tunneling, and NetWare/IP. The three techniques represent increasing levels of integrating between NetWare and TCP/IP. When a Novell server is used as an IP gateway, Novell protocols and TCP/IP share the same Ethernet, but are not integrated at any higher level. In IP tunneling, the TCP/IP network becomes the transport network for Novell packets by encapsulating them inside IP datagrams. NetWare/IP takes this a step further by making TCP/IP the native transport protocol of the Novell protocol stack. Before we get into the details of these different solutions, we need to know more about the NetWare protocols.

NetWare Protocols

NetWare is a LAN technology that is optimized for PCs. NetWare networks are server-based, with the bulk of the network knowledge and the configuration burden handled by the server. The client portion of NetWare is simple enough to run on a primitive PC, so NetWare is suitable for a very broad market.

Novell has built a successful company selling NetWare to people who want to build PC LANs. However, NetWare can do more. It can be used to build an internet of NetWare networks because it has some of the internetworking features that we are familiar with in TCP/IP. A close look at the NetWare protocol suite reveals a rich, complex protocol structure.

A comparison of Novell protocols and TCP/IP usually begins with Novell's *Internet Packet Exchange* (IPX) protocol and its *Sequenced Packet Exchange* (SPX) protocol—and for good reason. These protocols are very similar in function to *Internet Protocol* (IP) and *Transmission Control Protocol* (TCP).

Sequenced Packet Exchange

Like TCP, SPX provides reliable, sequenced packet delivery. (It's good to mention this first so that people don't panic when IPX is described as unreliable!) SPX is a connection-oriented protocol that creates a virtual circuit between the sending and the receiving systems. It provides packet sequencing information to ensure that packets arrive in order, and it requires acknowledgement of the packets received to guarantee that all packets are delivered. It does these things by adding 12 bytes of information to the basic 30-byte IPX header. Among other things, the added information includes:

Source Connection ID
> The sender uses this two-byte field to identify the virtual circuit connection. The sender assigns a unique value to the circuit for the life of the connection.

Destination Connection ID
> This two-byte field contains the virtual circuit identifier assigned by the remote system. When a system replies to an SPX packet, it uses the *Source Connection ID* from the received packet as the *Destination Packet ID* of the packet it sends. There is one exception to this: when the connection is initially established, the system that originates the connection cannot know what value the remote system will use as a connection ID. In this case, the sender uses FFFF as the *Destination Connection ID* for the very first packet and then uses the value received from the remote system for all subsequent packets. Figure 11-1 shows the exchange of packets, called a *handshake*, used to create an SPX connection.

Sequence Number
> SPX packets are numbered sequentially; this two-byte field holds the sequence number. Each time a new packet is sent the *Sequence Number* is incremented.

The field is not incremented if a packet has to be resent. The receiving station uses this field to check that it is receiving packets in the proper order and that it has received all packets.

Acknowledgement Number

This two-byte field contains the sequence number of the *next* packet the receiving station expects. It is used in the acknowledgement packet. When the station that has been sending out data receives an acknowledgement, it checks this value to make sure that the system receiving data expects the packet it plans to send next. If the system sending data detects an error in the *Acknowl-edgement Number,* it assumes that data has been lost and retransmits the last unacknowledged packet.

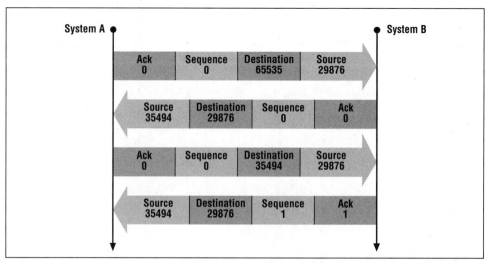

Figure 11–1: SPX Handshake

As of Novell release 3.11, SPX does not provide support for *sliding window* acknowledgements.[*] Each packet must be acknowledged before the next packet is sent. This creates performance problems when NetWare is used over low-speed lines, but it is not generally a problem for LANs operating at Ethernet speeds, and it makes SPX simple enough to run in the most primitive PCs. As the quality of the PC hardware installed at the user's desktop continues to improve, it is likely that Novell will favor protocol functionality over simplicity and that we will see sliding windows and other advanced features included in the next version of SPX.

---

* How sliding windows are used by TCP/IP is explained in Chapter 1 of *TCP/IP Network Administration.*

IPX Addressing and Routing

Like IP, IPX is an unreliable, connectionless datagram protocol. Each datagram travels the network independent of any other. IPX makes a "best effort" to deliver data, but it cannot guarantee delivery because it does not include error detection or correction. IPX depends on the underlying network or the upper layer protocols to provide reliable delivery.

IPX defines a hierarchical address structure that, within reason, is independent of the underlying physical network. This independent structure allows NetWare to route packets between networks and to pass packets over dissimilar physical networks. These are both features IPX shares with IP.

A Novell address is ten bytes long. The first four bytes identify the network and the remaining six bytes identify the host on that network. The host address is simply the physical layer address.[*] It is 6 bytes long to accommodate a full 48-bit Ethernet address.

The four-byte network address is an arbitrary value assigned by the network administrator. Take care to ensure that each network has a unique address. Routing cannot work if there are duplicate network addresses, though the addresses only need to be unique among the networks that can actually communicate with each other. Assigning unique addresses is not a problem when NetWare is used for isolated PC LANs. If you have one isolated network, you can choose any address you want. If you have an isolated enterprise network comprised of ten NetWare LANs, only the ten network addresses need to be coordinated. However, global NetWare communications require global network address coordination.

Novell maintains an address registry to provide the necessary coordination. Every organization that has been assigned an official IP address by the InterNIC has a registered Novell network address. Novell reserves an official IPX network address for every official IP network address. Our imaginary nut packing company has the network address 128.66; therefore, its reserved Novell address is 00804200. The illustration in Figure 11-2 shows how Novell derived this address.

Figure 11-2 shows that the four-byte IP address is shifted to the right 8 bits to become the four-byte IPX network address. The first byte of an IPX address created in this way is always zero. Shifting the four-byte IP address into the lower three bytes of the IPX network address is not a problem. The network portion of an IP address is never longer than three bytes, which is the case with a class C address. Class A addresses and class B addresses have network portions that are only one and two bytes long, respectively. The host portion of the IP address can be discarded because the IPX address provides a separate six-byte field for identifying the host. Following this simple guideline, the IP address 128.66.12.1 produces the IPX network address 0080420C.

---

* The physical layer address is usually called the MAC (Media Access Control) layer address.

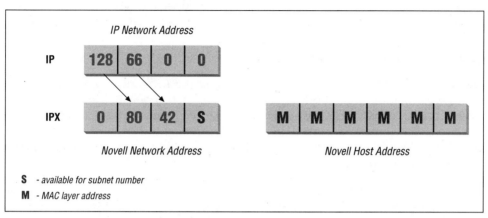

Figure 11–2: IP to IPX Address Mapping

Don't confuse the IPX network address with the internal network number. The *IPX network address* is the same for every system on an IPX subnet. The *internal network number* must be different on every NetWare server. The internal network is a logical network that exists inside of the server and is used by the server to route packets to the physical networks. All servers running NetWare version 3.0 or higher require that a unique internal network number be provided during the initial installation. An easy way to ensure uniqueness is to use the system's IP address as its internal network number. No two systems have the same IP address, so the number won't conflict with any other server, and it won't conflict with the IPX network address because that address uses only three bytes of the IP address. Using the example above, a server with the IP address 128.66.12.1 should be assigned an IPX network address of 0080420C and an internal network number of 80420C01.

IPX routes packets based on the network portion of the destination address. The network address is used in a table lookup to determine how a datagram is routed. The routing table points to the "next-hop" on the path to the remote network. IPX does not know the end-to-end path that a datagram will take. It counts on the router at the next-hop to know how to forward the datagram on toward its destination. Sound familiar? It should. It is very similar to the way IP handles routes.

The protocol used to distribute routes among servers and routers is the familiar *Routing Information Protocol* (RIP).[*] RIP works in much the same way on a Novell network as it does on a TCP/IP network. Routers, which can be thought of as NetWare servers that connect to more than one network, periodically broadcast routes to the networks to which they are attached. This information is used by other routers to update their routing tables and is, in turn, passed on by them to still

---

[*] The TCP/IP version of RIP is covered in detail in Chapter 7 of *TCP/IP Network Administration.*

other routers. Thus the routing information is disseminated router by router throughout the Novell network.

Service Advertising Protocol

The importance of distributing routes throughout the network is obvious; without routes we wouldn't know how to get from point A to point B. On a Novell network it is also important to disseminate information about servers. Everything on a Novell network centers on the servers.* Workstations need to know what servers are available and what services they offer. The *Service Advertising Protocol* (SAP) provides this information.

Servers and routers maintain a database of information called the *bindery*, which contains information about all of the servers on the network. Periodic SAP broadcasts are used to distribute this information to other servers and routers on the local network. As routers broadcast this information over each of the networks they are connected to, the information eventually is distributed throughout the entire network.

A client queries its server for bindery information using a SAP service query. The server responds to the client's specific request with a SAP service response. SAP combines broadcasts and directed unicasts to cover the full range of needs for server information. Broadcasts distribute a global picture of all of the services on the network to every server. The clients then query their local servers and get information about any service on the network. The client doesn't need to know about all of the remote servers because its local server does.

In a large internet, the overhead of broadcast protocols like RIP and SAP can be significant. Both of these protocols broadcast complete updates. For RIP, the update is a full routing table; for SAP, it is a complete set of bindery information. Complete updates can generate a substantial amount of data.

Novell realizes this is a potential problem and is developing a version of the OSI *Intermediate System to Intermediate System* (IS-IS) routing protocol specifically for NetWare. The NetWare version of the protocol is called *NetWare Link Services Protocol* (NLSP). NLSP carries both routing and service advertising information. It still uses periodic broadcasts to distribute the data, but it only sends changes, not complete databases, which dramatically reduces network overhead.

IPX, SPX, RIP, and even SAP are all low-level support protocols. They provide the addressing, routing, and transport services that are necessary for the operation of a Novell network. They do not provide direct user services or the applications interface required by user programs. These services are provided by the *NetWare Core Protocol* and the *Workstation Shell*.

---

* *NetWare Lite* is a peer-to-peer network similar to the NetBIOS networks discussed in Chapter 7. However, traditional Novell networks are strict client/server networks.

NetWare Core Protocol

Most of the protocols discussed so far are derived from the *Xerox Network System* (XNS) protocols and are almost identical to the originals. But NetWare is much more than a reimplementation of XNS for PCs. The real functionality of NetWare lies above these low-level protocols in the *NetWare Core Protocol* (NCP).

NCP provides the file and print services that make NetWare so useful, but it is not limited to file and print services. NCP handles connection services, accounting services, bindery services, directory services, job queue services, and several other things.[*] NCP is literally the core of NetWare. It is the protocol that clients use to request services and that the server uses to reply to those requests.

NCP is a request-response protocol. (We saw examples of this type of protocol when we worked with SMTP in Chapter 9.) Each request elicits a response, thus simplifying the protocol implementation, and in particular the implementation of error recovery. An NCP client simply times out and reissues a request if it does not receive a response. Using this simple error recovery technique, NCP can run directly over IPX without requiring the reliability of SPX.

Requiring a request and a response to exchange data is inefficient in some circumstances. It is particularly inefficient if reading a large file requires an exchange of packets for each block. Novell addresses this performance issue with *burst mode* transfers.

Burst mode is an NCP *Request Type* that is designed to make reading files more efficient. A single burst-mode NCP request can retrieve up to 64K bytes of data. The actual amount of data transferred is based on the packet size negotiated by the two systems and the number of burst-mode packet buffers configured on the client.[†] Transfers of 8K bytes at a time are easily achieved by systems on an Ethernet.

NCP is implemented in the *Workstation Shell*—also called the *NetWare Shell*. The shell is the TSR named NETx.COM, which intercepts DOS software interrupts 21h, 24h, and 17h. It examines the application's request and decides if it should be processed locally by DOS or processed remotely by the NetWare server. The shell converts requests that are bound for the server into NCP messages and passes them to IPX for delivery.

Most applications talk to the Novell network through the shell, but not all. Some Novell applications interface directly to SPX; others interface directly to IPX. Novell even provides a NetBIOS emulator so that NetBIOS applications can run over the Novell network. Figure 11-3 shows these various interfaces.

---

[*] A list of NCP service requests is contained in *Novell's Guide to NetWare LAN Analysis*, by Laura Chappell, Novell Press, 1993.

[†] The number of burst-mode packet buffers is defined by the pb buffers = *n* statement in the client's NET.CFG file. The maximum value for *n* is 10.

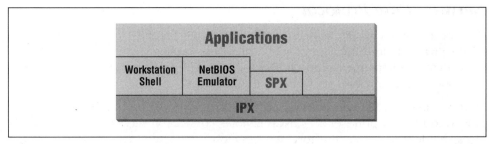

Figure 11–3: Novell Application Interfaces

The variety of application interfaces provides developers with a great deal of flexibility, but they also complicate things. It is not as simple to run NCP over TCP/IP
as it is to run NetBIOS over TCP/IP. The fact that some applications bypass NCP
and go directly to SPX or IPX means that it isn't simple to replace SPX and IPX
with TCP and IP. Novell has made several attempts to address NetWare and TCP/IP
integration, which is why there are so many different ways to handle it. We begin
our discussion of Novell integration techniques with their TCP/IP subsystem.

TCP/IP Transport Services

Novell includes TCP/IP in the standard NetWare package.[*] The software, usually
called the *TCP/IP subsystem*, is not a full suite of TCP/IP protocols. It doesn't turn
a Novell server into an NFS server, an FTP server, a Telnet login host, or any of the
other things you might expect on a TCP/IP server. Instead it provides transport
services and applications interfaces for other separately priced products that do
provide those services. The TCP/IP subsystem provides:

*   Transport services to support TCP/IP applications

*   BSD socket libraries and *Transport Layer Interface* (TLI) Streams libraries to
    support TCP/IP applications development

*   *IP Tunneling* to transport IPX datagrams between NetWare systems that are
    separated by a TCP/IP internet

*   TCP/IP routing services that include forwarding IP datagrams through IPX
    routers and supporting IP routing updates in the RIP protocol

*   Support for the *Simple Network Management Protocol* (SNMP)

This list of services doesn't cover everything you might want, but it does provide
some tools for integrating Novell networks into a TCP/IP environment. It is possible to use the transport services to host TCP/IP services, such as NFS and LPD, on
a NetWare server to support UNIX workstation clients. That approach is suitable if

---

* Novell began this practice with NetWare 3.11. If your users are using an earlier version of
NetWare, they should upgrade before connecting to your TCP/IP internet.

you have a large Novell network and very few UNIX workstations. *Novell's Guide to Integrating UNIX and NetWare Networks* deals with this approach. We, on the other hand, assume that you have a large TCP/IP network with a few Novell servers. In our environment, the Novell server's ability to act as an IP router and to tunnel IPX packets through a TCP/IP network are more important for integrating NetWare and TCP/IP. We discuss how these two features are used to deal with the following types of networks:

- A mixture of TCP/IP and NetWare systems on a single network

- A Novell subnet on a TCP/IP internet

- A NetWare internet overlayed on top of a TCP/IP internet

NetWare and TCP/IP can coexist on the same physical network without problems. It is possible for a Novell server and its clients to operate on the same Ethernet with a group of TCP/IP hosts without either group interfering with, or even noticing, the other. In this case, two logical networks, one NetWare and one TCP/IP, exist on the same physical Ethernet network.

Only slightly more effort is required to configure the clients so that they can interact with both the Novell server and the TCP/IP hosts that share the network. Using ODI, NDIS, or packet drivers, it is possible for a single network interface to support more than one protocol stack.[*] With an ODI driver in place, the client can send an NCP message with one packet and an IP datagram with the next.

Figure 11-4 shows a client sending NetWare and TCP/IP packets out of the same network interface. However, even with two protocol stacks in the client, the logical separation between NetWare and TCP/IP still exists. The client cannot interact with the Novell server using TCP/IP or with the TCP/IP host using NetWare. Novell's introduction of the ODI driver was an important first step in integrating PC clients into multi-protocol environments, but it is not a complete solution.

The coexistence of TCP/IP and NetWare on a single network does not require the installation of TCP/IP software in the server. In Figure 11-4, the Novell server speaks pure NetWare; only the clients speak both NetWare and TCP/IP. This level of integration has been available ever since the introduction of the NDIS, ODI, and packet drivers. The server does not need the TCP/IP subsystem unless it runs optional TCP/IP services or acts as a gateway to a TCP/IP network.

Novell's IP Gateway

A Novell network can be connected to a TCP/IP internet through its server. The server can act as an IP router because Novell's TCP/IP subsystem supports IP packet forwarding and IP routing protocols. Figure 11-5 shows this topology.

---

* ODI, NDIS, and packet drivers are covered in Chapter 4.

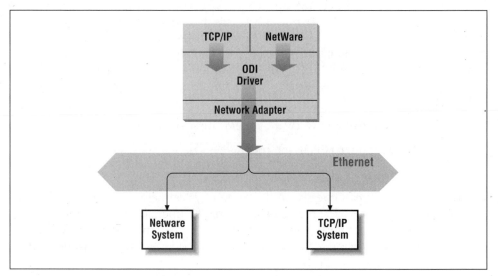

Figure 11-4: NetWare TCP/IP Coexistence

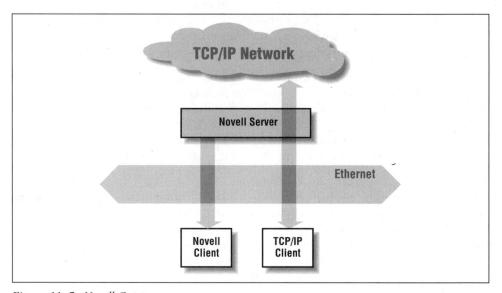

Figure 11-5: Novell Gateway

In the topology shown in Figure 11-5, NetWare traffic stays on the Novell subnet, and the Novell gateway passes IP traffic to the TCP/IP internet. Clients located on the Novell subnet communicate through the server to hosts located on the TCP/IP network. The clients must run both a NetWare and a TCP/IP protocol stack to use both Novell and TCP/IP services, but it is possible for a pure TCP/IP client located behind the Novell router to successfully communicate with remote TCP/IP hosts without running NetWare at all.

Configuring the Gateway

The TCP/IP subsystem is not part of the default Novell server installation; it is an option. As such, you need to take a few steps to add it to the server:

1. Modify the network interface driver to use a physical network framing technique that is compatible with TCP/IP.

2. Load the TCP/IP program.

3. Bind the TCP/IP protocol to the network interface.

Ethernet interfaces on NetWare systems default to 802.3 framing. Most UNIX systems, and therefore most TCP/IP networks, use Ethernet II framing. Edit the server configuration to add the correct framing for your network. (See the box *When Is Ethernet Ethernet?* in Chapter 4.)

The SYS:SYSTEM\AUTOEXEC.NCF file that is created during the initial installation contains the basic Novell server configuration. Edit the file and then add FRAME=ETHERNET_II to the **LOAD** *lan_driver* statement[*] as in this example:

```
LOAD NE2000 PORT=300 INT=3 FRAME=ETHERNET_II NAME=NUTS-NET
```

The **LOAD** command is followed by the name of the ODI driver, NE2000 in the example, and a variable group of configuration parameters. Several drivers, such as NE2000, NE3200, 3C503, etc., are included with the Novell software. Others are obtained directly from the network adapter manufacturers.

The specific configuration parameters differ between network adapter boards, but most of the parameters are the same configuration values, such as I/O Port (PORT) and IRQ interrupt (INT). The few Novell-specific parameters are easily explained. We know what the FRAME parameter is for because we just added it. The NAME parameter is a logical name that is used within the configuration to refer to this interface. We use the name later in the configuration to bind TCP/IP to the interface. NAME is an arbitrary string of up to 17 characters; in the example we use NUTS-NET as the interface name. Any string you think is descriptive will do.

None of these parameters is specific to the TCP/IP subsystem except for the FRAME parameter. All of the other values are already in the configuration file from the initial installation of NetWare. We are only adding the correct framing to make the interface compatible with our TCP/IP Ethernet.

The second installation step is to load the TCP/IP module. A NetWare program is called a *NetWare Loadable Module* (NLM). The TCP/IP module is TCPIP.NLM. It is loaded using the **LOAD** command, which can be as simple as LOAD TCPIP.

---

[*] The **LOAD** *lan_driver* statement is explained in great detail in the Novell *NetWare Version 3.11 System Administration* manual.

This works in most cases, but it is not exactly what we want. The default configuration of the TCP/IP module runs the RIP routing protocol and collects SNMP information for local processing, which are both things we want to do. It does not, however, forward IP packets, which we must do to use the server as an IP router. To get the functions we want, enter the following command:

```
LOAD TCPIP FORWARD=YES
```

The TCPIP command line has three options: FORWARD, TRAP, and RIP. **FORWARD=YES** is used when the Novell server acts as an IP router. **FORWARD=NO**, which is the default, is used when the Novell server has only one network interface. It prevents the server from forwarding IP packets and thus from acting as a router. In that case, the server relies on an external router to forward packets to other networks.

The TRAP option is used to direct SNMP information to the SNMP monitoring station. Enter the address of your network monitoring station in the form **TRAP=***ip-address*, e.g., **TRAP=128.66.3.7.**[*] If no value is entered, the system assumes that SNMP information is processed locally on the Novell server and viewed using the TCP/IP Console (TCPCON) program. See *NetWare v3.11 TCP/IP Transport Supervisor's Guide* for information on TCPCON.

The RIP parameter enables (**RIP=YES**) or disables (**RIP=NO**) the RIP routing protocol. If no RIP parameter is entered, the protocol is enabled by default. When RIP is enabled, the server listens to routing updates, and when RIP is enabled and **FORWARD=YES**, the server also sends out routing updates.

The Novell server normally learns all of its routing information through RIP, but it is possible to add information to the routing table manually even when RIP is running. This is usually done to add a temporary default route that is used during startup or information about a router that does not send out RIP updates. The IPCONFIG NLM is used to add the routes. IPCONFIG has no command-line options. To execute it, place a **LOAD IPCONFIG** in the AUTOEXEC.NCF file.

When IPCONFIG is executed it reads the SYS:ETC\GATEWAYS file and installs any routes that are defined there in the routing table. The format of this file is familiar to every UNIX system administrator because it is the same as the */etc/gateways* file that is read by the UNIX **routed** command.[†] The SYS:ETC\GATEWAYS file is typically used to define a temporary default route. A sample default route is shown below:

```
net 0.0.0.0 gateway 128.66.12.3 active
```

NetWare uses the default route when no specific route to a destination is found in the routing table. The keyword net is followed by the address of the destination network. 0.0.0.0 is a special address used for the default route. The keyword

---

[*] All IP addresses in the Novell configuration file must be in dotted decimal notation.
[†] Static routes, **routed**, and */etc/gateways* are covered in Chapter 7 of *TCP/IP Network Administration*.

`gateway` indicates that the following address is the gateway used to reach the destination; in this example it is 128.66.12.3. The keyword `active` permits RIP to modify this route based on the information received in the RIP updates. Therefore if RIP receives a default route in an update, it uses it to replace this temporary route. If the keyword `passive` is used, it prevents RIP from updating this route. Avoid using a passive default route; it defeats the purpose of dynamic routing and makes troubleshooting more difficult.

The last step in installing the TCP/IP subsystem is binding TCP/IP to the network interface. Novell's **BIND** command performs many of the same functions that the **ifconfig** command performs on a UNIX system. It defines most of the TCP/IP configuration parameters. A sample command shows this:

```
BIND IP TO NUTS-NET ADDR=128.66.12.1 MASK=255.255.255.0 BCAST=128.66.12.255
```

The command binds TCP/IP to the network interface identified earlier in the configuration as NUTS-NET. The sample command-line parameters are the IP address (ADDR), subnet mask (MASK), and broadcast address (BCAST) that we are so familiar with. Other less frequently used configuration parameters can be entered on the BIND command line as well. Two of these are the same seldom-used parameters found on the **ifconfig** command line: ARP and METRIC.

The default configuration enables the *Address Resolution Protocol* (ARP). **ARP=NO** disables ARP. Never disable ARP; it is needed to map IP addresses to physical network addresses.

METRIC is used to prefer one interface over another. The higher the METRIC number, the higher the "cost" of an interface, and therefore the less it is preferred. This parameter is only useful if the server has two interfaces that can reach the same destination, and there is something about one of the interfaces (higher speed, lower usage charges, etc.) that makes it "better" than the other interface.

A third obscure parameter is POISON, which enables *poison reverse* processing for RIP updates. Poison reverse is a rarely used feature that can increase routing stability and eliminate loops in complex IP internets. Don't build complex IP internets out of Novell servers and don't use POISON. While these three parameters, ARP, METRIC, and POISON, can be ignored, there are two other BIND parameters that are sometimes used. They are:

GATE

> This parameter defines a static default route. It should only be used if RIP is disabled (**RIP=NO**) on this interface. Use a default static route only when there is only one path to the outside world. Don't use one when the local network has multiple routers.

DEFROUTE

> This parameter tells the Novell server to advertise itself as the default gateway. It is used only if FORWARD is set to YES, and then only if the Novell server is the local subnet's sole path to the outside world. If **DEFROUTE=YES**, the

server advertises itself as the default route in RIP updates. If **DEFROUTE=NO**, the server sends out "normal" RIP updates that include only specific routing information.

This discussion of the various options and commands may make TCP/IP configuration appear more complex than it is, but a typical configuration is very simple. On most systems, the AUTOEXEC.NCF file contains the following commands for the TCP/IP subsystem:

```
LOAD 3C509 FRAME=ETHERNET_II NAME=SALES-NET
LOAD TCPIP TRAP=128.66.7.3
BIND IP TO SALES-NET ADDR=128.66.7.1 MASK=255.255.255.0 BCAST=128.66.7.255
```

These entries contain all of the basic configuration information we have come to expect with a TCP/IP installation. The one thing missing is the list of domain name servers. The reason is that the TCP/IP subsystem does not use DNS; it relies on local database files for that type of information.

TCP/IP Database Files

Novell's TCP/IP subsystem uses the same database files as a UNIX system. They are even located in the same directory—the ETC directory—though the UNIX path is */etc* and the Novell path is SYS:\ETC. The database files are:

HOSTS
This file maps hostnames to IP addresses.

NETWORKS
This file maps network names to network numbers.

SERVICES
This file maps network services to port numbers.

PROTOCOLS
This file maps transport protocols to protocol numbers.

All of these files have the exact same syntax and purpose as their UNIX counterparts, which are covered in detail in *TCP/IP Network Administration*. These files are also the same as the ones that Novell uses with its *LAN Workplace* DOS software, which is covered in Chapter 4. Most of these files can be ignored because they come preconfigured with all the values you need. The HOSTS file is the only one that you are likely to modify. HOSTS file modifications are generally limited to adding the address of the local host and the addresses of a few other frequently used hosts. The file can be modified with any standard text editor. See Chapter 4 for details of the syntax of this file.

IP Tunneling

One of the advantages of NetWare is that, like TCP/IP, it is a logical network that runs over a variety of physical networks. The physical network merely provides the delivery service for the Novell packets. This makes it possible to run NetWare over a TCP/IP network by replacing the driver for the physical network with a driver for a TCP/IP network; thus the TCP/IP network provides the delivery service. This is called *IP tunneling* or *IPX/IP tunneling* because the Novell packets "tunnel" through the TCP/IP network without interacting with it. A tunnel is a means to get from one place to another, nothing more.

IP tunneling is implemented in the IPTUNNEL driver that is provided as part of the Novell TCP/IP subsystem. IPTUNNEL is a network driver that functions just like an Ethernet driver. The difference is that it passes packets to a TCP/IP network instead of to an Ethernet. It is installed and used like any other driver. The steps to install IP Tunneling are:

- Install the TCP/IP subsystems.

- Load the IPTUNNEL driver.

- Bind IPX to the driver.

Figure 11-6 shows a network in which a few Novell subnets are interconnected through a TCP/IP enterprise network.

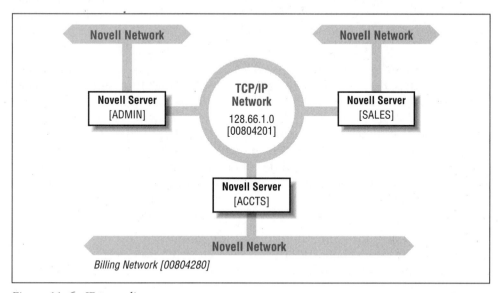

Figure 11-6: IP tunneling

A section of the AUTOEXEC.NCF file for the server named ACCTS in Figure 11-6 shows the three IP tunneling installation steps:

```
FILE SERVER NAME ACCTS
IPX INTERNAL NET 80420105
LOAD NE2000 PORT=300 INT=3 NAME=BILLING
LOAD 3C509 FRAME=ETHERNET_II NAME=BACKBONE
LOAD TCPIP
BIND IPX TO BILLING NET=00804280
BIND IP TO BACKBONE ADDR=128.66.1.5 MASK=255.255.255.0 BCAST=128.66.1.255
LOAD IPTUNNEL LOCAL=128.66.1.5 PEER=128.66.1.8
LOAD IPTUNNEL LOCAL=128.66.1.5 PEER=128.66.1.14
BIND IPX TO IPTUNNEL NET=00804201
```

The ACCTS server connects the BILLING subnet to the company TCP/IP network. The first line of the file loads the driver for the local Ethernet, the second line loads the Ethernet driver for the company's enterprise network, and the third line loads the TCP/IP software. So far this is exactly the type of configuration we saw in the previous section.

Next, IPX is bound to the interface of the BILLING network, which is a pure NetWare network. The next BIND command connects TCP/IP to the interface with the backbone network. None of this directly relates to IP tunneling, but it is all necessary preliminary configuration.

Finally, we load the IPTUNNEL driver and bind IPX to it. Binding IPX to the IPTUNNEL driver confuses some administrators, because they think they should bind TCP/IP to the driver. If you remember that you want to send IPX datagrams out over this interface, the reason for binding IPX to the IP tunnel becomes quite clear.

The BIND command also assigns a Novell network number to the TCP/IP network. From the point of view of the Novell servers, the TCP/IP network *is* a Novell network in the same way that a local Ethernet is a Novell network. For that reason, the TCP/IP network needs a Novell network number. All servers that attach to the TCP/IP network must use the same number. As discussed earlier, it is easier to keep the network numbers straight if you base them on the TCP/IP address. In our example the TCP/IP backbone is subnet 128.66.1.0. Based on the IP network number-to-Novell network number mapping described earlier, the decimal numbers 128, 66, and 1 are converted to hexadecimal and stored in the lower three bytes of the Novell address. Therefore, the Novell network number we use is 00804201.

The only configuration command that we haven't seen before is **LOAD IPTUNNEL**. This command has several command-linc options:

PEER=*IP-address*

    The PEER parameter specifies the address of a remote IPX router or server with which this system communicates. A Novell network depends on broadcasts to distribute RIP and SAP information. However, broadcasts cannot be used over a large IP internet; most IP routers do not forward broadcasts, and some physical network technologies do not support them. Therefore a Novell network running over TCP/IP must have some way to distribute SAP and RIP information that does not depend on broadcasts. That is where the PEER parameter comes in. Every time IPX sends out a broadcast packet it also addresses a packet containing the same information to every server identified as a PEER.

You may list up to 10 peers; each peer is listed on a separate IPTUNNEL command. The sample configuration shows three Novell servers connected to the TCP/IP network. One, of course, is the local system. The remaining two servers are this system's peers, so we have two IPTUNNEL commands.

CHKSUM=YES | NO

In IP tunneling, NetWare packets are encapsulated inside of UDP datagrams. This parameter turns on the UDP checksum so that the system can detect if the UDP packet becomes corrupted. The default is CHKSUM=YES. CHKSUM=NO disables UDP checksums. Unless you have an old system on your network that cannot properly handle checksums, let this value default to YES.

LOCAL=*IP-address*

The LOCAL parameter associates the IPTUNNEL with a specific network interface. If the LOCAL parameter is not used, the IPTUNNEL is associated with the first network interface to which TCP/IP was bound.

PORT=*port-number*

The PORT parameter assigns a UDP port number to be used for IP tunneling. UDP port 213 is officially assigned for tunneling IPX datagrams. The PORT parameter is used only if you don't want to use the officially assigned port. Of course, changing the port prevents the tunnel from working unless all of the computers using that tunnel use the same non-standard port number.

SHOW=YES | NO

The SHOW parameter is used to view the current configuration of the IPTUNNEL. Enter **LOAD IPTUNNEL SHOW=YES** to see the current configuration.

The PEER option is the most commonly used. Identify every Novell server and router in the group with a PEER command. In the sample, there are three Novell servers. Each one is configured with two PEER statement—one for each of the other servers.

The LOCAL parameter is also useful, though it is not required. The system will assign a default IP address to the LOCAL parameter, and everything will run fine. However, it is better to be explicit. It gives you more control, and it is easier to troubleshoot when the configuration is clearly defined in the configuration file.

The Limitations of Tunneling

Tunneling works through *encapsulation*. The Novell packets are enclosed inside of IP datagrams. As far as the TCP/IP network is concerned, the NetWare packets are just "data," and as far as the Novell network is concerned, the TCP/IP network is just a delivery service. Figure 11-7 illustrates encapsulation and shows how tunneling adds overhead. The IPX datagram is encapsulated in a UDP packet and in an IP datagram. Then the whole thing is encapsulated in the frame of some physical network for delivery. The additional layers of encapsulation require processing at both ends.

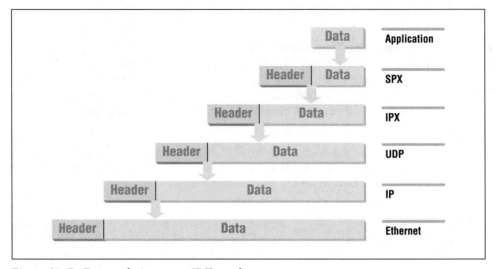

Figure 11-7: Encapsulation in an IP Tunnel

The overhead of tunneling makes it a poor choice for some applications. It can connect a client to a remote server, but it should only be used to do that in limited cases. If a client depends on the remote server for daily file and print services, the overhead of tunneling is an unacceptable burden. A better use of tunneling is to interconnect servers in such a way that clients get the bulk of their services from a local server and only tunnel to the remote server for occasional, specialized services.

IP tunneling is most often used to reach a remote location that cannot be reached directly by IPX. TCP/IP is a popular WAN technology; it runs over a wider variety of physical networks than any other protocol. In a TCP/IP enterprise network, tunneling may be the only way to get from here to there. Tunneling can even be used to reach a site on the other side of the world through the global Internet.

IP tunneling is functionally similar to the NetBIOS over TCP/IP service covered in Chapter 7. It works well but has its problems. As we have pointed out, it adds overhead. In addition, its solution for NetWare's dependence on broadcasts does not scale well: the maximum number of peers is ten, and the number of peers cannot simply be increased because a packet must be sent to each peer every time a broadcast is sent. Updating a large number of peers would overwhelm a server. But Novell saw these problems and developed another solution—NetWare/IP.

NetWare/IP

The last Novell TCP/IP integration product that we discuss is NetWare/IP. NetWare/IP replaces IPX with UDP and IP, which permits NCP to run directly over IP. It is functionally similar to tunneling in that it allows Novell networks, clients, and servers to communicate over a TCP/IP network, but with two big advantages:

- Lower overhead

- Reduced broadcast dependence

Overhead is reduced because there are fewer layers of encapsulation. A packet passed through an IP tunnel has all of the Novell layers plus all of the TCP/IP layers. Tunneling *adds* the lower layers of TCP/IP to the lower layers of NetWare, while NetWare/IP *replaces* the lower Novell layers with the lower layers of TCP/IP. Fewer layers, less encapsulation, less processing. Figure 11-8 shows the layers of encapsulation in NetWare/IP. Compare this to the layers shown in Figure 11-7, and you'll easily see that there is less protocol overhead.

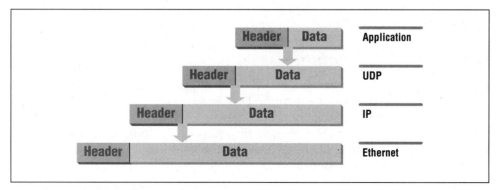

Figure 11–8: NetWare Encapsulation

To operate, a Novell network must disseminate server information and routing information. On a LAN, the SAP and RIP information is distributed via broadcasts, but as we noted earlier, networks that depend on broadcasts cannot work over a large TCP/IP internet. Tunneling solves the problem of broadcast dependence by defining a list of peer servers to which broadcast information is directly addressed. That solution, however, does not scale well, so Novell limits the list of peers to ten entries. NetWare/IP overcomes the scaling and distribution problem by creating a new central server specifically designed to gather and distribute RIP and SAP information. The new server is called the *Domain SAP/RIP Service* (DSS) server.

DSS is a simple and elegant solution. All RIP and SAP information is collected by the central server. Clients then query the central DSS server for that information. Packets are sent directly to and received directly from the DSS server. Broadcasts are not necessary.

The DSS system requires very little configuration. The system administrator does not enter server and routing information into the DSS server because its databases are automatically configured by the other systems on the network. Here's how:

- The DSS server is known to every system in the DSS domain.

- All Novell servers in the DSS domain send their RIP and SAP updates directly to the DSS server.

- The DSS server uses the updates to build a complete database of the Novell network without any input from the network administrator.

- Servers and routers that require RIP or SAP information query the DSS server directly. There is no need for internet-wide broadcasts.

The advantage of the NetWare/IP DSS server over the list of peers used by IP tunneling is obvious. Ten servers update the DSS server with ten packets. Ten servers each updating the other nine servers that are their peers send out a total of 90 packets.

To operate successfully, DSS depends on all of the servers knowing which system is the DSS server. NetWare/IP advertises the DSS server using features that exist in the standard TCP/IP domain name service.

Defining a DSS Domain

DSS shares some of the concepts of DNS. It has primary and secondary servers, and the Novell systems that share a DSS server are grouped together in a "domain." The unique thing about a DNS domain created to support DSS is that it only contains nameserver (NS) records that identify the primary and secondary DSS servers. It does not contain any other entries because its only purpose is to identify the DSS servers to their clients.

The DSS domain is created as a subdomain of an existing DNS domain. For example, our imaginary company has the domains *nuts.com*, *sales.nuts.com* and *plant.nuts.com*. It is possible to create DSS domains within any of these existing DNS domains. Imagine that the marketing department wants to create a DSS domain within *sales.nuts.com*. Furthermore, they have decided to call the DSS domain *netip.sales.nuts.com*. To create the new domain, the domain administrator adds the following entries to the *sales.nuts.com* zone file:

```
netip.sales.nuts.com.    IN   NS    cash.sales.nuts.com.
                         IN   NS    money.sales.nuts.com.
                         IN   NS    dollars.sales.nuts.com.
```

These entries create a subdomain called *netip* within the *sales.nuts.com* domain and define the master servers for this new domain as *cash*, *money* and *dollars*. Normally the master servers in a DNS domain maintain database files of host information for the systems in the domain. Not in this case. There are no host entries for the *netip* domain. In fact, none of these servers are even required to run DNS. They are DSS servers. This new domain is only used by DSS clients to find out who their servers are.

Each DSS client is configured with a NetWare/IP domain name. In our example all of the clients are given the DSS domain name of *netip.sales.nuts.com*. The DSS domain name does not replace the DNS domain name. All of these clients are also given a DNS domain name; in our example it would be *sales.nuts.com*. The DNS domain name is used in queries for the normal hostname information that DNS is always used for on a TCP/IP network. The DSS domain name is only used to locate the DSS servers. Once the servers are located, DSS queries are sent directly to the DSS servers and DNS is not involved.

A NetWare/IP server can act as a DNS master server and as a DSS master server, but it is not a good idea to put all of these tasks on one system. Doing it all in one system is only suitable for very small networks. On a larger network the workload of DNS and DSS can interfere with the file and print services that are the real work of a Novell server. If possible, offload DNS and DSS to other systems. When adding NetWare/IP to an existing TCP/IP network you already have access to operational DNS servers. Create the DSS subdomain on the existing primary DNS server and use the existing servers to provide DNS service to the NetWare/IP systems. If you have a large number of NetWare/IP clients you may also want to purchase an extra PC to act exclusively as a DSS server.

Configuring NetWare/IP

NetWare/IP depends on the TCP/IP subsystem for transport services. The first step in installing NetWare/IP is to install the NetWare server and the TCP/IP subsystem as outlined earlier in this Chapter. Next run the **INSTALL** program to load NetWare/IP from the installation diskette. After the software is loaded, it is configured using the UNICON utility.[*]

UNICON is a "universal console" utility that is used to configure a number of different Novell products. It presents menus that the system administrator uses to set various configuration values. DOS and UNIX people who like the directness of command line input may be frustrated working through the menus. However, the configuration procedure is very similar to those used to configure Windows products, and most people find it simple to work with and easy to understand. The configuration menus cover a lot of different things. Only a few of these are absolutely necessary to get a NetWare/IP server up and running.

---

[*] The UNICON utility is covered in detail in Novell's *NetWare/IP Administrator's Guide*.

Enter **LOAD UNICON** at the console to start the UNICON utility. Select **Configure Server Profile** from the main menu. The configuration template is shown in Figure 11-9. The window shown in the Figure contains most of the configuration values that are required by TCP/IP. The values in this template are the ones we have come to know so well, and they require very little explanation. There are two small points that need clarification. People sometimes confuse DSS with DNS. The *Domain* field on this template is the DNS domain. The DSS domain is defined on another template.

```
┌─────────────────────────────────────────────────────────────┐
│  ┌───────────────────────────────────────────────────────┐  │
│  │                   Server Profile                      │  │
│  ├───────────────────────────────────────────────────────┤  │
│  │  Host IP Name               : accts                   │  │
│  │  Primary IP Address         : 128.66.1.3              │  │
│  │  Primary Subnet Mask        : 255.255.255.0           │  │
│  │  Operating System Version   : Netware 4.0             │  │
│  │  Time Zone                  : Eastern Standard Time   │  │
│  │  Synchronization Interval   : 60 Seconds              │  │
│  │  DNS Access                 : <enabled>               │  │
│  │     Domain                  : sales.nuts.com          │  │
│  │     Primary Server          : 128.66.12.1             │  │
│  │     Secondary Server        : 128.66.7.3              │  │
│  │     Tertiary Server         : 128.66.3.1              │  │
│  │                                                       │  │
│  └───────────────────────────────────────────────────────┘  │
└─────────────────────────────────────────────────────────────┘
```

Figure 11-9: Server Profile

The other item that needs explanation is the *Synchronization Interval*, which is a Novell specific parameter. RIP and SAP databases are normally updated every 60 seconds. This value can be increased to reduce the amount of network traffic generated by the RIP and SAP protocols. However, increasing the interval allows this server's database to be out of synch with neighboring servers and routers for an increased period of time. The default value is adequate and does not usually require modification.

Use the arrow keys to select a field that you want to change and enter the new value. When finished with a template press the escape key (**Esc**) and select **Yes** when prompted to save your changes. This returns you to the main menu.

To define the DSS domain for this server select **Manage Services** from the main menu. This displays a menu that offers selections for *DNS Server*, *Hosts*, and *Net-Ware/IP*. Ignore the first two entries. DNS is already running on other servers on the TCP/IP network. Running another DNS server on the Novell server is just a waste of the Novell server's resources. Furthermore, you don't need to configure anything about DNS in this menu because the values required by the resolver, the domain name, and the list of name servers are defined in the *Configure Server Profile* template. Select **NetWare/IP** from this menu and **Configure NetWare/IP Server**

from the next menu that appears. This causes the window shown in Figure 11-10
to appear.

```
┌─────────────────────────────────────────────────────────────────┐
│  ┌───────────────────────────────────────────────────────────┐  │
│  │            NetWare/IP Server Configuration                 │  │
│  ├───────────────────────────────────────────────────────────┤  │
│  │   NetWare/IP Domain           : netip.sales.nuts.com.      │  │
│  │   Preferred IP Address        : 128.66.1.3                 │  │
│  └───────────────────────────────────────────────────────────┘  │
└─────────────────────────────────────────────────────────────────┘
```

Figure 11-10: NetWare IP Server Configuration

Enter the DSS domain name in the NetWare/IP Domain field of this template. In
Figure 11-10 the DSS name is *netip.sales.nuts.com.*, which is the domain name that
our system uses to locate its DSS server. If your system has more than one network interface, you will also see the Preferred IP Address field. Figure 11-10
shows this field because the sample Novell server is the IP gateway between the
Novell network and the TCP/IP backbone. The address should be the IP address
of the interface that attaches to the network that this system shares with its DSS
server. In the example the shared network is the TCP/IP backbone.

That's it! For an average server all you need to do is configure the basic TCP/IP
parameters, and the DSS domain name. Configuring the DSS servers requires some
additional effort.

Configuring DSS

Configuring the DSS master servers is surprisingly easy to do. The DSS database
information comes from the Novell servers that gather it on their local networks
and forward it to the DSS server. Therefore you don't need to provide it. All you
have to do is tell the system that it is a master DSS server. Do that through the
UNICON utility.

First make sure that the DSS domain is properly delegated in the primary DNS
name server, and that the NetWare, TCP/IP and NetWare/IP software is properly
installed and configured on the local server. Then start the UNICON utility. Select
Manage Services from the main menu and **NetWare/IP** from the **Manage Services**
menu. The NetWare/IP Server Administration menu shown in Figure 11-11
appears. To configure the primary DSS server, select **Configure Primary DSS** from
this menu.

The Primary DSS Configuration template is shown in Figure 11-12. The NetWare/IP
Domain field contains the name of the DSS domain, *netip.sales.nuts.com.* The *Primary DSS Host Name* field contains the DNS domain name of the local host.
(Remember the local host *is* the primary DSS server.) In Figure 11-12, the local
host is *money.sales.nuts.com.* The NetWare/IP configuration requires fully qualified

```
+-----------------------------------------------------------------+
|   +---------------------------------------------------------+   |
|   |        NetWare/IP Server Administration                 |   |
|   +---------------------------------------------------------+   |
|   |   Configure NetWare/IP Server                           |   |
|   |   Configure Primary DSS                                 |   |
|   |   Configure Secondary DSS                               |   |
|   +---------------------------------------------------------+   |
+-----------------------------------------------------------------+
```

Figure 11–11: NetWare/IP Server Administration

```
+-----------------------------------------------------------------+
|   +---------------------------------------------------------+   |
|   |             Primary DSS Configuration                   |   |
|   +---------------------------------------------------------+   |
|   |  NetWare/IP Domain:            netip.sales.nuts.com.    |   |
|   |  Primary DSS Host Name:        money.sales.nuts.com.    |   |
|   |  IPX Network Number (in hex):  804201ff                 |   |
|   |  Tunable Parameters:           <see list>               |   |
|   +---------------------------------------------------------+   |
+-----------------------------------------------------------------+
```

Figure 11–12: Primary DSS Configuration

domain names. The domain names used in all of the UNICON templates are fully qualified, which is why they all end with a dot (.).

The IPX Network Number field is the external IPX network used by DSS. This should be a unique IPX network number that is not used by any server as an internal number or by any IPX subnet as an external number. In our example we choose an unused IP host address and coverted it to an IPX address.

Selecting the last field in the template brings up a list of configurable parameters. These are:

UDP Port Number for NetWare/IP Service
> This parameter assigns the port numbers that are used by the DSS service. The defaults are 43981 and 43982. Don't change them. The only reason for changing these values is if they conflict with some other application already installed in your network.

SAP/RIP Database Synchronization Interval
> This parameter controls how often NetWare/IP servers query the DSS server for updates. The default is 5 minutes. This value generally does not need to be changed. Possible values range from 1 minute to 60 minutes.

Maximum UDP Retransmissions
> This parameter specifies how many times a DSS packet is re-sent if it is unacknowledged. The default is 3, which is usually adequate for any local area network. If the network includes poor-quality wide area network links and it

appears that remote servers are not receiving proper updates, increase this value. This value can range from 1 to 48 retries.

UDP Checksum

This parameter enables (YES) or disables (NO) UDP checksums. The default is NO. If your network includes some poor quality connections, enabling checksums may increase the system's ability to detect errors.

Completing this template is all that is necessary to set up the primary DSS server. The secondary servers are just as easy to configure and are also set up through the NetWare/IP Server Administration menu, see Figure 11-11. On secondary servers, select the **Configure Secondary DSS** menu item. The template shown in Figure 11-13 appears.

```
+-------------------------------------------------------------+
|  +-------------------------------------------------------+  |
|  |            Secondary DSS Configuration                |  |
|  +-------------------------------------------------------+  |
|  | NetWare/IP Domain:           netip.sales.nuts.com.    |  |
|  | Primary DSS Host:            money.sales.nuts.com.     |  |
|  +-------------------------------------------------------+  |
+-------------------------------------------------------------+
```

Figure 11-13: Secondary DSS Configuration

The Secondary DSS Configuration template, shown in Figure 11-13, contains two fields: the NetWare/IP Domain field and the Primary DSS Hosts field. Enter the DSS domain name in the first field. It is *netip.sales.nuts.com.* in Figure 11-13. In the next field, enter the DNS domain name of the primary DSS server. In the Figure it is *money.sales.nuts.com..* The only time it is necessary to enter the name of the primary server directly into the NetWare/IP configuration is when you configure a secondary server. All other systems locate the master servers via DNS. However, nothing in the DNS database identifies which DSS server is primary and which servers are secondary. They are all master servers and are all expected to have valid information. There is no way that the secondary servers can determine who is primary simply by querying the DNS database. The name of the primary server must be defined directly in the secondary servers' configuration.

That's it. DSS configuration, like the configuration of any NetWare/IP server, is actually quite simple.

Summary

Novell's NetWare is the leading PC LAN protocol. Novell networks are strict client/server networks. The server provides the clients with file and print services, routes packets, and handles most of the network configuration. The client/server protocol that provides these services is the *NetWare Core Protocol* (NCP).

The transport protocols that carry the NCP messages, *Sequenced Packet Exchange* (SPX) and *Internet Packet Exchange* (IPX), are based on the *Xerox Network System* (XNS) protocols. SPX, like TCP, provides reliable, sequenced packet delivery. IPX, like IP, is a connectionless datagram protocol. IPX defines the ten-byte Novell address structure. The first four address bytes identify the network and the remaining six bytes identify the host.

Despite some similarities, NetWare and TCP/IP are different and incompatible protocols. Special effort is required to integrate Novell networks into a TCP/IP internet. Novell offers several ways to do this. Two of these are: Novell's TCP/IP subsystem and NetWare/IP.

The TCP/IP subsystem provides the Novell server with TCP/IP transport services that coexist with the NetWare protocols. The subsystem allows the server to run TCP/IP services for TCP/IP clients, to act as an IP router, and to tunnel IPX packets through a TCP/IP network. IP tunneling works by enclosing the IPX datagrams inside of IP datagrams. The encapsulated IPX datagrams pass untouched through the TCP/IP network using the IP protocol as a delivery service.

NetWare/IP replaces the Novell transport protocols with the UDP and IP protocols from the TCP/IP protocol suite. NetWare/IP allows NCP to run directly over TCP/IP. This is more efficient than IP tunneling. NetWare/IP has other advantages that allow it to be used to construct larger "NetWare over TCP/IP" networks than are possible with IP tunneling.

Regardless of the integration technique used, Novell services are only available to Novell clients. Only clients that run NCP can use NCP services. TCP/IP is only an alternate transport protocol for Novell clients and servers.

Installation Planning Form

The form contained in this appendix is a useful planning tool for installing TCP/IP on a personal computer. Use it as a reminder of the required configuration values. It is divided into several major topics. Some are needed for installation, and some are useful as a historical record for future troubleshooting efforts.

The network administrator provides the information for the TCP/IP installation such as the hostname, the IP address and the list of servers, but most of the information (the operating system release, the MAC address, etc.) is taken from the system on which TCP/IP is being installed, and therefore must be provided by the installer. Copies of the startup files and the configuration files are an important part of this information. The files are very helpful for future debugging.

A sample of a completed form is provided at the end of this appendix. The sample clarifies the values requested for each field.

PC Information Form

Basic Information

The information in this section is provided by the network administrator. If you have any questions about it, please contact the administrator before beginning the installation.

Hostname: _____

IP address: _____

Subnet mask: _____

Broadcast address: _____

Default gateway address: _____

Domain Information

The information in this section is provided by the domain administrator. If you have any questions about it, please contact the administrator before beginning the installation.

Domain: _____

Name server: _____

Name server: _____

Name server: _____

Network Adapter Information

The following information must be provided by the network adapter installer.

Manufacturer: _____

Model: _____

MAC address: _____

IRQ: _____

I/O port address: _____

Adapter memory: _____

DRQ: _____

License Information

The following information must be provided by the software installer.

Software vendor: _____

Version number: _____

License number: _____

Authentication code: _____

System Information

The following information must be provided by the software installer.

Computer manufacturer: _____

Model: _____

Bus: _____

Operating system: _____

O/S version: _____

Attachments

After the system is configured and running, print out and attach the appropriate DOS and Windows startup files and a copy of the TCP/IP configuration file. List the names of the attached files below.

DOS files attached: _____

_____

Windows files attached: _____

_____

TCP/IP configuration file: _____

Sample Form

Basic Information

The information in this section is provided by the network administrator. If you have any questions about it, please contact the administrator before beginning the installation.

Hostname: peanut

IP address: 128.66.12.3

Subnet mask: 255.255.255.0

Broadcast address: 128.16.12.255

Default gateway address: 128.66.12.1

Domain Information

The information in this section is provided by the domain administrator. If you have any questions about it, please contact the administrator before beginning the installation.

Domain: nuts.com

Name server: 128.66.12.1

Name server: 128.66.7.3

Name server: _____

Network Adapter Information

The following information must be provided by the network adapter installer.

Manufacturer: 3COM

Model: 3C509

MAC address: 00:20:AF:33:7A:E5

IRQ: 10

I/O port address: 300

Adapter memory: none

DRQ: none

License Information

The following information must be provided by the software installer.

Software vendor: SuperTCP

Version number: 4.00_R2

License number: 010-043-81

Authentication code: 515-66a-18

System Information

The following information must be provided by the software installer.

Computer manufacturer: Intelicom System (clone)

Model: 486/33

Bus: ISA

Operating system: Windows

O/S version: 3.1

Attachments

After the system is configured and running, print out and attach the appropriate DOS and Windows startup files and a copy of the TCP/IP configuration file. List the names of the attached files below.

DOS files attached: CONFIG.SYS

                              AUTOEXEC.BAT

Windows files attached: WIN.INI

                              SYSTEM.INI

TCP/IP configuration file: none

B

Contacts and References

This appendix contains contact information for the various software packages mentioned in the text. It also contains a list of books and RFCs referenced in this book.

This book provides examples from several different TCP/IP implementations, but it doesn't try to list all of the available packages or compare the features of the packages. If you want that kind of information, try *TCP/IP for the Internet: The Complete Buyer's Guide to Micro-based TCP/IP Software* by Marshal Breeding, Mecklermedia, 1995.

Software Vendors

Beame & Whiteside Software
706 Hillsborough Street
Raleigh, NC 27603
919-831-8989

Castle Rock Computing, Inc.
20863 Steven Creek Blvd
Suite 530
Cupertino, CA 95014
800-331-7667

Distinct Corporation
14082 Loma Rio Drive
Saratoga, CA 95070
408-741-0781

Frontier Technologies Corporation
10201 N. Port Washington Road
Mequon, WI 53092
414-241-4555

FTP Software, Inc.
2 High Street
North Andover, MA 01845
508-685-4000

Microsoft
One Microsoft Way
Redmond, WA 98052-6399
800-426-9400

NetManage
20823 Steven Creek Blvd.
Cupertino, CA 95014
408-973-7171

Novell, Inc.
2180 Fortune Drive
San Jose, CA 95131
800-243-8526

SPRY, Inc.
316 Occidental Avenue South
Seattle, WA 98104
206-286-1412

SunSoft
Two Elizabeth Drive
Chelmsford, MA 01824
800-786-7638

The Wollongong Group
1129 San Antonio Road
Palo Alto, CA 94303
800-872-8649

Trumpet Software International
GPO Box 1649
Hobart, Tasmania
Australia 7001
011-61-02-487049

Publications

Books

DNS and BIND, Paul Albitz & Cricket Liu, O'Reilly & Associates, 1992

LAN Protocol Handbook, Mark Miller, M&T Books, 1990

Managing Internet Information Services, Cricket Liu, Jerry Peek, Russ Jones, Bryan Buus & Adrian Nye, O'Reilly & Associates, 1994

Managing Internetworks with SNMP, Mark Miller, M&T Books, 1993

Managing NFS and NIS, Hal Stern, O'Reilly & Associates, 1991

Networking Windows NT, John Ruley, et al., Wiley, 1994

Novell's Guide to Integrating UNIX and NetWare Networks, James Gaskin, Novell Press, 1993

Novell's Guide to NetWare LAN Analysis, Laura Chappell, Novell Press, 1993

sendmail, Bryan Costales, Eric Allman & Neil Rickert, O'Reilly & Associates, 1993

SNMP, SNMPv2, and CMIP, William Stallings, Addision-Wesley, 1993

TCP/IP Network Administration, Craig Hunt, O'Reilly & Associates, 1992

The Mosaic Handbook for Microsoft Windows, Dale Dougherty & Richard Koman, O'Reilly & Associates, 1994

The Simple Book, Marshall Rose, Prentice Hall, 1991

The Whole Internet User's Guide and Catalogue, Ed Krol, O'Reilly & Associates, 1994 (2nd edition)

Total SNMP, Sean Harnedy, CBM Books, 1994

Unveiling Windows 95, Roger Jennings with Matthew Harris, Que, 1994

Request For Comments (RFCs)

RFC 821, *Simple Mail Transfer Protocol*, J. Postel, 1982

RFC 822, *Standard for the Format of ARPA Internet Text Messages*, D. Crocker, 1982, (see also RFCs 1327 & 987)

RFC 826, *An Ethernet Address Resolution Protocol—or—Converting Network Protocol Addresses to 48.bit Ethernet Addresses for Transmission on Ethernet Hardware*, D. Plummer, 1982

RFC 903, *A Reverse Address Resolution Protocol*, Finlayson, Mann, Mogul & Theimer, 1984

RFC 937, *Post Office Protocol— Version 2*, Butler, et al., 1985

RFC 951, *Bootstrap Protocol (BOOTP)*, Croft & Gilmore, 1985, (see also RFCs 1395, 1532 & 1497)

RFC 1001, *Protocol Standard for a NetBIOS Service on a TCP/UDP Transport: Concepts and Methods*, Aggarwal, Auerbach, et al., 1987

RFC 1002, *Protocol Standard for a NetBIOS Service on a TCP/UDP Transport: Detailed Specifications*, Aggarwal, Auerbach, et al., 1987

RFC 1042, *Standard for the Transmission of IP Datagrams Over IEEE 802 Networks*, Postel & Reynolds, 1988

RFC 1048, *BOOTP Vendor Information Extensions*, P. Prindeville, 1988

RFC 1056, *PCMAIL: A Distributed Mail System for Personal Computers*, M. Lambert, 1988

RFC 1065, *Structure and identification of management information for TCP/IP-based internets*, K. McCloghrie and M. Rose, 1988

RFC 1122, *Requirements for Internet Hosts—Communication Layers*, R. Braden, 1989

RFC 1155, *Structure and Identification of Management Information for TCP/IP-based Internets*, K. McCloghrie and M. Rose, 1990

RFC 1176, *Interactive Mail Access Protocol— Version 2*, M. Crispin, 1990

RFC 1178, *Choosing a Name for Your Computer*, D. Libes, 1990

RFC 1213, *Management Information Base for Network Management of TCP/IP-based Internets: MIB-II*, K. McCloghrie and M. Rose, 1991

RFC 1425, *SMTP Service Extensions*, Klensin, et al., 1993

RFC 1521, *MIME (Multipurpose Internet Mail Extensions) Part One: Mechanism for Specifying and Describing the Format of Internet Messages*, Bodies, Borenstein & Freed, 1993, (see also RFC 1590)

RFC 1541, *Dynamic Host Configuration Protocol*, R. Droms, 1993

RFC 1652, *SMTP Service Extension for 8bit-MIMEtransport*, Klensin, et al., 1994

RFC 1653, *SMTP Service Extension for Message Size Declaration*, Klensin, et al., 1994

RFC 1700, *Assigned Numbers*, Reynolds & Postel, 1994

RFC 1725, *Post Office Protocol— Version 3*, M. Rose, 1994

ISO Standards

Standard 8824, *Specification of Abstract Syntax Notation One (ASN.1)*

Standard 8825, *Specification of Basic Encoding Rules for Abstract Syntax Notation One (ASN.1)*

Sendmail Configuration

This appendix contains a complete, commented listing of the *sendmail.cf* file described in Chapter 9. The file is based on the sample *tcpproto.cf* file from the **sendmail** software release. It has been modified according to the examples in Chapter 10 of *TCP/IP Network Administration* and in Chapter 9 of this text. The comments from the original *tcpproto.cf* file are boxed in pound signs (#). The comments added by *TCP/IP Network Administration* are boxed in plus signs (+) and the comments added by this text are boxed in asterisks (*). Comments that reference Chapter 10 are referring to Chapter 10 in the *TCP/IP Network Administration* book, and those that refer to Chapter 9 are referring to Chapter 9 in this book.

The sample configuration has only been tested on a Sun system running SunOS. It was written explicitly for this book and is only intended as an example. The configuration makes certain assumptions:

* The configuration is for a Sun system attached to an Ethernet. The mailer paths and the various file paths in the *Options* section might not be appropriate for other operating systems.

* The local Ethernet supplies this host with direct access to the Internet. The host does not have direct access to a UUCP network.

* The host handles mail for computers in the domain *nuts.com*.

This appendix also includes some shell scripts mentioned in Chapter 9. The *Shell Scripts* section contains a script for building *firstname.lastname* aliases from the gcos field of the */etc/passwd* file, and a script for building the *sendmail.cw* file from DNS data.

A Sample sendmail.cf

```
############################################################
############################################################
#####
#####            SENDMAIL CONFIGURATION FILE
#####
############################################################
############################################################
#++++++++++++++++++++++++++++++++++++++++++++++++++++++
#Like most sendmail configuration files, the first few sections of the
#file contain the data that is most likely to require custom
#configuration. In this file, the sections are titled "Local
#information," "General Macros," "Classes," and "Version Number."
#++++++++++++++++++++++++++++++++++++++++++++++++++++++


#######################
#   Local information   #
#######################
#++++++++++++++++++++++++++++++++++++++++++++++++++++++
#The "w" macro defines the system's hostname. This value is defined
#internally by sendmail and does not usually require modification. If
#your host is known by more than one hostname, the multiple hostnames
#can be defined here by creating a class "w" that contains all of the
#names for your host.
#++++++++++++++++++++++++++++++++++++++++++++++++++++++
#*****************************************************
#When the system acts as a mail server the names of all of the hosts
#that this system will accept mail for are defined in the "w" class.
#In this sample we load the host aliases from the sendmail.cw file.
#A script for creating sendmail.cw is found later in this appendix.
#See the "Host Aliases" section of Chapter 9 for more information.
#*****************************************************
# Load other hostnames that we accept mail for from sendmail.cw
Fw/usr/lib/sendmail.cw


####################
#   General Macros   #
####################
#++++++++++++++++++++++++++++++++++++++++++++++++++++++
#   The "D" macro contains the name of the local domain.
#++++++++++++++++++++++++++++++++++++++++++++++++++++++
# local domain name
DDnuts.com


#++++++++++++++++++++++++++++++++++++++++++++++++++++++
#If an MX record exists for the domain that this host is in, the domain
#name is defined in the "A" macro. If no MX record exists, the host
#name ($j) is used. "A" is used for rewriting the sender "From" address
#on outbound mail to hide the true hostname, and to address outbound
#mail as if it was from the MX server. This will only work if the
#MX mail server knows how to deliver mail to the users of this host.
#*****************************************************
#This system is the MX server. It delivers mail addressed
```

```
#to "user@nuts.com", so we use the "A" macro.
#***************************************************
#The "A" macro was created as part of the debugging example in Chapter
#10 of "TCP/IP Network Administration". In other sendmail configurations,
#"A" will have another meaning.
#++++++++++++++++++++++++++++++++++++++++++++++++++++
#  MX mail domain name
DAnuts.com


#++++++++++++++++++++++++++++++++++++++++++++++++++++
#The "R" macro contains the name of the mail relay that can deliver UUCP
#mail for this host. This should be the name of closest host to your
#site that will make the delivery for you. If you have such a host on
#your local network, use that host.
#++++++++++++++++++++++++++++++++++++++++++++++++++++
# UUCP relay host
DRuunet.uu.net


#++++++++++++++++++++++++++++++++++++++++++++++++++++
#All references to CSNET have been commented out. It
#would be cleaner to remove the lines completely, but because
#they were discussed in Chapter 10 they are left here for reference.
#++++++++++++++++++++++++++++++++++++++++++++++++++++
# csnet relay host
#DCYOUR_CSNET_RELAY_GOES_HERE


#++++++++++++++++++++++++++++++++++++++++++++++++++++
#The "B" macro contains the name of a host that can relay Bitnet mail.
#Use a host on your local network, if you have one that is connected to
#Bitnet. Otherwise use one of the well-known Bitnet relays. There are
#several: pucc.princeton.edu, mitvma.mit.edu, umrvmb.umr.edu, vm1.nodak.edu,
#cunyvm.cuny.edu, ricevm1.rice.edu, uicvm.uic.edu, uga.cc.uga.edu,
#cornellc.cit.cornell.edu, vtvm1.cc.vt.edu, and brownvm.brown.edu.
#++++++++++++++++++++++++++++++++++++++++++++++++++++
# bitnet relay host
DBcunyvm.cuny.edu


#++++++++++++++++++++++++++++++++++++++++++++++++++++
#The "j" macro contains the full hostname. On my system, the internal
#value set for "w" is the full hostname, which includes the domain.
#Therefore, the value of "w" can be used to set "j." If your system does
#not internally set "w" to the full hostname, use Dj$w.$D to set the
#value of "j."
#
#To find out if your sendmail.cf sets the correct value for "j," start
#sendmail and:
#       telnet localhost 25
#This telnet command will connect to your sendmail. sendmail will
#display a single line of output. The value of "j" is the second field
#displayed on this line. After you check the value, type "quit" to
#disconnect from sendmail.
#++++++++++++++++++++++++++++++++++++++++++++++++++++
# my official hostname
Dj$w
```

```
##############
#   Classes   #
##############
#++++++++++++++++++++++++++++++++++++++++++++++++++++++++
#Class "I" contains special internal domain names. These names are used
#for rewriting the mail that must be passed to the mail relays. See the
#"Modifying Classes" section in Chapter 10.
#++++++++++++++++++++++++++++++++++++++++++++++++++++++++
# Internal ("fake") domains that we use in rewriting
CIUUCP BITNET


#**********#
# NIS Map #
#**********#
#****************************************************
#The value for macro "G" is set to the passwd.byname map.
#We use this NIS map to re-write sender addresses to the
#"firstname.lastname" format. See "Rewriting Sender Addresses"
#in Chapter 9 for more details.
#****************************************************
# Define password map for GCOS information
DGpasswd.byname


####################
#   Version Number   #
####################
#++++++++++++++++++++++++++++++++++++++++++++++++++++++++
#Macro Z contains the configuration file's version number. It is
#modified every time the file is updated. Keep a record of your
#modifications.
#++++++++++++++++++++++++++++++++++++++++++++++++++++++++
# 2.0  modified by Craig, per Chapter 10
#         - modified local information and general macros
#         - changed path for aliases and sendmail.st
#         - removed all references to CSNET and to .arpa
# 2.1  added macro A for MX mail domain
#         - modified S14 and S24 to delete class N and use macro A
# 3.0  added ruleset 18 to rewrite the username to the user's real
#         first and last name, per Chapter 9
#         - modified S17 to call S18
DZ3.0


####################
#   Special Macros   #
####################
#++++++++++++++++++++++++++++++++++++++++++++++++++++++++
#In the following sections, "Special Macros," "Options," "Message
#Precedences," "Trusted Users," "Format of Headers," and "Rewriting
#Rules," changes are not usually required.
#++++++++++++++++++++++++++++++++++++++++++++++++++++++++
# my name
DnMAILER-DAEMON
# UNIX header format
DlFrom $g  $d
```

```
# delimiter (operator) characters
Do.:%@!^=/[]
# format of a total name
Dq$g$?x ($x)$.
# SMTP login message
De$j Sendmail $v/$Z ready at $b


##############
#   Options   #
##############
#+++++++++++++++++++++++++++++++++++++++++++++++++++++++
#In Chapter 10, we changed the value of option "A" to "/etc/aliases" and
#the value of option "t" to "EST,EDT" (Eastern Standard and Eastern
#Daylight Time). We also deleted option "W."  These changes were made
#primarily as examples and are not usually required.
#+++++++++++++++++++++++++++++++++++++++++++++++++++++++
# location of alias file
OA/etc/aliases
# wait up to ten minutes for alias file rebuild
Oa10
# substitution for space (blank) characters
OB.
# (don't) connect to "expensive" mailers
#Oc
# default delivery mode (deliver in background)
Odbackground
# temporary file mode
OF0600
# default GID
Og1
# location of help file
OH/usr/lib/sendmail.hf
# log level
OL9
# default network name
ONARPA
# default messages to old style
Oo
# queue directory
OQ/usr/spool/mqueue
# read timeout -- violates protocols
Or2h
# status file
OS/usr/lib/sendmail.st
# queue up everything before starting transmission
Os
# default timeout interval
OT3d
# time zone names (V6 only)
OtEST,EDT
# default UID
Ou1
# load average at which we just queue messages
Ox8
```

```
# load average at which we refuse connections
OX12


##########################
#   Message Precedences   #
##########################

Pfirst-class=0
Pspecial-delivery=100
Pbulk=-60
Pjunk=-100


###################
#   Trusted Users   #
###################

Troot
Tdaemon
Tuucp


#######################
#   Format of Headers   #
#######################
H?P?Return-Path: <$g>
HReceived: $?sfrom $s $.by $j ($v/$Z)
        id $i; $b
H?D?Resent-Date: $a
H?D?Date: $a
H?F?Resent-From: $q
H?F?From: $q
H?x?Full-Name: $x
HSubject:
# HPosted-Date: $a
# H?l?Received-Date: $b
H?M?Resent-Message-Id: <$t.$i@$j>
H?M?Message-Id: <$t.$i@$j>



##########################
###   Rewriting Rules   ###
##########################


##############################
#  Sender Field Pre-rewriting  #
##############################
S1
#R$*<$*>$*        $1$2$3                defocus


################################
#  Recipient Field Pre-rewriting  #
################################
S2
#R$*<$*>$*        $1$2$3                defocus
```

```
##################################
#  Final Output Post-rewriting  #
##################################
S4


R@                    $@                        handle <> error addr


# resolve numeric addresses to name if possible
R$*<@[$+]>$*         $:$1<@$[[$2]$]>$3          lookup numeric internet addr


# externalize local domain info
R$*<$+>$*            $1$2$3                      defocus
R@$+:@$+:$+          @$1,@$2:$3                  <route-addr> canonical


# UUCP must always be presented in old form
R$+@$-.UUCP          $2!$1                       u@h.UUCP => h!u


# delete duplicate local names
R$+%$=w@$=w           $1@$w                      u%host@host => u@host
R$+%$=w@$=w.$D        $1@$w                      u%host@host => u@host


###########################
#  Name Canonicalization  #
###########################
S3


# handle "from:<>" special case
R$*<>$*              $@@                         turn into magic token


# basic textual canonicalization -- note RFC733 heuristic here
R$*<$*<$*<$+>$*>$*>$*  $4                        3-level <> nesting
R$*<$*<$+>$*>$*       $3                         2-level <> nesting
R$*<$+>$*            $2                          basic RFC821/822 parsing


# make sure <@a,@b,@c:user@d> syntax is easy to parse -- undone later
R@$+,$+              @$1:$2                      change all "," to ":"


# localize and dispose of route-based addresses
R@$+:$+              $@$>6<@$1>:$2               handle <route-addr>


# more miscellaneous cleanup
R$+                  $:$>8$1                     host dependent cleanup
R$+:$*;@$+           $@$1:$2;@$3                 list syntax
R$+:$*;              $@$1:$2;                    list syntax
R$+@$+               $:$1<@$2>                   focus on domain
R$+<$+@$+>           $1$2<@$3>                   move gaze right
R$+<@$+>             $@$>6$1<@$2>                already canonical


# convert old-style addresses to a domain-based address
R$+^$+               $1!$2                       convert ^ to !
R$-!$+               $@$>6$2<@$1.UUCP>           resolve uucp names
R$+.$-!$+            $@$>6$3<@$1.$2>             domain uucps
R$+!$+               $@$>6$2<@$1.UUCP>           uucp subdomains
R$+%$+               $:$>9$1%$2                  user%host
```

```
R$+<@$+>                 $@$>6$1<@$2>          already canonical
#*************************************************************
# This rule will re-write first.last aliases into last@first!
# To avoid this problem, comment it out. See "Username
# Aliases" in Chapter 9 for a discussion of this change.
#*************************************************************
#R$-.$+                  $@$>6$2<@$1>          host.user


###############################
#   special local conversions   #
###############################

S6
R$*<@$=w>$*              $:$1<@$w>$3           get into u@$w form
R$*<@$=w.$D>$*           $:$1<@$w>$3
R$*<@$=U.UUCP>$*         $:$1<@$w>$3


###############################
#    Change rightmost % to @.   #
###############################

S9
R$*%$*                   $1@$2                 First make them all @'s.
R$*@$*@$*                $1%$2@$3              Undo all but the last.
R$*@$*                   $@$1<@$2>             Put back the brackets.


##################
###   Mailers   ###
##################
#+++++++++++++++++++++++++++++++++++++++++++++++++++++++
#The mailers do not usually require modification. However in Chapter
#10, we did make some changes to the S and R rulesets of one of the
#mailers. These changes will be noted later in this file.
#+++++++++++++++++++++++++++++++++++++++++++++++++++++++
#*****************************************************
#Additional changes were made in Chapter 9. Those changes are
#also noted where they occur.
#*****************************************************


#########################################################
#########################################################
#####
#####          Local and Program Mailer specification
#####
#########################################################
#########################################################


Mlocal, P=/bin/mail, F=rlsDFMmn, S=10, R=20, A=mail -d $u
Mprog,  P=/bin/sh,   F=lsDFMe,   S=10, R=20, A=sh -c $u


S10
R@                       $n                    errors to mailer-daemon
```

```
############################################################
############################################################
#####
#####          Local Domain SMTP Mailer specification
#####
#####    Messages processed by this specification are delivered
#####    by the local server.
#####
############################################################
############################################################


Mtcpld, P=[IPC], F=mDFMueXLC, S=17, R=27, A=IPC $h, E=\r\n


S17

# cleanup forwarding a bit
R$*<$*>$*              $1$2$3              defocus
R$*                    $:$>3$1             canonicalize
R$*%$*<@$w>            $:$>9$1%$2          user%localhost@localdomain

# pass <route-addr>'s through
R<@$+>$*               $@<@$[$1$]>$2       resolve <route-addr>

# map colons to dots everywhere
R$*:$*                 $1.$2               map colons to dots

# output local host as user@host.domain
#*********************************************************
# Changes made to call ruleset 18 for first.last rewrite.
# The change rewrites sender addresses to the form
# firstname.lastname@domain, hiding both the username and
# the hostname. See "Rewriting Sender Addresses", Chapter 9
#*********************************************************
# No hostname? Add the domain name and call ruleset 18
#*********************************************************
R$-                    $@$>18$1<@$A>         user w/o host
#*********************************************************
# This host? Convert the hostname to the domain name and
# call ruleset 18
#*********************************************************
R$+<@$w>               $@$>18$1<@$A>         this host
#*********************************************************
# A hostname alias? Send the username and the hostname to
# ruleset 18. If it finds the user in the passwd file it
# will convert the username to the first.last format and
# the hostname to the domain name. Otherwise it will
# return the original username and hostname.
#*********************************************************
R$+<@$=w>              $@$>18$1<@$2>         or an alias
#*********************************************************
# Perhaps it's a CNAME. Ask the nameserver to make the
# name canonical.
#*********************************************************
R$+<@$->               $:$1<@$[$2$]>         ask nameserver
```

```
#*******************************************************
# If the name server returns this host's name as the
# canonical name convert it to the domain name and
# call rulset 18. Otherwise don't bother ruleset 18.
#*******************************************************
R$+<@$w>                 $@$>18$1<@$A>          this host
R$+<@$->                 $@$1<@$2.$D>           if nameserver fails

# if not local, and not a "fake" domain, ask the nameserver
R$+<@$+.$~I>             $@$1<@$[$2.$3$]>       user@host.domain
R$+<@[$+]>               $@$1<@[$2]>            already ok

# output fake domains as user%fake@relay
R$+<@$+.BITNET>          $@$1%$2.BITNET<@$B>    user@host.bitnet
#R$+<@$+.CSNET>          $@$1%$2.CSNET<@$C>     user@host.CSNET
R$+<@$+.UUCP>            $@$2!$1<@$w>           user@host.UUCP


#*******************************************************
# This ruleset uses the username as an index into the passwd.byname
# NIS map. NIS returns the user's real name in the gcos field.
# See "Rewriting Sender Addresses in Chapter 9 for a full description
#*******************************************************
S18
#*******************************************************
# If the username is not in the passwd.byname map return without
# modifying the address. We defined macro G as the passwd.byname
# map so the test is "not in G"--$!G.
#*******************************************************
R$!G<@$+>                $@$1<@$2>              return, not in passwd
#*******************************************************
# Convert the username to the entire passwd record for that user
# and ensure that the hostname is replaced by the MX domain
#*******************************************************
R$-<@$+>                 $:${G$1$}<@$A>         user=>passwd entry
#*******************************************************
# Fields in the passwd record are separated by colons. The
# gcos field in the fifth field.
#*******************************************************
R$+:$+:$+:$+:$+          $5                     align on the gcos field
#*******************************************************
# Use the first value in the gcos field as the first name and
# the second value as the lastname. Return an address in the
# form of firstname.lastname@domain
#*******************************************************
R$-$-$+<@$+>             $:$1.$2<@$4>           gcos=>first.last@mxdomain


S27


# cleanup
R$*<$*>$*                $1$2$3                 defocus
R$*                      $:$>3$1                now canonical form
R$*%$*<@$w>              $:$>9$1%$2             user%localhost@localdomain
```

```
# pass <route-addr>'s through
R<@$+>$*              $@<@$[$1$]>$2          resolve <route-addr>


# map colons to dots everywhere
R$*:$*                $1.$2                  map colons to dots


# output local host as user@host.domain
R$-                   $@$1<@$w>              user w/o host
R$+<@$w>              $@$1<@$w>              this host
R$+<@$=w>             $@$1<@$w>              or an alias
R$+<@$->              $:$1<@$[$2$]>          ask nameserver
R$+<@$w>              $@$1<@$w>              this host
R$+<@$->              $@$1<@$2.$D>           if nameserver fails


# if not local, and not a "fake" domain, ask the nameserver
R$+<@$+.$~I>          $@$1<@$[$2.$3$]>       user@host.domain
R$+<@[$+]>            $@$1<@[$2]>            already ok


# output fake domains as user%fake@relay

R$+<@$+.BITNET>       $@$1%$2.BITNET<@$B>    user@host.BITNET
#R$+<@$+.CSNET>       $@$1%$2.CSNET<@$C>     user@host.CSNET
R$+<@$+.UUCP>         $@$2!$1                user@host.UUCP


###########################################################
###########################################################
#####
#####           Internet Relay Mailer specification
#####
#####   Messages processed by this specification are assumed to leave
#####   the local domain for delivery by a remote mail relay.
#####
###########################################################
###########################################################


Mtcp,   P=[IPC], F=mDFMueXLC, S=14, R=24, A=IPC $h, E=\r\n


S14


# pass <route-addr>'s through
R<@$+>$*              $@<@$[$1$]>$2          resolve <route-addr>


# map colons to dots everywhere
R$*:$*                $1.$2                  map colons to dots


# output local host in user@host.domain syntax
#+++++++++++++++++++++++++++++++++++++++++++++++++++++
#This ruleset referenced class "N", which is not defined in this
#configuration file. The rule referencing "N" was commented out. This
#ruleset also had a rule that would rewrite the sender address using the
#"% kludge" (u%h@gateway). That rule was commented out and replaced with
#a rule that rewrites the sender address into user@domain using the MX
#domain name we stored in macro "A."
#+++++++++++++++++++++++++++++++++++++++++++++++++++++
```

```
R$-                     $1<@$w>                 user w/o host
R$+<@$=w>               $:$1<@$w>               this host
R$+<@$->                $:$1<@$[$2$]>           canonicalize into dom
R$+<@$->                $:$1<@$2.$D>            if nameserver fails
#R$+<@$=N.$D>           $@$1<@$2.$D>            nic-reg hosts are ok
#R$+<@$*.$D>            $@$1%$2.$D<@$A>         else -> u%h@gateway
R$+<@$*.$D>             $@$1<@$A>               else -> user@domain


# if not local, and not a "fake" domain, ask the nameserver
R$+<@$+.$~I>            $@$1<@$[$2.$3$]>        user@host.domain
R$+<@[$+]>              $@$1<@[$2]>             already ok


# output internal ("fake") domains as "user%host@relay"

R$+<@$+.BITNET>         $@$1%$2.BITNET<@$B>     user@host.BITNET
#R$+<@$+.CSNET>         $@$1%$2.CSNET<@$C>      user@host.CSNET
R$+<@$+.UUCP>           $@$2!$1<@$w>            user@host.UUCP



S24


# put in <> kludge
R$*<$*>$*               $1$2$3                  defocus
R$*                     $:$>3$1                 now canonical form


# pass <route-addr>'s through
R<@$+>$*                $@<@$[$1$]>$2           resolve <route-addr>


# map colons to dots everywhere.....
R$*:$*                  $1.$2                   map colons to dots


# output local host in user@host.domain syntax
#+++++++++++++++++++++++++++++++++++++++++++++++++++++++
#The same modifications for the class "N" and macro "A" as noted in
#ruleset 14 were made here. It is common for the same rule to occur in
#multiple rulesets.
#+++++++++++++++++++++++++++++++++++++++++++++++++++++++
R$-                     $1<@$D>                 user w/o host
R$+<@$=w>               $:$1<@$w>               this host
R$+<@$->                $:$1<@$[$2$]>           canonicalize into dom
R$+<@$->                $:$1<@$2.$D>            if nameserver fails
#R$+<@$=N.$D>           $@$1<@$2.$D>            nic-reg hosts are ok
#R$+<@$*.$D>            $@$1%$2.$D<@$A>         else -> u%h@gateway
R$+<@$*.$D>             $@$1<@$A>               else -> u%h@gateway


# if not local, and not a "fake" domain, ask the nameserver
R$+<@$+.$~I>            $@$1<@$[$2.$3$]>        user@host.domain
R$+<@[$+]>              $@$1<@[$2]>             already ok


# Hide fake domains behind relays

R$+<@$+.BITNET>         $@$1%$2.BITNET<@$B>     user@host.BITNET
#R$+<@$+.CSNET>         $@$1%$2.CSNET<@$C>      user@host.CSNET
R$+<@$+.UUCP>           $@$2!$1                 user@host.UUCP
```

```
####################
###   Rule Zero   ###
####################
############################################################
############################################################
#####
#####              RULESET ZERO PREAMBLE
#####
#####   The beginning of ruleset zero is constant through all
#####   configurations.
#####
############################################################
############################################################


S0


# first make canonical
R$*<$*>$*              $1$2$3                  defocus
R$+                    $:$>3$1                 make canonical

# handle special cases
R$*<@[$+]>$*           $:$1<@$[[$2]$]>$3       numeric internet addr
R$*<@[$+]>$*           $#tcp$@[$2]$:$1@[$2]$3  numeric internet spec
R$+                    $:$>6$1
R$-<@$w>               $#local$:$1
R@                     $#error$:Invalid address   handle <> form

# canonicalize using the nameserver if not internal domain
R$*<@$*.$~I>$*         $:$1<@$[$2.$3$]>$4
R$*<@$->$*             $:$1<@$[$2$]>$3
R$*<@$->$*             $:$1<@$2.$D>$3          if nameserver fails

# now delete the local info
R<@$w>:$*              $@$>0$1                 @here:... -> ...
R$*<@$w>               $@$>0$1                 ...@here -> ...


###################################
#  End of ruleset zero preamble   #
###################################


##############################################
###   Machine dependent part of Rule Zero   ###
##############################################
#++++++++++++++++++++++++++++++++++++++++++++++++++++++
#This section contains the part of ruleset 0 that reflects the mail
#delivery capability of this host. This section would be different for
#a host that is only connected to a UUCP network or for one that is
#connected to both UUCP and TCP/IP.
#
#As noted in Chapter 10, references to CSNET and the old ".arpa" domain
#are commented out.
#++++++++++++++++++++++++++++++++++++++++++++++++++++++


# resolve fake top level domains by forwarding to other hosts
```

```
R$*<@$+.BITNET>$*          $#tcp$@$B$:$1<@$2.BITNET>$3      user@host.BITNET
#R$*<@$+.CSNET>$*          $#tcp$@$C$:$1<@$2.CSNET>$3       user@host.CSNET


# forward non-local UUCP traffic to our UUCP relay
R$*<@$*.UUCP>$*            $#tcpld$@$R$:$1<@$2.UUCP>        uucp mail

# hide behind our internet relay when talking to people in the arpa domain
#R$*<@$*.arpa>$*           $#tcp$@$2.arpa$:$1<@$2.arpa>$3  user@host.arpa

# but speak domains to them if they speak domains too
R$*<@$*>$*                 $#tcpld$@$2$:$1<@$2>$3           user@host.domain

# remaining names must be local
R$+                        $#local$:$1                      everything else
```

Shell Scripts

Building Aliases

Chapter 9 of this book contains a script for building *firstname.lastname* aliases from data contained in the */etc/passwd* file. The script shown below builds a file named *local.aliases* that contains only the *firstname.lastname* aliases. Special aliases, mailing lists, and all of the other things found in a complete *aliases* file are added separately by the system administrator.

```
#! /bin/sh
#
# Eliminate "non-login" accounts
#
grep -v '*' /etc/passwd | \
#
# Replace delimiting colons with whitespace
#
sed 's/:/ /g' | \
#
# Output first.last: username aliases to local.aliases
#
awk '{ print $5"."$6":", $1 }' > /etc/local.aliases
```

Building aliases from the *passwd* file is completely dependent on the format of that file. The file MUST have a consistent format for the *gcos* field and a consistent way to identify a "non-user" account. A "non-user" account is not used by a user to login or to collect email. It is normally a system account used by system or application software. A classic example is the *uucp* account. Every system has some way to mark that these accounts are not used for user logins. Some systems use an asterisk in the password field, some use an exclaimation mark, other systems use the letters NP, and still others use something else. The sample script assumes that an asterisk is used. Print out your *passwd* file to find out what it uses and modify the script accordingly.

The sample script also assumes that the first two values in the *gcos* field are the user's first and last name separated by a blank. If the beginning of the *gcos* field is in any other format, the script produces garbage. The procedure you use to add new users to your system should produce a consistent *gcos* field. Inconsistentcy is the enemy of automation. The sample below shows a file that has inconsistencies, and the bad aliases it produces.

```
% cat /etc/passwd
root:oRd1L/vMzzxno:0:1:System Administrator:/:/bin/csh
nobody:*:65534:65534::/:
daemon:*:1:1::/:
sys:*:2:2::/:/bin/csh
bin:*:3:3::/bin:
uucp:*:4:8::/var/spool/uucppublic:
news:*:6:6::/var/spool/news:/bin/csh
ingres:*:7:7::/usr/ingres:/bin/csh
audit:*:9:9::/etc/security/audit:/bin/csh
craig:1LrpKlz8sYjw:198:102:Craig Hunt:/home/craig:/bin/csh
dan:RSU.NY1KuFqzh2:214:885:Dan Scribner:/home/dan:/bin/csh
becca:monfTHdnjj:101:102:"Becky_Hunt":/home/becca:/bin/csh
dave:lniuhugfds:121:885:David H. Craig:/home/dave:/bin/csh
kathy:TUVigddehh:101:802:Kathleen S McCafferty:/home/kathy:/bin/csh
% bldalias
System.Administrator: root
Craig.Hunt: craig
Dan.Scribner: dan
"Becky_Hunt"./home/becca: becca
David.H.: dave
Kathleen.S: kathy
```

Your *passwd* file may have grown over time under the control of several different system administrators, and may be full of inconsistencies. If it is, clean it up before you run the script to build email aliases and then maintain it consistently in the future. Because the clean up is a one-time event, do it manually with a text editor. There is no point in automating a simple edit that will not be repeated.

The sample *passwd* file shown above has *gcos* data in three different formats from the three administrators that have run this system. Let's use it to provide a general outline of the steps you take in cleaning up a *passwd* file:

1. Copy the *passwd* file to a temporary work file called *passwd.work*:

   ```
   cp passwd passwd.work
   ```

2. Edit the work file and globally remove unwanted data from the *gcos* field. For the sample file, we remove quote marks (**sed 's/"//g'**), replace each underscore character with a single space (**sed 's/_/ /g'**), and remove the middle initial in both forms—with and without a period:

   ```
   sed 's/ [A-Z] / /g' | sed 's/ [A-Z]\. / /g'
   ```

3. Compare the password field in the original *passwd* file with the password field in the work file to make sure that no passwords were accidentally modified.

The script shown below helps with this task. If any passwords have been modified, correct the passwords in the work file using the passwords from the original *passwd* file and rerun the comparison to double check the work file. When you are 100% sure the work file is correct, copy *passwd* to *passwd.org* and copy the *passwd.work* file to *passwd*.

A script for comparing the work file and the original file is shown below.

```
#! /bin/sh
echo "If a password error is found, the username of the"
echo "record that contains the error is displayed below"
echo "along with the correct password for that username."
echo
cat /etc/passwd | awk -F: '{ print $1, $2 }' >/tmp/org.words
cat passwd.work | awk -F: '{ print $1, $2 }' >/tmp/work.words
diff /tmp/org.words /tmp/work.words | \
awk '/^</ { print $2 "\t\t" $3 } \
END { if ( NR <= 1 ) print "*** No errors found! ***" }'
rm /tmp/*.words
```

The edits for your *passwd* file won't be exactly the same as the ones mentioned above. However, you will follow similar steps in cleaning up your file.

Building the sendmail.cw File

A script can build the host aliases for the *sendmail.cw* file from data in the DNS database. The following script assumes that the system is the MX server for all hosts within the *sales.nuts.com* domain. The script converts every hostname from the domain into an entry in *sendmail.cw* file. *sendmail.cw* is read into the *w* class by the *sendmail.cf* file. See the notes near the beginning of the sample *sendmail.cf* file earlier in this appendix.

```
#! /bin/sh
#
# List all of the hostnames in this zone
#
echo ls sales.nuts.com | nslookup | \
#
# Use the network address as a filter to
# skip all of the headers and any servers
# that are located outside of the domain
#
grep '128\.66\.7\.' | \
#
# Sort the names for future convenience
#
sort | \
#
# Output the hostnames and the hostnames plus
# the domain name in proper sendmail.cw format

    '{ print $1, $1".sales.nuts.com" }' > sendmail.cw
```

Changes to System Files

DOS and Windows 3.1 are configured at startup through a series of system files. Installing a network changes these startup files because the network must be linked into the operating system and restarted every time the system reboots. The principal systems files affected by installing TCP/IP are:

CONFIG.SYS   Loads TCP/IP device drivers under DOS

AUTOEXEC.BAT Loads TCP/IP TSR programs under DOS

SYSTEM.INI   Provides network hardware information to Windows

WIN.INI   Stores a variety of information for network applications running under Windows

PROGMAN.INI Holds information about the TCP/IP program groups for the Windows *Program Manager*

Examples of how CONFIG.SYS and AUTOEXEC.BAT are changed to install TCP/IP under DOS are provided in Chapter 4. This appendix shows the changes made to those files and to the Windows initialization files when TCP/IP is installed on a Windows system. We use *SuperTCP Pro* for our examples.

File Modifications

Installing *SuperTCP Pro* changes all five of the system files listed above, and it adds several other .INI files to the C:\WINDOWS directory. The additional .INI files are used to configure individual TCP/IP applications. Each version of TCP/IP has its own set of applications and its own set of application initialization files. If you decide to remove TCP/IP from your system, you can simply delete the TCP/IP application initialization files, but you can't delete the system initialization files. The system files must be returned to their original condition. For this reason, it is very important to make a copy of the original system files and to know what changes the TCP/IP installation made to those files. Each of the following sections provides advice on how to remove TCP/IP from from the system files.

CONFIG.SYS

Device drivers that run under DOS are installed through this file. The sample *SuperTCP* installation adds the following three statements:

```
Device=c:\supertcp\protman.dos /i:c:\supertcp
Device=c:\supertcp\ELNK3.DOS
Device=c:\supertcp\stcpndis.dos
```

The *Protocol Manager* (*protman.dos*) and the NDIS driver (*stcpndis.dos*)[*] allow multiple protocols to share the 3C509 network adapter (ELNK3.DOS). This configuration allows NetBIOS and TCP/IP to share the same network interface.

Cleaning these statements out of the CONFIG.SYS file is simple because they all contain the C:\SUPERTCP pathname. Of course, the NDIS driver, the Protocol Manager, and the 3COM adapter driver are not specific to *SuperTCP*. These drivers could come from other directories, and they could be needed for NetBIOS networking even after TCP/IP is removed. Use judgement based on the pathname of the driver and your knowledge of how the PC is being used before you remove any device driver.

AUTOEXEC.BAT

The AUTOEXEC.BAT file is used by *SuperTCP* to set DOS environment variables and to load TSRs. The sample installation adds the following lines to that file:

```
SET TZ=est5edt
REM Frontier Begin Modifications
SET PATH=%PATH%;C:\SUPERTCP
SET SUPERTCP=C:\WINDOWS\SUPERTCP.INI
c:\supertcp\netbind.com
REM Frontier End Modifications
```

The NETBIND.COM TSR is used to add NetBIOS support. It is required for the shared NDIS drivers we installed in CONFIG.SYS. PATH is the standard DOS environment variable that defines the execution path. This statement adds the directory C:\SUPERTCP to the execution path. The other two variables, TZ and SUPERTCP, are specific to the *SuperTCP* installation. TZ sets the time zone, and SUPERTCP points to *SuperTCP's* initialization file.

Cleaning up this file is simple because most of the statements added by SuperTCP are surrounded by remarks (REM) that clearly state that these modifications were made for *SuperTCP*. Many vendors highlight the modifications they make to the system files in this manner. If your vendor doesn't, it's a good idea to insert these comments yourself.

---

[*] This is a *SuperTCP* implementation. Normally the NDIS driver is named NDIS.DOS.

The TZ variable is an exception; it isn't included between the remarks. But even if it is not removed when *SuperTCP* is deleted from the system, it does not cause a boot problem. Environment variables are generally harmless, and this one does not even reference the C:\SUPERTCP directory.[*]

SYSTEM.INI

SuperTCP adds the following devices to the [386Enh] section of the SYSTEM.INI file:

```
device=C:\WINDOWS\SYSTEM\win32s\w32s.386
device=C:\SUPERTCP\ftctcpip.386
```

The *SuperTCP* VxD is easy to identify. It is C:\SUPERTCP*ftctcpip.386*. The path name clearly gives it away. The other driver, W32S.386, provides support for 32-bit applications; it doesn't really have anything to do with *SuperTCP*. The only reason *SuperTCP* added it was that it needed it to support some applications. Only remove the driver that contains C:\SUPERTCP in its path to cleanup this file. The W32S.386 driver is useful for many other applications.

WIN.INI

Our sample installation changes the load= statement in the [windows] section of the WIN.INI file to:

```
load=C:\SUPERTCP\MSERVICE.EXE
```

This load= statement causes *SuperTCP Master Services* to run when Windows is started.

WIN.INI is often used to store application specific configuration information. SuperTCP adds the following section to the file:

```
[Frontier Technologies Corporation]
Last Diskette=A:\
0x00000008=0ff-0a0-77,b22-01e-2c
SEC_Package=0x50ceff2a
Company name=ORA
User name=Craig Hunt
MailBox=C:\SUPERTCP\MAILBOX\
MailLeft=C:\SUPERTCP\EMAIL.EXE
NumPackages=1
Package1=SUPERTCP.INF
SUPERTCP.INF=C:\SUPERTCP
SuperTCP Name=SuperTCP Pro for Windows
SuperTCP Version=Version 1.00
```

Another vendor's implementation would add a completely different section to WIN.INI. The commands shown above are only significant to *SuperTCP*.

---

[*] Unused environment variables should be removed to conserve memory.

Cleaning up this file is easy. Having C:\SUPERTCP in the path of the load= statement makes that easy to identify. And the section that is dedicated to Frontier Technologies software can be removed in its entirety.

PROGMAN.INI

Any application that adds a program group to the *Program Manager* modifies the PROGMAN.INI file. *SuperTCP Pro* adds the following two groups to the [Groups] section of that file:

```
Group6=C:\WINDOWS\SUPERX.GRP
Group7=C:\WINDOWS\SUPERTCP.GRP
```

You don't have to edit this file to clean it up. From Windows, highlight the group you want to delete in the *Program Manager* and select **Delete** from the **File** menu.

E

Public Domain Software

The bulk of the examples in this book are based on commercial PC software. Most PC support staffs favor commercial software, because:

- *It's already integrated.* Integration is a difficult task, and it is difficult for documentation to provide any real help. Incompatibilities are undocumented because they are unknown to the developer of the software. TCP/IP developers try to write compatible software, but they do not know the exact combination of software you are using. The Winsock standard addresses some integration issues, but not all. And Winsock is limited to Windows; it doesn't do anything for DOS users.

  Most commercial packages contain the TCP/IP stack and a full suite of applications. This eliminates the need to integrate software from several different sources. All of the components come from the same source and are tested for compatibility. Integration is not an issue.

  Sticking with one software vendor does have problems, however. You're dependent on one source for software, which can mean waiting for the vendor to commercialize important new software that is already available from some other source.

- *It's supported.* Commercial software generally comes with technical support or offers technical support as an extra cost option. This support often leaves a lot to be desired, but at least there is someone at the other end of the phone who will attempt to answer your questions. Public domain software sometimes has better quality support because the developer answers the questions and provides the fixes. However when the developer loses interest, is assigned to another project, or the amount of support requested grows too large for the developer to handle, support for the public domain software may decline or disappear all together.

- *It's documented*. Documentation is always inadequate, but commercial packages usually have the edge.

Interestingly, the same people who love UNIX public domain software shy away from many PC public domain packages. The reason is that PC packages frequently do not include source code. The ability to modify source code is a key part of "self support." Even when source is provided, the wide variety of languages and compilers used on PCs can mean trouble compiling the code. Without source, you can't fix the problem yourself, and you're completely dependent on someone else for support.

These reasons lead most businesses to use commercial software. For them, time is money; for others, it's a different story. The home hobbyist has no money and enjoys spending time tinkering with the computer. The educational organization has little money and many students who need to spend time learning about computers. There are many more examples of people and organizations for whom public domain software makes good financial sense.

Low initial cost is not the only advantage of public domain software. Another advantage is that public domain software is often at the leading edge of TCP/IP network technology. New protocols and services are frequently first implemented as public domain software. Organizations that want to be on the leading edge of networking sometimes must turn to public domain software because no commercial version of the protocol they seek is yet available.

There is a lot of great public domain software. It comes in several different forms; three are used in this book:

- *Freeware* is software that is available for free. It costs nothing to use and can be freely copied and distributed.

- *Shareware* is software that is available for a nominal "registration" fee. The software can be freely copied and distributed but can only be used for an extended period if the user sends a small registration fee to the author. Shareware falls somewhere between free software and commercial software. Some of the most widely used PC programs are shareware.

- *Bookware* is my term for software that is included with a book. Buy the book and get the software. The software attached to the book can be freeware or shareware. If it is shareware, an additional registration fee beyond the price of the book may be requested.

  I like this way of obtaining public domain software because I love good hardcopy documentation. The problem with bookware is that it quickly gets out of date. The Mosaic used in Chapter 5 is bookware, and the packet driver, TCP/IP, and mailer used in this appendix are available as bookware from *Internet CD*, by Vivian Neou, Prentice Hall, 1994.

In this appendix, we build a fully operational TCP/IP system under Windows 3.1 using:[*]

Crynwr packet drivers

A packet driver is a piece of software that provides the *Network Access Layer* connection between IP and a network adapter. Because the packet driver must be specifically tailored for the network hardware, each adapter uses a different packet driver. The *Crynwr* packet drivers were previously called the *Clarkson* packet drivers because they were developed at Clarkson University.

Trumpet TCP/IP

Trumpet is a Winsock-compliant version of TCP/IP for Windows. It provides the basic TCP/IP stack and several network applications.

Eudora

Eudora is a mailer. We use the freeware version 1.4. A more complete commercial version is available from QUALCOMM, the company that sells *Eudora*.

The *Crynwr* packet drivers are freeware. Information is available from:

Crynwr Software
11 Grant Street
Potsdam, NY 13676

Trumpet is shareware. Licensing and registration information is available from:

Trumpet Software International
GPO Box 1649
Hobart, TAS Australia 7001
Phone: 61-02-487049

The commercial version of *Eudora* is available from:

QUALCOMM Incorporated
6455 Lusk Blvd.
San Diego, CA 92121-2779
Phone: (619)587-1121
Email: *eudora-sales@qualcomm.com*

We should also mention **PKZIP** and **PKUNZIP**. These are shareware programs that compress and decompress files. They have nothing to do with networking, but **PKUNZIP** is used repeatedly in this text. Information about registering **PKUNZIP** can be obtained from:

PKWARE, Inc.
9025 N. Deerwood Drive
Brown Deer, WI 53223
Phone: (414)354-8699

---

[*] These instructions only work for Windows 3.1. Windows for Workgroups is discussed later in the appendix.

Installing a Packet Driver

The public domain TCP/IP that we are using relies on TSRs. As Chapter 5 points out, there are advantages and disadvantages to TSRs, but the main reason that they are used in public domain Windows software is that they already existed for DOS. Public domain software is a cooperative effort. Developers build on each others' work to create the finished product. Packet drivers already existed to run TCP/IP under DOS, so when people started to implement TCP/IP for Windows they naturally took advantage of them.

The *Crynwr* packet drivers are available from many sources. Some manufacturers provide a packet driver with their network adapter software. On the *Internet CD*, the drivers are found in the \SRC\PC\CRYNWR directory. I downloaded them from the */SimTel/msdos/pktdrvr* directory at *oak.oakland.edu* where they are contained in the *pktd11.zip* file.[*]

Create a directory to hold the drivers, in the example it's called PKTDRVR. Download PKTD11.ZIP into it. **PKUNZIP** the file, and delete the original zipped file.

```
C:\>mkdir pktdrvr
C:\>cd pktdrvr
C:\pktdrvr>ftp oak.oakland.edu
Connected to oak.oakland.edu.
220 oak.oakland.edu FTP server ready.
User (oak.oakland.edu:(none)): anonymous
331 Guest login ok, use e-mail address as password.
Password:
ftp> bin
200 Type set to I.
ftp> get /SimTel/msdos/pktdrvr/pktd11.zip
200 PORT command successful.
150 Opening BINARY mode data connection for pktd11.zip (435420 bytes).
226 Transfer complete.
435420 bytes received in 50.15 seconds (8.68 Kbytes/sec)
ftp> quit
C:\pktdrvr>pkunzip pktd11.zip
  plenty of information printed by PKUNZIP
C:\pktdrvr>del pktd11.zip
```

At the time of this writing there are more than 50 drivers in the file, as this DIR listing shows. You only need a few of these files. After the installation you can delete the unneeded files.

```
C:\pktdrvr>dir /w
 Directory of C:\pktdrvr
[.]              [..]             3C501.COM        3C503.COM        3C507.COM
3C507.DOC        3C509.COM        3C523.COM        AQUILA.COM       AR450.COM
ARCETHER.COM     AT&T.COM         AT&T_LP.COM      AT1500.COM       AT1700.COM
BIBLIO.DOC       BUGS.DOC         CHANGES.DOC      COPYING.DOC      CRYNWR.WAV
```

---

[*] This name will change over time as new drivers are added. Look for *pktd??.zip* if you don't find this exact name.

```
CTRONDNI.COM    DAVIDSYS.COM    DE600.COM       DEPCA.COM       DK86960.COM
GPL.DOC         DK86965.COM     EN301.COM       ES3210.COM      ETHERSL.COM
ETHIIE.COM      EXOS205.COM     EXP16.COM       GOPHER.DOC      HOWTOGET.IT
HPPCLAN.COM     HPPCLANP.COM    IBMTOKEN.COM    INSTALL.DOC     INSTALL.PS
IPXPKT.COM      IPXPKT.DOC      IPXPKT.NOT      IPXSTAT.EXE     ISOLAN.COM
ISOLINK.COM     KODIAK16.COM    KODIAK8.COM     KODIAKK.COM     MANIFEST.DOC
NB.COM          MYLEX.COM       NE1000.COM      NE2.COM         NE2000.COM
NE2100.COM      NI5010.COM      NI5210.COM      NI6510.COM      NI9210.COM
NOVELL.DOC      NOVELL.NOT      ORDER.DOC       PACKET.DOC      PACKET_D.109
PDIPX103.ZIP    PKTCHK.COM      PKTD35.SYS      PKTD40A.SYS     PKTSTAT.COM
PKTTRAF.COM     PKTWATCH.COM    PLIP.COM        PLIP.DOC        PROMBOOT.NOT
READ.ME         SLIP8250.COM    SMC_WD.COM      SNMP.NOT        SOFTWARE.DOC
SUPPORT.DOC     TCENET.COM      TERMIN.COM      TIARA.COM       UBNICPC.COM
UBNICPS2.COM    UUNET.DOC       VAXMATE.COM     WD8003E.COM     WINPKT.COM
WORKERS.DOC     ZNOTE.COM       DLLPKT.NOT      ARCETHER.DOC
         92 file(s)        944,851 bytes
          2 dir(s)     401,604,608 bytes free
```

Each driver is named for the network adapter it is designed to work with. Use the NE2000.COM driver for an NE2000 adapter, the 3C509.COM driver for a 3C509 adapter, and so on.

The command-line arguments vary slightly from driver to driver. The variation is caused by the fact that the configuration of each board varies slightly. The syntax of the NE2000 command is a good example of an "average" driver command line:

NE2000 [*options*] *sw_int* [*irq*] [*io_port*]

options

> −d   Used for PCs that boot from the network instead of from a local disk.

> −n   Used to specify Novell IEEE 802.3 framing. Don't use on a TCP/IP network.

> −p   Disables promiscuous mode.

> −w   Don't use this option. It is obsolete because of the **WINPKT** program, which is described later.

> −i   Used to specify IEEE 802.3 framing. This option can be used on a TCP/IP network if required, but most TCP/IP networks use Ethernet II framing.

sw_int

> The *sw_int* is a hexadecimal value in the range of 0x60 to 0x7f. It is the software interrupt vector for the driver. It is the only required parameter.

irq

> The IRQ of this network adapter. Some adapter boards do not require that the IRQ is specified on the command line. In this case, the NE2000 driver defaults to IRQ 2 if no value is specified. Use the value you assigned to the card when it was installed.

io_port

>The I/O Port Address for this adapter. Some network cards do not require this configuration value on the command line. The NE2000 defaults to using 0x300. The possible I/O Port Addresses are hexadecimal values from 0x100 to 0x3ff, but most network adapters do not support the full range of values. Use the value you assigned to the card when it was installed.

Install the packet driver through the AUTOEXEC.BAT file, just like any other TSR. Our sample system has a 3C509 card. We add the following lines to AUTOEXEC.BAT:

```
REM Begin Trumpet Winsock Modifications
C:\PKTDRVR\3C509 0x60
REM End Trumpet Winsock Modifications
```

The software interrupt is the only argument needed on this command line. This packet driver obtains the adapter's configuration directly from the card. A packet driver for a different network adapter would have different arguments. See the *Crynwr* INSTALL.DOC file and the various notes files (*.NOT) that come with the packet drivers for information on individual drivers.

Reboot the system, and the packet driver is installed. Next we install a TCP/IP stack to take advantage of the new driver.

Installing Trumpet

Trumpet Winsock can be ordered directly from *Trumpet*, obtained from a CD, or downloaded from any number of sites on the Internet. No matter how it is obtained, *Trumpet Winsock* is NOT FREE. See the final section of the *Trumpet* INSTALL.TXT document for instructions on how to pay for your copy.

For the examples in this section, I downloaded *twsk20b.zip* from the */pub3/win3/winsock* directory on *oak.oakland.edu*.[*] Create a directory for the file and use **PKUNZIP** to decompress it.

```
C:\>mkdir trumpet
C:\>cd trumpet
C:\trumpet>ftp oak.oakland.edu
Connected to oak.oakland.edu.
220 oak.oakland.edu FTP server ready.
User (oak.oakland.edu:(none)): anonymous
331 Guest login ok, send your e-mail address as password.
Password:
ftp> bin
200 Type set to I.
ftp> get /pub3/win3/winsock/twsk20b.zip
200 PORT command successful.
150 Opening BINARY mode data connection for twsk20b.zip (179015 bytes).
226 Transfer complete.
```

---

[*] The filename will change as the file is updated.

```
179015 bytes received in 27.13 seconds (6.60 Kbytes/sec)
ftp> quit
221 Goodbye.
C:\trumpet>pkunzip twsk20b.zip
 plenty of information printed by PKUNZIP
C:\trumpet>del *.zip
C:\trumpet>dir /w
 Volume in drive C has no label
 Volume Serial Number is 1D3D-2141
 Directory of C:\trumpet
[.]             [..]            README.MSG       DISCLAIM.TXT     INSTALL.DOC
INSTALL.TXT     WINPKT.COM      WINSOCK.DLL      TCPMAN.EXE       SENDREG.EXE
PINGW.EXE       SERVICES        PROTOCOL         HOSTS            LOGIN.CMD
BYE.CMD         SETUP.CMD
        15 file(s)        457,540 bytes
         2 dir(s)     401,031,168 bytes free
```

The directory now contains the **TCPMAN** program, the Winsock DLL, the documentation, and the tools necessary to complete the *Trumpet Winsock* installation. **WINPKT** is one of these tools.

The packet driver installed in the previous section supports TCP/IP for DOS. To make it work for Windows we need to use a *shim*. A shim is a piece of software that slightly modifies the function or interface of another piece of software so that it can be put to a different use. Shims are very popular in public domain software because they allow previously developed software to be put to a new use. The **WINPKT** shim provided with the *Trumpet* software helps the DOS packet driver work more effectively with Windows. Its syntax is very simple:

WINPKT *sw_int*

sw_int, the software interrupt, is the same as the one defined on the packet driver command line. The software interrupt is the only configuration value required by the **WINPKT** TSR.

The shim is a TSR. Install it through AUTOEXEC.BAT. Also add a PATH statement to AUTOEXEC.BAT to make the programs in the *Trumpet* directory easily accessible to your users. Add the two new lines to the section of the AUTOEXEC.BAT file that contains the *Trumpet Winsock* modifications. The completed *Trumpet Winsock* section is shown below:

```
REM Begin Trumpet Winsock Modifications
SET PATH=%PATH%;C:\TRUMPET
C:\PKTDRVR\3C509 0x60
C:\TRUMPET\WINPKT 0x60
REM End Trumpet Winsock Modifications
```

Reboot the system and type **PATH** at the DOS prompt. C:\TRUMPET should be part of the execution path that is displayed. If it is, type **WIN** to start Windows 3.1.

Select **Run** from the **File** menu in the Program Manager and enter **TCPMAN** in the dialogue box to run *Trumpet Winsock*. The first time it runs, the configuration window shown in Figure E-1 appears.

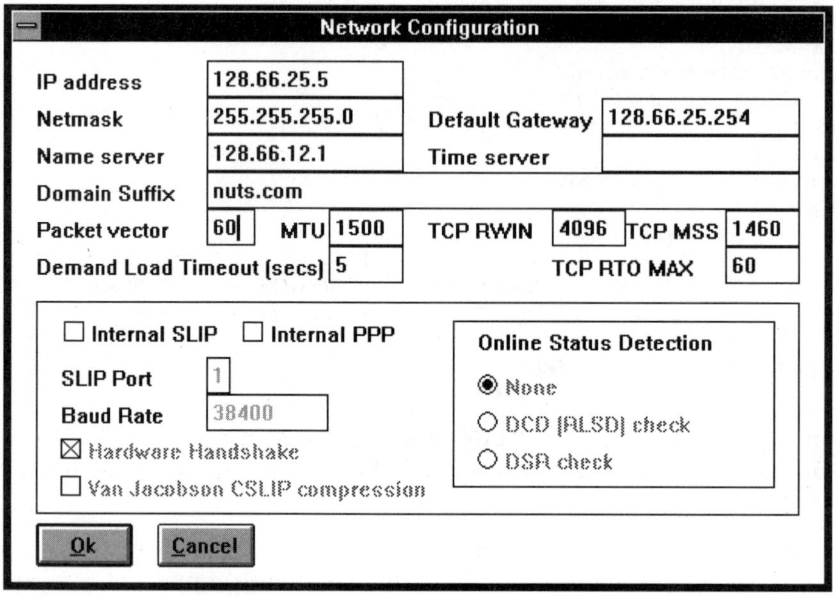

Figure E-1: TCPMAN Configuration

Most of the configuration values in Figure E-1 are familiar. By now, we all know what the IP address, subnet mask, name server, domain name and default gateway are. One note about the Name server field: you can specify more than one server by separating the server addresses with a blank space. The *MTU* (Maximum Transmission Unit), the *TCP RWIN* (TCP Receive Window), the *TCP MSS* (TCP Maximum Segment Size), and the *TCP RTO MAX* (TCP Read Time Out) all default to the correct values for the Ethernet interface and do not need to be changed.

Set the Packet Vector to the software interrupt vector used by the packet driver. In the sample AUTOEXEC.BAT file we used 0x60, so we set the value here to 60. *Trumpet Winsock* defaults to 00, which means that the system will search for the correct value. It's best to provide the correct value yourself.

The lower half of the window is only used for *Trumpet*'s internal SLIP driver. This section of the window is never used if a packet driver is installed, even if it is a SLIP packet driver. It is only used when *Trumpet* provides its own SLIP service. We'll discuss this later; for now, we can ignore it.

The configuration is stored in the TRUMPWSK.INI file in the TRUMPET directory. Do not edit that file directly. Use the configuration window.

When all of the values are set, click **OK**. The Trumpet Winsock window is displayed. To make sure that all of the values are set correctly, exit this copy of *Trumpet* by selecting **Exit** from the **File** menu, and rerun **TCPMAN** from the *Program Manager*. This time *Trumpet Winsock* should start without prompting for any configuration information.

If you get an error message about not being able to load TCP or not being able to locate the packet driver, go back and make sure everything is installed correctly in the AUTOEXEC.BAT. Reboot the system with echo on. Check the messages displayed during the boot to make sure the drivers start and that no error messages are displayed. See Chapter 3 for hints on troubleshooting the boot process and resolving memory conflicts.

If **TCPMAN** runs without error messages, test your connection with the ping program included with *Trumpet Winsock*. Run **PINGW** by selecting **Run** from the **File** menu in the *Program Manager*. In the window that appears, enter the name of the host you want to ping at the *Host:* prompt. End the ping with a CRTL-C. If the ping fails, use the ping error message as a guide to troubleshooting your TCP/IP configuration. Chapter 3 provides guidance on how the error messages relate to specific configuration problems. If you receive an unusual error message, such as *ICMP transmit error*, suspect the packet driver.

If **TCPMAN** runs without errors and the ping is successful, you're ready to run! Install your applications and use the network.

Trumpet provides several basic network applications. They can be found on the *Internet CD* in the \SRC\PC\TRUMPET\WINAPPS directory. Simply copy them to the C:\TRUMPET directory and use them. Telnet, FTP, **ping**, **traceroute**, **chat**, and other programs are included. The notable exception is a mail program. To complete our Windows 3.1 TCP/IP system, we install *Eudora* on top of *Trumpet Winsock*.

Installing Trumpet Under WfW

Suppose the user of our sample system upgrades to Windows for Workgroups 3.11, and decides to use both NetBIOS networking and TCP/IP. WfW installs without a hitch, and the NetBIOS networking runs without a problem, but the *Trumpet* TCP/IP stops working. Ping now fails with a "ICMP transmit error" message.

You can't just put WfW on top of a running TCP/IP system.[*] You must reinstall TCP/IP after installing WfW, selecting a new set of drivers and shims. The process of selecting and installing the right drivers for a specific situation is the kind of thing a commercial installation program does for you automatically and can also take hours of your time when done manually. Luckily, some stalwarts of public domain software have developed an installation kit for *Trumpet* that makes it as easy to install under WfW 3.11 as a commercial package.

The installation kit is available from *ftp.trumpet.com.au* where it is stored in the file */ftp/pub/winsock/wfwsetup/twswfwg.zip*. Get the file and unzip it into the C:\TRUMPET directory. The README.TXT file contains the installation instruc-

---

[*] Old versions of *Trumpet* do not run under WfW. Make sure you have *Trumpet Winsock* version 2.0b or later.

tions. Compare it to the Microsoft TCP/IP installation in Chapter 7. Basically the installation is the same as it is for any standard WfW network.

Start Windows for Workgroups and run **Network Setup** from the Network program group. Click **Driver** and then **Add Protocol**. In the Add Protocol dialogue box, highlight Unlisted or Updated Protocol and click **OK**. Enter the path of the new files (C:\TRUMPET in Figure E-2) in the Install Driver dialogue box and click **OK**. A dialogue box that lists *Trumpet TCP/IP* as the protocol is displayed. Click **OK**. Now the Network Drivers window shows that *Trumpet TCP/IP* is one of the installed networks.

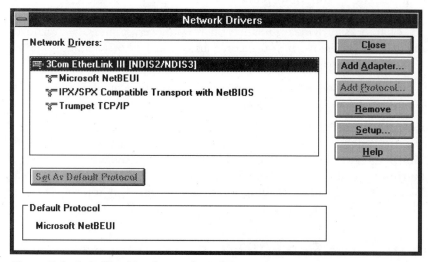

Figure E-2: Installing Trumpet under WfW

No further configuration is required at this time. If you highlight Trumpet TCP/IP and click **Setup**, you might be surprised. Remember, this installation package installs the drivers and shims that **TCPMAN** needs. This **Setup** button is used to define the driver values, such as the software interrupt vector, that we defined in the AUTOEXEC.BAT file when we installed *Trumpet* under Windows 3.1. The TCP/IP configuration values are still set through **TCPMAN**, just as they were under Windows 3.1, so just ignore the **Setup** button and click **OK**.

A warning message about the changes that the installation program made to AUTOEXEC.BAT, PROTOCOL.INI, and SYSTEM.INI is displayed. Reboot the system and restart Windows for Workgroups. Run **TCPMAN** from the **File** menu in the *Program Manager*. The first time you run it you'll be prompted for the TCP/IP configuration. See the Installing Trumpet section for information on entering these values.

Trumpet's Internal SLIP/PPP Support

The internal SLIP/PPP driver installation is almost identical to the *Trumpet* installation covered earlier in this appendix. The biggest difference is that the internal SLIP/PPP driver does not require a *Crynwr* packet driver or the **WINPKT** shim. Skip those installation steps. Simply get the files from TWSK20B.ZIP into the C:\TRUMPET directory, add that directory to the execution path, and run **TCPMAN** from the **File** menu in the *Program Manager*. This time, when the Network Configuration window appears, select either the **Internal SLIP** or the **Internal PPP** checkbox.

```
┌──────────────────────────────────────────────────────────────┐
│ ─                     Network Configuration                    │
├──────────────────────────────────────────────────────────────┤
│  IP address      128.66.25.5                                   │
│  Netmask         0.0.0.0        Default Gateway  0.0.0.0        │
│  Name server     128.66.12.1    Time server                    │
│  Domain Suffix   nuts.com                                       │
│  Packet vector   00    MTU 1500   TCP RWIN 4096  TCP MSS 1460   │
│  Demand Load Timeout (secs) 5              TCP RTO MAX   60      │
│                                                                │
│   □ Internal SLIP  ⊠ Internal PPP    ┌─ Online Status Detection ─┐│
│                                      │                          ││
│   SLIP Port      1                   │  ○ None                  ││
│   Baud Rate      38400               │  ⊙ DCD (RLSD) check       ││
│   ⊠ Hardware Handshake               │  ○ DSR check             ││
│   □ Van Jacobson CSLIP compression   └──────────────────────────┘│
│                                                                │
│   [ Ok ]   [ Cancel ]                                          │
└──────────────────────────────────────────────────────────────┘
```

Figure E-3: Trumpet SLIP/PPP Configuration

Figure E-3 shows the window used to configure SLIP or PPP. PPP is preferable, though not as widely supported as SLIP. If PPP isn't available, SLIP is certainly adequate. Selecting one of the internal serial line drivers activates the lower half of the window and changes the upper half of the window. In the upper half, neither the subnet mask nor the default gateway are required. In the lower half, several new fields request values:

SLIP Port

Enter the number of the COM port that is connected to the modem. Use a 1 for COM1, a 2 for COM2, a 3 for COM3, and a 4 for COM4.

Baud Rate

Enter the baud rate of your serial line connection. Speeds up to 115200 bps can be entered. Of course, the correct equipment is needed to actually drive a connection at that speed. It requires a V.34 modem operating at 28.8K bps with maximum data compression connected to a serial port on the PC that has a buffered UART (Universal Asynchronous Receiver/Transmitter), such as the 16550.

Hardware Handshake

Select this checkbox; it enables hardware flow control. Only disable it if your modem, link, or remote server cannot support it.

Van Jacobsen CSLIP compression

If your SLIP server provides CSLIP, check this box. Header compression gives better throughput. It has no effect if you are using PPP.

Online Status Detection

Select either **DCD** (Data Carrier Detect) or **DSR** (Data Set Ready) depending on which signal your modem uses to indicate the connection status of the line. DCD is most commonly used. Read your modem manual to find out what signal it uses and how you enable it in the modem. My MultiTech modem uses DCD, which is enabled on my modem with the AT&C1 command. If your modem does not provide a signal for line state, choose **None**.

When all of the values are set, click **OK** to return to the *Trumpet Winsock* window. You're ready to try your first connection. Select **Manual Login** from the **Dialler** menu. Type the modem commands, username, password, and SLIP/PPP commands that are required to set up the connection directly into the *Trumpet Winsock* window, as shown in Figure E-4. When the connection is made press the ESC (Escape) key.

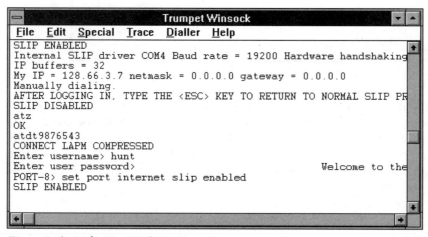

Figure E-4: Making a SLIP/PPP Connection

Use **PINGW** to test the connection. If the ping is not successful, remember that most SLIP/PPP problems are caused by the modem configuration. Your modem configuration must be compatible with the remote server's modem. See Chapter 5 for advice on SLIP/PPP modem configuration. The *Trumpet* dialer defaults to 8-bit, no parity. You may need to change this through Dialler Options. Refer to the section Installing Trumpet for additional troubleshooting hints.

If everything works right, you may want to use a script for future logins. Select **Edit Scripts** from the **Dialler** menu to edit the login script, which is in the file LOGIN.CMD found in the C:\TRUMPET directory. Figure E-5 shows the script editor.

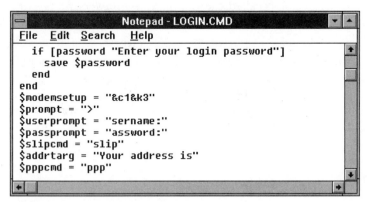

Figure E-5: Trumpet SLIP/PPP Editor

The default script asks the user for the telephone number, username, and password to access the remote server. It then uses these values to respond to prompts from the remote system. The script makes assumptions about those prompts. As we saw in Chapter 5, those assumptions may not be correct for your server. Put the correct values in the $userprompt, $passprompt, $slipcmd and $pppcmd variables. For example, in Chapter 5, note that the correct commands to start SLIP and PPP on our imaginary server are set port internet slip enabled and set port ppp enabled respectively. Therefore, we would change $slipcmd and $pppcmd to these values.

When all of the values are set, save the file and exit the editor. Test the script by selecting **Login** from the **Dialler** menu. The interaction between the script and the remote server is displayed in the *Trumpet Winsock* window. If the login fails, the trace shows where. If you need to modify the script extensively, see the information on the scripting language found in the INSTALL.TXT document in the C:\TRUMPET directory. And remember, you can always use the manual dialing feature to get connected. If the login works, you're in business.

Chameleon's Free SLIP Implementation

This appendix emphasizes *Trumpet Winsock*, but there are many choices in the world of low-cost and no-cost network software. As we have seen, some commercial vendors even provide no-cost versions of their software. Microsoft TCP/IP, discussed in Chapter 7, is a no-cost TCP/IP stack that runs under Windows for Workgroups. The *Eudora* software used in this appendix is a free version of a commercial mailer. The *Chameleon* software used extensively in this book is also available in a free "SLIP-only" version called the *Chameleon Sampler* and is available from *ftp.netmanage.com* in the file */pub/demos/sampler/sampler.exe*.

Create a directory for the *Sampler* and download it. SAMPLER.EXE is a self-exploding file. Enter **SAMPLER** at the DOS prompt to explode it into its component parts—about 80 files! In addition to the stack, the *Sampler* includes a ping program, a very nice FTP program, a good Telnet program, and a fine mailer. It also includes configuration files for SLIP and PPP access to a large number of different Internet service providers.

```
C:\>mkdir sampler
C:\>cd sampler
C:\SAMPLER>ftp ftp.netmanage.com
Connected to sunny1.netmanage.com.
220 sunny1 FTP server ready.
Name (ftp.netmanage.com:craig): anonymous
331 Guest login ok, send ident as password.
Password:
230 Guest login ok, access restrictions apply.
ftp> bin
200 Type set to I.
ftp> cd /pub/demos/sampler
250 CWD command successful.
ftp> get sampler.exe
200 PORT command successful.
150 Binary data connection for sampler.exe (754372 bytes).
226 Binary Transfer complete.
local: sampler.exe remote: sampler.exe
754372 bytes received in 22 seconds (33 Kbytes/s)
ftp> quit
221 Goodbye.
C:\SAMPLER>sampler
```

Installing the *Sampler* is just like installing any commercial Windows software. Install it using the **SETUP** program that is found in the *Sampler* directory. **SETUP** creates a C:\NETMANAG directory, copies the files into it, creates the *Chameleon Sampler* program group, and modifies the necessary initialization files.

SETUP automatically handles the installation. You must handle the configuration. This is done by opening the Custom icon from the *Chameleon Sampler* program group. Two things to note:

- The configuration program only allows you to select SLIP, CSLIP, or PPP interfaces.

- The maximum baud rate available for the port configuration is 19.2K bps.

The details of the installation process, the TCP/IP configuration, and the creation of SLIP and PPP login scripts are covered in Chapter 5. There is no need to rehash those topics here. Refer to Chapter 5 if you decide to use the *Sampler*.

The *Sampler* is a fine freeware package that includes three very nice applications. It is a good choice for software to provide home access to the Internet. Of course, it does not begin to approach the capability of the full commercial package, and it does have the limitations noted above. No software package is right for every situation. If you have a PC and modem that can push more than 19.2K bps through the serial port, you might want to use *Trumpet*'s internal SLIP or PPP driver.[*]

Installing Eudora

Eudora is a commercial mail program, based on the *Eudora* mailer originally developed for Macintosh computers. Version 1.4 is available at no cost, and though limited when compared to the commercial version, it is a good mailer. We use version 1.4 for Windows in this section.

Eudora 1.4 is available from many sources on the Internet. I downloaded the copy used in these examples from *oak.oakland.edu*, where it is found in the file */pub3/win3/eudora/eudora14.zip*. It can also be found in the \SRC\PC\EUDORA directory of the *Internet CD*.

Create a directory for *Eudora*, download the file into the directory, and unzip it. This unpacks the file into its component parts: WEUDORA.EXE (the program), README.TXT (the installation document), and CHANGES (a change history).

```
C:\>mkdir eudora
C:\>cd eudora
C:\EUDORA>ftp oak.oakland.edu
Connected to oak.oakland.edu.
220 oak.oakland.edu FTP server ready.
Name (oak.oakland.edu:craig): anonymous
331 Guest login ok, send your e-mail address as password.
Password:
ftp> bin
200 Type set to I.
ftp> cd /pub3/win3/eudora
250 CWD command successful.
ftp> get eudora14.zip
200 PORT command successful.
150 Opening BINARY mode data connection for eudora14.zip (259927 bytes).
226 Transfer complete.
```

---

[*] According to the WfW installation kit documentation, the internal SLIP and PPP drivers do not work under WfW 3.11.

```
local: eudora14.zip remote: eudora14.zip
259927 bytes received in 10 seconds (24 Kbytes/s)
ftp> quit
221 Goodbye.
C:\EUDORA>pkunzip eudora14.zip
```

Installing *Eudora* requires a small modification to the AUTOEXEC.BAT file. *Eudora* needs a temporary directory for its operations. Make the directory and add to AUTOEXEC.BAT an environment variable named TMP that points to the new directory. Here are the lines for AUTOEXEC.BAT given a temporary directory named C:\TMP:

```
REM TMP variable added for Eudora
SET TMP=C:\TMP
```

Reboot the system and then run Windows. Start C:\EUDORA\WEUDORA.EXE by selecting **Run** from the **File** menu in the Program Manager. The first time *Eudora* runs, it displays the configuration window shown in Figure E-6.

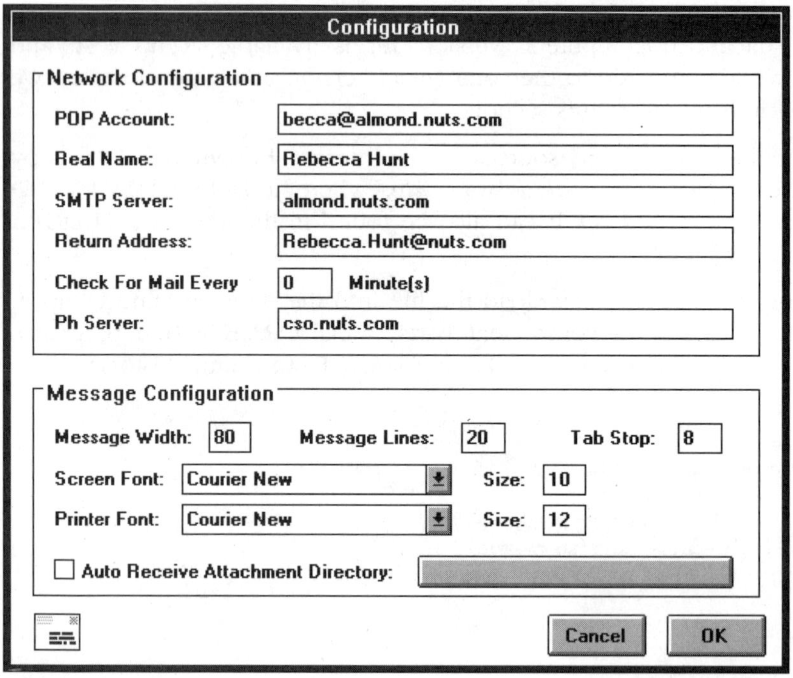

Figure E-6: Eudora Configuration

The upper half of the window in Figure E-6 provides most of the required POP configuration. Enter your username from the POP server and the hostname of the POP server in the form of an email address in the POP Account box. Enter the name of your mail relay host in the SMTP Server field. (On most networks this is the same system as the POP server.) In the Return Address field, enter the simplified email address you want to advertise to the world. You can also tell Eudora how often to check the server for mail; use a time that balances your need for frequent access to your mail against the load on the POP server. Unless told otherwise by the administrator of the POP server, try 20 minutes. The default value of 0 means that *Eudora* will not automatically check for mail. The last field only needs a value if your network has a *CSO Phonebook* server that you want to use. *CSO Phonebook* is an email directory service.

Most of the lower half of the window is used to configure the display. It defines the size of the mail window and the fonts used to display mail. One interesting item in this subwindow is the **Auto Receive Attachment Directory** checkbox. Check this box and provide the path to the directory that you want all attached files written to. This permits you to force attached files into a specific directory—this is a security feature designed to prevent attachments from accidentally overwriting important files.

All of the values set through the configuration window are stored in the EUDORA.INI file found in the EUDORA directory. Don't edit that file directly; use the window to set the configuration.

When everything is set, click **OK** to display the "normal" *Eudora* window. Recall the configuration window at any time by selecting **Configuration** from the **Special** menu in the *Eudora* window. One thing that appears to be missing from the configuration window is the password for accessing the POP server. Don't worry, you'll be asked for the password when the PC first accesses the server.

Eudora is ready to run. Add *Eudora* to one of the program groups in the *Program Manager* to make it more user friendly. First, open the group that you want to add it to, for example Applications. Next, select **New** from the **File** menu in the *Program Manager*. In the dialogue box that appears, check **Program Item** and click **OK**. The dialogue box shown in Figure E-7 appears. Fill in the Description and the Command Line and click **OK**. A new icon that looks like a piece of mail appears in the Applications program window. A double-click on that icon runs *Eudora*. Use this same process to create an icon for *Trumpet* and the other network applications.

That's it. We have installed *Crynwr* packet drivers, *Trumpet Winsock*, and *Eudora* email on a Windows 3.1 system. This installation does take more manual effort than installing the commercial Windows packages we used earlier. The commercial installation programs handle most of these manual tasks. Despite that, this installation is only slightly more difficult than installing a commercial package. This sample installation is a "plain vanilla" installation on a clean Windows 3.1 system. A change in the system environment changes the installation.

Figure E–7: Creating a Program Item

Summary

There is a wide variety of quality public domain TCP/IP software available for PCs. It is available at no-cost (freeware) or low-cost (shareware) from many different sources. Some commercial software houses even offer free versions of their products as a form of advertising.

The decision to use public domain software is a business decision based on an investment of time versus an initial outlay of money. Businesses and people who view the PC as a tool usually prefer commercial software. Technical educational institutions and people who view the PC as an end in itself generally prefer public domain software. You should not, however, base your decision on generalities. Select the software that is right for you.

Glossary

10Base2

An IEEE standard for Ethernet on thin coaxial cable. Also called *thinnet*, *cheapernet*, or *black cable* Ethernet.

10Base5

An IEEE standard for Ethernet on thick coaxial cable. Also called *thicknet* or *yellow cable* Ethernet.

10BaseT

An IEEE standard for Ethernet on unshielded twisted pair (UTP) cable that uses standard Category 3 telephone twisted pair cable. Ethernet does not run on untwisted telephone cable.

API

An Application Program Interface standardizes the way that an application communicates with a service program or a physical device.

application interface

See API.

ARP

Address Resolution Protocol is a standard protocol that maps IP addresses to physical network addresses.

ASCII

American Standard Code for Information Interchange is a standard character set. 7-bit ASCII, which is often used in data communications, has 128 distinct characters and uses only the lower order 7 bits of the transmitted octet.

AUTOEXEC.BAT

A DOS initialization file that loads TSR programs, sets environment variables, and starts programs at boot time.

backbone

A backbone network interconnects local area networks within a campus or building. Generally, hosts are not directly connected to the backbone.

baud rate

This is a measurement of the speed at which data can be carried over an analog serial line. The term "baud" derives from Baudot, a very early teletype character set named for its inventor. In this book, baud rate is synonymous with "bit rate," though that is not strictly true. A 9600 baud modem cannot transmit faster than 9600 baud, but with data compression it may be able to transmit 19200 bits per second. When configuring the COM port for such a modem, specify the port speed as 19200 even if prompted for the baud rate. The terms are confused and used interchangeably. This book does nothing to lessen the confusion because we also use the terms interchangeably.

BIND

Berkeley Internet Name Domain is the most popular implementation of Domain Name Service.

BIOS

Basic Input Output System is the low level software interface to the PC hardware. It is implemented in ROM BIOS and in the BIOS software loaded at boot time. DOS BIOS software is stored on the boot disk in a hidden file with a name like IBMBIOS.COM or IO.SYS.

BNC

The bayonet connector used for thin Ethernet.

boolean

A argument that can only be either true or false.

boot server

A computer that boots another computer. Generally used to boot diskless devices. The term "boot server" is occasionally used to refer to a "configuration server."

broadcast

A transmission addressed to every computer on the network.

broadcast area

A collection of physical networks through which a broadcast is propagated.

broadcast medium

A physical network that supports broadcasts—not all networks do. The network must have a physical layer broadcast capability for a broadcast at the IP level to work.

BSD

Berkeley Software Distribution is the version of UNIX that was distributed by the University of California at Berkeley.

buffers

Areas of memory that provide temporary storage for I/O devices. Some I/O adapters have on-board buffers to store arriving data so that none is lost when the PC is too busy to immediately service the adapter.

bundled

Software included with an operating system or as part of a package of other software. For example: Microsoft bundles TCP/IP with Windows NT and Net-Manage bundles many applications with its TCP/IP stack.

cache

Information saved in memory for later use. For example: DNS servers save answers learned from other servers in a cache, and WfW systems save addresses read at startup from the LMHOSTS file in a cache. The term is also used as a verb: "The system cached the answer."

checksum

A value used to verify that data is not corrupted. It is calculated from the sum of the binary values of each byte transmitted.

CISC

A Complex Instruction Set Computer uses complex machine language instructions that can take several clock cycles to execute.

client/server

A process divided between a front-end client that handles the interface and a back-end server that handles the bulk of the data processing. UNIX users apply this term to systems implemented through *RPC* (Remote Procedure Calls). PC LAN users use this term for server-based networks, such as a Novell network.

collisions

A condition that occurs on an Ethernet when more than one device transmits at the same time. Ethernet is a CSMA/CD (Carrier Sense Multiple Access with Collision Detection) network. An Ethernet device listens for a clear carrier and transmits when it is detected. The device then listens to the return of its own transmission. If the first 512 bits return undamaged, it continues transmitting to the end of the frame. If the bits are damaged, the device knows its transmission has collided with another transmission. It stops transmitting and backs off for a random amount of time before attempting to retransmit.

COM port

A serial port on a PC. Serial ports have only one transmit line and one receive line. Therefore data is sent over the line as a series of bits. Thus the name "serial line."

commodity PC

A low-cost system that is purchased solely on the basis of cost with no regard for features. This type of system has minimal equipment and no pre-installed network hardware or software.

concentrator

A device that concentrates several network connections at a single point.

CONFIG.SYS

A startup file used by DOS to load hardware device drivers.

configuration server

A computer that provides configuration information to another network device. It is used in this book to refer to servers that configure TCP/IP software on their clients.

conventional memory

The first 1M bytes of memory on a DOS system.

CP/M-86

Control Program for Microprocessors. An operating system that predates DOS.

CRC

A Cyclic Redundancy Check is calculated from the data transmitted between systems. It ensures that the data has arrived without any errors.

daemon

A UNIX process that continues running in the background providing service on demand. Daemons never die; they must be killed.

datagram

The unit of data transmitted by IP. A datagram can be thought of as an IP packet.

device driver

A piece of software used to control a piece of hardware.

DIP

Dual In-line Packaging is the most common way computer chips are packaged. The chip is mounted in a rectangle of plastic with two rows of "legs" that provide the solder connections. DIP switches are micro switches mounted on such a package.

disk partition

A logical division of a physical disk into separate filesystems. In DOS, each partition is given a different logical drive name, e.g., drive E:, F:, and G: could all be on one hard drive.

DMA

Direct Memory Access is a technique for writing data into or reading data from memory at high speed.

DNS

Domain Name Service is used by TCP/IP to map hostnames to IP addresses.

DOS memory

The lower 640K bytes of memory on a DOS computer.

drivers

See **device driver**.

DSS

A Domain SAP Server is a server that provides service access information and routing information on a Novell network.

dynamic routing

Routing that automatically adjusts to reflect changing network conditions. Routing protocols exchange information and use that information to update the system's internal routing table. See **static routing**.

ECU

An EISA configuration utility is a program for configuring the hardware on an EISA bus PC.

EISA

The Extended Industry Standard Architecture bus is an enhancement of the PC bus.

EMM386

A memory manager that is included with DOS.

EMS

The Expanded Memory Specification is a way to make use of memory beyond the 1M byte limit. It is designed for older PCs and it requires a special hardware board. EMS has been superseded by newer standards.

encapsulation

Wraps the data and headers from one protocol inside of another protocol. It happens within a single protocol stack, e.g., UDP is encapsulated in IP; and between protocol stacks, e.g., IPX encapsulated in UDP and IP.

encoding technique

The process of preparing data for transmission. In this book, it is used to refer to the process necessary to prepare binary data for transmission.

exporting

The *NFS* (Network File System) term for when a server offers to share a filesystem with its clients.

FAT

The File Allocation Table is the native filesystem of DOS. Other systems, such as NT, provide FAT filesystems for compatibility with DOS.

file server

A computer that shares its disk storage with other systems on the network.

filter

A process that selects data that meets certain criteria or modifies data to meet specific criteria. An example of a filter that selects data is a filter on a protocol analyzer that captures only those packet flowing between two specific systems. An example of a filter that modifies data is an **lpd** printer filter.

flow control

A technique for signaling the remote system to stop its transmission until the receiving system is ready to handle more data. In-band flow control uses characters inserted in the data stream, e.g., XON and XOFF. Out-of-band flow control uses a control signal sent separately from the primary data channel, e.g., RTS and CTS.

framing

Ethernet packets are called *frames*. In this book, framing is used to refer to the technique used to construct the header for an Ethernet frame.

gateway

This term is used differently in different contexts. An IP gateway is an IP router. It forwards data between IP networks. An application gateway translates data between dissimilar applications; e.g., an SMTP gateway is necessary to send Novell MHS mail to a remote SMTP mail site.

gcos

The field in the */etc/passwd* file that contains comments, such as the user's real name. The term "gcos" is used for historical reasons. GCOS, also called GECOS, stands for the General Comprehensive Operating System, which was the operating system of Honeywell 6000 and GE 600 computers. Multics, the father of UNIX, was originally developed on these computers.

GID

The Group ID is a numeric value used by UNIX to identify user who are members of the same group.

gif The Graphics Interchange Format standard is used for exchanging graphics between systems.

gopher

A menu-driven document retrieval system that was originally developed at the University of Minnesota.

GUI

A Graphical User Interface is a fancy way for a user to give commands to the computer. It is usually a window system accessed through a pointing device such as a mouse. Variations on how the mouse interacts with the objects on the screen give rise to the descriptions "a point and click interface" or "a drag and drop interface." The antithesis of a GUI is a command-line interface.

header

The delivery and control information prepended to the data being transmitted. Each layer in a protocol stack adds its own header.

high memory

This refers to the 64K bytes of memory just above the top of conventional memory. This memory can only be used when address line 21 is enabled.

host

Any device connected to a TCP/IP network that does not forward datagrams between networks. Traditional TCP/IP terminology identifies only hosts and gateways (IP routers). Most hosts support the protocol stack up through the applications layer.

HPFS

The High Performance File System is the native filesystem of OS/2.

hub

A multipurpose network device that lies at the center of a star topology network. Most hubs do the same job as concentrators. Concentrators, however, have a dedicated purpose and are usually not very expandable. Hubs support a variety of different interface cards, from concentrator cards to router cards. Hubs are also expandable within a single chassis. Despite these differences, the terms "hub" and "concentrator" are often used interchangeably.

ICMP

The Internet Control Message Protocol is a part of the TCP/IP protocol stack. It provides control and error messages for the Internet Protocol.

IEEE 802.3

The Institute of Electrical and Electronic Engineers 802 standards committee standardizes network technologies. 802.3 is the 802 standard that most closely resembles Ethernet.

internet

An internet (with a lowercase "i") is any collection of networks interconnected by a common protocol. You can build your own internet by interconnecting the networks in your organization with TCP/IP. The Internet (with an uppercase "I") is the worldwide collection of networks that grew out of the original ARPANET.

InterNIC

Is the network information center for the Internet.

interrupt

An event that suspends the currently active process to switch the CPU to a new process.

interrupt driven

An system that is controlled by interrupts.

interrupt handler

The software that processes interrupts.

IP Internet Protocol is the heart of TCP/IP. It defines the datagram, the basic unit of information transmitted over a TCP/IP network. It defines the addressing used by TCP/IP and routes packets.

IPX

Internet Packet Exchange is Novell's internet layer protocol.

IS-IS

Intermediate System to Intermediate System routing protocol is an OSI protocol that passes routing information between routers, which are called "intermediate systems" in OSI terminology.

ISA

The Industry Standard Architecture bus is the most commonly used PC bus. It was developed for the PC AT.

ISDN

Integrated Services Digital Network is a digital telephone service standard. The ISDN Basic Rate Interface (BRI) service provides two 64K bps digital channels that can be used to transmit voice or data, or both simultaneously.

jpeg

The Joint Photographic Experts Group standard for encoding and compressing still graphic images.

legacy systems

A system that already exists and cannot be easily replaced or ignored.

library

A collection of software routines available to all programs. Some libraries are linked into the program at compile time. Dynamically linked libraries are called at run time.

MAC

The Media Access Control layer is one of the sublayers of the Physical Layer. It defines the protocol used to access the physical media of the network. In this book, MAC is sometimes used to describe things that are related to the Ethernet protocol.

MAC address

The physical layer address of a network, e.g., an Ethernet address.

machine language

The low level instructions directly executed by the CPU. Assembly language is the closest programming language to machine language. The terms "assembly language" and "machine language" are often used interchangeably.

macro

A symbolic reference to a group of instructions or values. The symbol is replaced by the actual instructions or values assigned to the symbol when the macro is expanded.

mail header

The delivery and control information that is located at the beginning of a mail message. SMTP mail headers are defined in RFC 822.

mailing lists

A group of email addresses that are referenced by a single address.

make

A program used on UNIX systems to control the compilation, linking, and installation of C language programs.

man pages

The online reference manual on a UNIX system.

MCA

Micro Channel Architecture is a bus developed by IBM for the PS/2 and currently used in the RS/6000.

memory manager

A program that optimizes the use of conventional memory on a DOS computer and provides access to memory beyond the 1M byte barrier.

message body

The part of an email message that occurs after the mail headers. It is the data being sent by the user.

mounting

When an NFS client attaches a filesystem offered by the server to its local filesystem.

mpeg

The Moving Pictures Experts Group standard for encoding and compressing moving video images.

multicast

A technique for simultaneously addressing a group of hosts.

NCP

NetWare Core Protocol is the heart of the Novell network. It is the protocol that defines the services provided by NetWare.

NetBEUI

An extension of NetBIOS that defines an expanded application interface, the Service Message Block (SMB) protocol, and the frame delivery mechanism.

NetBIOS

A network protocol design for very small networks limited to a single network segment. Over time, NetBIOS has evolved so that its application interface can be used with several different network transport protocols.

NetWare

Novell's network operating system.

network number

The portion of an address that identifies a single network on an internet. Internetworking protocols, like IP and IPX, interconnect many networks. Part of the address used by these protocols identifies the network. That portion of the address is called the network number.

NIC

In the PC networking world, NIC means the network interface card, e.g., the Ethernet adapter card. In Internet terminology, NIC means a Network Information Center. Look at the context to decide what is meant.

NIS

Network Information System is a network-accessible system administration database. It was originally developed by Sun Microsystems but is now widely used. It is sometimes called "yellow pages" or "YP."

NLM

NetWare Loadable Modules are programs that loaded and execute on a Novell server. See the LOAD command in Chapter 10.

NLSP

NetWare Link Service Protocol is a Novell protocol for distributing both routing and service advertising information.

NTAS

NT Advanced Server is the Windows NT server software. The name "Advanced Server" is not actually used in the current NT server product, but the acronym NTAS is still used to describe an NT server network.

NTFS

NT File System is the native filesystem of Windows NT.

octet

A contiguous group of 8 bits of data. It is similar to a byte but the term "octet" is preferred in data communications because it applies as easily to a transmitted stream of bits or bytes.

open protocol

A protocol that can be developed and used without any licensing fee. The protocol specifications are available to everyone.

OSI

Open Systems Interconnect was an international effort to develop an open standard for data communications. Much of the terminology used to describe data communications was developed in OSI and several popular protocols are founded on work originally done for OSI.

overlay

A template used to organize data. It is only used in this book to refer to the templates used to organize configuration data.

packet

A self-addressed block of data suitable for transmission over a network. It is the smallest unit of data delivered by a packet switched network. Packets are similar to datagrams but the term packet is more generic. "Datagram" is most closely associated with IP.

packet driver

Driver software that interfaces IP to the PC's network adapter card.

PAD

A packet-assembler/disassembler is used to interface to an X.25 network. As the name implies, it build packets for transmission on an X.25 network and decode the packets received from the network.

pair tester

Test equipment designed to test telephone cable. It is used to test UTP cable for 10BaseT Ethernet installations.

parameters

Arguments or options used on a command line or in a configuration file.

parity

A simple technique for checking the validity of data transmitted over an asynchronous connection. If 7-bit ASCII data is used, the eighth bit of the octet can be used for parity checking. Even parity requires that an even number of bits in the octet be set to ones. Odd parity requires an odd number of ones bits. The transmitting system sets the parity bit as appropriate. The receiving system checks for the proper parity. Because there is no error correction, parity checking has very limited utility. Most systems use 8-bit data with no parity in order to support a larger character set and binary data transmission.

PCI

Peripheral Component Interconnect is a high speed local bus for PCs, commonly found on Pentium systems.

PCM

Pulse coded modulation is a technique for digitally encoding and compressing audio signals.

PCMCIA

The Personal Computer Memory Card International Association provides a standard for expansion cards for laptop computers.

PDN

A public data network is a commercial X.25 network service that provides wide-area access to computer services.

peer

A co-equal system, program, or protocol.

peer-to-peer

Communications between equivalent systems. A "peer-to-peer" network is a network that does not have a server. Instead, each computer can provide services to any other.

physical address

The MAC address used to address a device on the physical network.

physical network

A network constructed from one type of network hardware. An Ethernet segment is a physical network. An Ethernet segment connected to an IBM token ring through an IP router is not a physical network. It is two physical networks: an Ethernet and a token ring. The IP router joins the two physical networks into a single logical IP network.

PIC

A Programmable Interrupt Controller is a device used to control access to devices that are external to the system board. In this book, it is used in reference to the 8259 PIC, which is a single chip controller that handles the hardware interrupts for the PC and the ISA buses.

pin-out

The electrical connections on a computer chip or a hardware interface connector.

POP

Post Office Protocol is mail protocol that allows a remote mail client to read mail from a server.

primitives

Simple commands used from within an application. Primitives are similar to options except they can usually be used together to create simple "programs."

print server

A computer that shares its printer with other systems on the network.

promiscuous mode

The state in which the network interface accepts all data from the network as if it were addressed to the local host.

proprietary protocol

Networking software that is the copyrighted, private property of one vendor.

protocol

A set of rules that computers use to communicate over a network.

public domain

In this book, it refers to any software that can be freely copied and distributed.

RAS

Remote Access Service is a Microsoft product that provides remote, asynchronous access to NetBIOS networks. At first it only supported NetBEUI; more recent versions of RAS also support TCP/IP through PPP and SLIP.

re-write rule

A command within the *sendmail.cf* file that is used to modify the format of an email address.

register

An area within the CPU where data and addresses can be directly manipulated.

RFC

Requests For Comments are the documents used to propose Internet protocols and procedures. RFCs provide the documentation for all TCP/IP protocols.

RIP

Routing Information Protocol is a widely-used protocol for distributing routing information on enterprise networks. It is used by both IP and IPX.

RISC

Reduced Instruction Set Computers use simple machine language instructions that execute in no more than one clock cycle.

RJ45

A modular connector used on UTP cable. It is used for 10BaseT Ethernet.

ROM shadowing

Read Only Memory is not as fast as Random Access Memory. In ROM shadowing, information stored in ROM is copied to RAM and accessed from there to speed processing.

ruleset

A collection of re-write rules in a *sendmail.cf* file.

SAP

Service Advertising Protocol disseminates information about servers on a Novell network.

shim

A piece of software that modifies the function of another piece of software so that it can be put to a new use.

SMB

Service Message Block protocol is an application interface. It is an extension of NetBIOS and is defined as part of NetBEUI.

SMTP

Simple Mail Transport Protocol is used to send mail over a TCP/IP network.

SNMP

Simple Network Management Protocol allows a network administrator to monitor the status of network equipment.

sockets

The TCP/IP application interface developed at Berkeley for BSD UNIX. The term "socket" refers to the unique identifier assigned to each TCP/IP network connection. "Sockets" refers to the software interface standard.

SPX

Sequential Packet Exchange is the Novell protocol used for reliable delivery.

start bits

The data bits in an asynchronous transmission are framed with bits that signal the beginning and the end of the data. The start bits are one or more bits sent before the data to ensure that the receiving modem is ready to receive it.

startup files

Initialization files that are read by the operating system during the boot process or by individual applications as they startup.

static routing

Manual routes installed by the system administrator in the routing table. Static routes do not adjust to changing network conditions.

stop bits

One or more bits sent after the data bits in an asynchronous transmission. Normally one stop bit is used. With one start and one stop bit, 10 bits are transmitted for each octet of data.

subnets

Logical networks created from a single IP network address. A mask is used to identify bits from the host portion of the address to be used for the subnet addresses.

system administrator

The person responsible for configuring and maintaining a multi-user computer system.

system context

The current state of the machine as viewed by the CPU, i.e., the current state of all machine registers.

system integration

The blending of hardware and software into a seamless operational system.

system memory

The 384K bytes of memory that lie just above user memory.

System V

The version of UNIX originally developed by AT&T and currently licensed from Novell.

tar The tape archive system is a BSD UNIX standard for storing data on tape. However, tape is not required. **tar** can be used to archived filesystems to disk files.

TCP

Transmission Control Protocol is the data transport protocol that provides reliable, connection-oriented data delivery in the TCP/IP protocol stack.

TDR

A Time Domain Reflectometer is a piece of test equipment that is used to verify the quality of a coaxial cable.

terminal emulator

Software that allows a PC to be used as a computer terminal.

thicknet

An Ethernet constructed from thick, yellow coaxial cable. Also called 10Base5.

thinnet

An Ethernet constructed of thin, black cable. Also called 10Base2.

trusted host security

A security system that trusts the remote system to verify the user. The local system does not request a password from the user.

trusted hosts

A remote computer that is trusted to grant access to the local system. Hosts are granted trust by being listed in a configuration file by the system administrator. The UNIX files that grant trust are: *hosts.equiv*, *.rhosts*, *hosts.lpd*, and *exports*.

TSR

Terminate and Stay Resident programs are DOS programs that stay in memory where they can be accessed immediately. TSRs are used to handle interrupts.

tunneling

Any technique for passing packets over an incompatible network by encapsulating them in packets that are compatible with the network. For example, IPX packets can be tunneled through a TCP/IP network by encapsulating them in UDP and IP.

UART

A Universal Asynchronous Receiver Transmitter is a single chip that controls asynchronous transmission for a serial port. PCs use the 8250, an unbuffered chip capability of speeds up to 19.2K bps, and the 16550, a buffered chip capable of much higher performance.

UDP

User Datagram Protocol is the TCP/IP transport protocol used for packet delivery service. It is a lightweight protocol because it does not have the overhead of creating connections and verifying delivery.

UID

The User ID is a numeric value used by UNIX to identify an individual user.

UMB

An Upper Memory Block is a piece of contiguous upper memory. UMBs are used by memory managers to relocate programs and data from user memory. See **upper memory**.

unshielded twisted pair

A standard telephone cable made up of insulated 24-gauge solid copper wires that are twisted together in pairs. The pairs of cable are bundled together in a insulating wrapper. The cable is not covered with a metal shield.

unzip

Decompressing a file with PKUNZIP.

upper memory

The 384K bytes of conventional memory that lie just above user memory.

user memory

The first 640K bytes of memory on a DOS system.

vector

An address that points to an interrupt handler. The interrupt table (or vector table) contains a vector for each interrupt available to the system. When an interrupt occurs, it is used as an index into the table to retrieve the vector. The system then jumps to the address pointed to by the vector and executes the instructions found there.

VESA

The Video Electronics Standards Association defined a local bus video adapter. It was the first PC local bus standard used for a peripheral device.

virtual machine

A simulated machine environment implemented in software. Intel processors, beginning with the 80386, provide an addressing technique that allows available memory to be segmented to support multiple virtual 8086 machines. Software running in each virtual machine can address its chunk of memory using real mode addressing as if it were a real DOS machine.

VT100

An intelligent terminal manufactured by Digital Equipment Corporation (DEC). The term often refers to the entire family of DEC intelligent terminals. Most PC terminal emulators offer VT100 emulation.

well-known port

A standard port number assigned to a specific network service. The *Assigned Numbers* RFC officially assigns these port numbers. For example, SMTP mail is always delivered to port 25, which is the well known port for email.

workgroup

A collection of related computers connected to a shared network. The computers are related in that they share common tasks and operate on shared data.

workstation

A computer that is designed for networking. It has network hardware and software already installed.

WWW

The World Wide Web is a networked information system for accessing hypertext information. It was originally developed at CERN. It is the information structure used by browsers such as Mosaic.

X.121

The addressing standard used for X.25.

X.25

A standard network protocol for wide-area, packet switched networks.

XMS

The Extended Memory Specification provides a standard technique for DOS systems to access memory above the 1M byte barrier without using special hardware.

XNS

The Xerox Network Services protocol suite was design by Xerox to run over Ethernet. Novell adapted the XNS protocols for NetWare.

zip Compressing a file with PKZIP.

Index

About the Author

Craig Hunt is an author, lecturer, and network administrator. Craig has worked with computer systems for more than 20 years. He spent the first few years after receiving his Bachelor's degree from American University running an outdoor camp for inner-city kids, but the call of computing was too strong. Craig went to work for the federal government as a programmer and then as a system programmer. He left the government to work for Honeywell on the WWMCCS network in the days before TCP/IP, back when the network used Network Control Protocol. After Honeywell, Craig went to work for the National Institute of Standards and Technology. He is still there today working on computer networking.

Craig lives with his wife and children in Gaithersburg, Maryland. He has a passion for rock and roll music. Craig loves the outdoors; he splits vacation time between the mountains and the sea. He has recently begun exploring the agonies of golf and has found it to be an excellent way to ruin a walk in the park.

Colophon

The animal on the cover of *Networking Personal Computers with TCP/IP* is a jerboa, a jumping rodent of the family Dipodidae. Jerboas live in the desert regions of Africa and Central Asia. There are more than 20 species of jerboa, ranging in size from 1.6 to 10 inches, with tails of an additional 2.7 to 11 inches. Their hind legs, which are used for jumping, are at least four times as long as their front legs, which are used only for gathering food or running short distances. Jerboas can jump five to ten feet in a single leap, or they can move using short hops. Their long tails are used for balance when jumping or standing.

Jerboas are nocturnal animals. Although they are not sociable, jerboas within a given area all emerge from their burrows at about the same time each evening and simultaneously head to their feeding grounds in search of food. The jerboa diet primarily consists of seeds, along with some insects and vegetation. They are able to manufacture water from their food, and so have no need to drink water.

The gestation period for jerboas is 25-42 days. Most females breed at least twice a season, giving birth to two to six per litter. The life expectancy of jerboas is less than two years. Jerboas hibernate both in the winter and in very hot or dry summer periods.

Edie Freedman designed the cover of this book, using a 19th-century engraving from the Dover Pictorial Archive. The cover layout was produced with Quark XPress 3.3 using the ITC Garamond font. Whenever possible, our books use RepKover™, a durable and flexible lay-flat binding. If the page count exceeds RepKover's limit, perfect binding is used.

The inside layout was designed by Edie Freedman, with modifications by Nancy Priest, and implemented in GNU gtroff by Lenny Muellner. The text and heading fonts are ITC Garamond Light and Garamond Book. The illustrations that appear in the book were created in Aldus Freehand 5.0 by Chris Reilley, and the screenshots were processed in Adobe PhotoShop. This colophon was written by Clairemarie Fisher O'Leary.

More Titles from O'Reilly

Network Administration

Virtual Private Networks

*By Charlie Scott, Paul Wolfe &
Mike Erwin
1st Edition February 1998
184 pages, ISBN 1-56592-319-7*

This book tells you how to plan and
build a Virtual Private Network (VPN),
a collection of technologies that creates
secure connections or "tunnels" over
regular Internet lines. It starts with general
concerns like costs and configuration and continues with detailed
descriptions of how to install and use VPN technologies that are
available for Windows NT and UNIX, such as PPTP and L2TP, the
AltaVista Tunnel, and the Cisco PIX Firewall.

DNS and BIND, 3rd Edition

*By Paul Albitz & Cricket Liu
3rd Edition September 1998
502 pages, ISBN 1-56592-512-2*

DNS and BIND discusses one of the
Internet's fundamental building blocks:
the distributed host information database
that's responsible for translating names
into addresses, routing mail to its proper
destination, and many other services.
The third edition covers BIND 4.9, on which most commercial
products are currently based, and BIND 8, which implements
many important new features and will be the basis for the
next generation of commercial name servers.

TCP/IP Network Administration, 2nd Edition

*By Craig Hunt
2nd Edition December 1997
630 pages, ISBN 1-56592-322-7*

A complete guide to setting up and
running a TCP/IP network for practicing
system administrators. Beyond basic
setup, this new second edition discusses
the Internet routing protocols and
provides a tutorial on how to configure
important network services. It now also includes Linux in
addition to BSD and System V TCP/IP implementations.

sendmail, 2nd Edition

*By Bryan Costales & Eric Allman
2nd Edition January 1997
1050 pages, ISBN 1-56592-222-0*

sendmail, 2nd Edition, covers sendmail
Version 8.8 from Berkeley and the standard
versions available on most systems. This
cross-referenced edition offers an expanded
tutorial, solution-oriented examples, and
new topics such as the #error delivery
agent, sendmail's exit values, MIME headers, and how to set up
and use the user database, *mailertable*, and *smrsh*.

Cracking DES

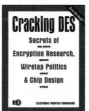

*By Electronic Frontier Foundation
1st Edition July 1998
272 pages, ISBN 1-56592-520-3*

The Data Encryption Standard withstood
the test of time for twenty years. *Cracking
DES: Secrets of Encryption Research,
Wiretap Politics & Chip Design* shows
exactly how it was brought down.
Every cryptographer, security designer,
and student of cryptography policy should read this book to
understand how the world changed as it fell.

The Networking CD Bookshelf

*By O'Reilly & Associates, Inc.
1st Edition April 1999 (est.)
Features CD-ROM
ISBN 1-56592-523-8*

Network administrator alert! Six bestselling
O'Reilly Animal Guides are now available
on CD-ROM, easily accessible with your
favorite Web browser: *TCP/IP Network
Administration, 2nd Edition*; *sendmail,
2nd Edition*; *sendmail Desktop Reference*; *DNS and BIND, 3rd
Edition*; *Practical UNIX & Internet Security, 2nd Edition*; and
Building Internet Firewalls. As a bonus, the new hardcopy version
of *DNS and BIND* is also included.

Network Administration

Using & Managing PPP

By Andrew Sun
1st Edition March 1999
444 pages, ISBN 1-56592-321-9

This book is for network administrators and others who have to set up computer systems to use PPP. It covers all aspects of the protocol, including how to set up dial-in servers, authentication, debugging, and PPP options. In addition, it contains overviews of related areas, like serial communications, DNS setup, and routing.

Managing IP Networks with Cisco Routers

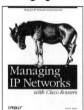

By Scott M. Ballew
1st Edition October 1997
352 pages, ISBN 1-56592-320-0

This practical guide to setting up and maintaining a production network covers how to select routing protocols, configure protocols to handle most common situations, evaluate network equipment and vendors, and setup a help desk. Although it focuses on Cisco routers, and gives examples using Cisco's IOS, the principles discussed are common to all IP networks.

Protecting Networks with SATAN

By Martin Freiss
1st Edition May 1998
128 pages, ISBN 1-56592-425-8

SATAN performs "security audits," scanning host computers for security vulnerabilities. This book describes how to install and use SATAN, and how to adapt it to local requirements and increase its knowledge of specific security vulnerabilities.

Managing Mailing Lists

By Alan Schwartz
1st Edition March 1998
288 pages, ISBN 1-56592-259-X

Mailing lists are an ideal vehicle for creating email-based electronic communities. This book covers four mailing list packages (Majordomo, LISTSERV, ListProcessor, and SmartList) and tells you everything you need to know to set up and run a mailing list, from writing the charter to dealing with bounced messages. It discusses creating moderated lists, controlling who can subscribe to a list, offering digest subscriptions, and archiving list postings.

Managing Usenet

By Henry Spencer & David Lawrence
1st Edition December 1997
512 pages, ISBN 1-56592-198-4

Usenet, also called Netnews, is the world's largest discussion forum, and it is doubling in size every year. This book, written by two of the foremost authorities on Usenet administration, contains everything you need to know to administer a Netnews system. It covers C News and INN, explains the basics of starting a Netnews system, and offers guidelines to help ensure that your system is capable of handling news volume today—and in the future.

Web Server Administration

Web Security & Commerce

By Simson Garfinkel
with Gene Spafford
1st Edition June 1997
506 pages, ISBN 1-56592-269-7

Learn how to minimize the risks of the Web with this comprehensive guide. It covers browser vulnerabilities, privacy concerns, issues with Java, JavaScript, ActiveX, and plug-ins, digital certificates, cryptography, web server security, blocking software, censorship technology, and relevant civil and criminal issues.

Web Server Administration

Stopping SPAM

By Alan Schwartz & Simson Garfinkel
1st Edition October 1998
204 pages, ISBN 1-56592-388-X

This book describes spam—unwanted email messages and inappropriate news articles—and explains what you and your Internet service providers and administrators can do to prevent it, trace it,stop it, and even outlaw it. Contains a wealth of advice, technical tools, and additional technical and community resources.

Writing Apache Modules with Perl and C

By Lincoln Stein & Doug MacEachern
1st Edition March 1999
746 pages, ISBN 1-56592-567-X

This guide to Web programming teaches you how to extend the capabilities of the Apache Web server. It explains the design of Apache, mod_perl, and the Apache API, then demonstrates how to use them to rewrite CGI scripts, filter HTML documents on the server-side, enhance server log functionality, convert file formats on the fly, and more.

Building Your Own WebSite™

By Susan B. Peck & Stephen Arrants
1st Edition July 1996
514 pages, Includes CD-ROM,
ISBN 1-56592-232-8

This is a hands-on reference for Windows® 95 and Windows NT™ users who want to host a site on the Web or on a corporate intranet. This step-by-step guide will have you creating live web pages in minutes. You'll also learn how to connect your web to information in other Windows applications, such as word processing documents and databases. The book is packed with examples and tutorials on every aspect of web management, and it includes the highly acclaimed WebSite™ 1.1 server software on CD-ROM.

Apache: The Definitive Guide, 2nd Edition

By Ben Laurie & Peter Laurie
2nd Edition February 1999
388 pages, includes CD-ROM
ISBN 1-56592-528-9

Written and reviewed by key members of the Apache group, this book is the only complete guide on the market that describes how to obtain, set up, and secure the Apache software on both UNIX and Windows systems. The second edition fully describes Windows support and all the other Apache 1.3 features. Includes CD-ROM with Apache sources and demo sites discussed in the book.

Web Performance Tuning

By Patrick Killelea
1st Edition October 1998
374 pages, ISBN 1-56592-379-0

Web Performance Tuning hits the ground running and gives concrete advice for improving crippled Web performance right away. For anyone who has waited too long for a Web page to display or watched servers slow to a crawl, this book includes tips on tuning the server software, operating system, network, and the Web browser itself.

Building Your Own Web Conferences™

By Susan B. Peck & Beverly Murray Scherf
1st Edition March 1997
270 pages, Includes CD-ROM
ISBN 1-56592-279-4

Building Your Own Web Conferences is a complete guide for Windows® 95 and NT™ users on how to set up and manage dynamic virtual communities that improve workgroup collaboration and keep visitors coming back to your site. The second in O'Reilly's "Build Your Own..." series, this book comes with O'Reilly's state-of-the-art WebBoard™ 2.0 software on CD-ROM.

Windows Programming

Access Database Design & Programming

By Steven Roman
1st Edition June 1997
270 pages, ISBN 1-56592-297-2

This book provides experienced Access users who are novice programers with frequently overlooked concepts and techniques necessary to create effective database applications. It focuses on designing effective tables in a multi-table application; using the Access interface or Access SQL to construct queries; and programming using the Data Access Object (DAO) and Microsoft Access object models.

VB & VBA in a Nutshell: The Languages

By Paul Lomax
1st Edition October 1998
656 pages, ISBN 1-56592-358-8

For Visual Basic and VBA programmers, this book boils down the essentials of the VB and VBA languages into a single volume, including undocumented and little documented areas essential to everyday programming. The convenient alphabetical reference to all functions, procedures, statements, and keywords allows VB and VBA programmers to use this book both as a standard reference guide to the language and as a tool for troubleshooting and identifying programming problems.

Learning VBScript

By Paul Lomax
1st Edition July 1997
616 pages, includes CD-ROM
ISBN 1-56592-247-6

This definitive guide shows web developers how to take full advantage of client-side scripting with the VBScript language. In addition to basic language features, it covers the Internet Explorer object model and discusses techniques for client-side scripting, like adding ActiveX controls to a web page or validating data before sending it to the server. Includes CD-ROM with over 170 code samples.

Visual Basic Controls in a Nutshell

By Evan S. Dictor
1st Edition July 1999 (est.)
686 pages (est.), ISBN 1-56592-294-8

This quick reference covers one of the crucial elements of Visual Basic: its controls, and their numerous properties, events, and methods. It provides a step-by-step list of procedures for using each major control and contains a detailed reference to all properties, methods, and events. Written by an experienced Visual Basic programmer, it helps to make painless what can sometimes be an arduous job of programming Visual Basic.

Learning Perl on Win32 Systems

By Randal L. Schwartz,
Erik Olson & Tom Christiansen
1st Edition August 1997
306 pages, ISBN 1-56592-324-3

In this carefully paced course, leading Perl trainers and a Windows NT practitioner teach you to program in the language that promises to emerge as the scripting language of choice on NT. Based on the "llama" book, this book features tips for PC users and new, NT-specific examples, along with a foreword by Larry Wall, the creator of Perl, and Dick Hardt, the creator of Perl for Win32.

Learning Word Programming

By Steven Roman
1st Edition October 1998
408 pages, ISBN 1-56592-524-6

This no-nonsense book delves into the core aspects of VBA programming, enabling users to increase their productivity and power over Microsoft Word. It takes the reader step-by-step through writing VBA macros and programs, illustrating how to generate tables of a particular format, manage shortcut keys, create FAX cover sheets, and reformat documents.

Windows Programming

Developing Windows Error Messages

By Ben Ezzell
1st Edition March 1998
254 pages, Includes CD-ROM
ISBN 1-56592-356-1

This book teaches C, C++, and Visual Basic programmers how to write effective error messages that notify the user of an error, clearly explain the error, and most important, offer a solution. The book also discusses methods for preventing and trapping errors before they occur and tells how to create flexible input and response routines to keep unnecessary errors from happening.

Inside the Windows 95 File System

By Stan Mitchell
1st Edition May 1997
378 pages, Includes diskette
ISBN 1-56592-200-X

In this book, Stan Mitchell describes the Windows 95 File System, as well as the new opportunities and challenges it brings for developers. Its "hands-on" approach will help developers become better equipped to make design decisions using the new Win95 File System features. Includes a diskette containing MULTIMON, a general-purpose monitor for examining Windows internals.

Win32 Multithreaded Programming

By Aaron Cohen & Mike Woodring
1st Edition December 1997
724 pages, Includes CD-ROM
ISBN 1-56592-296-4

This book clearly explains the concepts of multithreaded programs and shows developers how to construct efficient and complex applications. An important book for any developer, it illustrates all aspects of Win32 multithreaded programming, including what has previously been undocumented or poorly explained.

Windows NT File System Internals

By Rajeev Nagar
1st Edition September 1997
794 pages, Includes diskette
ISBN 1-56592-249-2

Windows NT File System Internals presents the details of the NT I/O Manager, the Cache Manager, and the Memory Manager from the perspective of a software developer writing a file system driver or implementing a kernel-mode filter driver. The book provides numerous code examples included on diskette, as well as the source for a complete, usable filter driver.

Inside the Windows 95 Registry

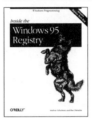

By Ron Petrusha
1st Edition August 1996
594 pages, Includes diskette
ISBN 1-56592-170-4

An in-depth examination of remote registry access, differences between the Win95 and NT registries, registry backup, undocumented registry services, and the role the registry plays in OLE. Shows programmers how to access the Win95 registry from Win32, Win16, and DOS programs in C and Visual Basic. VxD sample code is also included. Includes diskette.

Windows NT SNMP

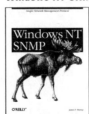

By James D. Murray
1st Edition January 1998
464 pages, Includes CD-ROM
ISBN 1-56592-338-3

This book describes the implementation of SNMP (the Simple Network Management Protocol) on Windows NT 3.51 and 4.0 (with a look ahead to NT 5.0) and Windows 95 systems. It covers SNMP and network basics and detailed information on developing SNMP management applications and extension agents. The book comes with a CD-ROM containing a wealth of additional information: standards documents, sample code from the book, and many third-party, SNMP-related software tools, libraries, and demos.

Windows Programming

Developing Visual Basic Add-Ins

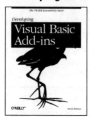

By Steven Roman
1st Edition December 1998
186 pages, ISBN 1-56592-527-0

A tutorial and reference guide in one, this book covers all the basics of creating useful VB add-ins to extend the IDE, allowing developers to work more productively with Visual Basic. Readers with even a modest acquaintance with VB will be developing add-ins in no time. Includes numerous simple code examples.

How to stay in touch with O'Reilly

1. Visit Our Award-Winning Web Site

http://www.oreilly.com/

★ "Top 100 Sites on the Web" —*PC Magazine*
★ "Top 5% Web sites" —*Point Communications*
★ "3-Star site" —*The McKinley Group*

Our web site contains a library of comprehensive product information (including book excerpts and tables of contents), downloadable software, background articles, interviews with technology leaders, links to relevant sites, book cover art, and more. File us in your Bookmarks or Hotlist!

2. Join Our Email Mailing Lists

New Product Releases

To receive automatic email with brief descriptions of all new O'Reilly products as they are released, send email to:
listproc@online.oreilly.com
Put the following information in the first line of your message (*not* in the Subject field):
subscribe oreilly-news

O'Reilly Events

If you'd also like us to send information about trade show events, special promotions, and other O'Reilly events, send email to:
listproc@online.oreilly.com
Put the following information in the first line of your message (*not* in the Subject field):
subscribe oreilly-events

3. Get Examples from Our Books via FTP

There are two ways to access an archive of example files from our books:

Regular FTP

*   ftp to:
    ftp.oreilly.com
    (login: anonymous
    password: your email address)
*   Point your web browser to:
    ftp://ftp.oreilly.com/

FTPMAIL

*   Send an email message to:
    ftpmail@online.oreilly.com
    (Write "help" in the message body)

4. Contact Us via Email

order@oreilly.com
To place a book or software order online. Good for North American and international customers.

subscriptions@oreilly.com
To place an order for any of our newsletters or periodicals.

books@oreilly.com
General questions about any of our books.

software@oreilly.com
For general questions and product information about our software. Check out O'Reilly Software Online at **http://software.oreilly.com/** for software and technical support information. Registered O'Reilly software users send your questions to: **website-support@oreilly.com**

cs@oreilly.com
For answers to problems regarding your order or our products.

booktech@oreilly.com
For book content technical questions or corrections.

proposals@oreilly.com
To submit new book or software proposals to our editors and product managers.

international@oreilly.com
For information about our international distributors or translation queries. For a list of our distributors outside of North America check out:
http://www.oreilly.com/www/order/country.html

O'Reilly & Associates, Inc.
101 Morris Street, Sebastopol, CA 95472 USA
TEL 707-829-0515 or 800-998-9938
     (6am to 5pm PST)
FAX 707-829-0104

International Distributors

UK, EUROPE, MIDDLE EAST AND AFRICA (EXCEPT FRANCE, GERMANY, AUSTRIA, SWITZERLAND, LUXEMBOURG, LIECHTENSTEIN, AND EASTERN EUROPE)

INQUIRIES

O'Reilly UK Limited
4 Castle Street
Farnham
Surrey, GU9 7HS
United Kingdom
Telephone: 44-1252-711776
Fax: 44-1252-734211
Email: josette@oreilly.com

ORDERS

Wiley Distribution Services Ltd.
1 Oldlands Way
Bognor Regis
West Sussex PO22 9SA
United Kingdom
Telephone: 44-1243-779777
Fax: 44-1243-820250
Email: cs-books@wiley.co.uk

FRANCE

ORDERS

GEODIF
61, Bd Saint-Germain
75240 Paris Cedex 05, France
Tel: 33-1-44-41-46-16 (French books)
Tel: 33-1-44-41-11-87 (English books)
Fax: 33-1-44-41-11-44
Email: distribution@eyrolles.com

INQUIRIES

Éditions O'Reilly
18 rue Séguier
75006 Paris, France
Tel: 33-1-40-51-52-30
Fax: 33-1-40-51-52-31
Email: france@editions-oreilly.fr

GERMANY, SWITZERLAND, AUSTRIA, EASTERN EUROPE, LUXEMBOURG, AND LIECHTENSTEIN

INQUIRIES & ORDERS

O'Reilly Verlag
Balthasarstr. 81
D-50670 Köln
Germany
Telephone: 49-221-973160-91
Fax: 49-221-973160-8
Email: anfragen@oreilly.de (inquiries)
Email: order@oreilly.de (orders)

CANADA (FRENCH LANGUAGE BOOKS)

Les Éditions Flammarion ltée
375, Avenue Laurier Ouest
Montréal (Québec) H2V 2K3
Tel: 00-1-514-277-8807
Fax: 00-1-514-278-2085
Email: info@flammarion.qc.ca

HONG KONG

City Discount Subscription Service, Ltd.
Unit D, 3rd Floor, Yan's Tower
27 Wong Chuk Hang Road
Aberdeen, Hong Kong
Tel: 852-2580-3539
Fax: 852-2580-6463
Email: citydis@ppn.com.hk

KOREA

Hanbit Media, Inc.
Sonyoung Bldg. 202
Yeksam-dong 736-36
Kangnam-ku
Seoul, Korea
Tel: 822-554-9610
Fax: 822-556-0363
Email: hant93@chollian.dacom.co.kr

PHILIPPINES

Mutual Books, Inc.
429-D Shaw Boulevard
Mandaluyong City, Metro
Manila, Philippines
Tel: 632-725-7538
Fax: 632-721-3056
Email: mbikikog@mnl.sequel.net

TAIWAN

O'Reilly Taiwan
No. 3, Lane 131
Hang-Chow South Road
Section 1, Taipei, Taiwan
Tel: 886-2-23968990
Fax: 886-2-23968916
Email: benh@oreilly.com

CHINA

O'Reilly Beijing
Room 2410
160, FuXingMenNeiDaJie
XiCheng District
Beijing, China PR 100031
Tel: 86-10-86631006
Fax: 86-10-86631007
Email: frederic@oreilly.com

INDIA

Computer Bookshop (India) Pvt. Ltd.
190 Dr. D.N. Road, Fort
Bombay 400 001 India
Tel: 91-22-207-0989
Fax: 91-22-262-3551
Email: cbsbom@giasbm01.vsnl.net.in

JAPAN

O'Reilly Japan, Inc.
Kiyoshige Building 2F
12-Bancho, Sanei-cho
Shinjuku-ku
Tokyo 160-0008 Japan
Tel: 81-3-3356-5227
Fax: 81-3-3356-5261
Email: japan@oreilly.com

ALL OTHER ASIAN COUNTRIES

O'Reilly & Associates, Inc.
101 Morris Street
Sebastopol, CA 95472 USA
Tel: 707-829-0515
Fax: 707-829-0104
Email: order@oreilly.com

AUSTRALIA

WoodsLane Pty., Ltd.
7/5 Vuko Place
Warriewood NSW 2102
Australia
Tel: 61-2-9970-5111
Fax: 61-2-9970-5002
Email: info@woodslane.com.au

NEW ZEALAND

Woodslane New Zealand, Ltd.
21 Cooks Street (P.O. Box 575)
Waganui, New Zealand
Tel: 64-6-347-6543
Fax: 64-6-345-4840
Email: info@woodslane.com.au

LATIN AMERICA

McGraw-Hill Interamericana
Editores, S.A. de C.V.
Cedro No. 512
Col. Atlampa
06450, Mexico, D.F.
Tel: 52-5-547-6777
Fax: 52-5-547-3336
Email: mcgraw-hill@infosel.net.mx

O'REILLY®